My Body / Our Rights

World War 3 Illustrated #53

Editors of this issue: **Paula Hewitt Amram, Sabrina Jones, Rebecca Migdal**
Asst Editor: **Seth Tobocman**

www.ww3.nyc   Order copies: **akpress.org**
Printed in Canada

World War 3 Illustrated #53

My Body / Our Rights

A Message from the Editors

We went through some changes while working on this issue, as you probably did, too. Threats to our bodies became more acute in 2022. Leaked documents foreshadowed the overturning of Roe v. Wade, ending 50 years of nation-wide legal abortion. Trigger laws in 13 states instantly made abortion a felony. The slow, steady erosion of our rights just took a great leap forward. You can't say they didn't warn us, but the shock is still visceral.

Nicole Schulman

We, the artist-editors of this issue, continued with our art, activism, and our intimate editorial conversations with the artists in this book as we all processed the change. And yet, through these changes, our original vision remains true.

My body is always mine alone. In pleasure and pain, sickness and health, until death do us part. Sexuality, pregnancy and abortion happen within my skin. Intimate experience shapes my relations to others. From growing up to growing old, no laws can change who I really am. But they can sure make life difficult.

Our rights are always social. We name and claim them in public. A fundamental right is deciding whether or not to have children, when, how many, and with whom. Empowering the bodily autonomy of all people is essential for healthy minds, families, and communities. From our threatened local clinics (where we still have them) to our legislatures and our courts, our right to care for our own body depends on our own public advocacy.

My Body/Our Rights is a collection of comics and graphic art in defense of abortion rights and appropriate healthcare for all people. We present testimony of abortions through the generations, the experience of healthcare providers, and challenges to our bodily autonomy. We bear witness to those resisting oppressive laws, embracing nontraditional families, and creating a culture of respect for all identities. We hope you are encouraged, enraged, and moved by these stories and images.

Issue #53 editors: **Paula Hewitt Amram, Sabrina Jones, Rebecca Migdal;** assistant editor: **Seth Tobocman**

CONTENTS

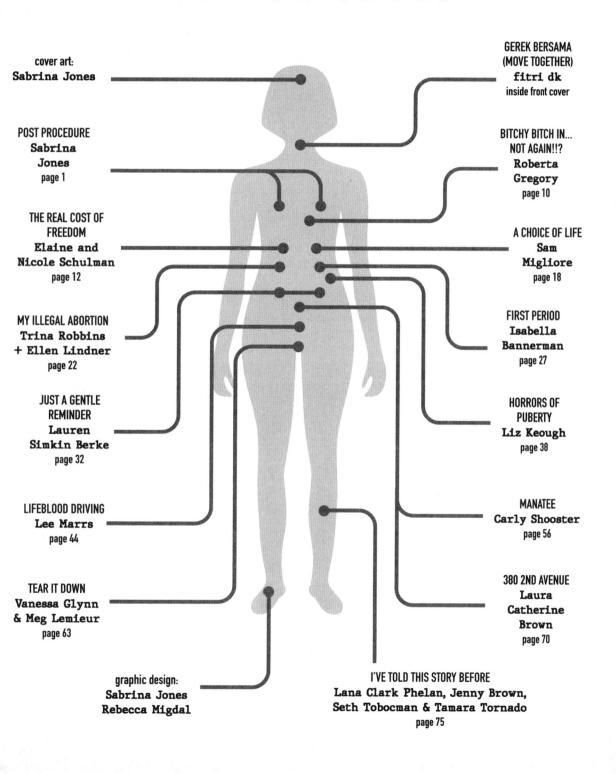

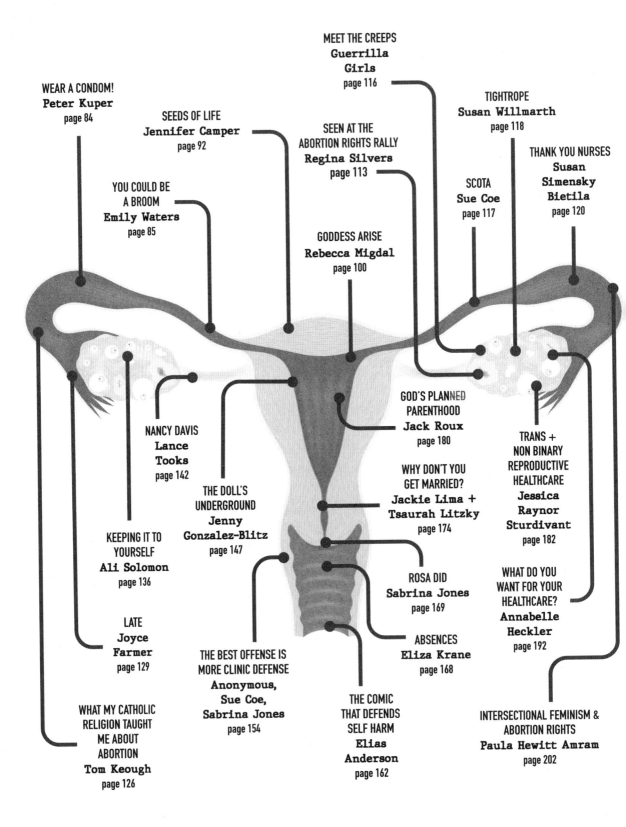

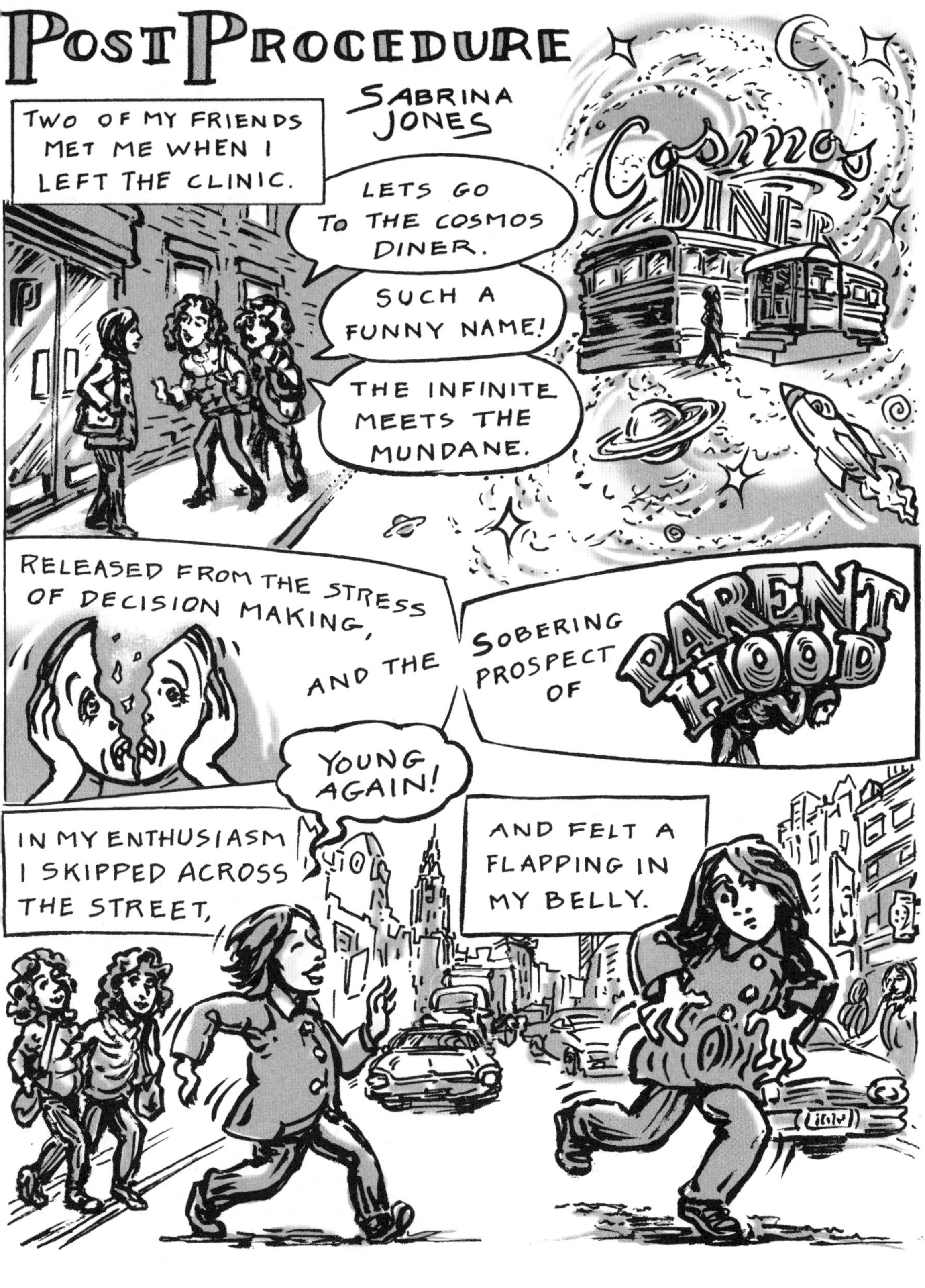
POST PROCEDURE
SABRINA JONES
TWO OF MY FRIENDS MET ME WHEN I LEFT THE CLINIC.
LETS GO TO THE COSMOS DINER.
SUCH A FUNNY NAME!
THE INFINITE MEETS THE MUNDANE.
Cosmos DINER
RELEASED FROM THE STRESS OF DECISION MAKING,
AND THE
SOBERING PROSPECT OF
PARENT HOOD
YOUNG AGAIN!
IN MY ENTHUSIASM I SKIPPED ACROSS THE STREET,
AND FELT A FLAPPING IN MY BELLY.

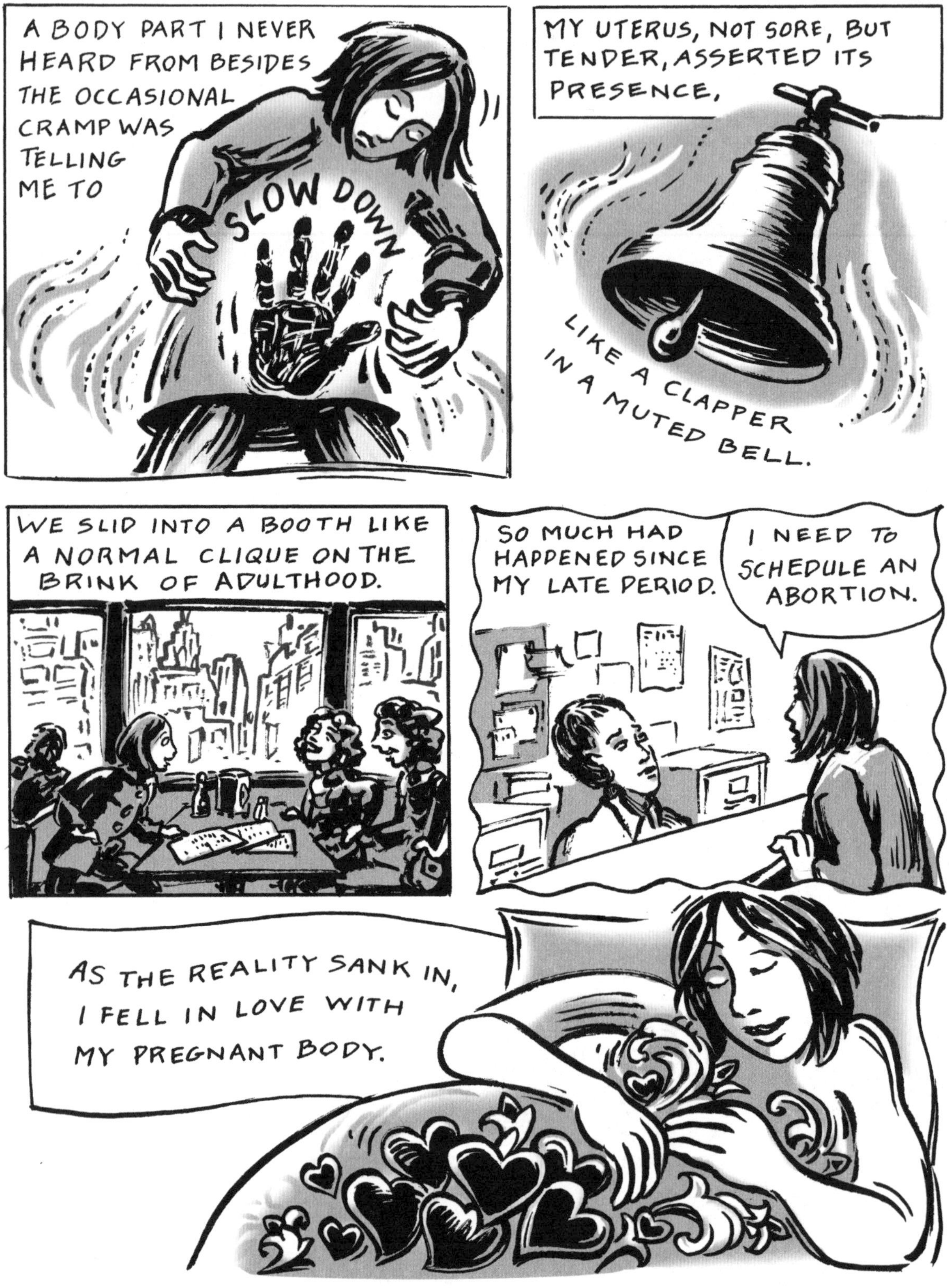
A BODY PART I NEVER HEARD FROM BESIDES THE OCCASIONAL CRAMP WAS TELLING ME TO
SLOW DOWN
MY UTERUS, NOT SORE, BUT TENDER, ASSERTED ITS PRESENCE,
LIKE A CLAPPER IN A MUTED BELL.
WE SLID INTO A BOOTH LIKE A NORMAL CLIQUE ON THE BRINK OF ADULTHOOD.
SO MUCH HAD HAPPENED SINCE MY LATE PERIOD.
I NEED TO SCHEDULE AN ABORTION.
AS THE REALITY SANK IN, I FELL IN LOVE WITH MY PREGNANT BODY.

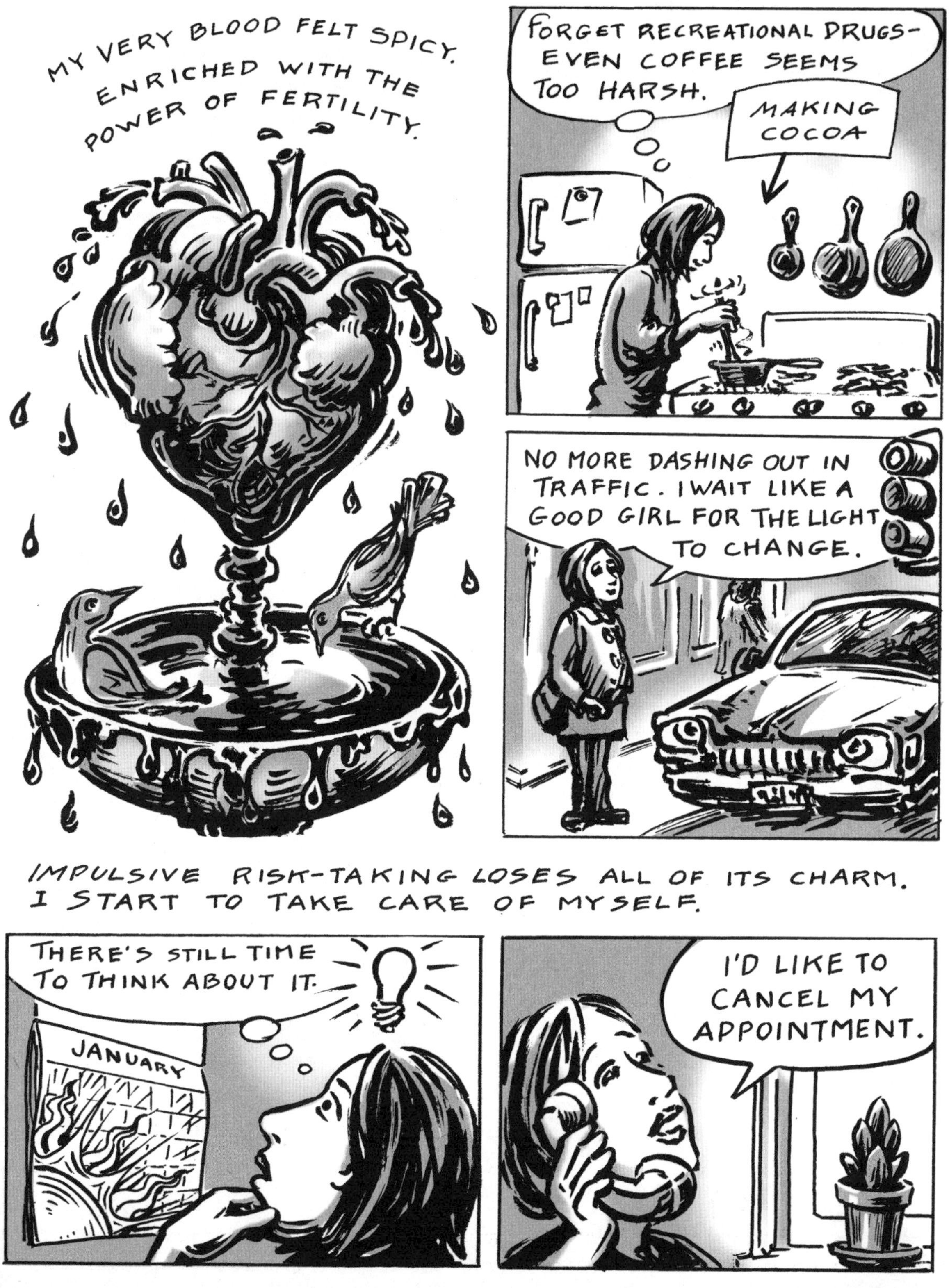
MY VERY BLOOD FELT SPICY. ENRICHED WITH THE POWER OF FERTILITY.
FORGET RECREATIONAL DRUGS- EVEN COFFEE SEEMS TOO HARSH.
MAKING COCOA
NO MORE DASHING OUT IN TRAFFIC. I WAIT LIKE A GOOD GIRL FOR THE LIGHT TO CHANGE.
IMPULSIVE RISK-TAKING LOSES ALL OF ITS CHARM. I START TO TAKE CARE OF MYSELF.
THERE'S STILL TIME TO THINK ABOUT IT.
JANUARY
I'D LIKE TO CANCEL MY APPOINTMENT.

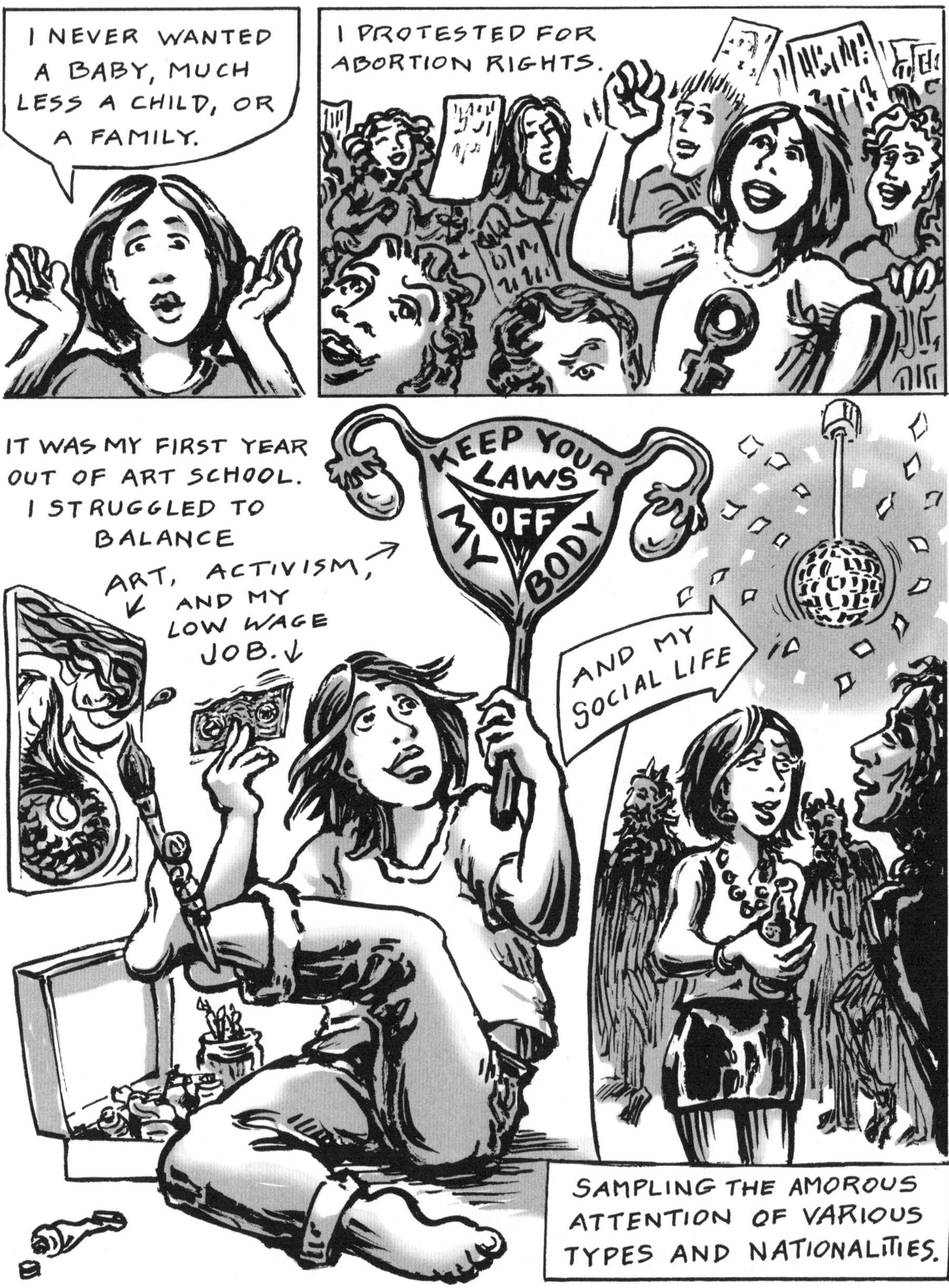
I NEVER WANTED A BABY, MUCH LESS A CHILD, OR A FAMILY.
I PROTESTED FOR ABORTION RIGHTS.
IT WAS MY FIRST YEAR OUT OF ART SCHOOL. I STRUGGLED TO BALANCE
ART,
ACTIVISM,
AND MY LOW WAGE JOB.
KEEP YOUR LAWS OFF MY BODY
AND MY SOCIAL LIFE
SAMPLING THE AMOROUS ATTENTION OF VARIOUS TYPES AND NATIONALITIES.

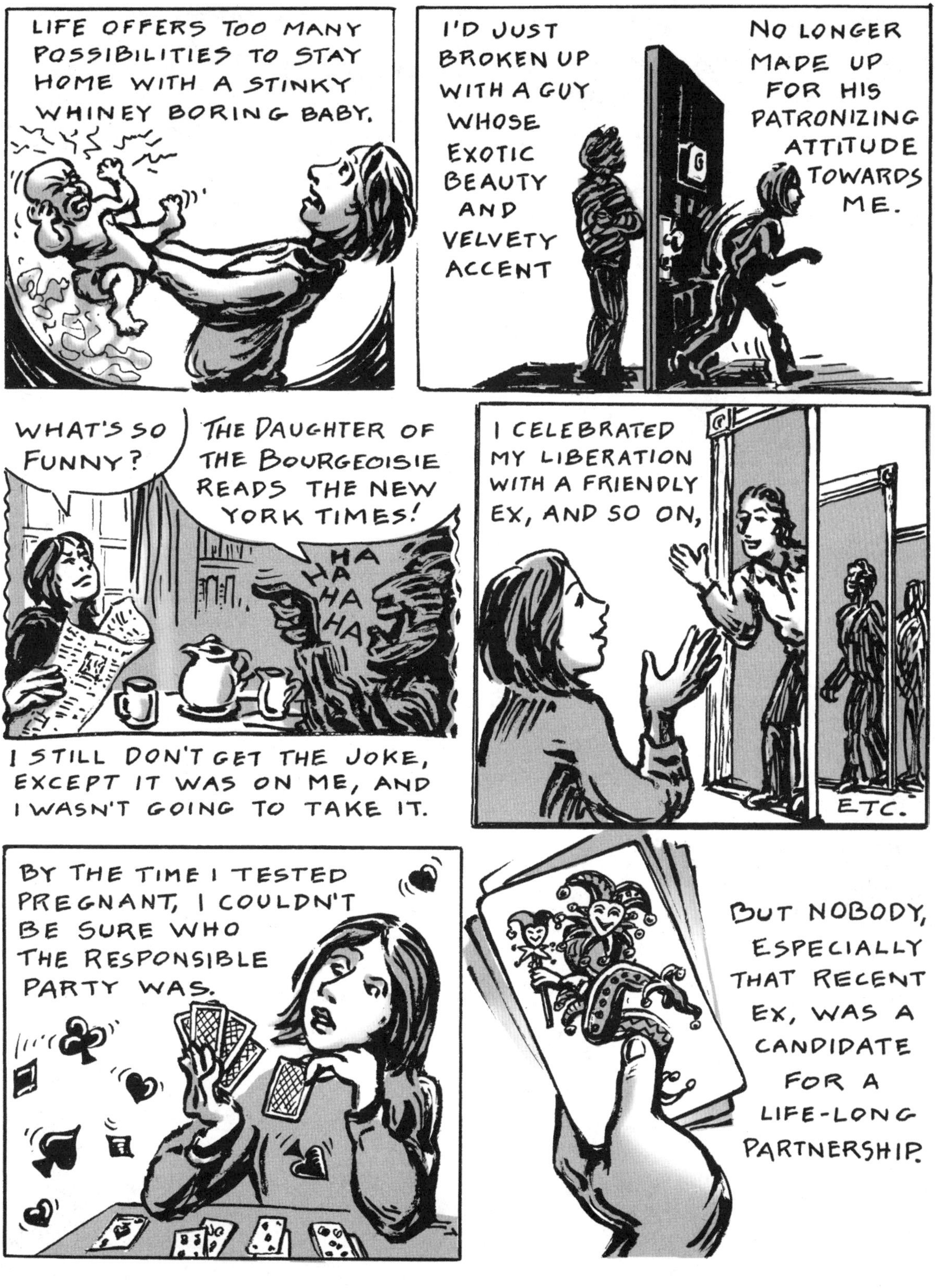
LIFE OFFERS TOO MANY POSSIBILITIES TO STAY HOME WITH A STINKY WHINEY BORING BABY.
I'D JUST BROKEN UP WITH A GUY WHOSE EXOTIC BEAUTY AND VELVETY ACCENT
NO LONGER MADE UP FOR HIS PATRONIZING ATTITUDE TOWARDS ME.
WHAT'S SO FUNNY?
THE DAUGHTER OF THE BOURGEOISIE READS THE NEW YORK TIMES!
HA HA HA HA HA
I STILL DON'T GET THE JOKE, EXCEPT IT WAS ON ME, AND I WASN'T GOING TO TAKE IT.
I CELEBRATED MY LIBERATION WITH A FRIENDLY EX, AND SO ON,
ETC.
BY THE TIME I TESTED PREGNANT, I COULDN'T BE SURE WHO THE RESPONSIBLE PARTY WAS.
BUT NOBODY, ESPECIALLY THAT RECENT EX, WAS A CANDIDATE FOR A LIFE-LONG PARTNERSHIP.

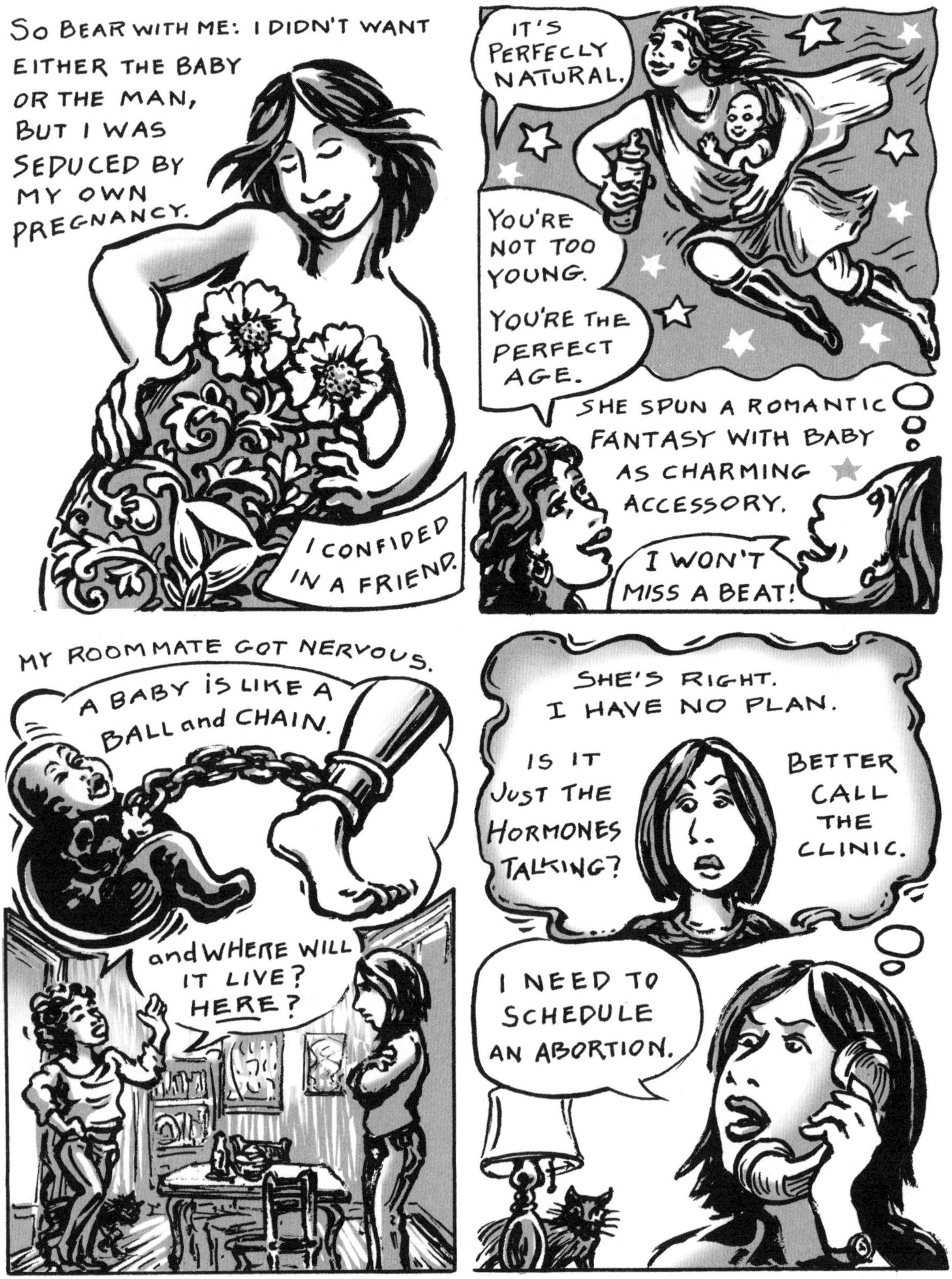

SO BEAR WITH ME: I DIDN'T WANT EITHER THE BABY OR THE MAN, BUT I WAS SEDUCED BY MY OWN PREGNANCY.
I CONFIDED IN A FRIEND.
IT'S PERFECLY NATURAL.
YOU'RE NOT TOO YOUNG.
YOU'RE THE PERFECT AGE.
SHE SPUN A ROMANTIC FANTASY WITH BABY AS CHARMING ACCESSORY.
I WON'T MISS A BEAT!
MY ROOMMATE GOT NERVOUS.
A BABY IS LIKE A BALL and CHAIN.
and WHERE WILL IT LIVE? HERE?
SHE'S RIGHT. I HAVE NO PLAN.
IS IT JUST THE HORMONES TALKING?
BETTER CALL THE CLINIC.
I NEED TO SCHEDULE AN ABORTION.

AFTER THE ABORTION, A FRIEND CALLED.

YOU WANT TO SUB FOR ME ON MY BABYSITTING JOB?

IT'LL CURE YOU OF ANY ILLUSIONS ABOUT SINGLE MOTHERHOOD.

OKAY

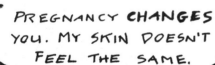

THE NEW MOTHER'S HOME WAS IN THE MIDST OF RENOVATION.

AND I'M TRYING TO HANG ON TO THE VESTIGES OF MY CAREER. IT'S EXHAUSTING!

PREGNANCY **CHANGES** YOU. MY SKIN DOESN'T FEEL THE SAME.

I CAN'T IMAGINE DOING IT ALONE. WHAT HAPPENS WHEN THE BABY GETS SICK, AND THEN **YOU** GET SICK?

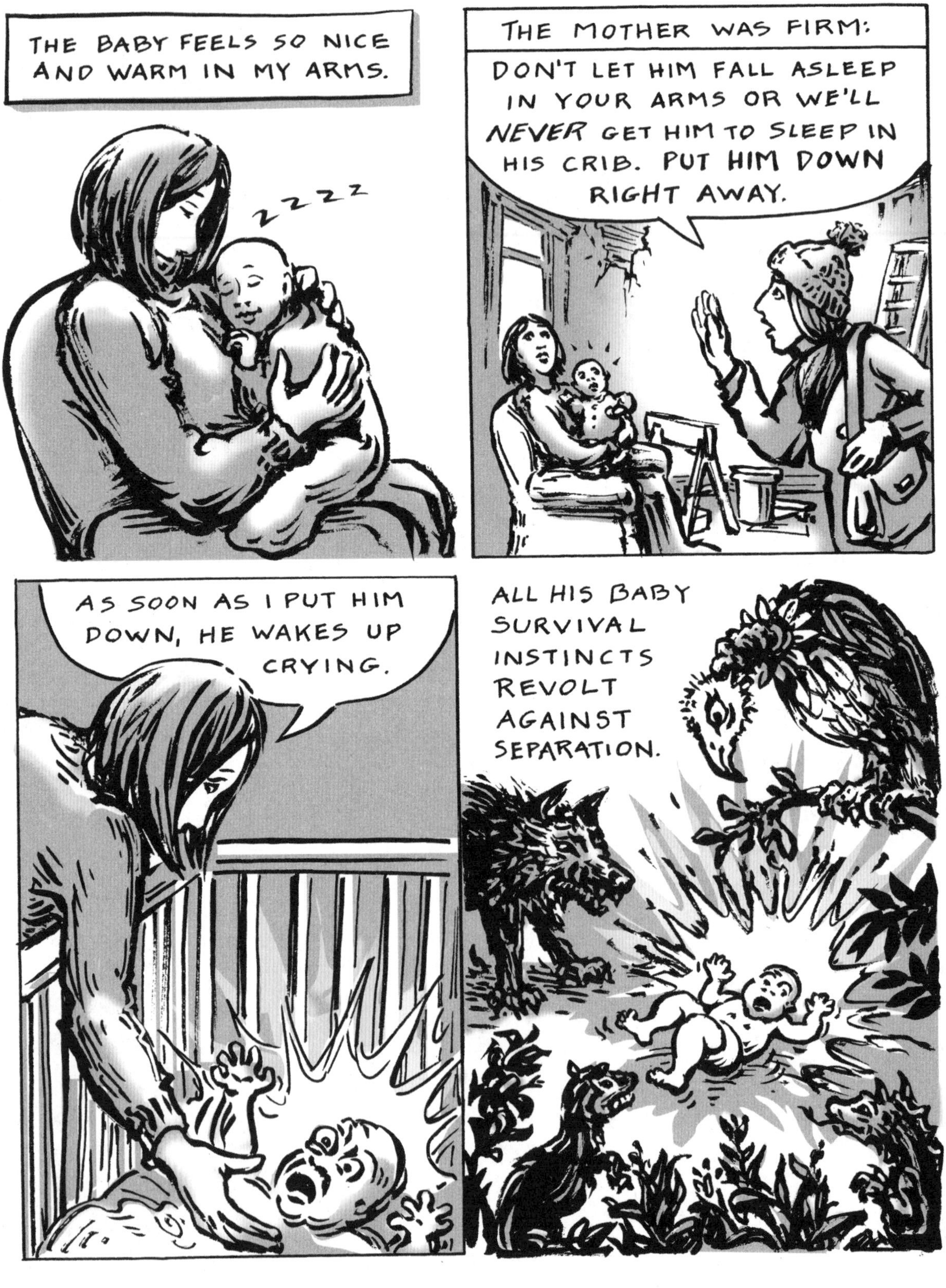
THE BABY FEELS SO NICE AND WARM IN MY ARMS.
ZZZZZ
THE MOTHER WAS FIRM:
DON'T LET HIM FALL ASLEEP IN YOUR ARMS OR WE'LL NEVER GET HIM TO SLEEP IN HIS CRIB. PUT HIM DOWN RIGHT AWAY.
AS SOON AS I PUT HIM DOWN, HE WAKES UP CRYING.
ALL HIS BABY SURVIVAL INSTINCTS REVOLT AGAINST SEPARATION.

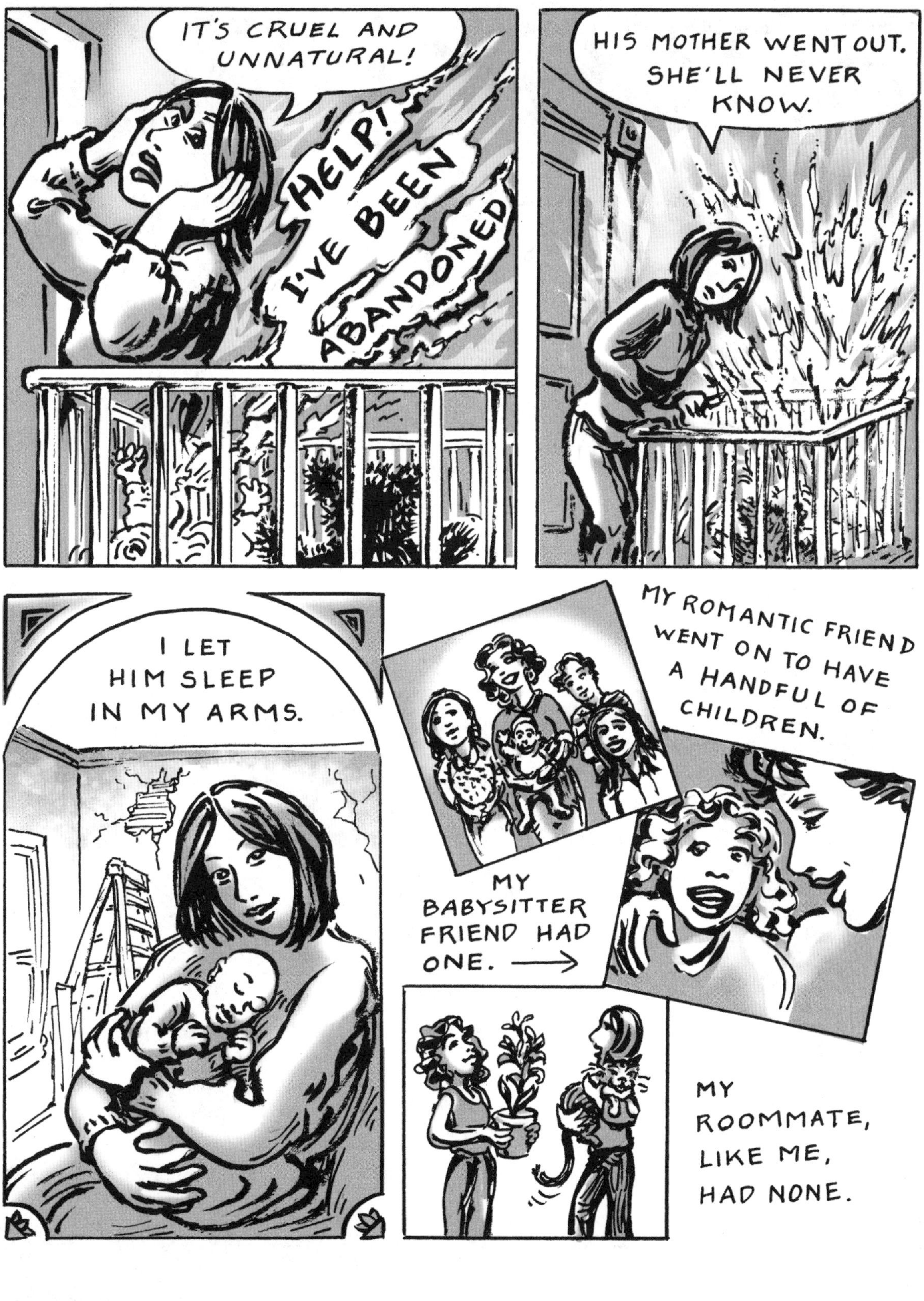
IT'S CRUEL AND UNNATURAL!
HELP! I'VE BEEN ABANDONED
HIS MOTHER WENT OUT. SHE'LL NEVER KNOW.
I LET HIM SLEEP IN MY ARMS.
MY ROMANTIC FRIEND WENT ON TO HAVE A HANDFUL OF CHILDREN.
MY BABYSITTER FRIEND HAD ONE.
MY ROOMMATE, LIKE ME, HAD NONE.

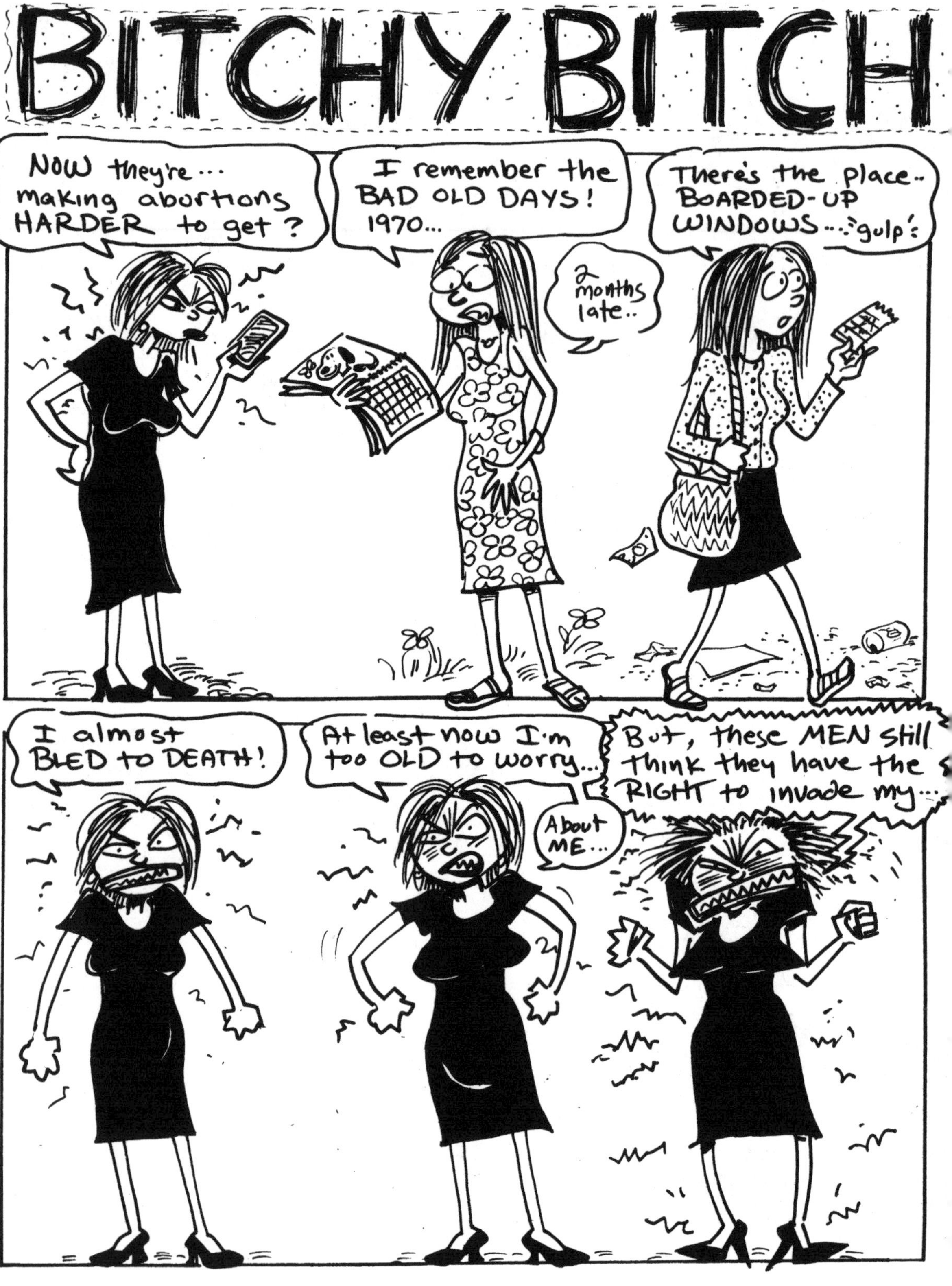
BITCHY BITCH
NOW they're… making abortions HARDER to get?
I remember the BAD OLD DAYS! 1970…
2 months late..
There's the place.. BOARDED-UP WINDOWS… gulp
I almost BLED to DEATH!
At least now I'm too OLD to worry…
About ME…
But, these MEN still think they have the RIGHT to invade my…

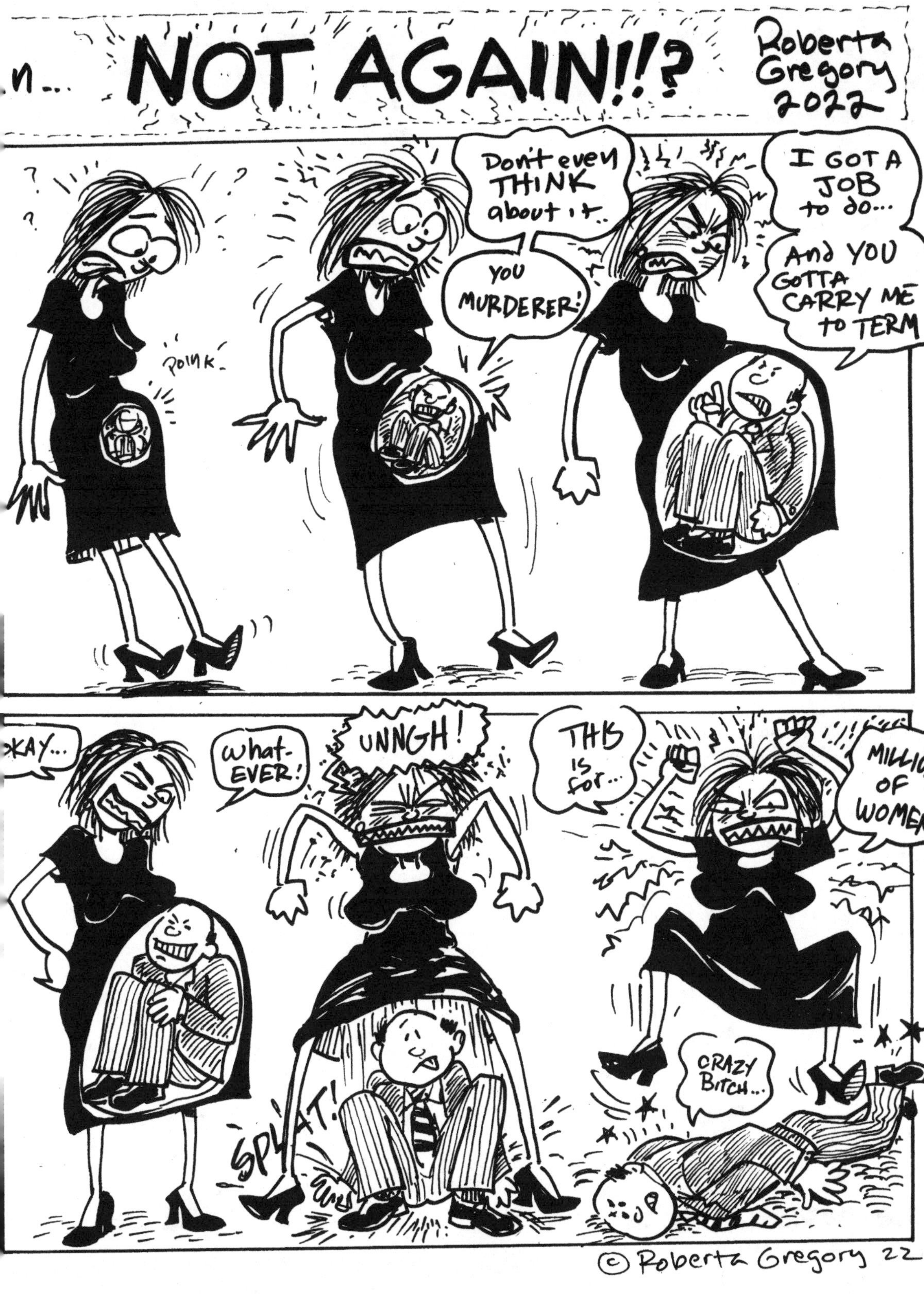
NOT AGAIN!!?
Roberta Gregory 2022
POINK
Don't even THINK about it..
YOU MURDERER!
I GOT A JOB to do...
And YOU GOTTA CARRY ME to TERM!
KAY...
what-EVER!
UNNGH!
SPLAT!
THIS is for...
MILLIONS OF WOMEN!
CRAZY BITCH...
© Roberta Gregory 22

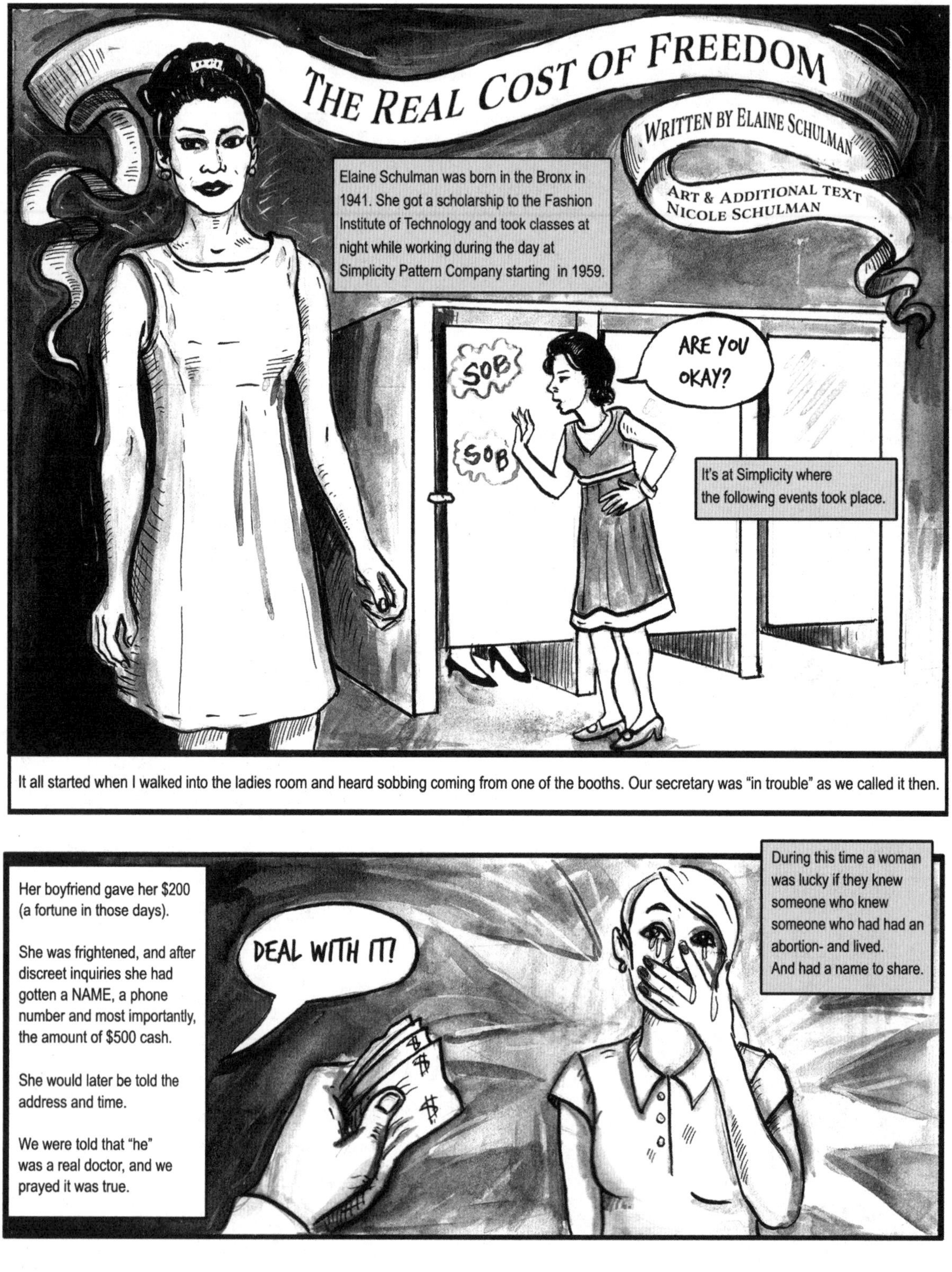
THE REAL COST OF FREEDOM
WRITTEN BY ELAINE SCHULMAN
ART & ADDITIONAL TEXT NICOLE SCHULMAN
Elaine Schulman was born in the Bronx in 1941. She got a scholarship to the Fashion Institute of Technology and took classes at night while working during the day at Simplicity Pattern Company starting in 1959.
SOB
SOB
ARE YOU OKAY?
It's at Simplicity where the following events took place.
It all started when I walked into the ladies room and heard sobbing coming from one of the booths. Our secretary was "in trouble" as we called it then.
Her boyfriend gave her $200 (a fortune in those days).
She was frightened, and after discreet inquiries she had gotten a NAME, a phone number and most importantly, the amount of $500 cash.
She would later be told the address and time.
We were told that "he" was a real doctor, and we prayed it was true.
DEAL WITH IT!
During this time a woman was lucky if they knew someone who knew someone who had had an abortion- and lived. And had a name to share.

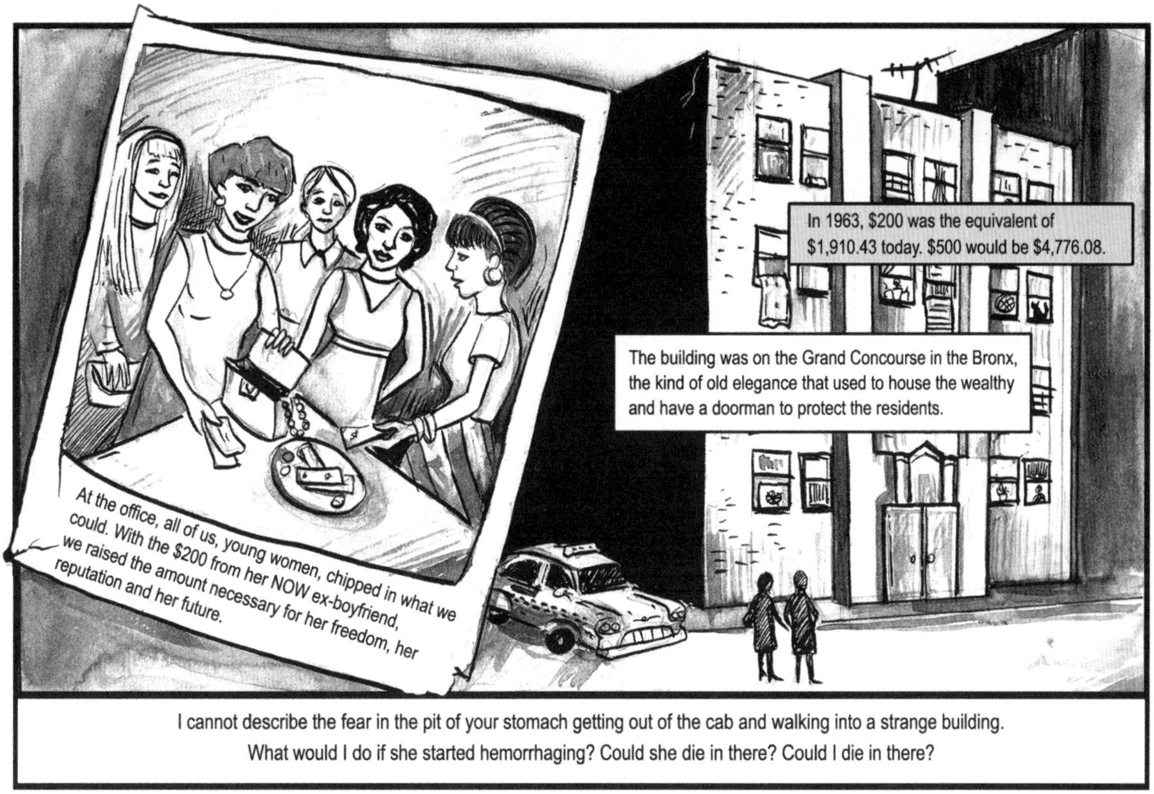
At the office, all of us, young women, chipped in what we could. With the $200 from her NOW ex-boyfriend, we raised the amount necessary for her freedom, her reputation and her future.
In 1963, $200 was the equivalent of $1,910.43 today. $500 would be $4,776.08.
The building was on the Grand Concourse in the Bronx, the kind of old elegance that used to house the wealthy and have a doorman to protect the residents.
I cannot describe the fear in the pit of your stomach getting out of the cab and walking into a strange building. What would I do if she started hemorrhaging? Could she die in there? Could I die in there?

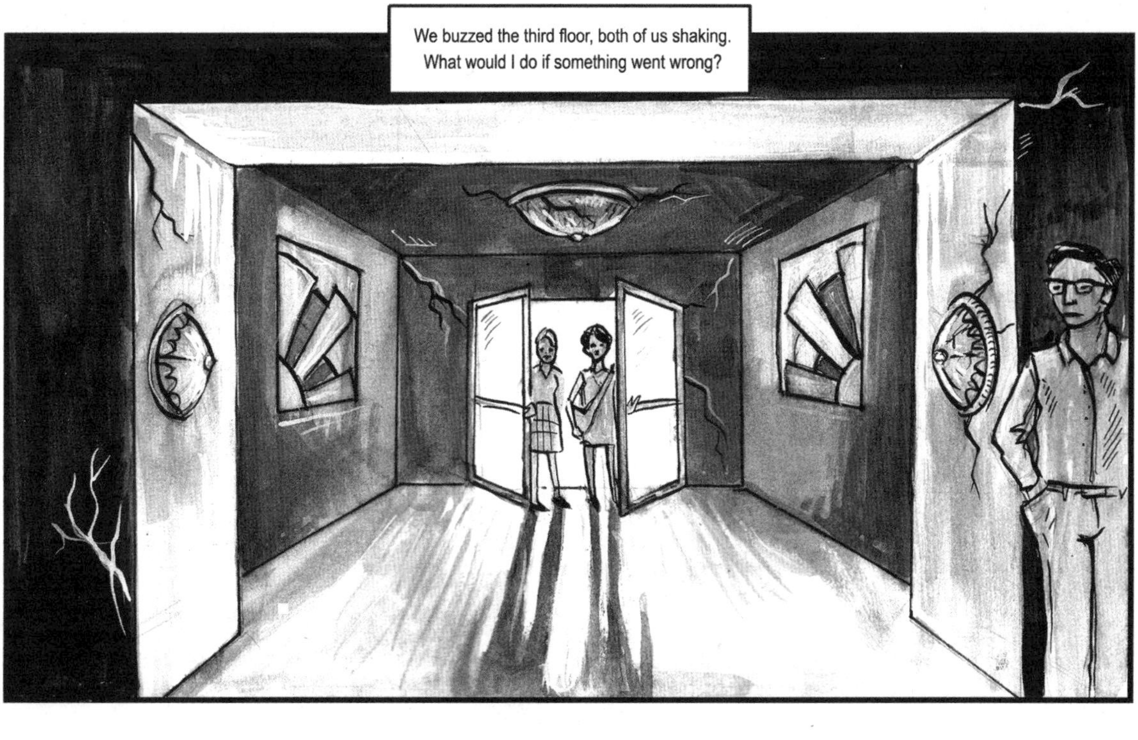
We buzzed the third floor, both of us shaking. What would I do if something went wrong?

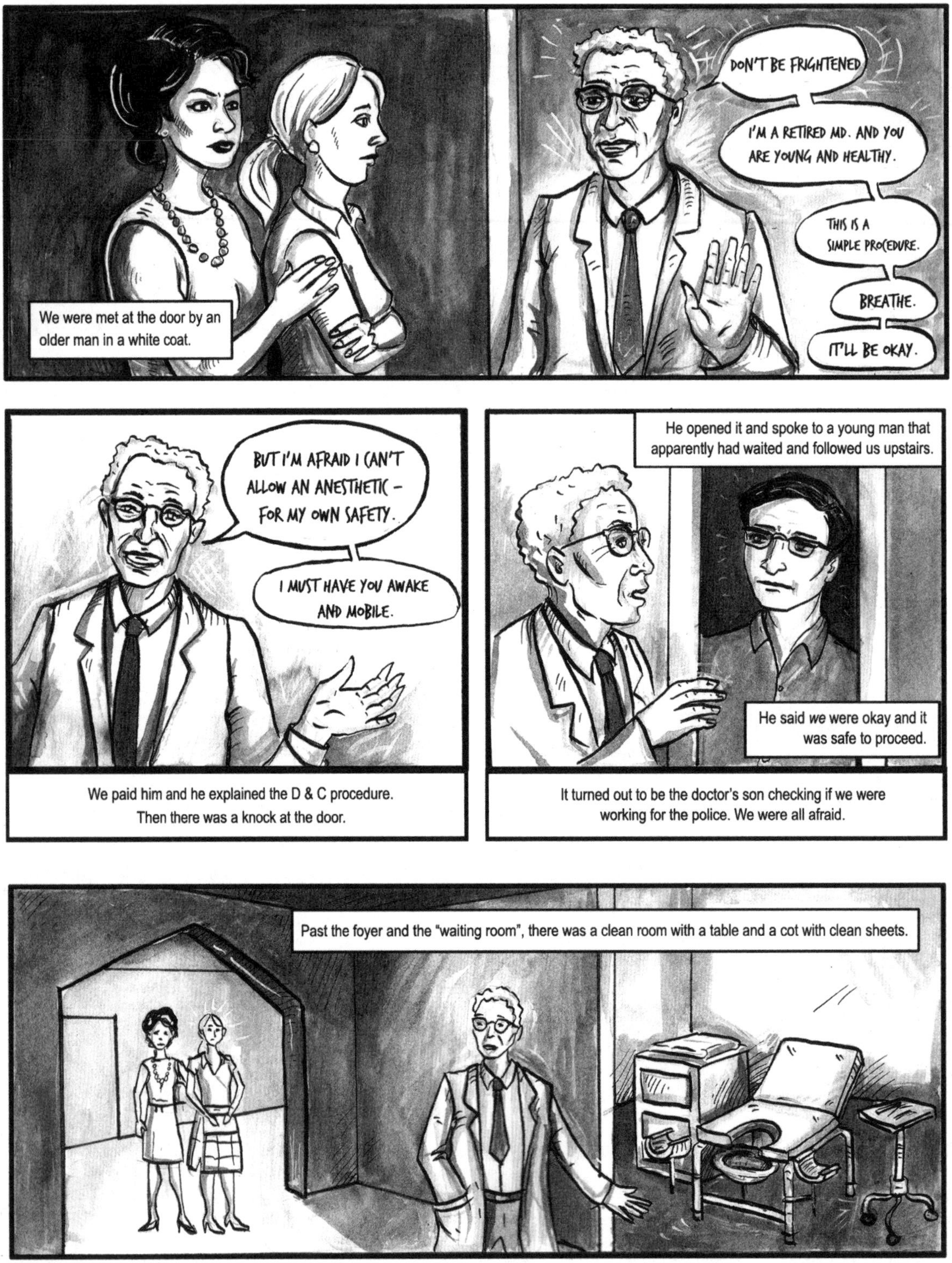
We were met at the door by an older man in a white coat.
DON'T BE FRIGHTENED
I'M A RETIRED MD. AND YOU ARE YOUNG AND HEALTHY.
THIS IS A SIMPLE PROCEDURE.
BREATHE.
IT'LL BE OKAY.
BUT I'M AFRAID I CAN'T ALLOW AN ANESTHETIC - FOR MY OWN SAFETY.
I MUST HAVE YOU AWAKE AND MOBILE.
We paid him and he explained the D & C procedure. Then there was a knock at the door.
He opened it and spoke to a young man that apparently had waited and followed us upstairs.
He said *we* were okay and it was safe to proceed.
It turned out to be the doctor's son checking if we were working for the police. We were all afraid.
Past the foyer and the "waiting room", there was a clean room with a table and a cot with clean sheets.

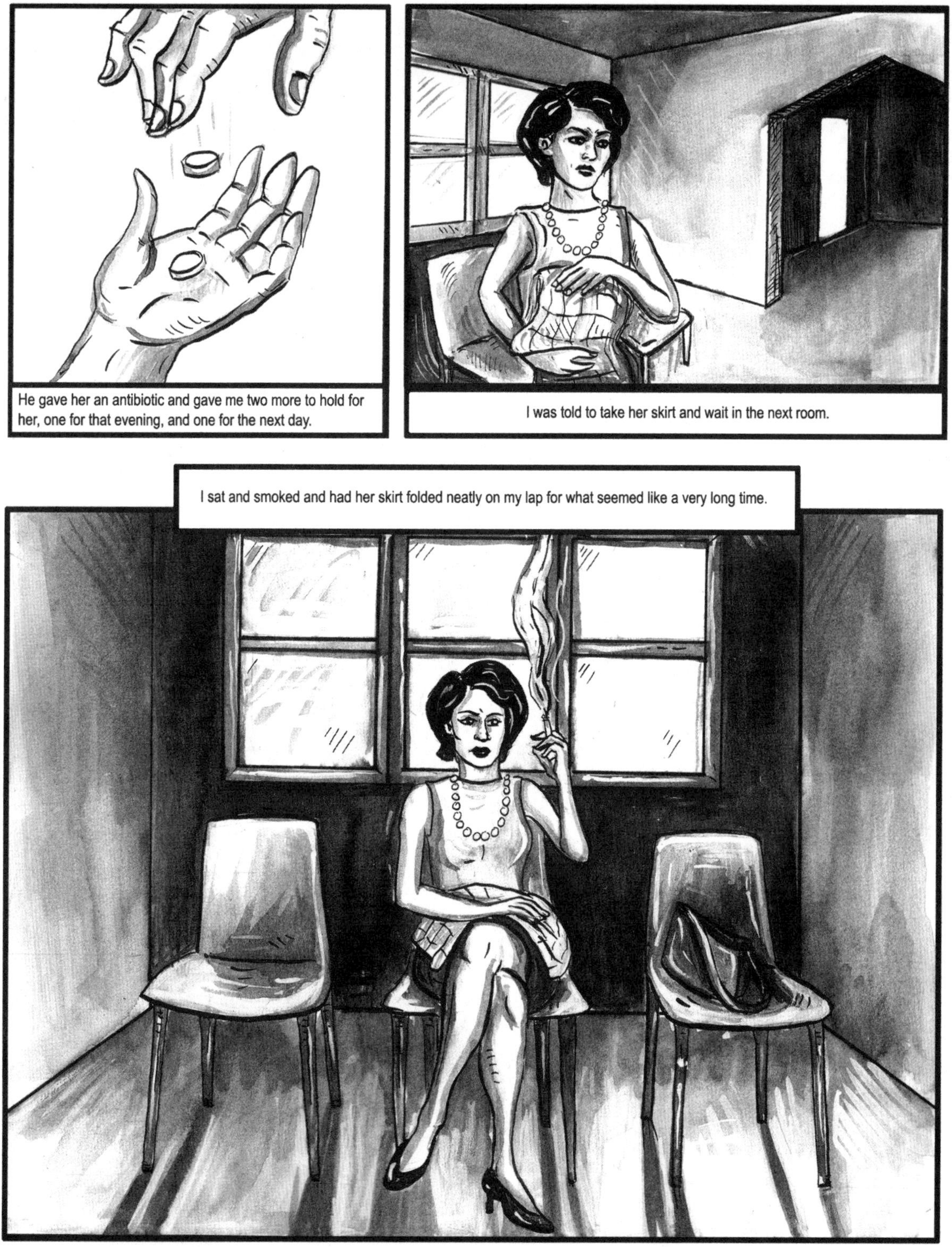
He gave her an antibiotic and gave me two more to hold for her, one for that evening, and one for the next day.
I was told to take her skirt and wait in the next room.
I sat and smoked and had her skirt folded neatly on my lap for what seemed like a very long time.

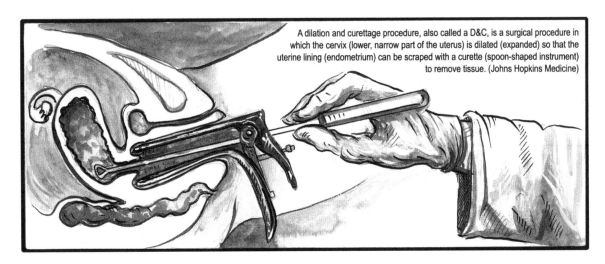

A dilation and curettage procedure, also called a D&C, is a surgical procedure in which the cervix (lower, narrow part of the uterus) is dilated (expanded) so that the uterine lining (endometrium) can be scraped with a curette (spoon-shaped instrument) to remove tissue. (Johns Hopkins Medicine)

Eventually, he came out and took his mask off...

...and smiled.

Everything had gone well and she was resting.

To calm herself during the D&C, she told the doctor about work and the girls there who had come together to help her.

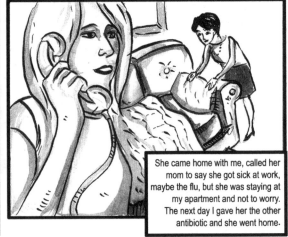

She came home with me, called her mom to say she got sick at work, maybe the flu, but she was staying at my apartment and not to worry. The next day I gave her the other antibiotic and she went home.

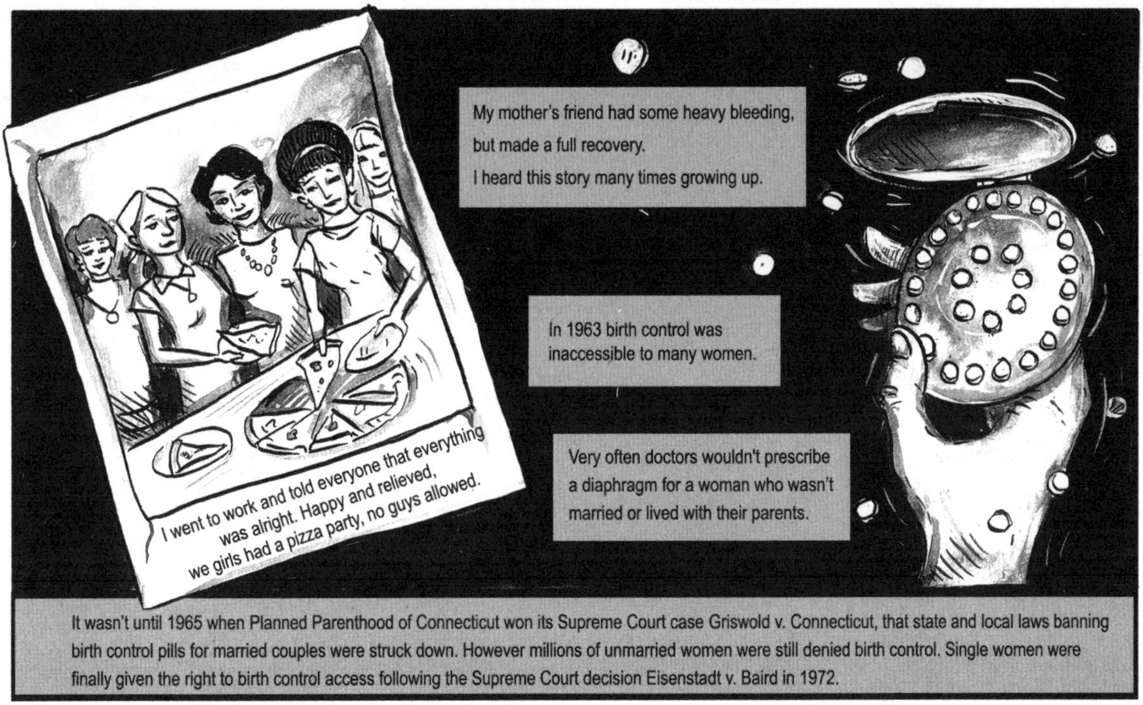
I went to work and told everyone that everything was alright. Happy and relieved, we girls had a pizza party, no guys allowed.
My mother's friend had some heavy bleeding, but made a full recovery.
I heard this story many times growing up.
In 1963 birth control was inaccessible to many women.
Very often doctors wouldn't prescribe a diaphragm for a woman who wasn't married or lived with their parents.
It wasn't until 1965 when Planned Parenthood of Connecticut won its Supreme Court case Griswold v. Connecticut, that state and local laws banning birth control pills for married couples were struck down. However millions of unmarried women were still denied birth control. Single women were finally given the right to birth control access following the Supreme Court decision Eisenstadt v. Baird in 1972.

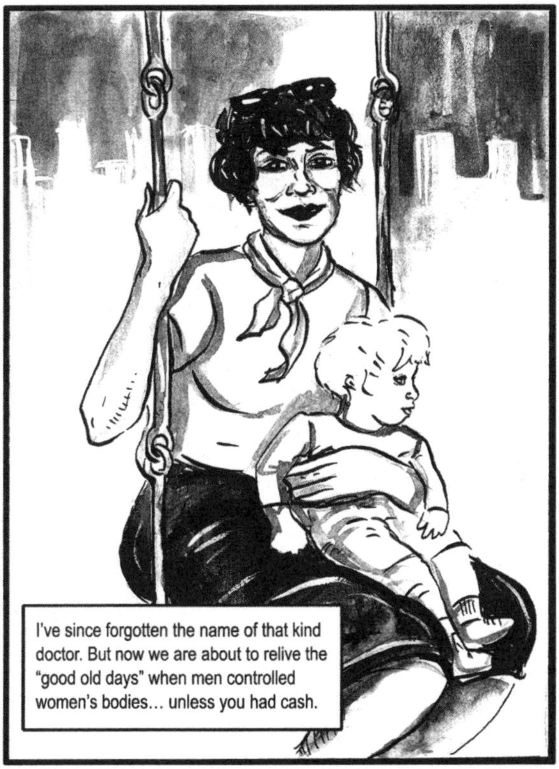
I've since forgotten the name of that kind doctor. But now we are about to relive the "good old days" when men controlled women's bodies… unless you had cash.

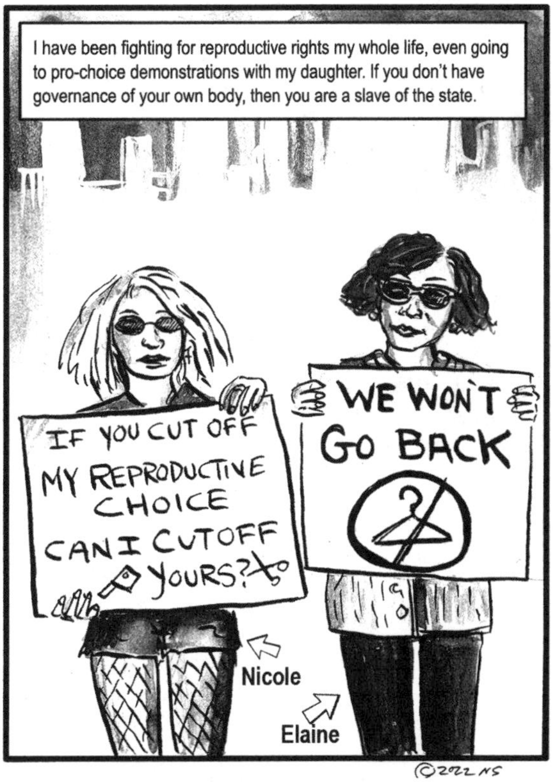
I have been fighting for reproductive rights my whole life, even going to pro-choice demonstrations with my daughter. If you don't have governance of your own body, then you are a slave of the state.
IF YOU CUT OFF MY REPRODUCTIVE CHOICE CAN I CUTOFF YOURS?
WE WON'T GO BACK
Nicole
Elaine

©2022 NS

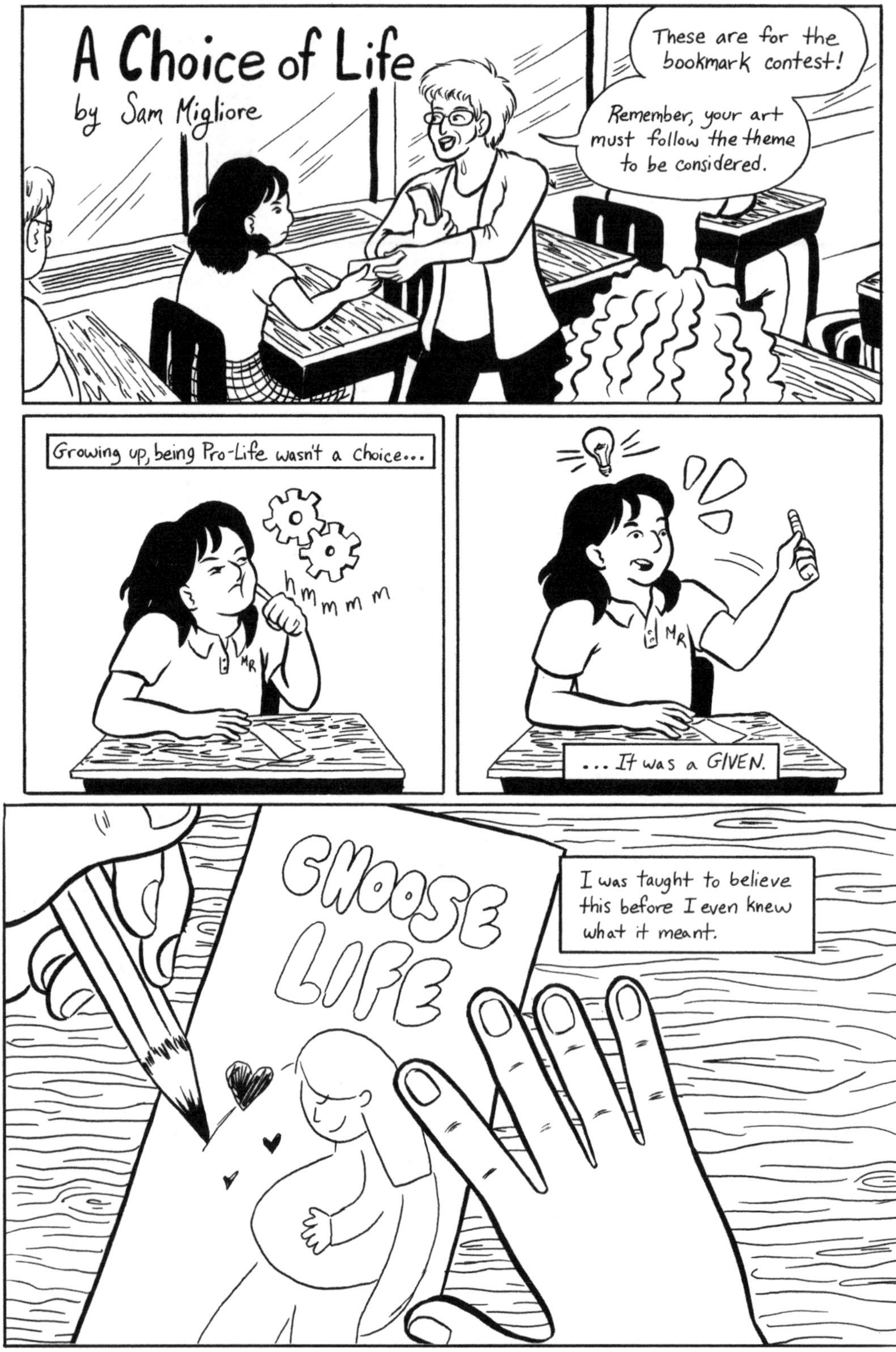
A Choice of Life
by Sam Migliore
These are for the bookmark contest!
Remember, your art must follow the theme to be considered.
Growing up, being Pro-Life wasn't a choice...
hmmmm
MR
MR
... It was a GIVEN.
CHOOSE LIFE
I was taught to believe this before I even knew what it meant.

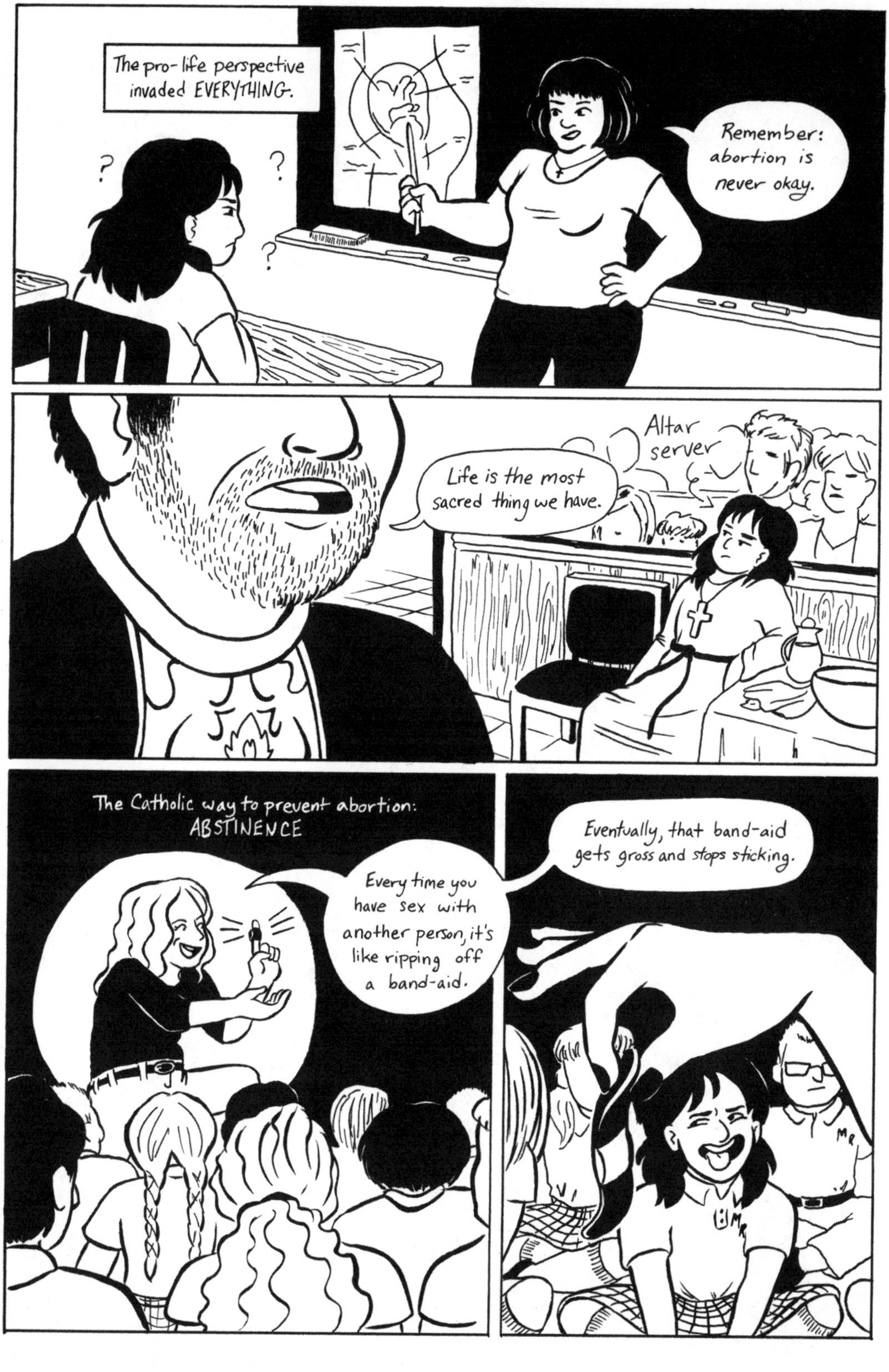

The pro-life perspective invaded EVERYTHING.
Remember: abortion is never okay.
Altar server
Life is the most sacred thing we have.
The Catholic way to prevent abortion: ABSTINENCE
Every time you have sex with another person, it's like ripping off a band-aid.
Eventually, that band-aid gets gross and stops sticking.

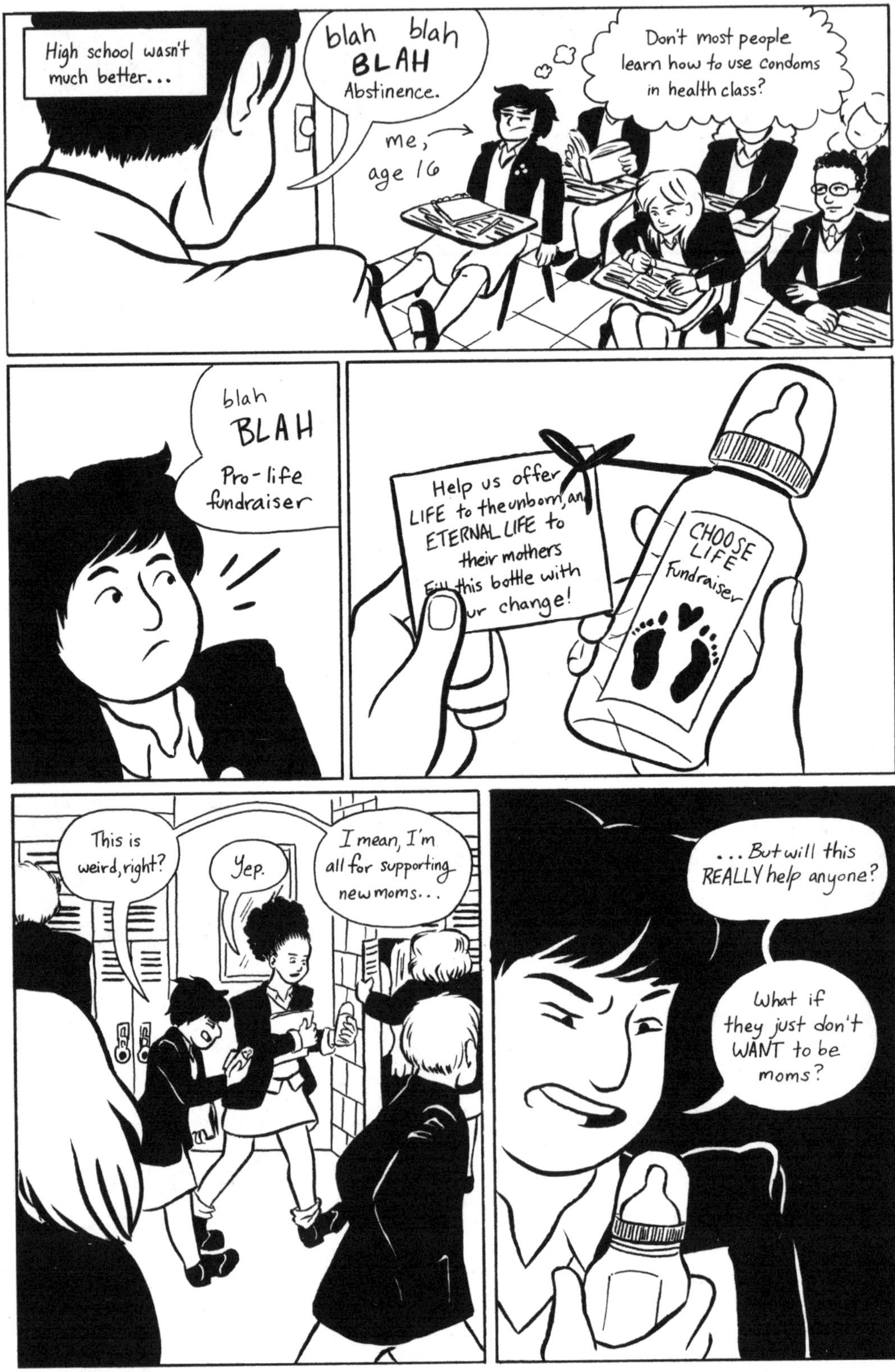

High school wasn't much better...
blah blah BLAH Abstinence.
me, age 16
Don't most people learn how to use condoms in health class?
blah BLAH Pro-life fundraiser
Help us offer
LIFE to the unborn, an
ETERNAL LIFE to
their mothers
this bottle with
ur change!
CHOOSE LIFE Fundraiser
This is weird, right?
Yep.
I mean, I'm all for supporting new moms...
...But will this REALLY help anyone?
What if they just don't WANT to be moms?

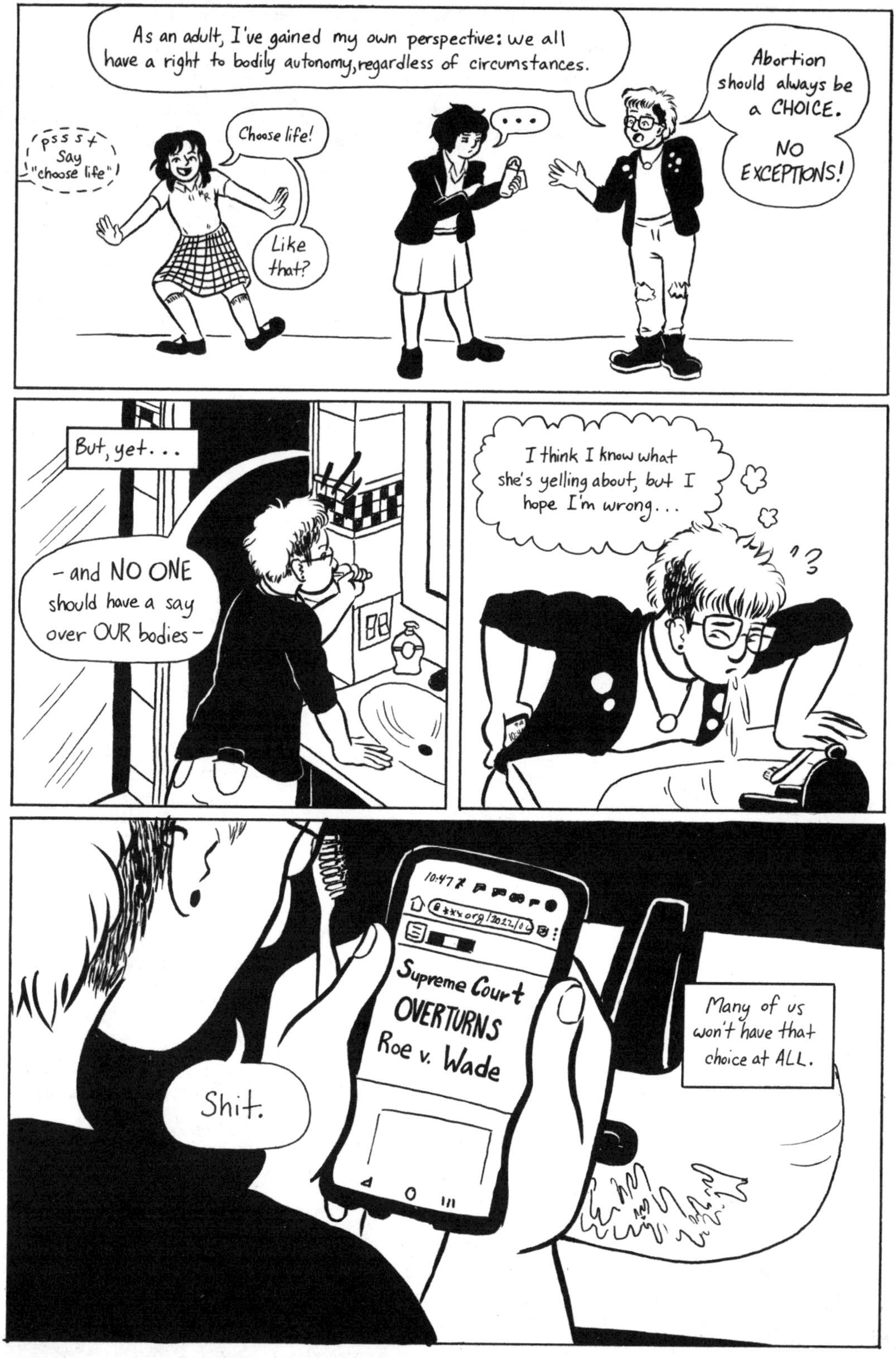
As an adult, I've gained my own perspective: we all have a right to bodily autonomy, regardless of circumstances.
psssst Say "choose life"
Choose life!
Like that?
...
Abortion should always be a CHOICE.
NO EXCEPTIONS!
But, yet...
- and NO ONE should have a say over OUR bodies -
I think I know what she's yelling about, but I hope I'm wrong...
Supreme Court OVERTURNS Roe v. Wade
Shit.
Many of us won't have that choice at ALL.

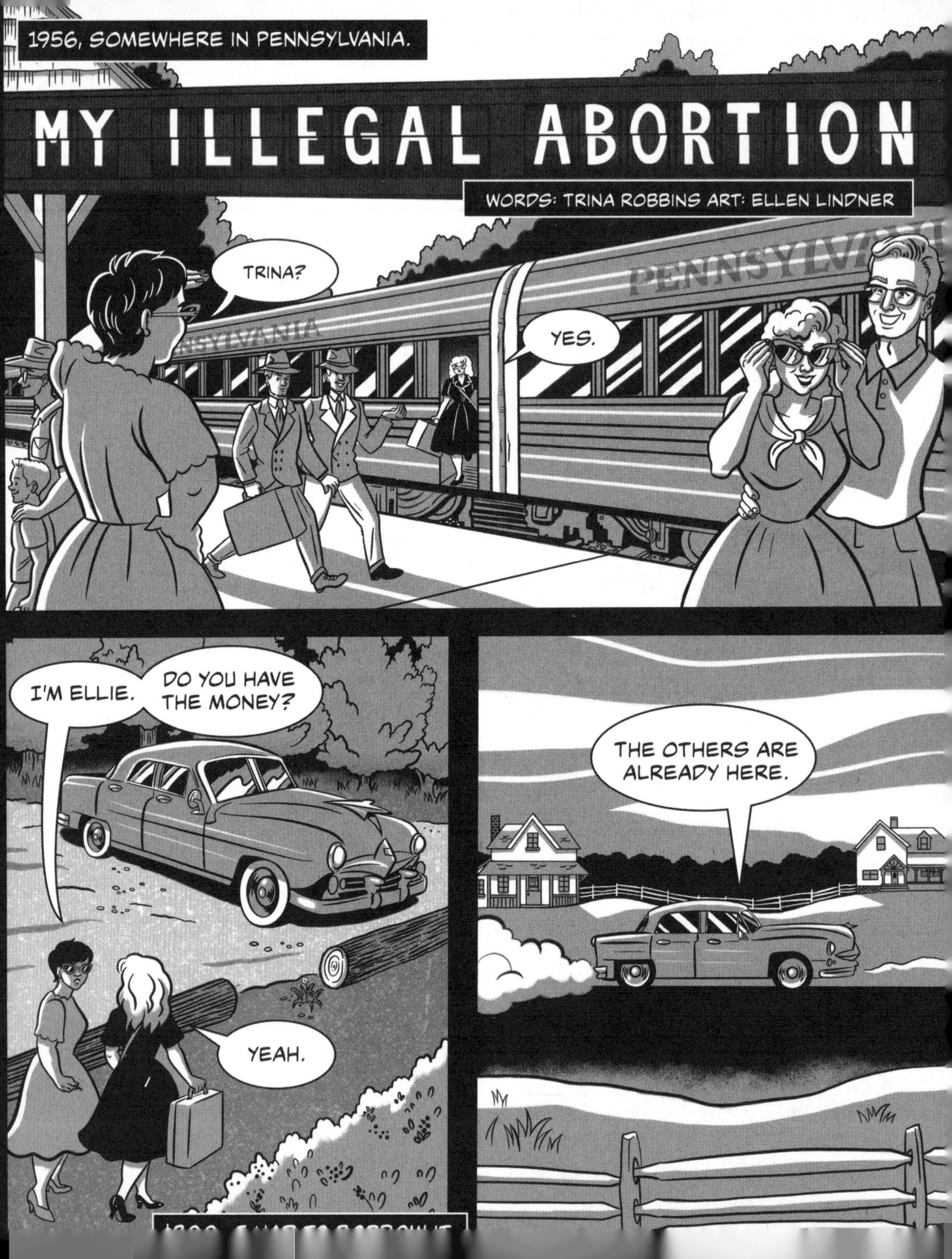
1956, SOMEWHERE IN PENNSYLVANIA.
MY ILLEGAL ABORTION
WORDS: TRINA ROBBINS ART: ELLEN LINDNER
TRINA?
YES.
I'M ELLIE.
DO YOU HAVE THE MONEY?
YEAH.
THE OTHERS ARE ALREADY HERE.

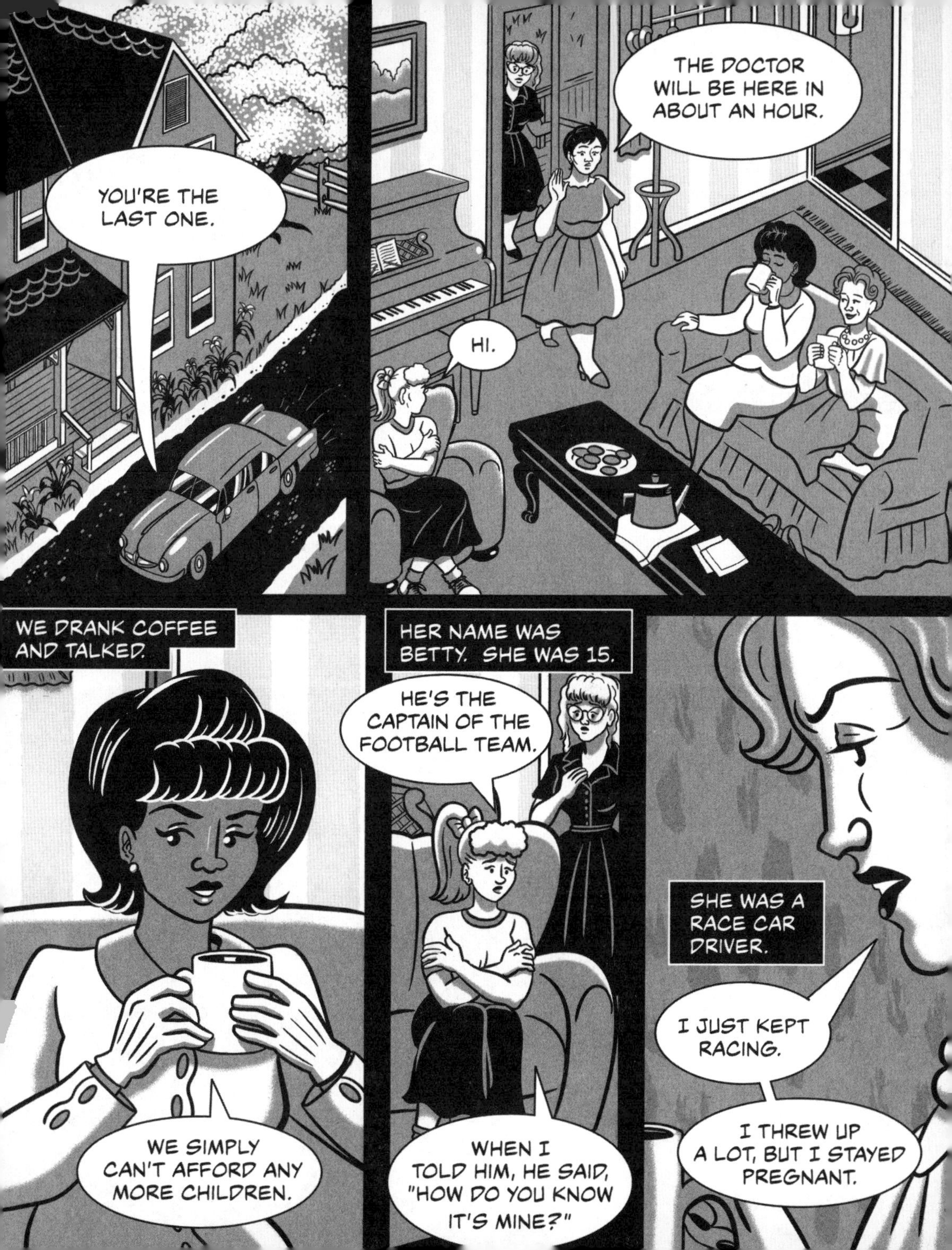

YOU'RE THE LAST ONE.
THE DOCTOR WILL BE HERE IN ABOUT AN HOUR.
HI.
WE DRANK COFFEE AND TALKED.
WE SIMPLY CAN'T AFFORD ANY MORE CHILDREN.
HER NAME WAS BETTY. SHE WAS 15.
HE'S THE CAPTAIN OF THE FOOTBALL TEAM.
WHEN I TOLD HIM, HE SAID, "HOW DO YOU KNOW IT'S MINE?"
SHE WAS A RACE CAR DRIVER.
I JUST KEPT RACING.
I THREW UP A LOT, BUT I STAYED PREGNANT.

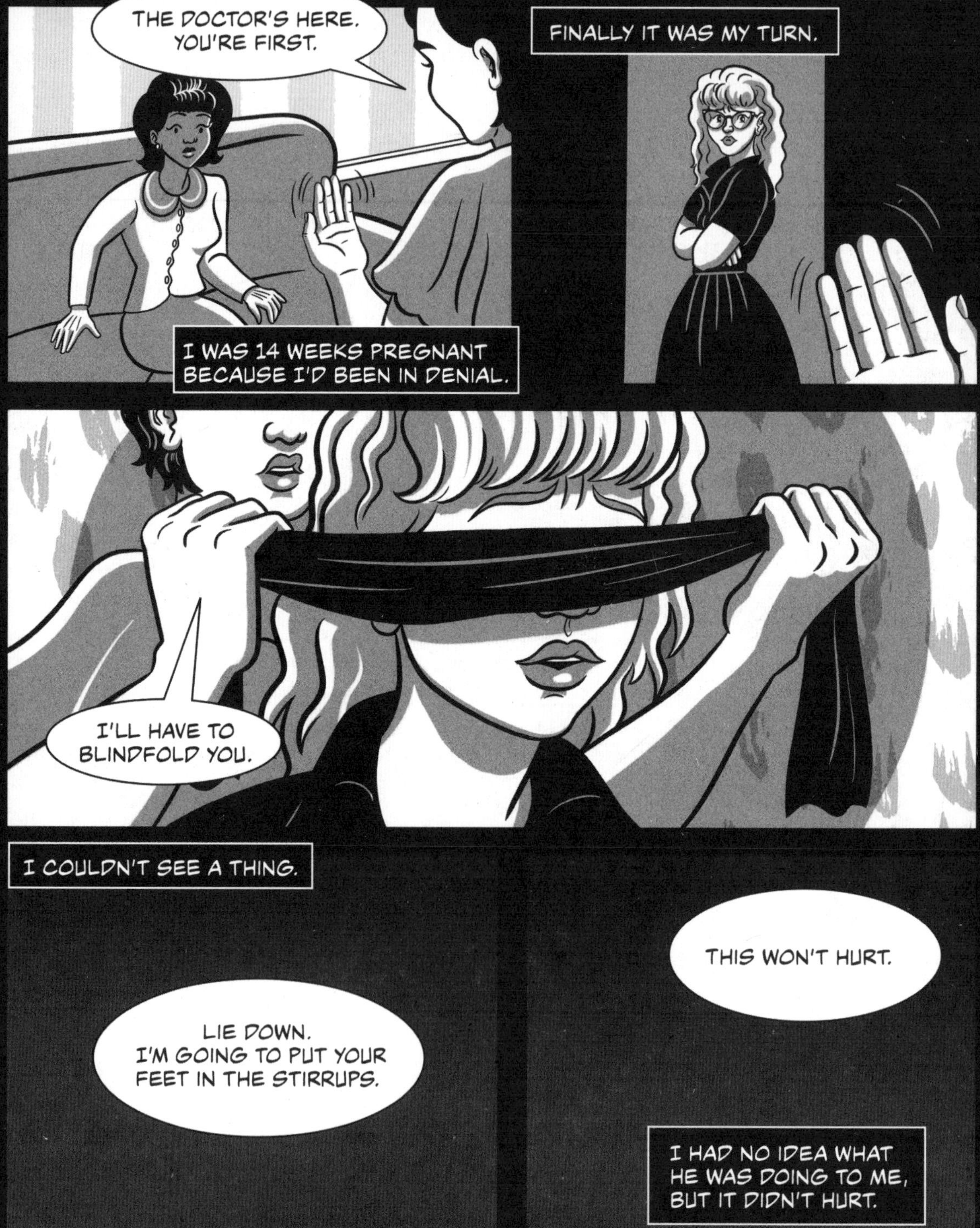
THE DOCTOR'S HERE. YOU'RE FIRST.
I WAS 14 WEEKS PREGNANT BECAUSE I'D BEEN IN DENIAL.
FINALLY IT WAS MY TURN.
I'LL HAVE TO BLINDFOLD YOU.
I COULDN'T SEE A THING.
LIE DOWN. I'M GOING TO PUT YOUR FEET IN THE STIRRUPS.
THIS WON'T HURT.
I HAD NO IDEA WHAT HE WAS DOING TO ME, BUT IT DIDN'T HURT.

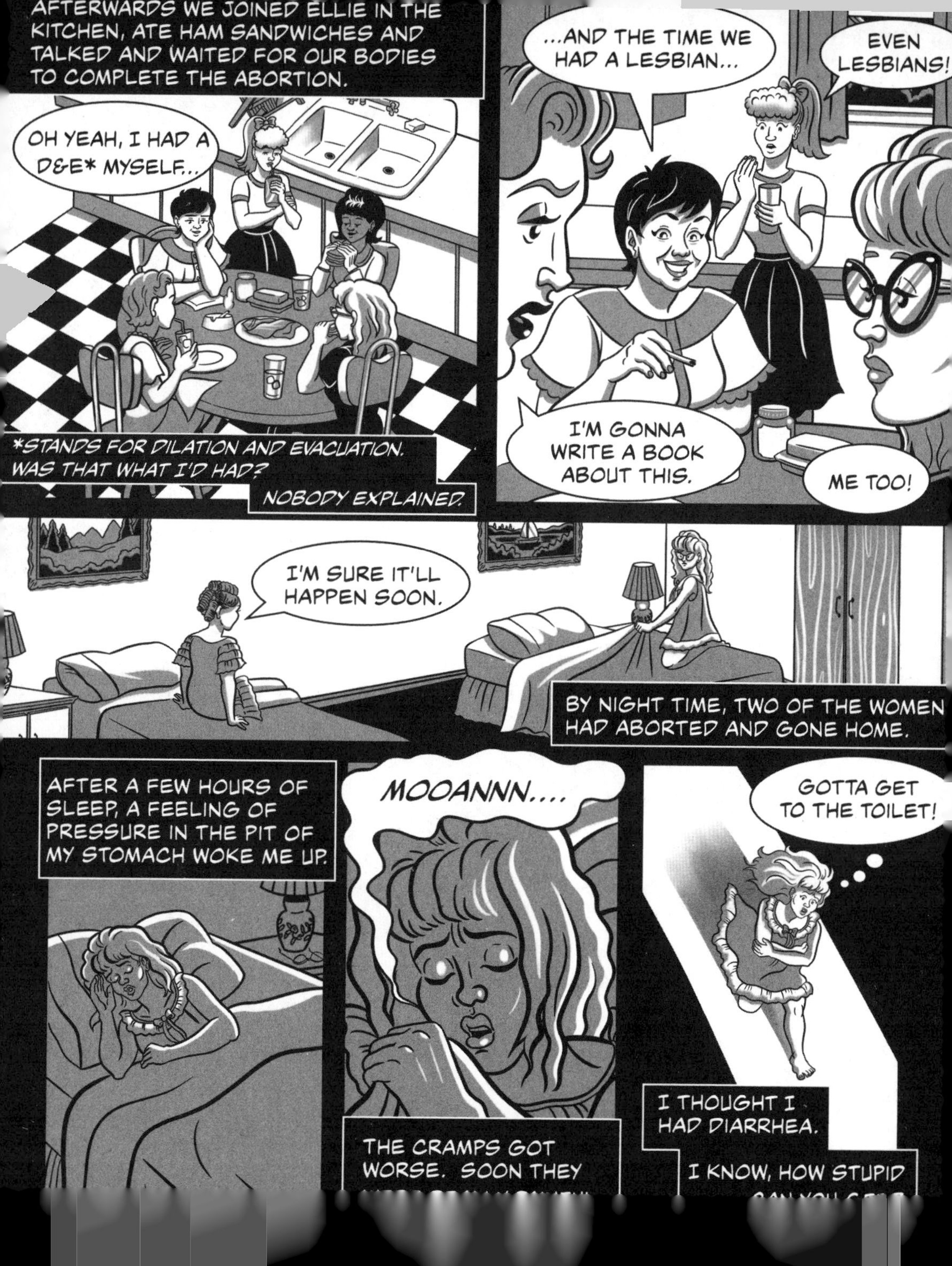
AFTERWARDS WE JOINED ELLIE IN THE KITCHEN, ATE HAM SANDWICHES AND TALKED AND WAITED FOR OUR BODIES TO COMPLETE THE ABORTION.
OH YEAH, I HAD A D&E* MYSELF...
*STANDS FOR DILATION AND EVACUATION. WAS THAT WHAT I'D HAD?
NOBODY EXPLAINED.
...AND THE TIME WE HAD A LESBIAN...
EVEN LESBIANS!
I'M GONNA WRITE A BOOK ABOUT THIS.
ME TOO!
I'M SURE IT'LL HAPPEN SOON.
BY NIGHT TIME, TWO OF THE WOMEN HAD ABORTED AND GONE HOME.
AFTER A FEW HOURS OF SLEEP, A FEELING OF PRESSURE IN THE PIT OF MY STOMACH WOKE ME UP.
MOOANNN....
THE CRAMPS GOT WORSE. SOON THEY
GOTTA GET TO THE TOILET!
I THOUGHT I HAD DIARRHEA.
I KNOW, HOW STUPID

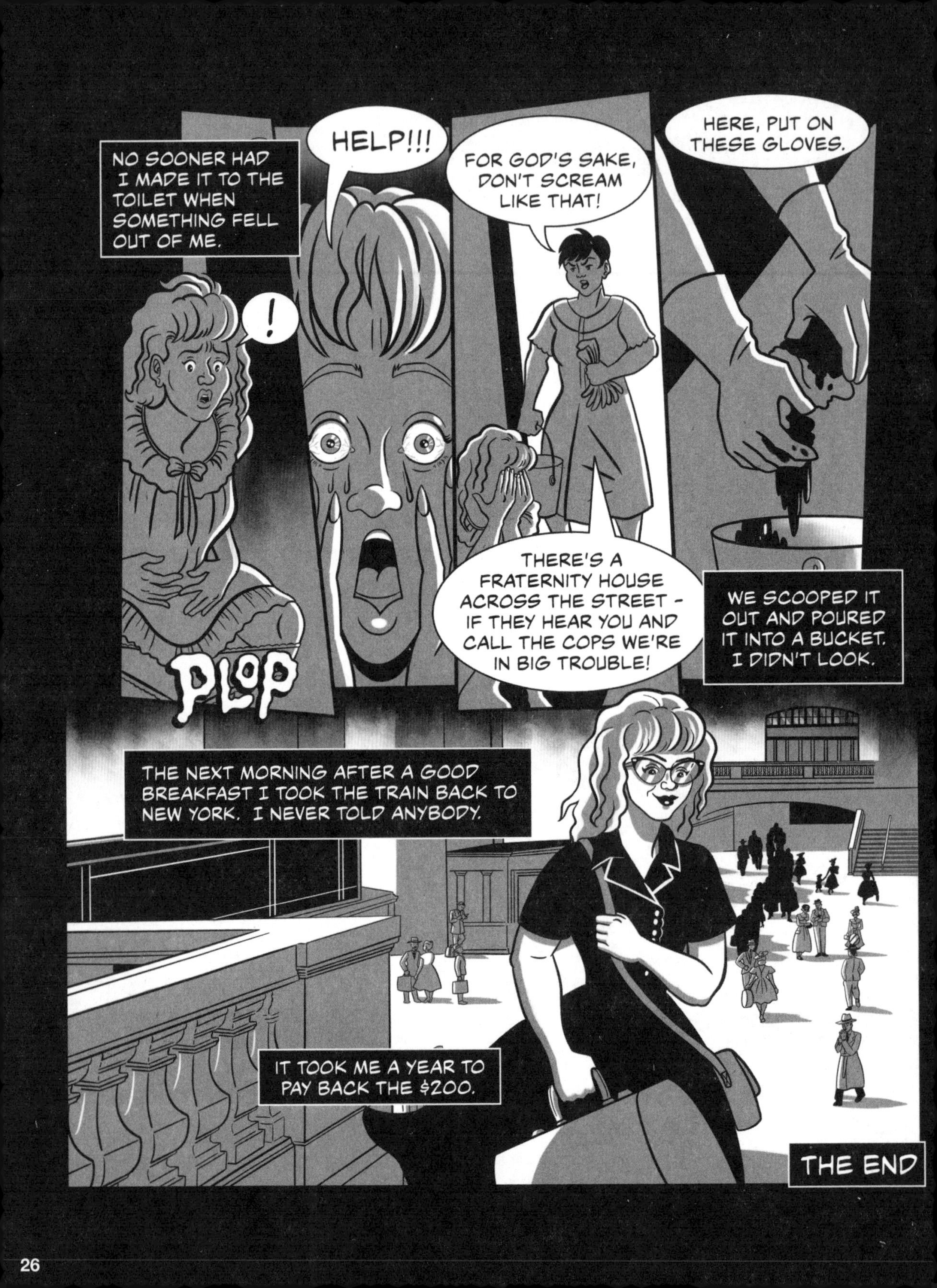
NO SOONER HAD I MADE IT TO THE TOILET WHEN SOMETHING FELL OUT OF ME.
!
PLOP
HELP!!!
FOR GOD'S SAKE, DON'T SCREAM LIKE THAT!
THERE'S A FRATERNITY HOUSE ACROSS THE STREET - IF THEY HEAR YOU AND CALL THE COPS WE'RE IN BIG TROUBLE!
HERE, PUT ON THESE GLOVES.
WE SCOOPED IT OUT AND POURED IT INTO A BUCKET. I DIDN'T LOOK.
THE NEXT MORNING AFTER A GOOD BREAKFAST I TOOK THE TRAIN BACK TO NEW YORK. I NEVER TOLD ANYBODY.
IT TOOK ME A YEAR TO PAY BACK THE $200.
THE END

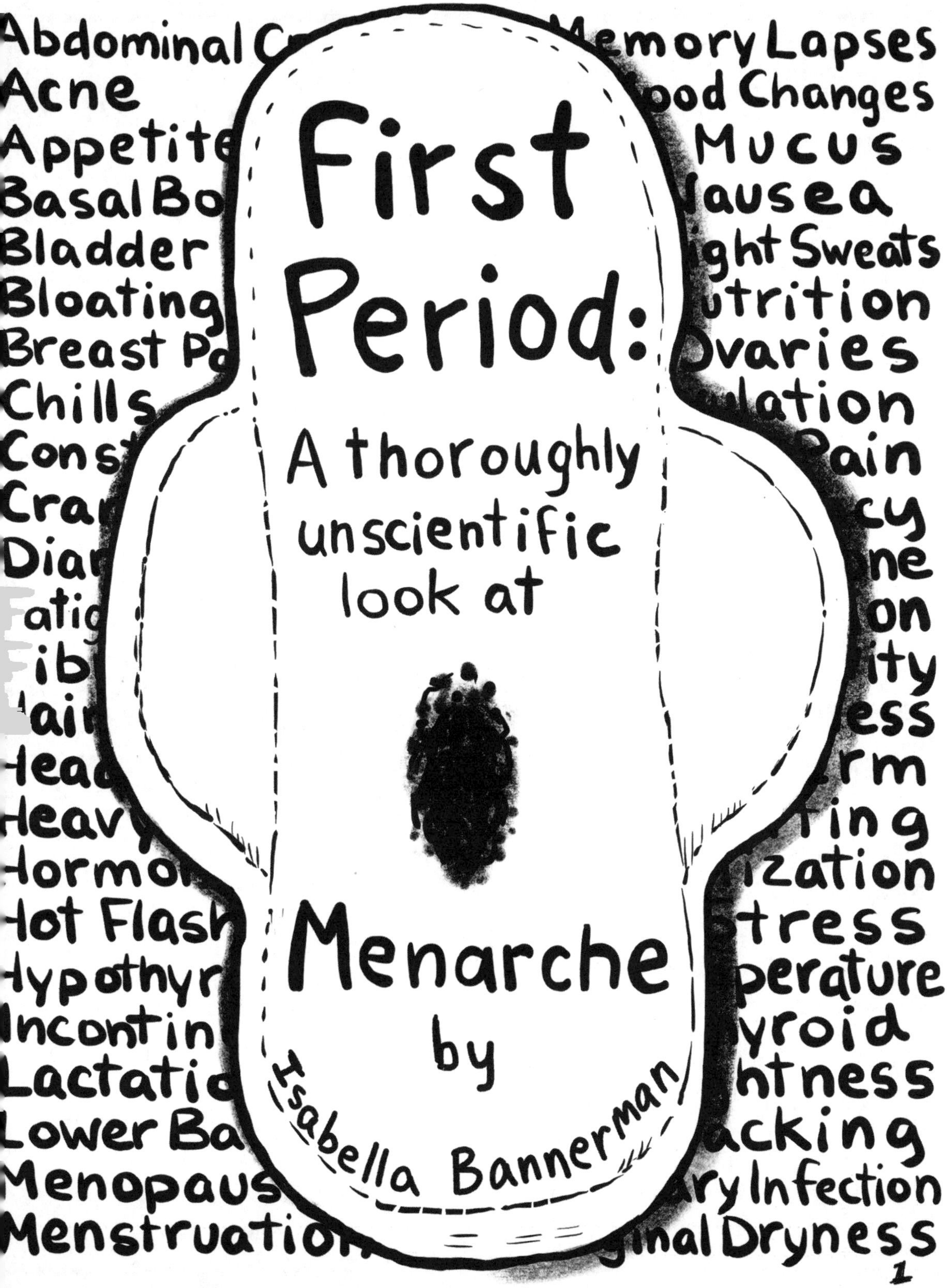

Abdominal C...   Memory Lapses
Acne   ...ood Changes
Appetite...   Mucus
BasalBo...   ...ausea
Bladder   ...ght Sweats
Bloating   ...utrition
Breast P...   Ovaries
Chills   ...lation
Cons...   ...Pain
Cra...   ...cy
Dia...   ...ne
...atio   ...on
...ib...   ...ty
...air   ...ess
...ead   ...rm
Heavy   ...ting
Hormor...   ...ization
Hot Flash...   ...tress
Hypothyr...   ...perature
Incontin...   ...yroid
Lactatio...   ...htness
Lower Ba...   ...acking
Menopaus...   ...ry Infection
Menstruation...   ...ginal Dryness

First Period:

A thoroughly unscientific look at

Menarche

by

Isabella Bannerman

1

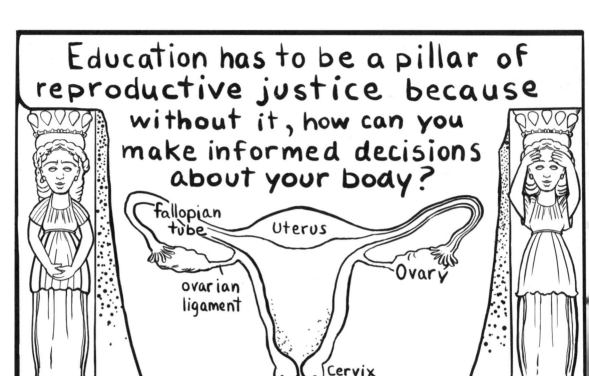

Education has to be a pillar of reproductive justice because without it, how can you make informed decisions about your body?

fallopian tube

Uterus

ovarian ligament

Ovary

Cervix

vagina

War disrupts education of every kind.

Both my mother and mother-in-law were separated from their mothers during World War II.

Italy, 1943 No one had told me anything, so I thought I was dying. I phoned my older sister and she laughed, and then she explained—a little. But nobody talked about periods in those days. I used cotton washcloths and rinsed them with bleach.

Sweden, 1945 No one had told me anything, so I thought I was bleeding to death. I called my mother. She said, *Isn't it wonderful?* I thought it was terrible. Then I told my grandmother, who I was living with at the time.

2

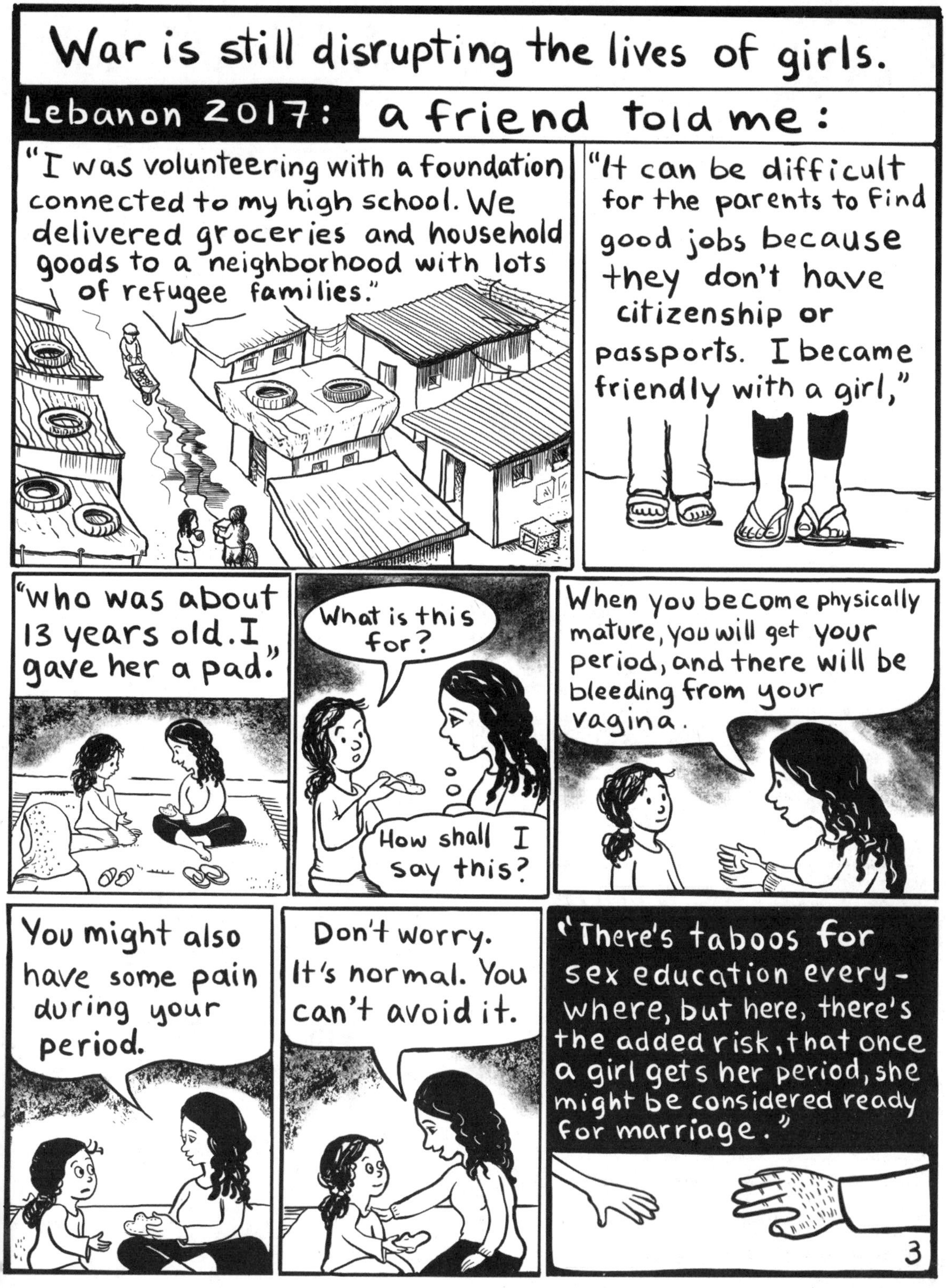
War is still disrupting the lives of girls.
Lebanon 2017: a friend told me:
"I was volunteering with a foundation connected to my high school. We delivered groceries and household goods to a neighborhood with lots of refugee families."
"It can be difficult for the parents to find good jobs because they don't have citizenship or passports. I became friendly with a girl,"
"who was about 13 years old. I gave her a pad."
What is this for?
How shall I say this?
When you become physically mature, you will get your period, and there will be bleeding from your vagina.
You might also have some pain during your period.
Don't worry. It's normal. You can't avoid it.
"There's taboos for sex education every-where, but here, there's the added risk, that once a girl gets her period, she might be considered ready for marriage."
3

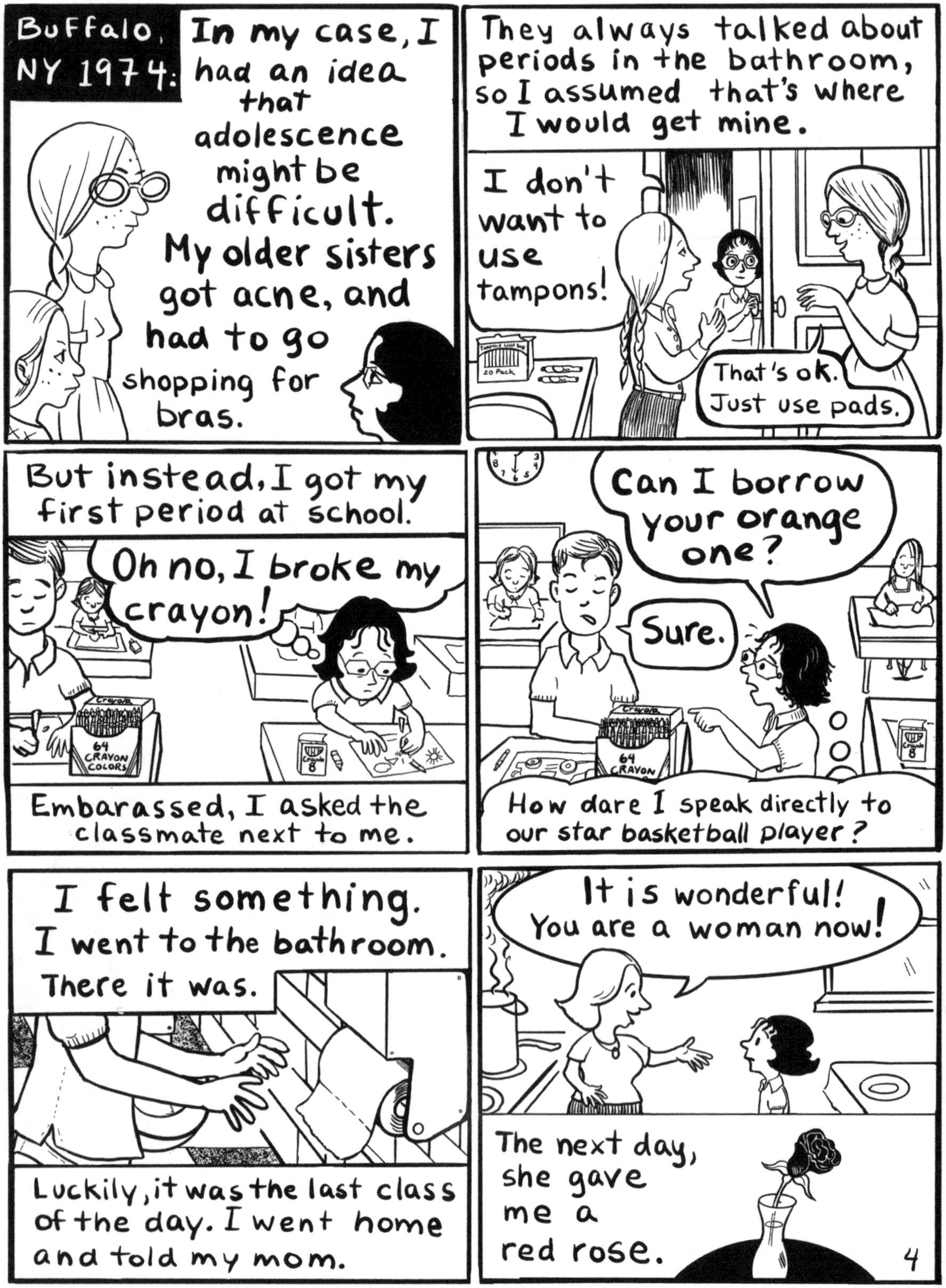

Buffalo, NY 1974:
In my case, I had an idea that adolescence might be difficult. My older sisters got acne, and had to go shopping for bras.
They always talked about periods in the bathroom, so I assumed that's where I would get mine.
I don't want to use tampons!
That's ok. Just use pads.
20 Pack
But instead, I got my first period at school.
Oh no, I broke my crayon!
Crayola
64 CRAYON COLORS
Embarassed, I asked the classmate next to me.
Can I borrow your orange one?
Sure.
Crayola
64 CRAYON
How dare I speak directly to our star basketball player?
I felt something. I went to the bathroom. There it was.
Luckily, it was the last class of the day. I went home and told my mom.
It is wonderful! You are a woman now!
The next day, she gave me a red rose.
4

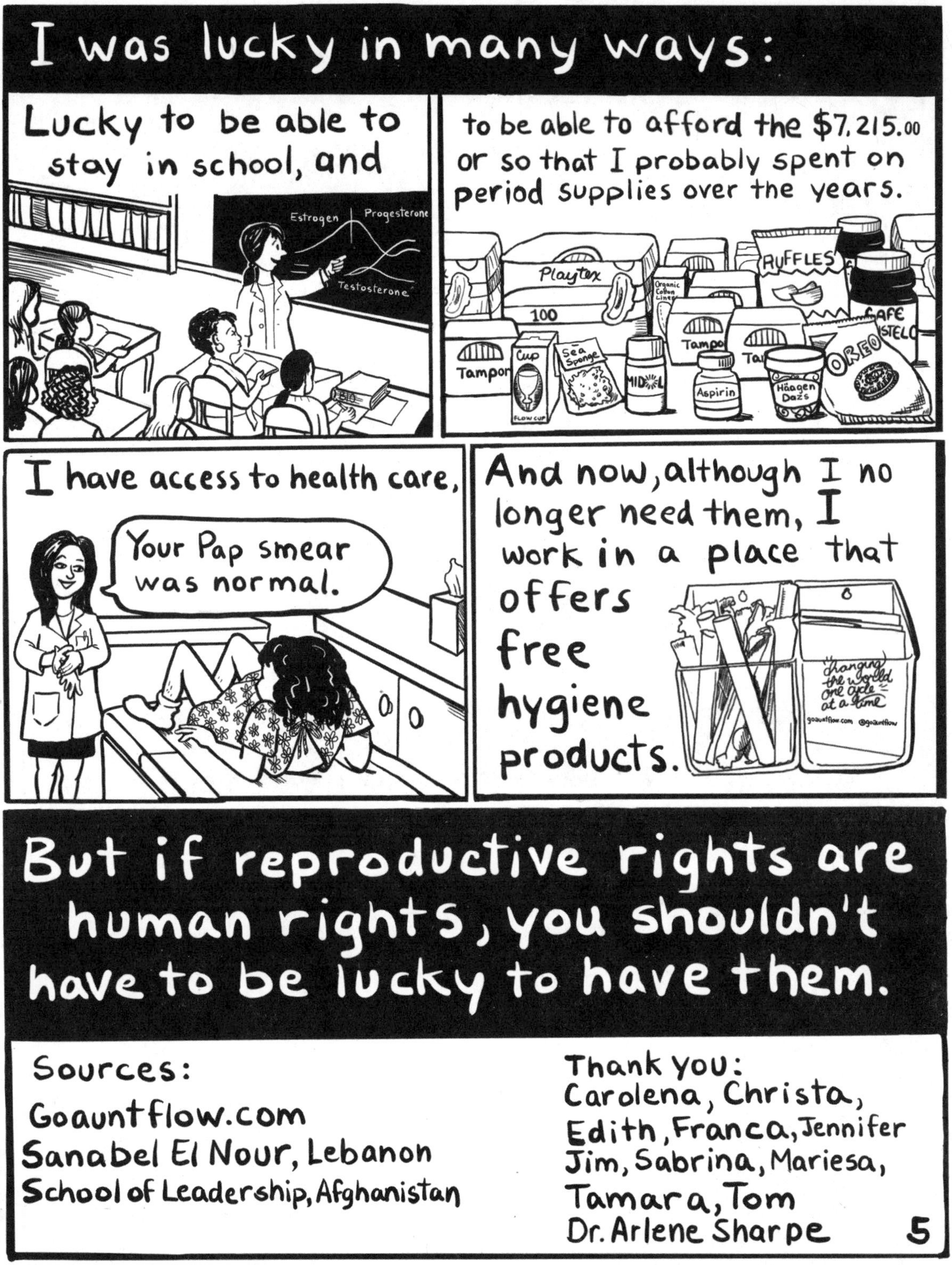

I was lucky in many ways:
Lucky to be able to stay in school, and
Estrogen
Progesterone
Testosterone
to be able to afford the $7,215.00 or so that I probably spent on period supplies over the years.
Playtex
100
Organic Cotton Liners
RUFFLES
Cup
FLOW CUP
Sea Sponge
Aspirin
Häagen Dazs
OREO
I have access to health care,
Your Pap smear was normal.
And now, although I no longer need them, I work in a place that offers free hygiene products.
changing the world one cycle at a time
goauntflow.com @goauntflow
But if reproductive rights are human rights, you shouldn't have to be lucky to have them.
Sources:
Goauntflow.com
Sanabel El Nour, Lebanon
School of Leadership, Afghanistan
Thank you:
Carolena, Christa, Edith, Franca, Jennifer Jim, Sabrina, Mariesa, Tamara, Tom
Dr. Arlene Sharpe
5

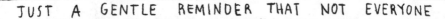

Just A Gentle Reminder...

LAUREN SIMKIN BERKE © 2022

JUST A GENTLE REMINDER THAT NOT EVERYONE

AND

WITH A UTERUS IS A WOMAN

NOT EVERY WOMAN HAS A UTERUS

SO WHEN YOU FRAME ABORTION ACCESS AS A "WOMEN'S ISSUE" YOU ARE MISSING A BUNCH OF PEOPLE

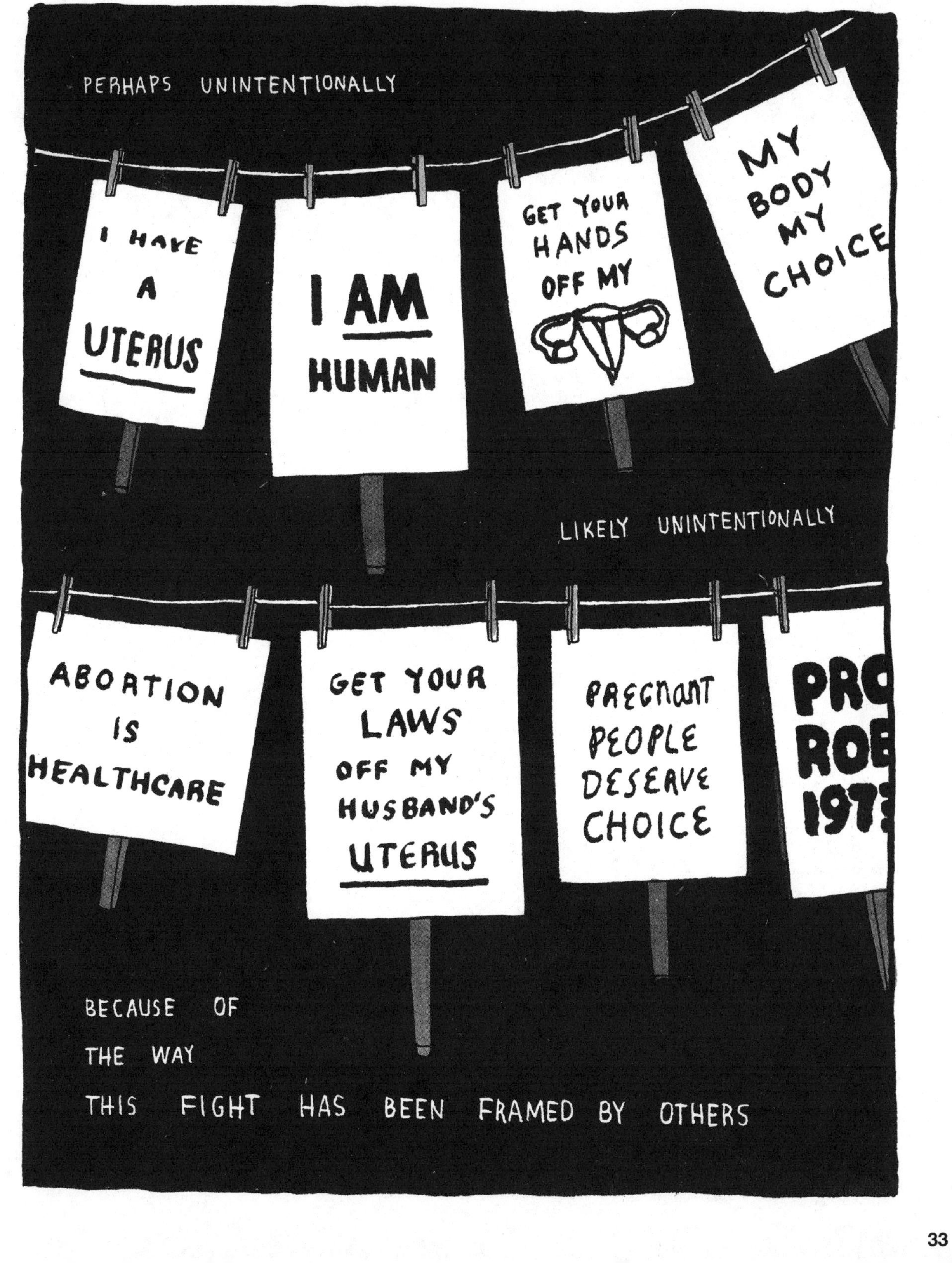
PERHAPS UNINTENTIONALLY
I HAVE A UTERUS
I AM HUMAN
GET YOUR HANDS OFF MY
MY BODY MY CHOICE
LIKELY UNINTENTIONALLY
ABORTION IS HEALTHCARE
GET YOUR LAWS OFF MY HUSBAND'S UTERUS
PREGNANT PEOPLE DESERVE CHOICE
BECAUSE OF
THE WAY
THIS FIGHT HAS BEEN FRAMED BY OTHERS

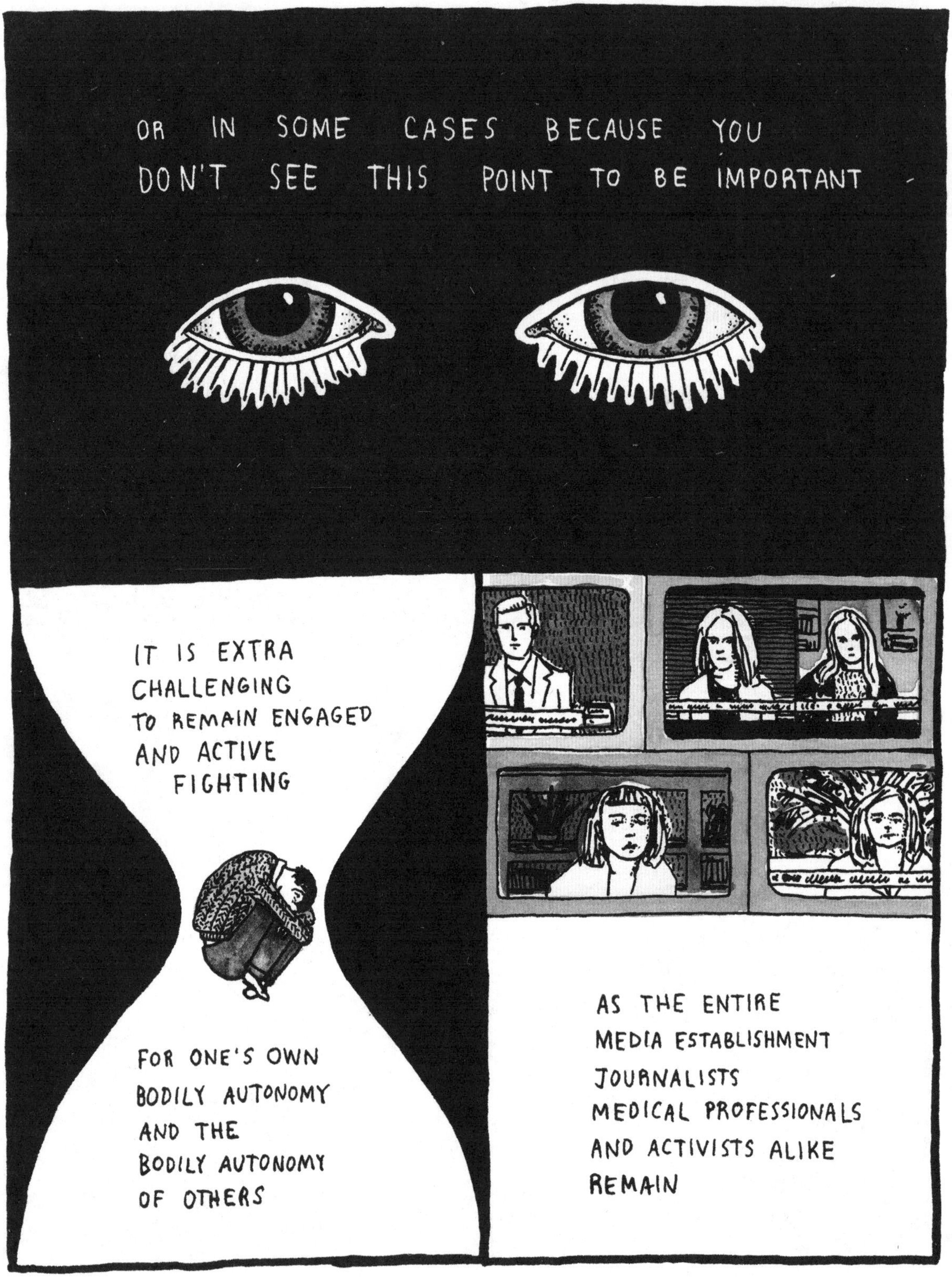

OR IN SOME CASES BECAUSE YOU DON'T SEE THIS POINT TO BE IMPORTANT -
IT IS EXTRA CHALLENGING TO REMAIN ENGAGED AND ACTIVE FIGHTING
FOR ONE'S OWN BODILY AUTONOMY AND THE BODILY AUTONOMY OF OTHERS
AS THE ENTIRE MEDIA ESTABLISHMENT JOURNALISTS MEDICAL PROFESSIONALS AND ACTIVISTS ALIKE REMAIN

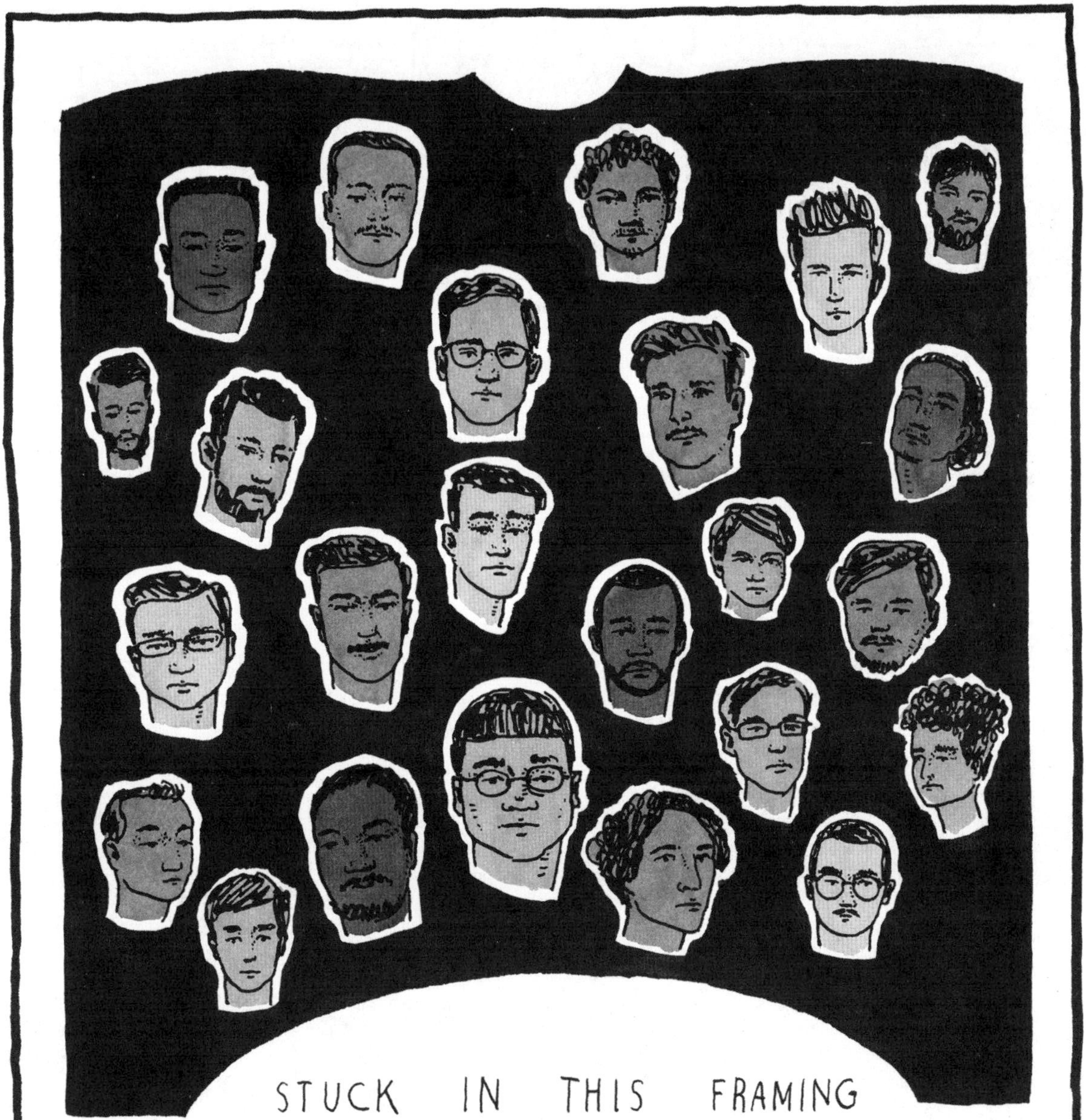
STUCK IN THIS FRAMING
THAT IGNORES THE AUTHENTICITY OF LIVED LIVES THAT DO NOT FIT INTO THEIR IDEA OF WHO A PERSON WITH A UTERUS IS

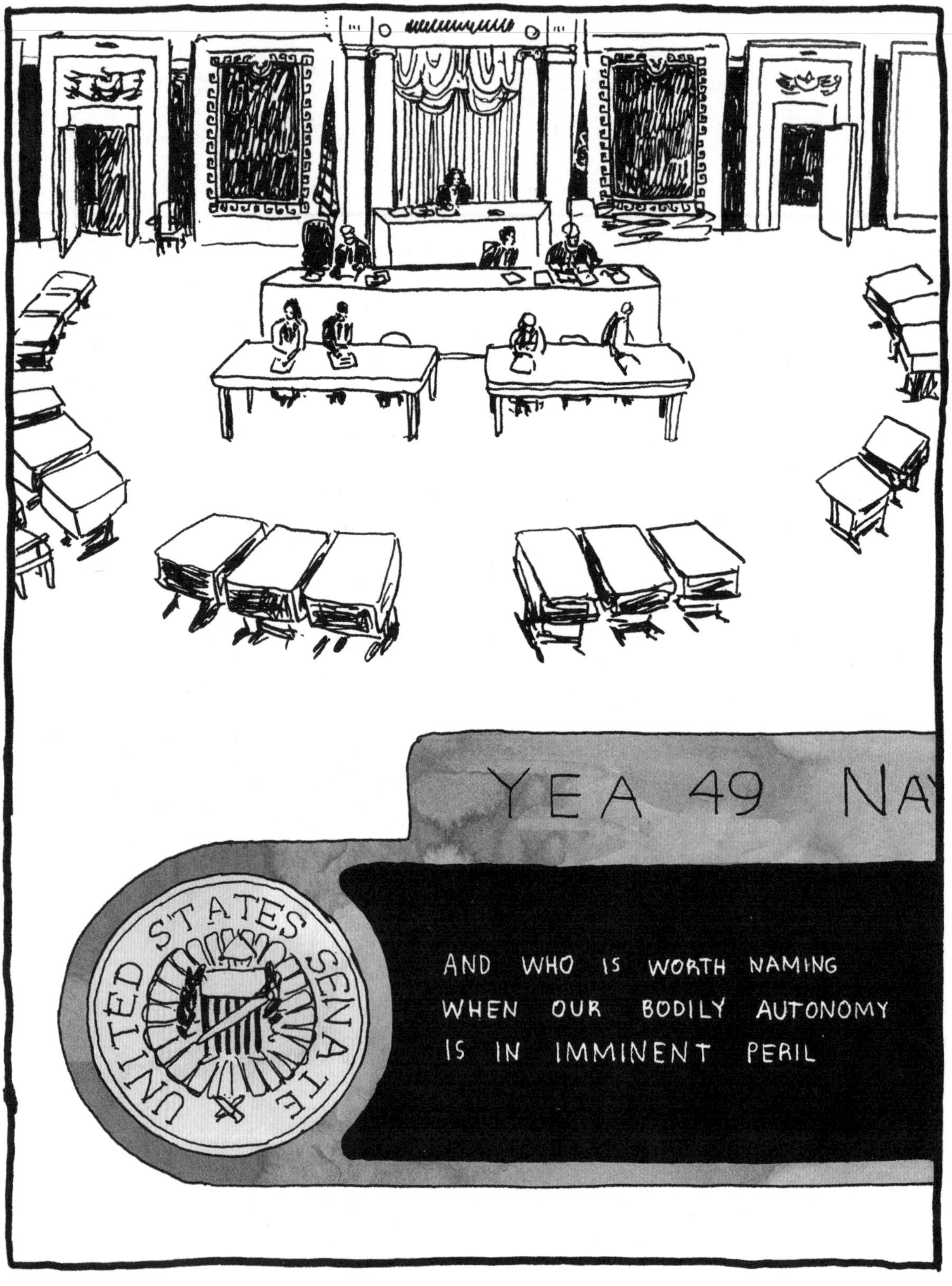
YEA 49 NAY
UNITED STATES SENATE
AND WHO IS WORTH NAMING
WHEN OUR BODILY AUTONOMY
IS IN IMMINENT PERIL

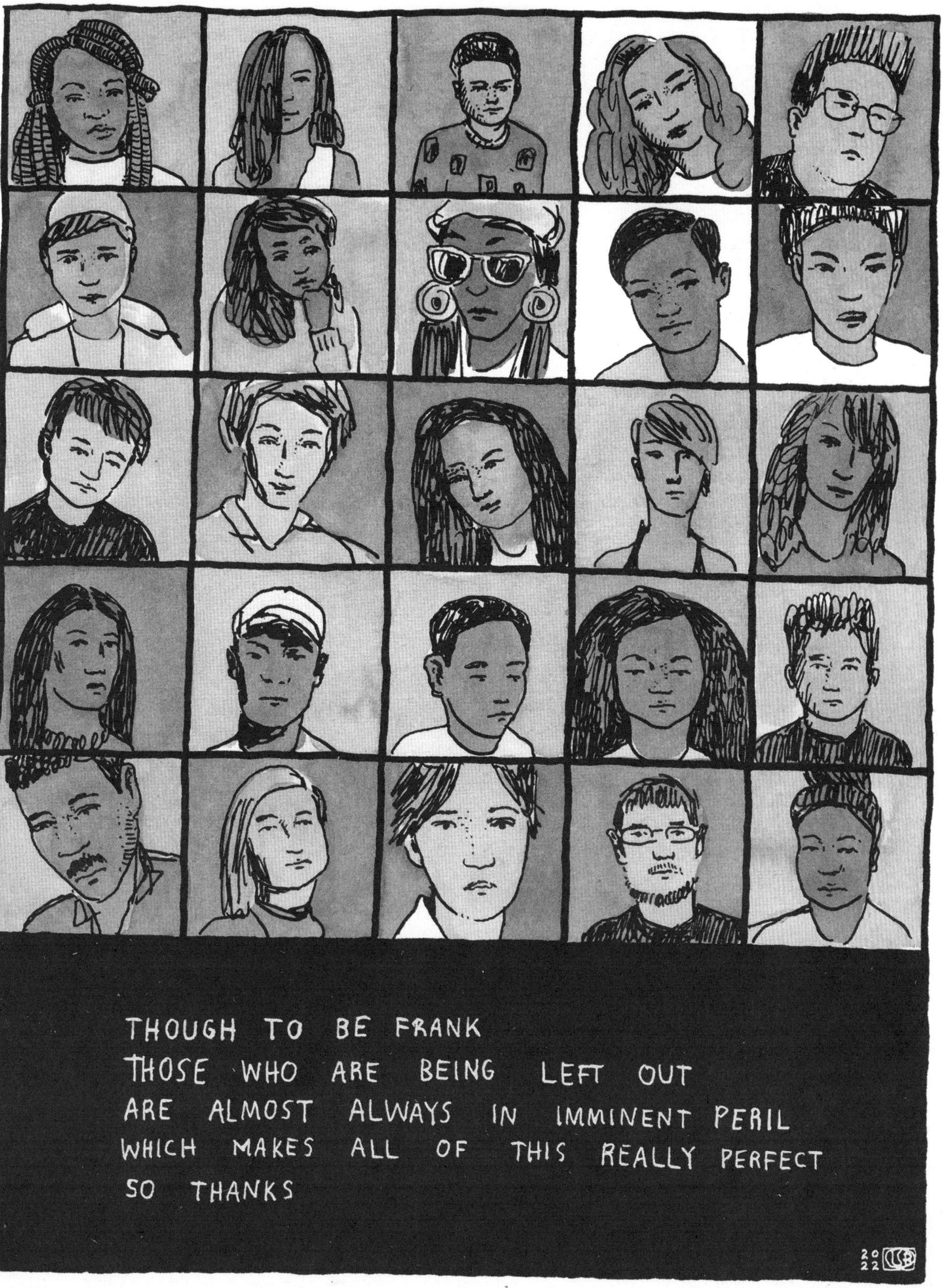
THOUGH TO BE FRANK
THOSE WHO ARE BEING LEFT OUT
ARE ALMOST ALWAYS IN IMMINENT PERIL
WHICH MAKES ALL OF THIS REALLY PERFECT
SO THANKS
2022

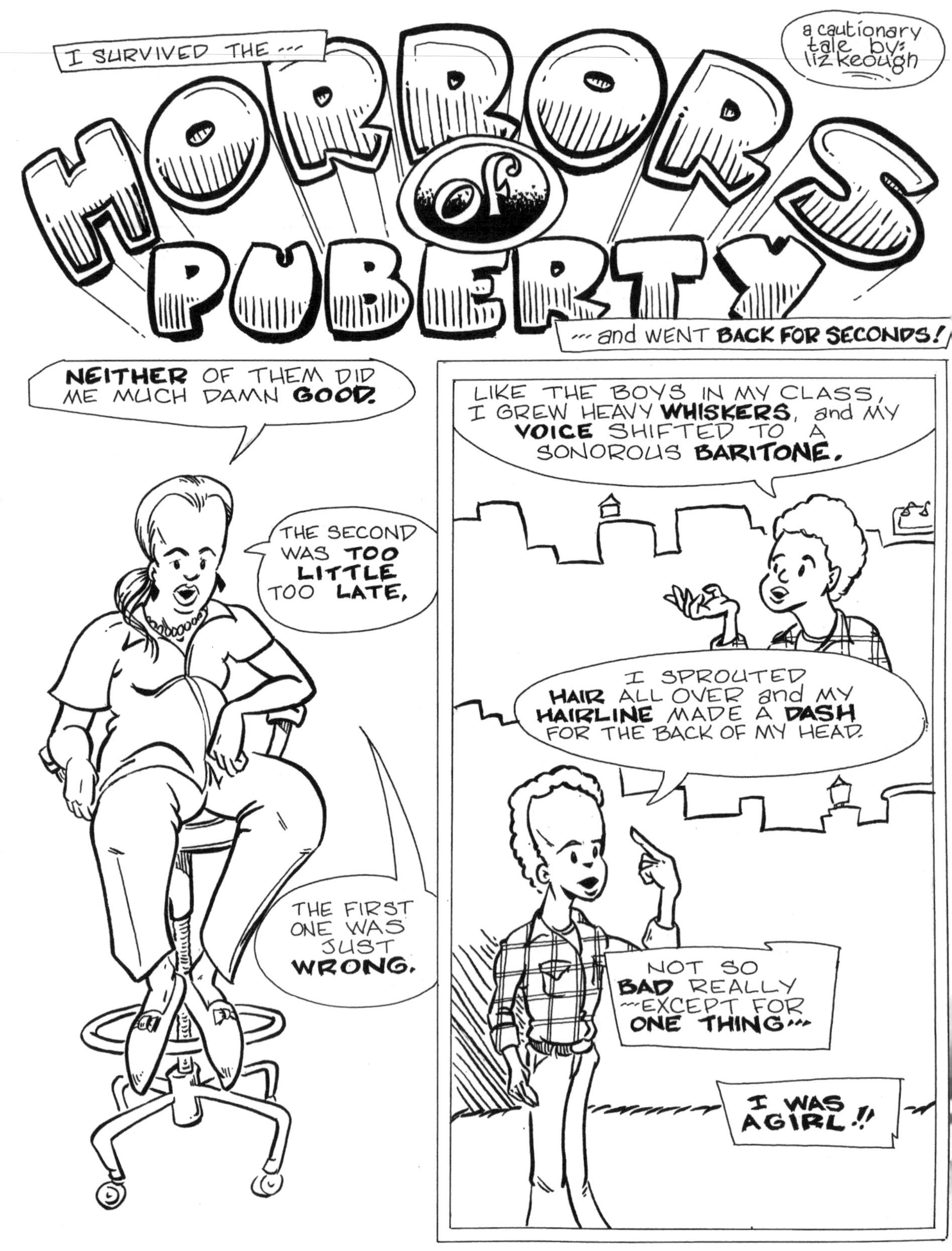
I SURVIVED THE ...
HORRORS of PUBERTY
a cautionary tale by: liz keough
... and WENT BACK FOR SECONDS!
NEITHER OF THEM DID ME MUCH DAMN GOOD.
THE SECOND WAS TOO LITTLE TOO LATE,
THE FIRST ONE WAS JUST WRONG.
LIKE THE BOYS IN MY CLASS, I GREW HEAVY WHISKERS, and MY VOICE SHIFTED TO A SONOROUS BARITONE.
I SPROUTED HAIR ALL OVER and MY HAIRLINE MADE A DASH FOR THE BACK OF MY HEAD.
NOT SO BAD REALLY ... EXCEPT FOR ONE THING...
I WAS A GIRL!!

THE GOOD NEWS!

↑ODAY THERE'S **APPROVED TREATMENT** FOR TRANSGENDER YOUTH!

Ⓖ UIDED BY MEDICAL **DOCTORS,** PSYCHOLOGISTS, AND PARENTS, YOUNG, TRANSGENDER FOLKS CAN **AVOID** THE **WRONG HORMONES** ALTERING THEIR BODIES.

THE BAD NEWS!

BUT NOT IN TEXAS!

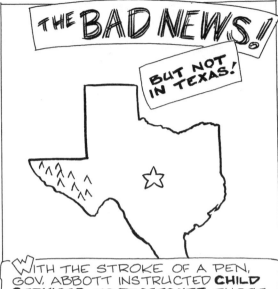

Ⓦ ITH THE STROKE OF A PEN, GOV. ABBOTT INSTRUCTED **CHILD SERVICES** TO **PROSECUTE** THOSE DOCTORS, COUNSELORS AND **PARENTS** FOR **CHILD ABUSE.**

Ⓣ HE TRANSGENDER **CHILDREN** WILL BE PLACED IN STATE-APPROVED **FOSTER CARE,** THE **PARENTS** and PROFESSIONALS WILL GO TO **JAIL.** IN SOME STATES, LAW MAKERS WANT TO **JAIL** THEM **FOR LIFE.**

Ⓘ 'M TOLD THAT THIS IS ONLY PANDERING FOR EASY **VOTES** FROM FEARFUL **BIGOTS** WHO ARE ENCOURAGED BY SUCH **NONSENSE.**

Ⓑ UT, TRANS **KIDS** AREN'T A POLITICAL ISSUE, THEY ARE **REGULAR,** LIVING, BREATH-ING **PEOPLE** WITHOUT MUCH MEANS TO **DEFEND** THEMSELVES.

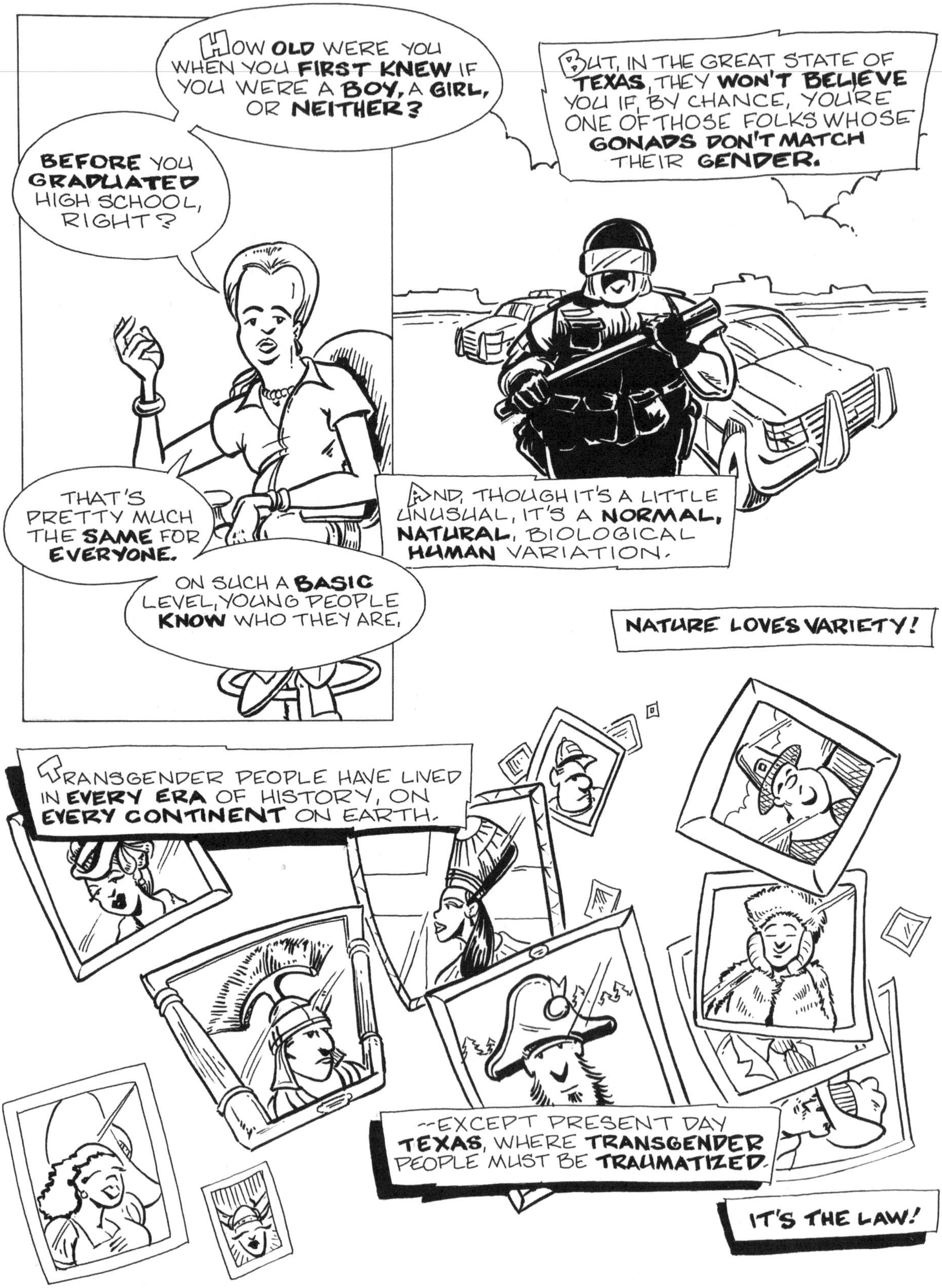
HOW OLD WERE YOU WHEN YOU FIRST KNEW IF YOU WERE A BOY, A GIRL, OR NEITHER?
BEFORE YOU GRADUATED HIGH SCHOOL, RIGHT?
THAT'S PRETTY MUCH THE SAME FOR EVERYONE.
ON SUCH A BASIC LEVEL, YOUNG PEOPLE KNOW WHO THEY ARE.
BUT, IN THE GREAT STATE OF TEXAS, THEY WON'T BELIEVE YOU IF, BY CHANCE, YOU'RE ONE OF THOSE FOLKS WHOSE GONADS DON'T MATCH THEIR GENDER.
AND, THOUGH IT'S A LITTLE UNUSUAL, IT'S A NORMAL, NATURAL, BIOLOGICAL HUMAN VARIATION.
NATURE LOVES VARIETY!
TRANSGENDER PEOPLE HAVE LIVED IN EVERY ERA OF HISTORY, ON EVERY CONTINENT ON EARTH.
--EXCEPT PRESENT DAY TEXAS, WHERE TRANSGENDER PEOPLE MUST BE TRAUMATIZED.
IT'S THE LAW!

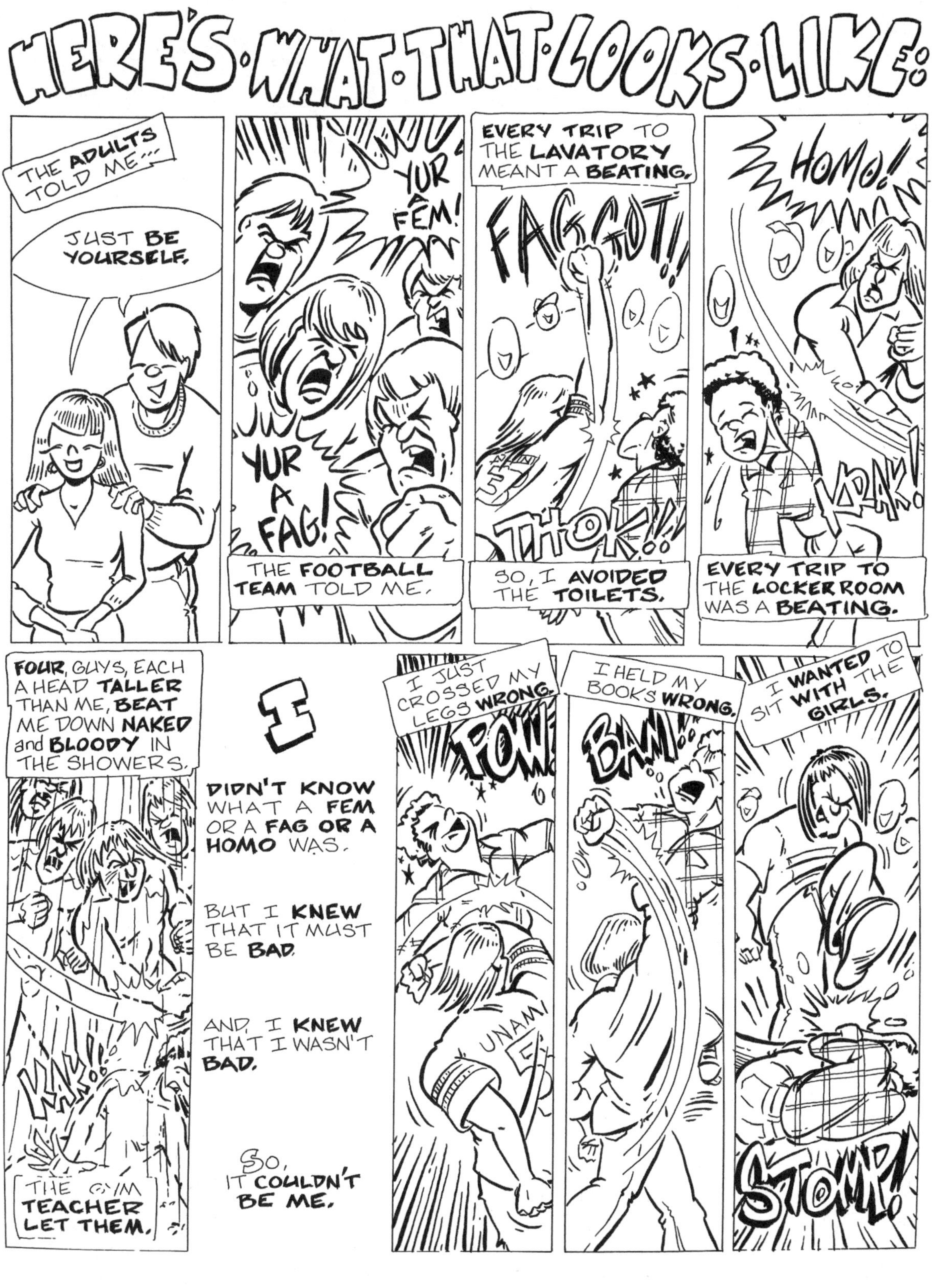
HERE'S WHAT THAT LOOKS LIKE:
THE ADULTS TOLD ME...
JUST BE YOURSELF.
YUR FEM!
YUR A FAG!
THE FOOTBALL TEAM TOLD ME.
EVERY TRIP TO THE LAVATORY MEANT A BEATING.
FAGGOT!!
THOK!!
SO, I AVOIDED THE TOILETS.
HOMO!
KRAK!
EVERY TRIP TO THE LOCKER ROOM WAS A BEATING.
FOUR GUYS, EACH A HEAD TALLER THAN ME, BEAT ME DOWN NAKED and BLOODY IN THE SHOWERS.
KAK!
THE GYM TEACHER LET THEM.
I
DIDN'T KNOW WHAT A FEM OR A FAG OR A HOMO WAS.
BUT I KNEW THAT IT MUST BE BAD.
AND, I KNEW THAT I WASN'T BAD.
SO, IT COULDN'T BE ME.
I JUST CROSSED MY LEGS WRONG.
POW!
I HELD MY BOOKS WRONG.
BAM!
I WANTED TO SIT WITH THE GIRLS.
STOMP!

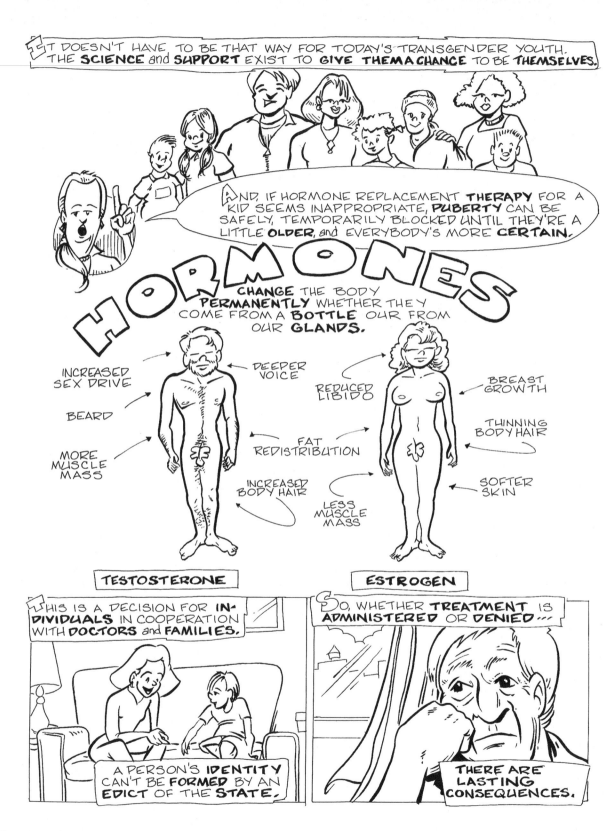

IT DOESN'T HAVE TO BE THAT WAY FOR TODAY'S TRANSGENDER YOUTH. THE **SCIENCE** and **SUPPORT** EXIST TO **GIVE THEM A CHANCE** TO BE **THEMSELVES.**

AND, IF HORMONE REPLACEMENT **THERAPY** FOR A KID SEEMS INAPPROPRIATE, **PUBERTY** CAN BE SAFELY, TEMPORARILY BLOCKED UNTIL THEY'RE A LITTLE **OLDER,** and EVERYBODY'S MORE **CERTAIN.**

HORMONES

CHANGE THE BODY **PERMANENTLY** WHETHER THEY COME FROM A **BOTTLE** OUR FROM OUR **GLANDS.**

INCREASED SEX DRIVE

DEEPER VOICE

BEARD

MORE MUSCLE MASS

FAT REDISTRIBUTION

INCREASED BODY HAIR

REDUCED LIBIDO

BREAST GROWTH

THINNING BODY HAIR

SOFTER SKIN

LESS MUSCLE MASS

TESTOSTERONE

ESTROGEN

THIS IS A DECISION FOR **IN-DIVIDUALS** IN COOPERATION WITH **DOCTORS** and **FAMILIES.**

A PERSON'S **IDENTITY** CAN'T BE **FORMED** BY AN **EDICT** OF THE **STATE.**

SO, WHETHER **TREATMENT** IS **ADMINISTERED** OR **DENIED** ···

THERE ARE LASTING CONSEQUENCES.

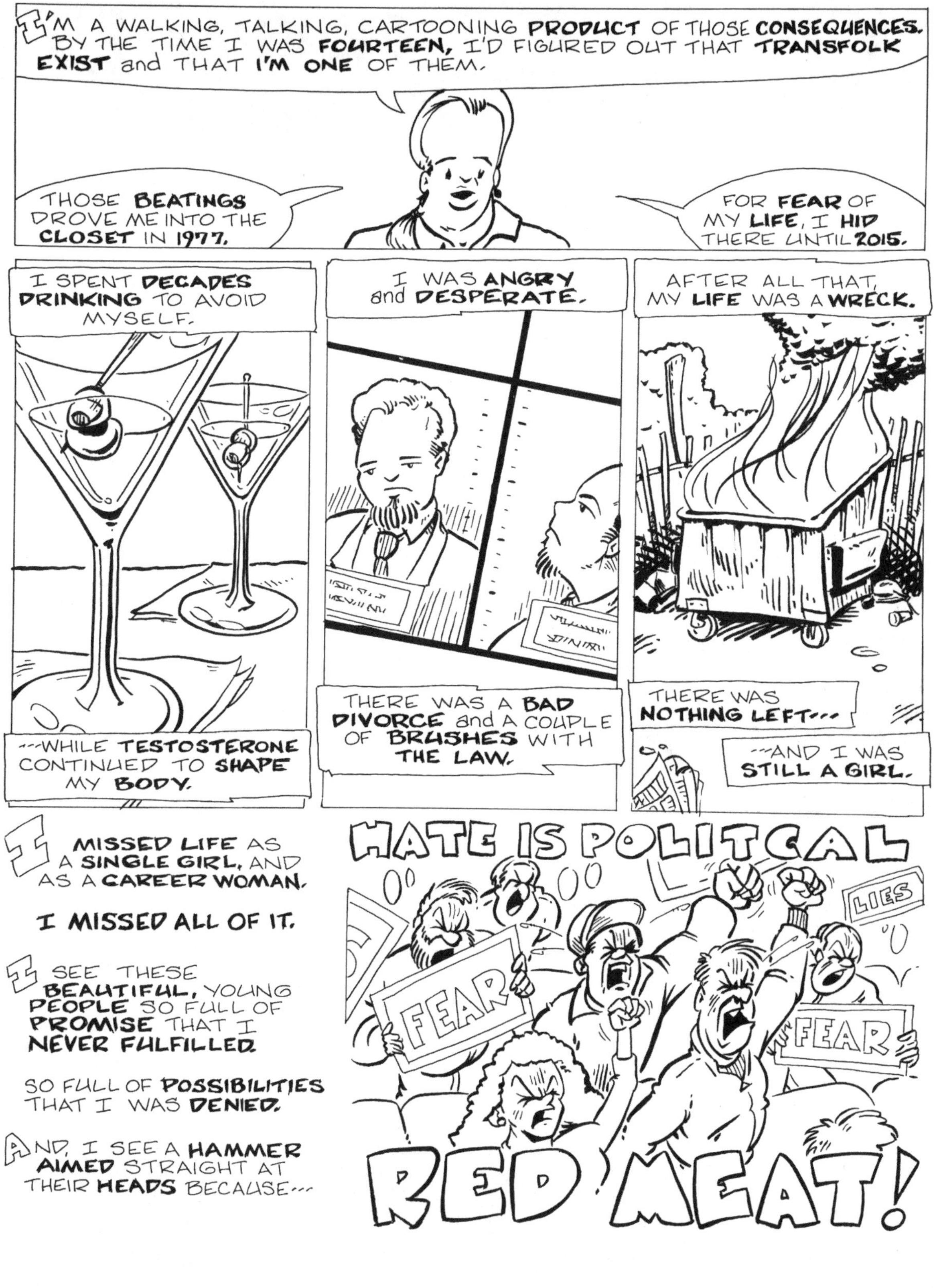
I'M A WALKING, TALKING, CARTOONING PRODUCT OF THOSE CONSEQUENCES. BY THE TIME I WAS FOURTEEN, I'D FIGURED OUT THAT TRANSFOLK EXIST and THAT I'M ONE OF THEM.
THOSE BEATINGS DROVE ME INTO THE CLOSET IN 1977.
FOR FEAR OF MY LIFE, I HID THERE UNTIL 2015.
I SPENT DECADES DRINKING TO AVOID MYSELF.
---WHILE TESTOSTERONE CONTINUED TO SHAPE MY BODY.
I WAS ANGRY and DESPERATE.
THERE WAS A BAD DIVORCE and A COUPLE OF BRUSHES WITH THE LAW.
AFTER ALL THAT, MY LIFE WAS A WRECK.
THERE WAS NOTHING LEFT---
---AND I WAS STILL A GIRL.
I MISSED LIFE AS A SINGLE GIRL, AND AS A CAREER WOMAN.
I MISSED ALL OF IT.
I SEE THESE BEAUTIFUL, YOUNG PEOPLE SO FULL OF PROMISE THAT I NEVER FULFILLED.
SO FULL OF POSSIBILITIES THAT I WAS DENIED.
AND, I SEE A HAMMER AIMED STRAIGHT AT THEIR HEADS BECAUSE---
HATE IS POLITCAL
LIES
FEAR
FEAR
RED MEAT!

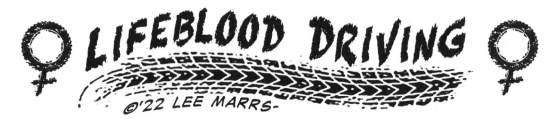

LIFEBLOOD DRIVING

A TRUE-TO-LIFE SAGA OF BIRTH, BLOOD, AND DEATH BROUGHT TO YOU BY THE ETERNAL FORCES OF OPPRESSION.

THE BAD OLE DAYS

IN THE 1950S, WHEN I WAS YOUNG, ABORTION WAS ILLEGAL IN AMERICA. TOTALLY QUITE ILLEGAL. AS IN, YOU COULD GET ARRESTED. FORTUNATE GIRLS/WOMEN COULD BE DRIVEN TO MEXICO, IF YOU LIVED CLOSE ENOUGH OR HAD TRANSPORTATION. AND ACCOMODATION. AND FOOD ...

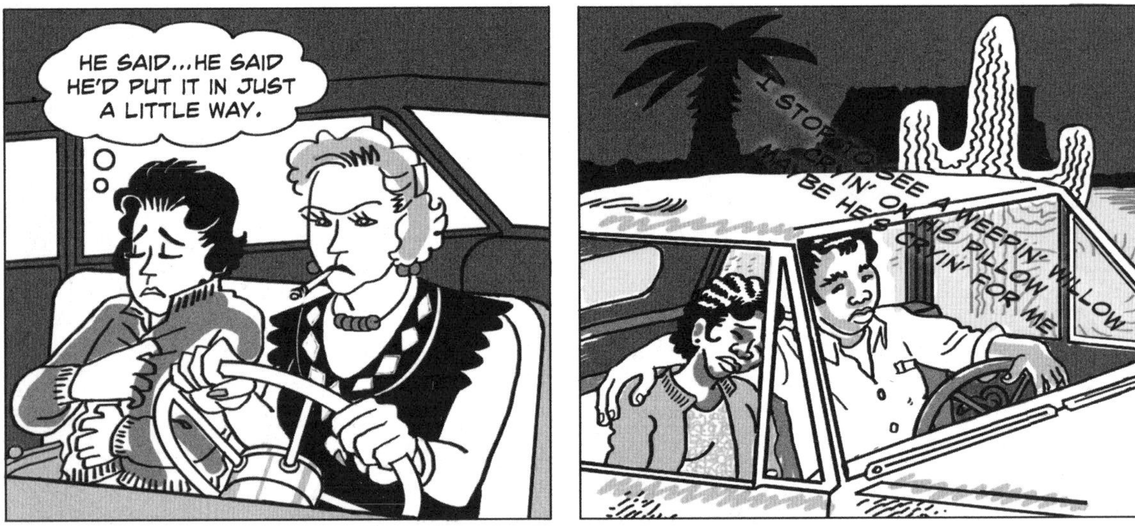
HE SAID...HE SAID HE'D PUT IT IN JUST A LITTLE WAY.
I STOP
SEE A WEEPIN' WILLOW
IN' ON HIS PILLOW
BE HE'S
IN' FOR ME

OTHERWISE...

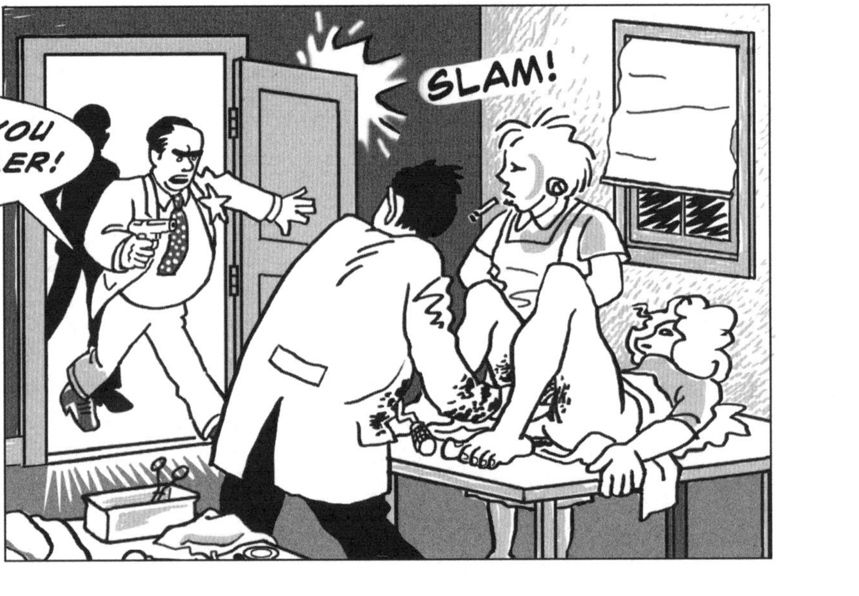
HANDS UP, YOU GODDAM KILLER!
SLAM!

THERE ***WERE*** FEMALE BIRTH CONTROL METHODS BUT VERY, VERY, VERY FEW GIRLS/WOMEN KNEW ABOUT THEM. HOWEVER, THE MYTHS WERE RAMPANT. EVERYBODY KNEW AT LEAST ONE METHOD.

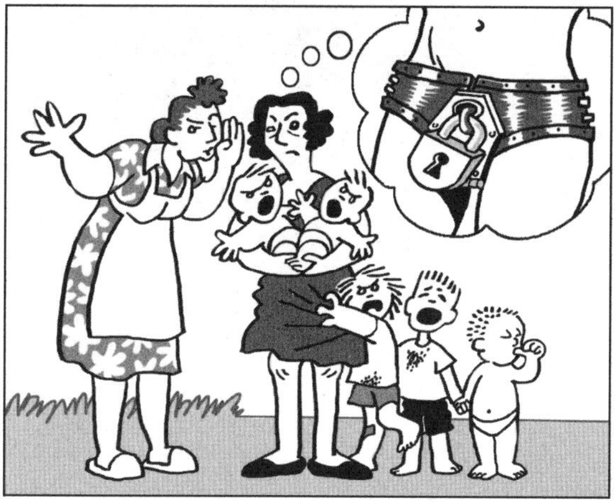

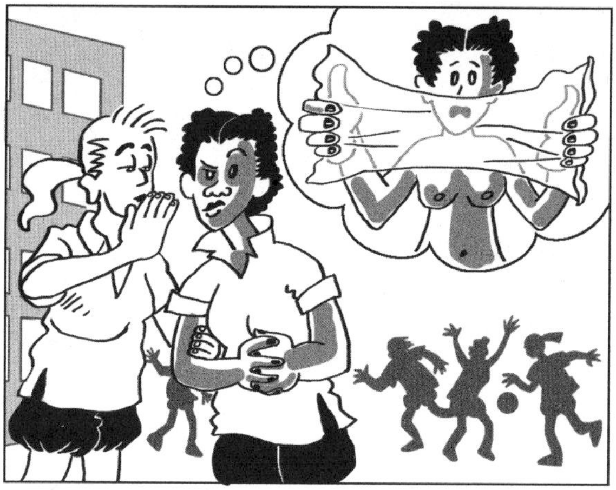

MOST WOMEN DIDN'T HAVE A DOCTOR OR ANYONE WHO COULD GIVE THEM CORRECT INFORMATION ABOUT NOT ONLY BIRTH CONTROL OR ABORTION BUT EVEN PERSONAL HEALTH. NO MATTER YOUR SITUATION, UNLESS YOU COULD AFFORD A SYMPATHETIC DOCTOR, YOU WERE TOAST.

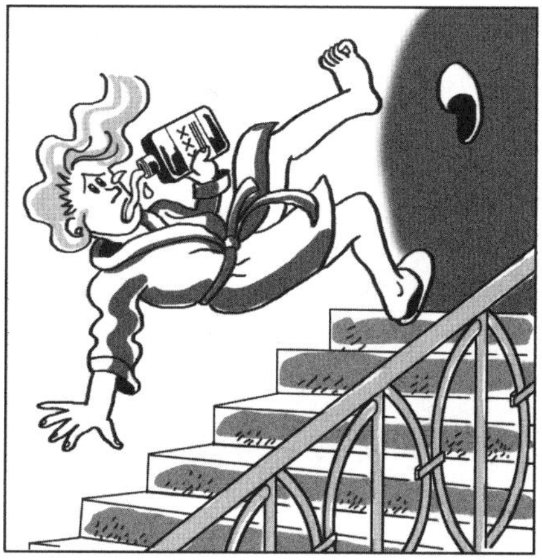

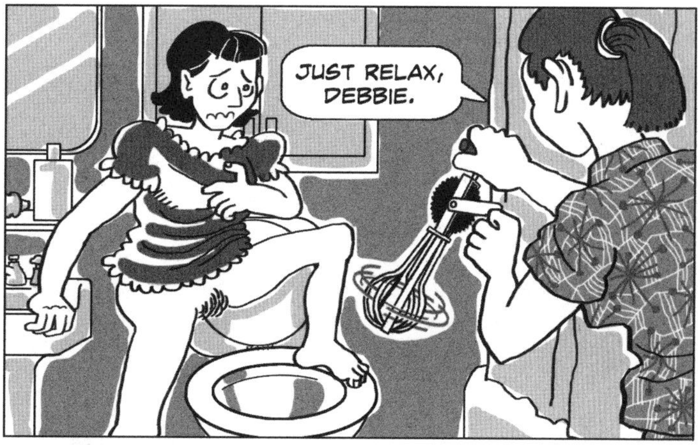
JUST RELAX, DEBBIE.

SO WE HAD TO DEPEND ON THE GUYS.

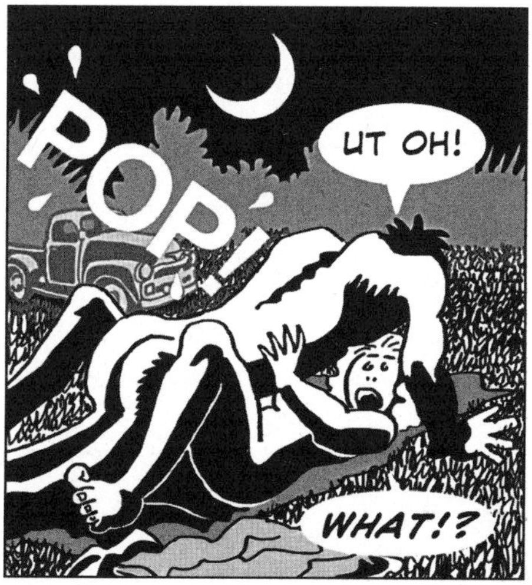
POP!
UT OH!
WHAT!?

AND THEIR CONDOMS.

WE ***SHOULD*** HAVE BEEN TAUGHT ABOUT OUR OWN HEALTH AND WELL-BEING. WE ***SHOULD*** HAVE OWNED OUR OWN BODIES. WE ***SHOULD*** HAVE HAD CONTROL OVER EVERY ASPECT OF OUR HEALTH.

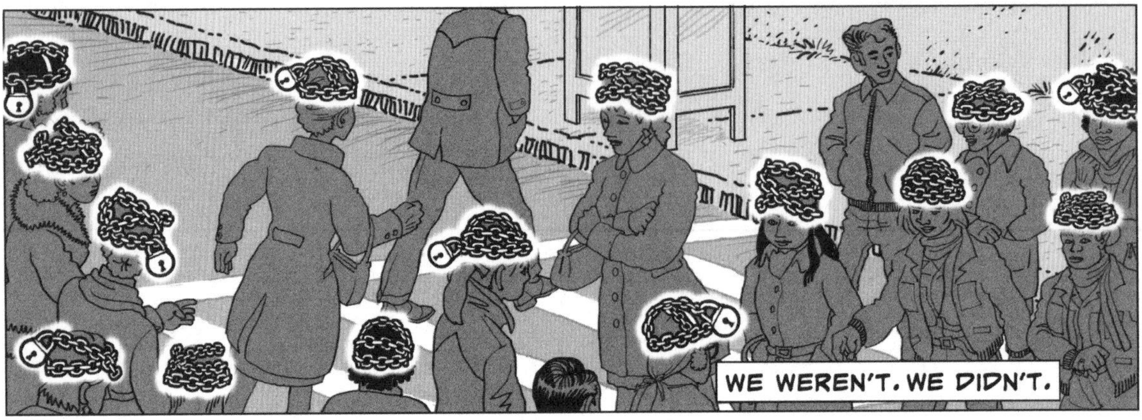
WE WEREN'T. WE DIDN'T.

HISTORICALLY, MIDWIVES STEEPED IN SUCH MATTERS WERE ALWAYS SUSPECT. LAY MIDWIVES WERE FINALLY OUTLAWED IN THE UNITED STATES DURING THE BEGINNING OF THE 20TH CENTURY, LOSING OUT TO "PROFESSIONAL" DOCTORS.

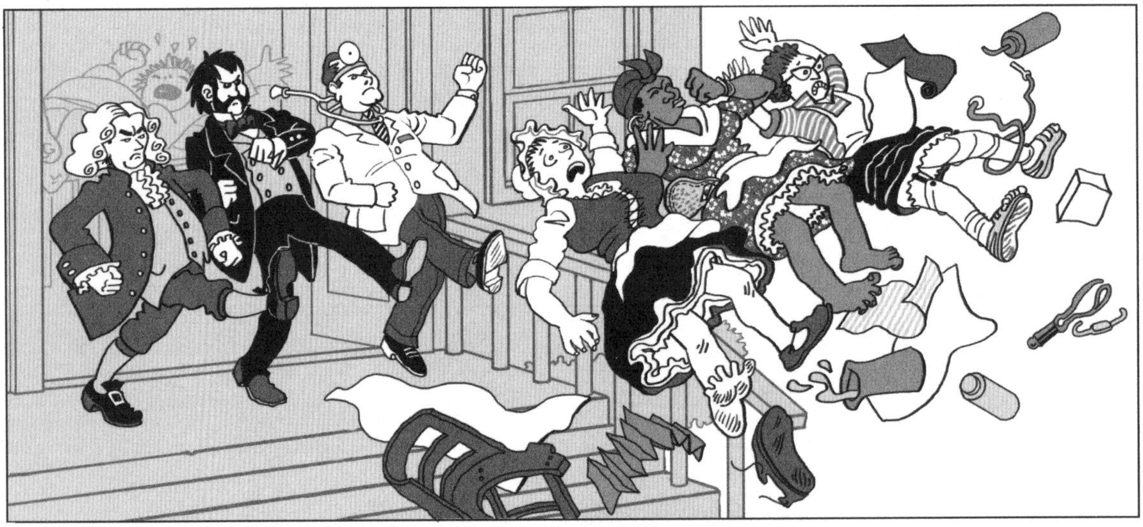

INSTEAD, BORROWING FROM FRIENDS, WE FOUND OURSELVES IN CARS DRIVING TO KINDLY DOCTORS OR DODGY ABORTIONISTS, HOPING AND PRAYING THAT WE WOULDN'T ***DIE***.

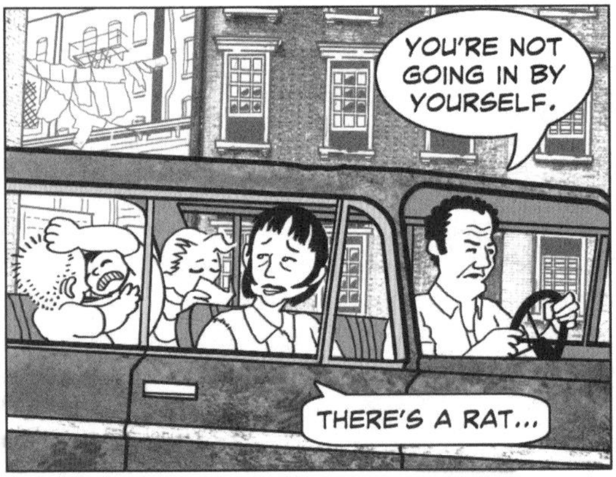
YOU'RE NOT GOING IN BY YOURSELF.
THERE'S A RAT...

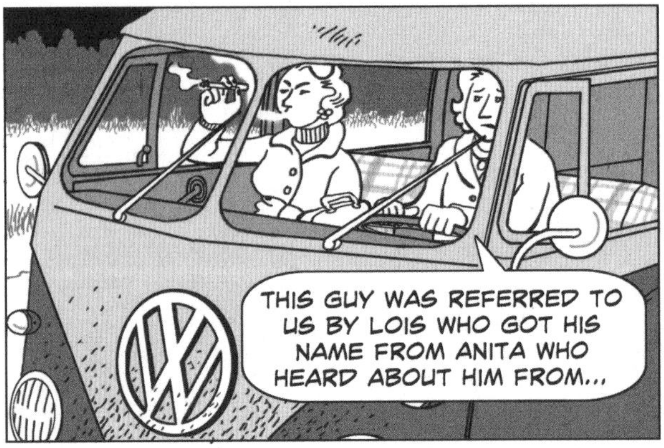
THIS GUY WAS REFERRED TO US BY LOIS WHO GOT HIS NAME FROM ANITA WHO HEARD ABOUT HIM FROM...

TRANSITION DAYS

IN 1960, FOR MANY OF US, THE ARRIVAL OF...

THE PILL

...CHANGED LIFE AS WE KNEW IT!

FOR THE FIRST TIME, WE DIDN'T HAVE TO DEPEND ON MEN FOR OUR REPRODUCTIVE FATES!

THE PHARMACEUTICAL INDUSTRY WAS MOVING WITH THE TIMES AND DECLARING PROFITS!

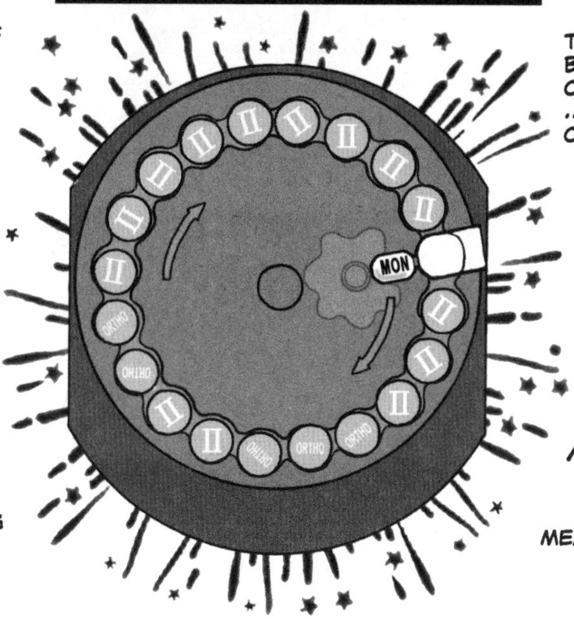
MON

THESE DAYS WERE SO BIZARRE. FEMALE BIRTH CONTROL WAS LEGAL ...SORTA...UNDER CERTAIN CIRCUMSTANCES.

(AFTER ALL, CONDOMS HAD BEEN AVAILABLE FOR DECADES! BUT WE WON'T GET INTO THE DETAILS OF THE PATRIARCHIAL BULLSHIT HERE. THAT'S FOR ANOTHER STORY.)

IF WE COULD AFFORD IT – AND MANY COULD ***NOT*** – WE WOULD OWN OUR OWN BODIES.

MEANWHILE, ABORTION WAS STILL ILLEGAL.

OF COURSE, EVEN FOR THOSE WITH MONEY, THE ACCESS TO THE PILL WAS RESTRICTED, CAUSING CONVOLUTED SCENARIOS TO BE CREATED. BIG LITTLE LIES.

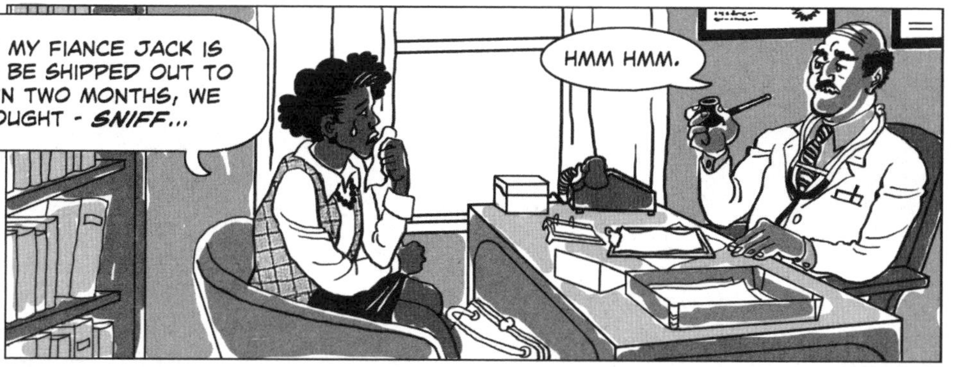
...BUT MY FIANCE JACK IS GONNA BE SHIPPED OUT TO 'NAM IN TWO MONTHS, WE THOUGHT - SNIFF...
HMM HMM.

FOR THE REST OF MERICA...

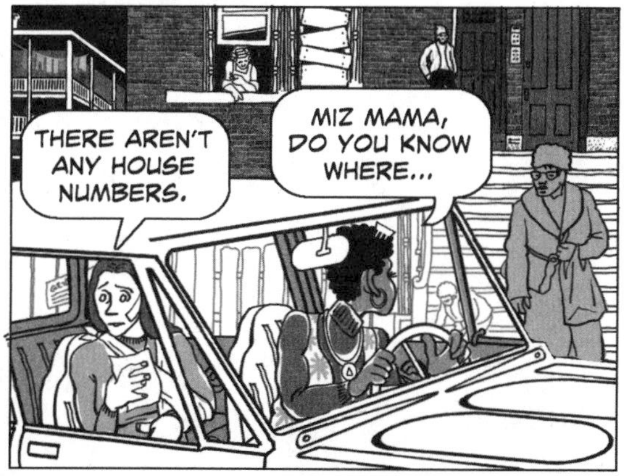
THERE AREN'T ANY HOUSE NUMBERS.
MIZ MAMA, DO YOU KNOW WHERE...

IN COLLEGE, MY ROOMMATE DROVE ME TO A RESPECTABLE DOCTOR THE WEEK AFTER I "WENT ALL THE WAY" WITH MY BOYFRIEND.

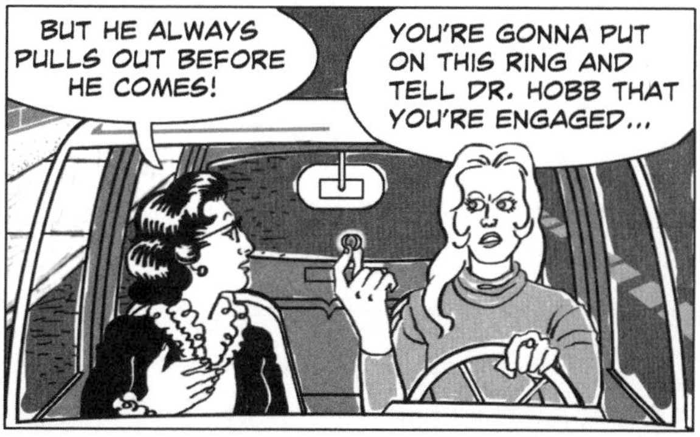
BUT HE ALWAYS PULLS OUT BEFORE HE COMES!
YOU'RE GONNA PUT ON THIS RING AND TELL DR. HOBB THAT YOU'RE ENGAGED...

A COUPLE OF YEARS LATER, WHILE I WAS ***ON THE PILL***, I BECAME PREGNANT!

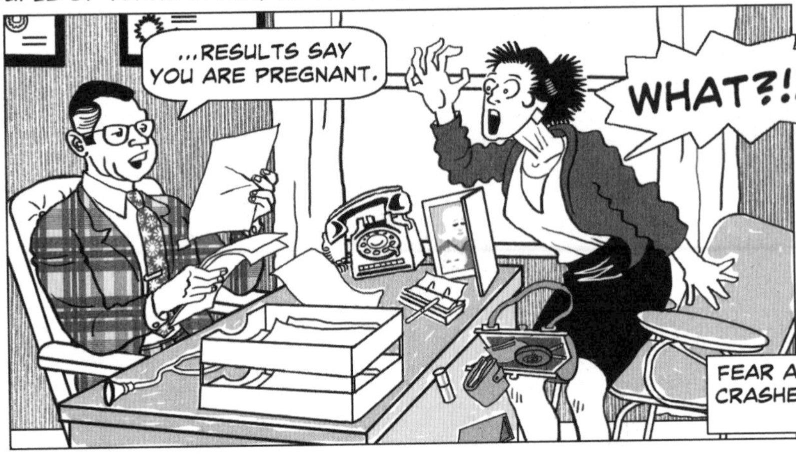
...RESULTS SAY YOU ARE PREGNANT.
WHAT?!!
FEAR AND HORROR CRASHED DOWN ON ME.

TRAPPED, INCAPABLE OF RAISING A BABY, I WAS STUCK WITH A GUY WHO DIDN'T WANT TO BE MARRIED. AND TO TELL MY PARENTS...

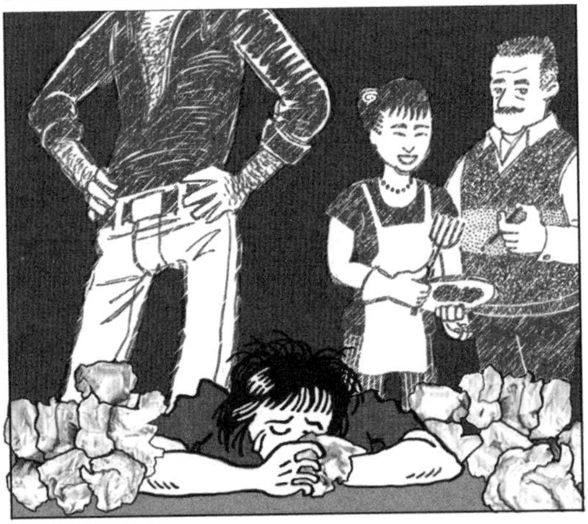

BUT BEFORE I HAD TO MAKE ANY DECISIONS...

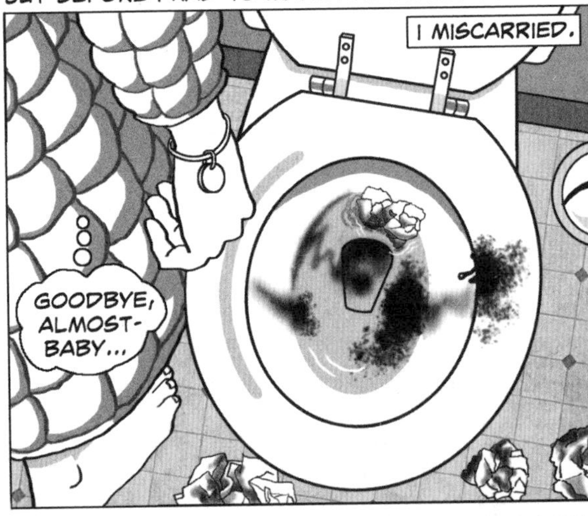
I MISCARRIED.
GOODBYE, ALMOST-BABY...

THAT MISCARRIAGE IGNITED AN AWARENESS, A COMMITTMENT THAT HAS LASTED MY WHOLE LIFE.

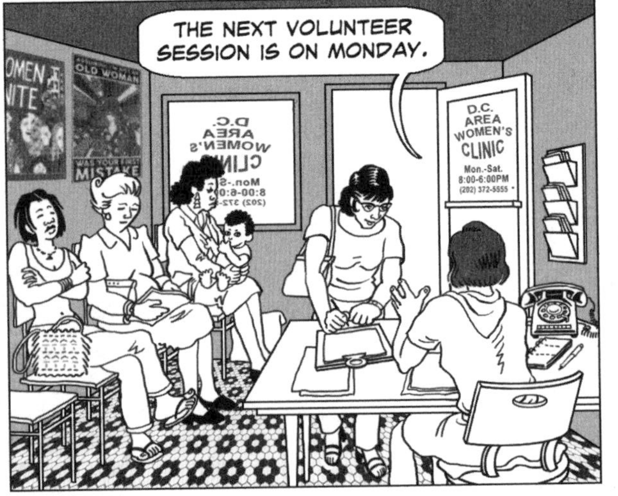
THE NEXT VOLUNTEER SESSION IS ON MONDAY.
OLD WOMAN
MISTAKE
D.C. AREA WOMEN'S CLINIC
Mon.-Sat. 8:00-6:00PM
(202) 372-5555

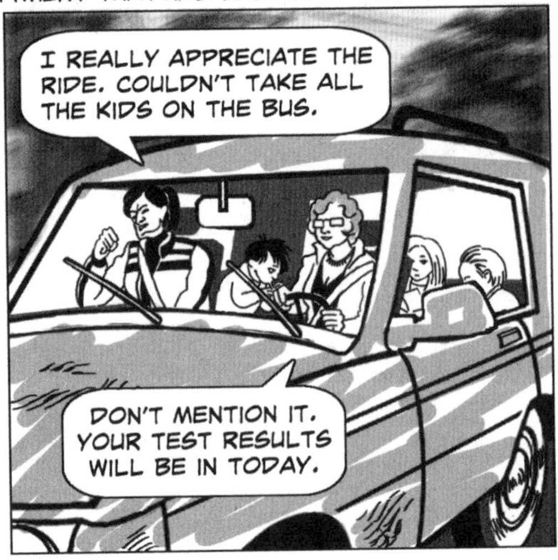
I REALLY APPRECIATE THE RIDE. COULDN'T TAKE ALL THE KIDS ON THE BUS.
DON'T MENTION IT. YOUR TEST RESULTS WILL BE IN TODAY.

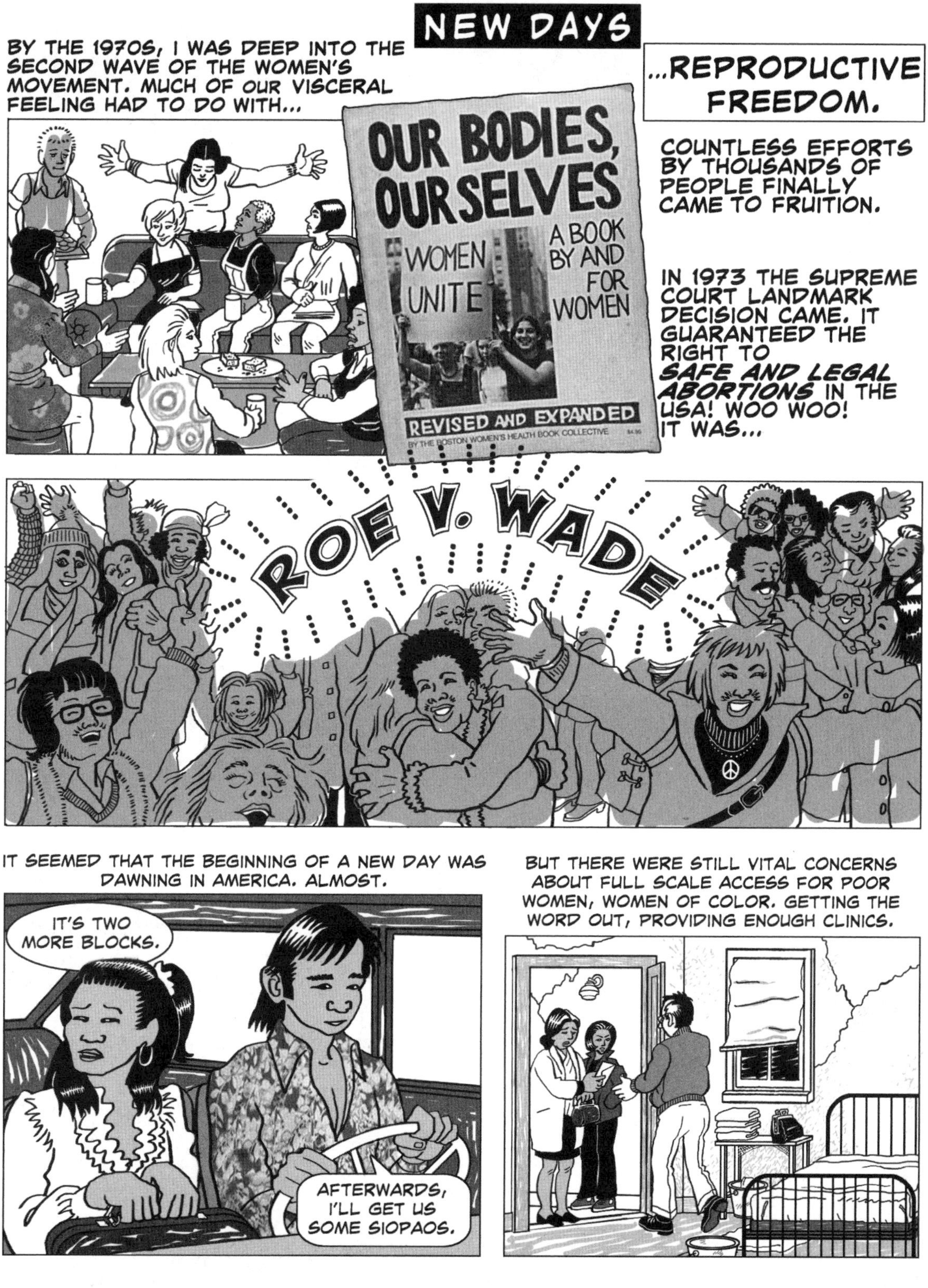
NEW DAYS
BY THE 1970S, I WAS DEEP INTO THE SECOND WAVE OF THE WOMEN'S MOVEMENT. MUCH OF OUR VISCERAL FEELING HAD TO DO WITH...
...REPRODUCTIVE FREEDOM.
OUR BODIES, OURSELVES
A BOOK BY AND FOR WOMEN
WOMEN UNITE
REVISED AND EXPANDED
BY THE BOSTON WOMEN'S HEALTH BOOK COLLECTIVE
COUNTLESS EFFORTS BY THOUSANDS OF PEOPLE FINALLY CAME TO FRUITION.
IN 1973 THE SUPREME COURT LANDMARK DECISION CAME. IT GUARANTEED THE RIGHT TO SAFE AND LEGAL ABORTIONS IN THE USA! WOO WOO! IT WAS...
ROE V. WADE
IT SEEMED THAT THE BEGINNING OF A NEW DAY WAS DAWNING IN AMERICA. ALMOST.
IT'S TWO MORE BLOCKS.
AFTERWARDS, I'LL GET US SOME SIOPAOS.
BUT THERE WERE STILL VITAL CONCERNS ABOUT FULL SCALE ACCESS FOR POOR WOMEN, WOMEN OF COLOR. GETTING THE WORD OUT, PROVIDING ENOUGH CLINICS.

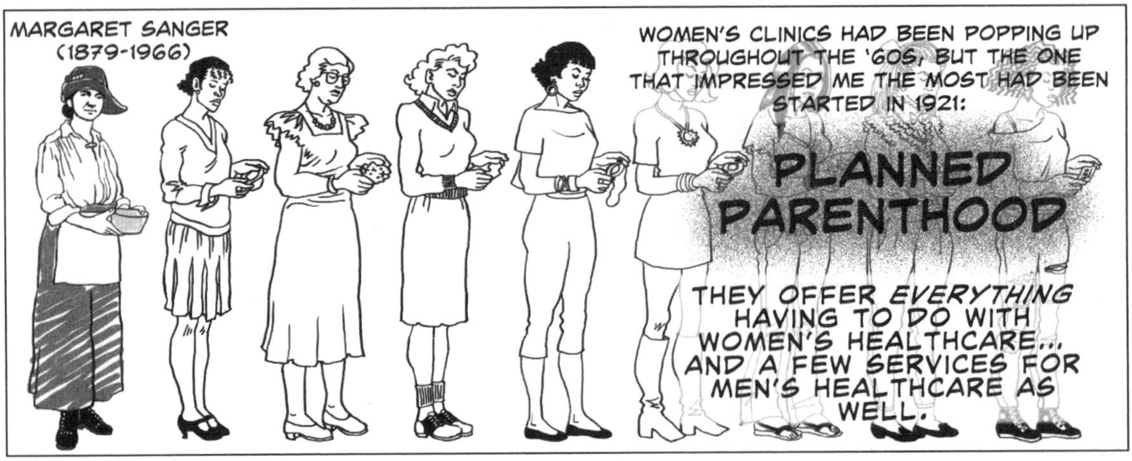
MARGARET SANGER (1879-1966)
WOMEN'S CLINICS HAD BEEN POPPING UP THROUGHOUT THE '60S, BUT THE ONE THAT IMPRESSED ME THE MOST HAD BEEN STARTED IN 1921:
PLANNED PARENTHOOD
THEY OFFER *EVERYTHING* HAVING TO DO WITH WOMEN'S HEALTHCARE... AND A FEW SERVICES FOR MEN'S HEALTHCARE AS WELL.

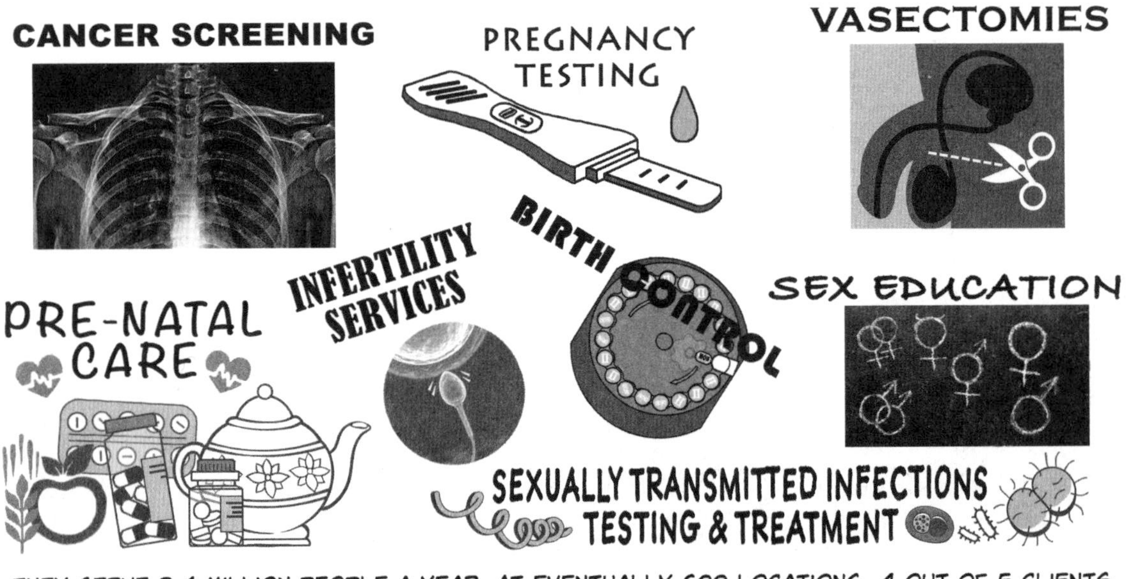
CANCER SCREENING
PREGNANCY TESTING
VASECTOMIES
INFERTILITY SERVICES
BIRTH CONTROL
SEX EDUCATION
PRE-NATAL CARE
SEXUALLY TRANSMITTED INFECTIONS TESTING & TREATMENT

THEY SERVE 2.4 MILLION PEOPLE A YEAR. AT EVENTUALLY 600 LOCATIONS, 4 OUT OF 5 CLIENTS ARE AT OR BELOW THE FEDERAL POVERTY LEVEL.

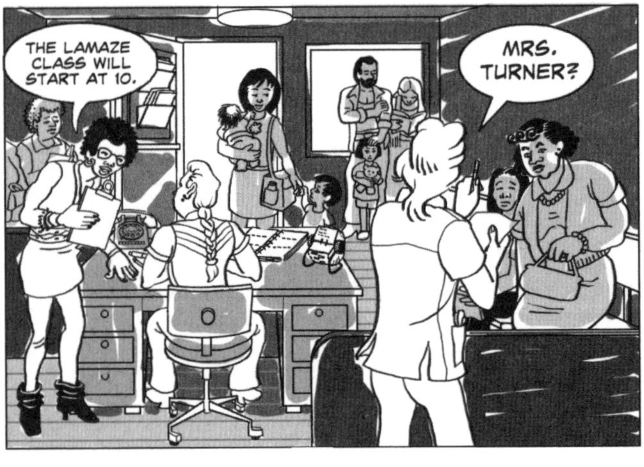
THE LAMAZE CLASS WILL START AT 10.
MRS. TURNER?

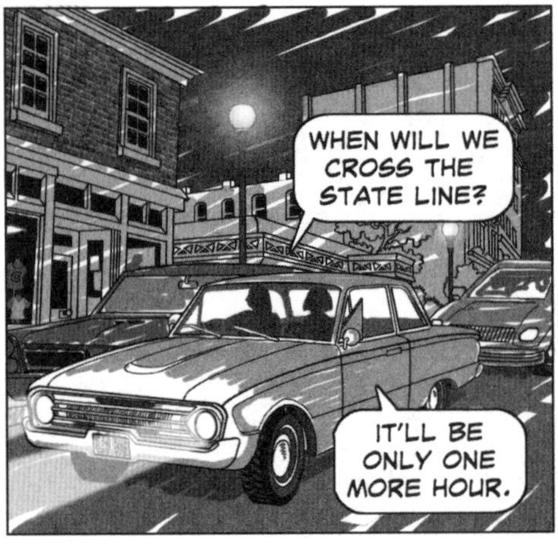
WHEN WILL WE CROSS THE STATE LINE?
IT'LL BE ONLY ONE MORE HOUR.

DUE TO THEIR ABORTION OFFERING, DESPITE THEIR USEFUL, GENEROUS RANGE OF SERVICES, WOMEN'S CLINICS – AND PARTICULARLY PLANNED PARENTHOOD – BECAME A TARGET. A TARGET FOR ANTI-ABORTION ACTIVISTS, RIGHT WING FANATICS... AND ***KILLERS.*** THESE FORCES USED A VARIETY OF METHODS, INCLUDING ...

HARASSMENT

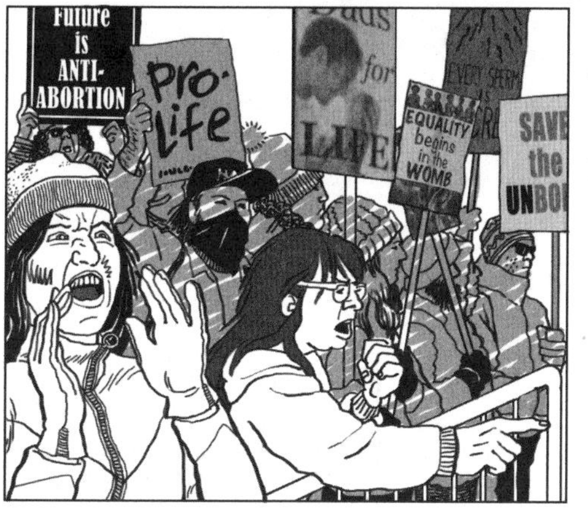
Future is ANTI-ABORTION
Pro-Life
EQUALITY begins in the WOMB

BOMBING

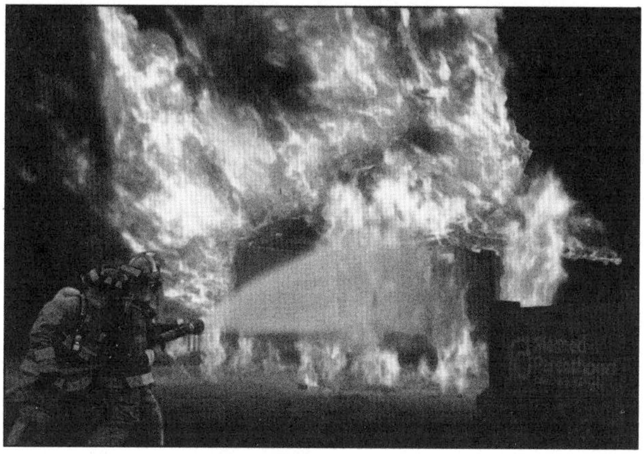

MURDER

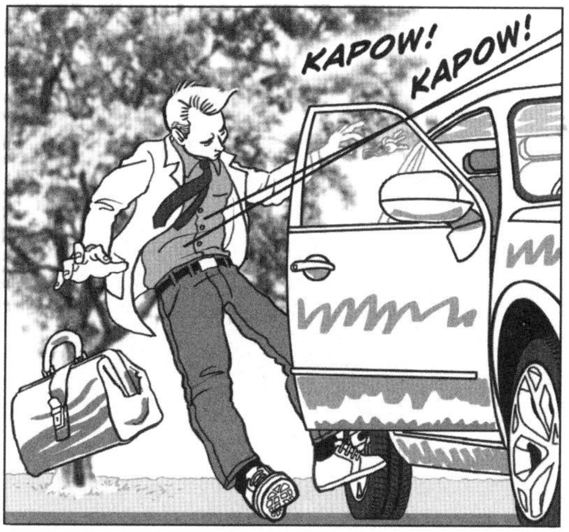
KAPOW!
KAPOW!

SLAUGHTER

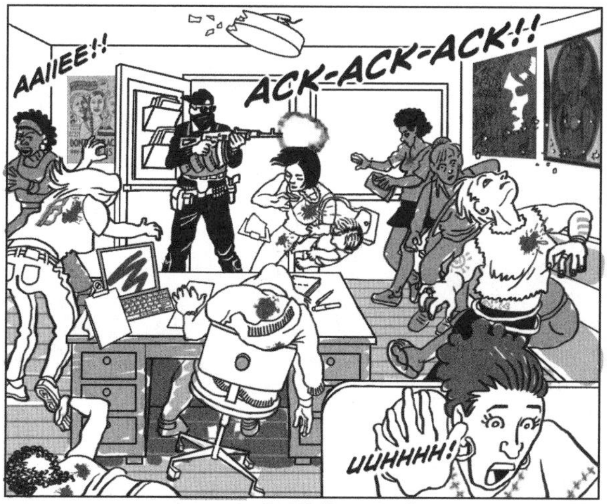
AAIIEE!!
ACK-ACK-ACK!!
UUHHHH!

ALL THIS MAYHEM WENT ON WHILE ABORTIONS WERE ... **LEGAL!**

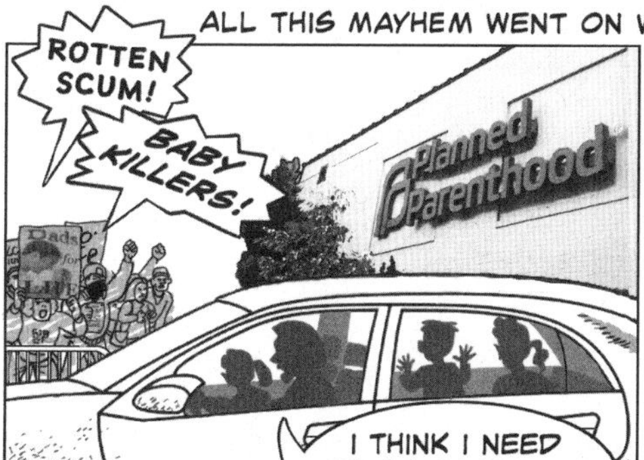
ROTTEN SCUM!
BABY KILLERS!
Planned Parenthood
I THINK I NEED TO RE-SCHEDULE MY CHECK-UP.

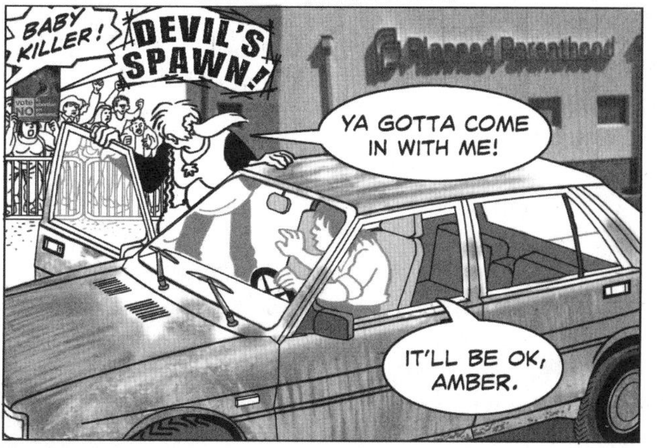
BABY KILLER!
DEVIL'S SPAWN!
Planned Parenthood
YA GOTTA COME IN WITH ME!
IT'LL BE OK, AMBER.

BAD NEW DAYS

THE NEGATIVE GOVERNMENTAL FORCES WERE PERSISTENTLY AT WORK.
ROE VS. WADE WAS UNDER CONSTANT ATTACK.

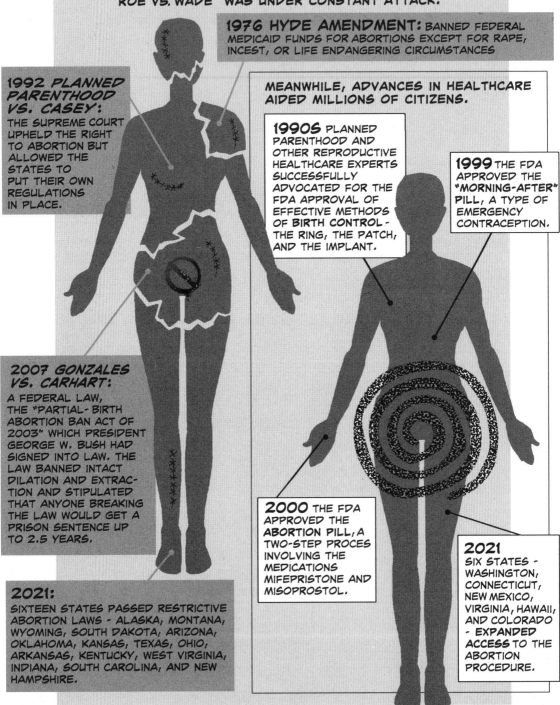

1976 HYDE AMENDMENT: BANNED FEDERAL MEDICAID FUNDS FOR ABORTIONS EXCEPT FOR RAPE, INCEST, OR LIFE ENDANGERING CIRCUMSTANCES

1992 PLANNED PARENTHOOD VS. CASEY: THE SUPREME COURT UPHELD THE RIGHT TO ABORTION BUT ALLOWED THE STATES TO PUT THEIR OWN REGULATIONS IN PLACE.

MEANWHILE, ADVANCES IN HEALTHCARE AIDED MILLIONS OF CITIZENS.

1990S PLANNED PARENTHOOD AND OTHER REPRODUCTIVE HEALTHCARE EXPERTS SUCCESSFULLY ADVOCATED FOR THE FDA APPROVAL OF EFFECTIVE METHODS OF BIRTH CONTROL - THE RING, THE PATCH, AND THE IMPLANT.

1999 THE FDA APPROVED THE "MORNING-AFTER" PILL, A TYPE OF EMERGENCY CONTRACEPTION.

2007 GONZALES VS. CARHART: A FEDERAL LAW, THE "PARTIAL- BIRTH ABORTION BAN ACT OF 2003" WHICH PRESIDENT GEORGE W. BUSH HAD SIGNED INTO LAW. THE LAW BANNED INTACT DILATION AND EXTRACTION AND STIPULATED THAT ANYONE BREAKING THE LAW WOULD GET A PRISON SENTENCE UP TO 2.5 YEARS.

2000 THE FDA APPROVED THE ABORTION PILL, A TWO-STEP PROCES INVOLVING THE MEDICATIONS MIFEPRISTONE AND MISOPROSTOL.

2021 SIX STATES - WASHINGTON, CONNECTICUT, NEW MEXICO, VIRGINIA, HAWAII, AND COLORADO - EXPANDED ACCESS TO THE ABORTION PROCEDURE.

2021: SIXTEEN STATES PASSED RESTRICTIVE ABORTION LAWS - ALASKA, MONTANA, WYOMING, SOUTH DAKOTA, ARIZONA, OKLAHOMA, KANSAS, TEXAS, OHIO, ARKANSAS, KENTUCKY, WEST VIRGINIA, INDIANA, SOUTH CAROLINA, AND NEW HAMPSHIRE.

ROTTEN CURRENT DAYS

ON JUNE 24, 2022 THE SUPREME COURT OVERTURNED ROE V. WADE IN A 6-3 DECISION, ELIMINATING THE CONSTITUTIONAL RIGHT TO AN ABORTION AFTER ALMOST 50 YEARS. THE RULING MAKES THE U.S.A. ONE OF ONLY FOUR COUNTRIES TO REMOVE PROTECTIONS FOR LEGAL ABORTION IN THE PAST 25 YEARS.

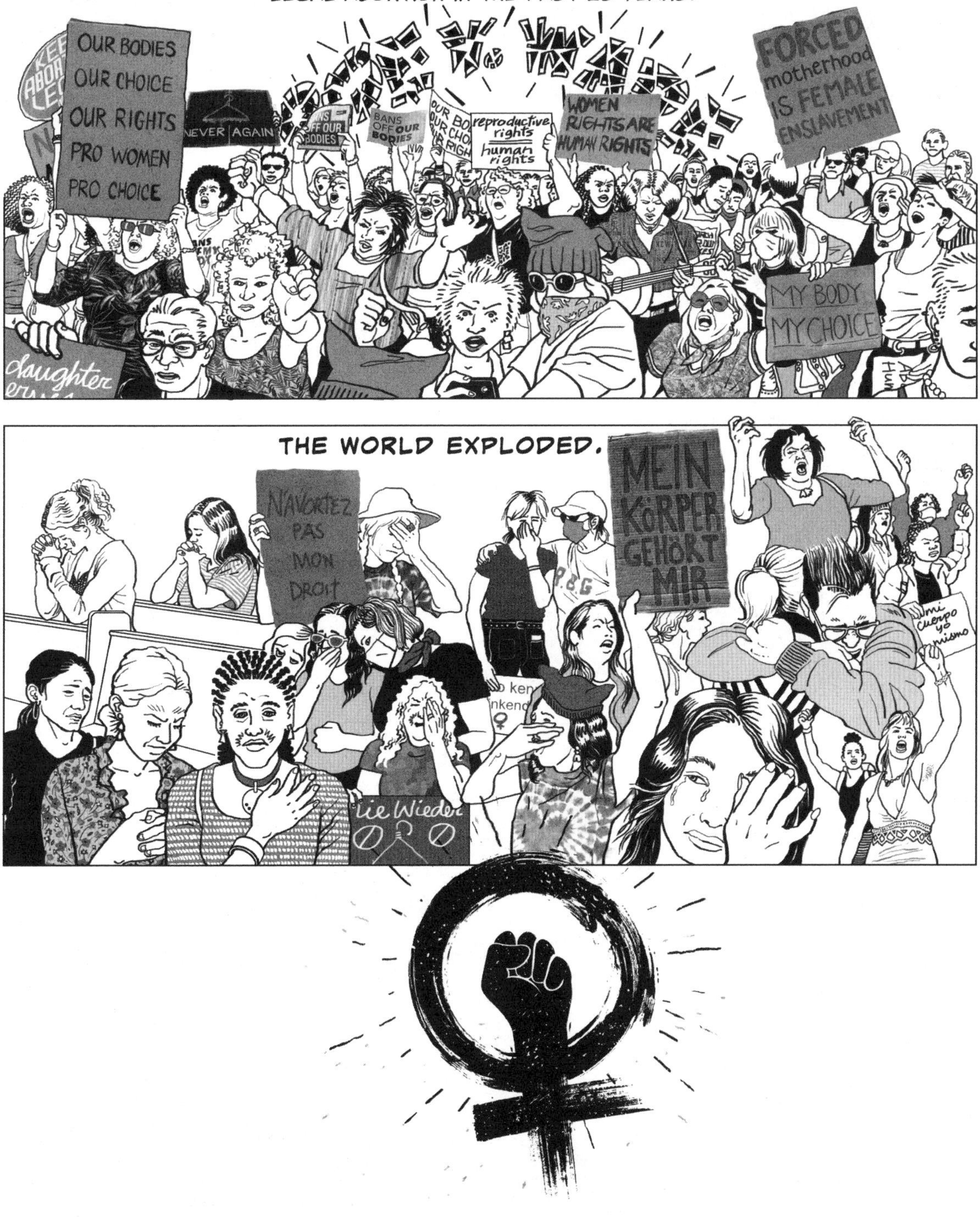

OUR BODIES OUR CHOICE OUR RIGHTS PRO WOMEN PRO CHOICE
NEVER AGAIN
BANS OFF OUR BODIES
reproductive rights = human rights
WOMEN RIGHTS ARE HUMAN RIGHTS
FORCED motherhood IS FEMALE ENSLAVEMENT
MY BODY MY CHOICE
daughter
THE WORLD EXPLODED.
N'AVORTEZ PAS MON DROIT
MEIN KÖRPER GEHÖRT MIR
mi cuerpo yo mismo

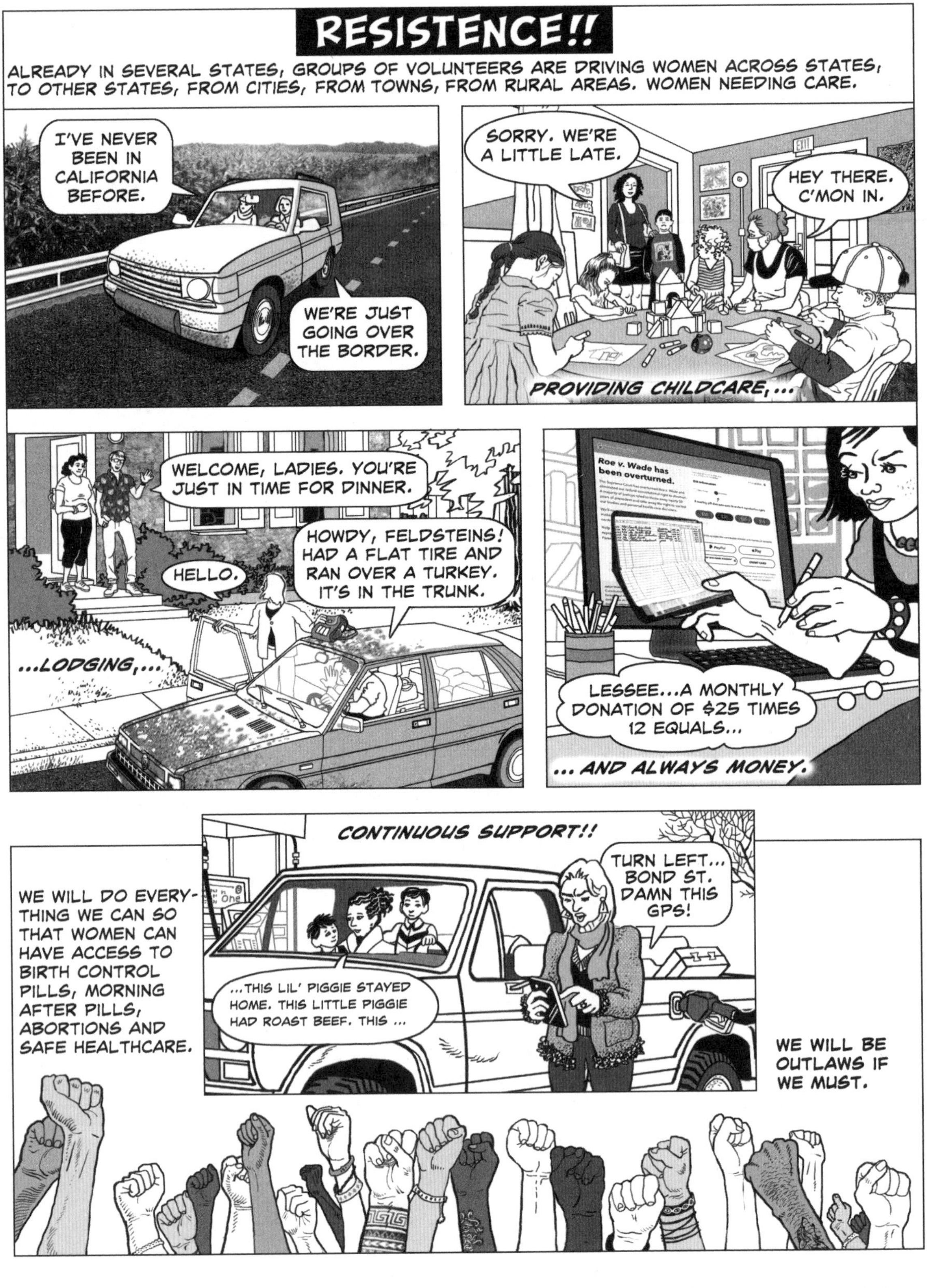
RESISTENCE!!
ALREADY IN SEVERAL STATES, GROUPS OF VOLUNTEERS ARE DRIVING WOMEN ACROSS STATES, TO OTHER STATES, FROM CITIES, FROM TOWNS, FROM RURAL AREAS. WOMEN NEEDING CARE.
I'VE NEVER BEEN IN CALIFORNIA BEFORE.
WE'RE JUST GOING OVER THE BORDER.
SORRY. WE'RE A LITTLE LATE.
HEY THERE. C'MON IN.
PROVIDING CHILDCARE,...
WELCOME, LADIES. YOU'RE JUST IN TIME FOR DINNER.
HELLO.
HOWDY, FELDSTEINS! HAD A FLAT TIRE AND RAN OVER A TURKEY. IT'S IN THE TRUNK.
...LODGING,...
Roe v. Wade has been overturned.
LESSEE...A MONTHLY DONATION OF $25 TIMES 12 EQUALS...
...AND ALWAYS MONEY.
CONTINUOUS SUPPORT!!
WE WILL DO EVERY-THING WE CAN SO THAT WOMEN CAN HAVE ACCESS TO BIRTH CONTROL PILLS, MORNING AFTER PILLS, ABORTIONS AND SAFE HEALTHCARE.
TURN LEFT... BOND ST. DAMN THIS GPS!
...THIS LIL' PIGGIE STAYED HOME. THIS LITTLE PIGGIE HAD ROAST BEEF. THIS ...
WE WILL BE OUTLAWS IF WE MUST.

WE WILL NOT BE STOPPED. OUR BODIES BELONG TO US. WE WILL DECIDE WHEN TO HAVE CHILDREN OR NOT. FOR OURSELVES. AND THE GENERATIONS TO COME WILL DECIDE FOR THEMSELVES. WOMEN AND MALE ALLIES ARE DRIVING. DRIVING EVERY DAY. FROM COUNTIES TO COUNTIES, FROM STATE TO STATE.

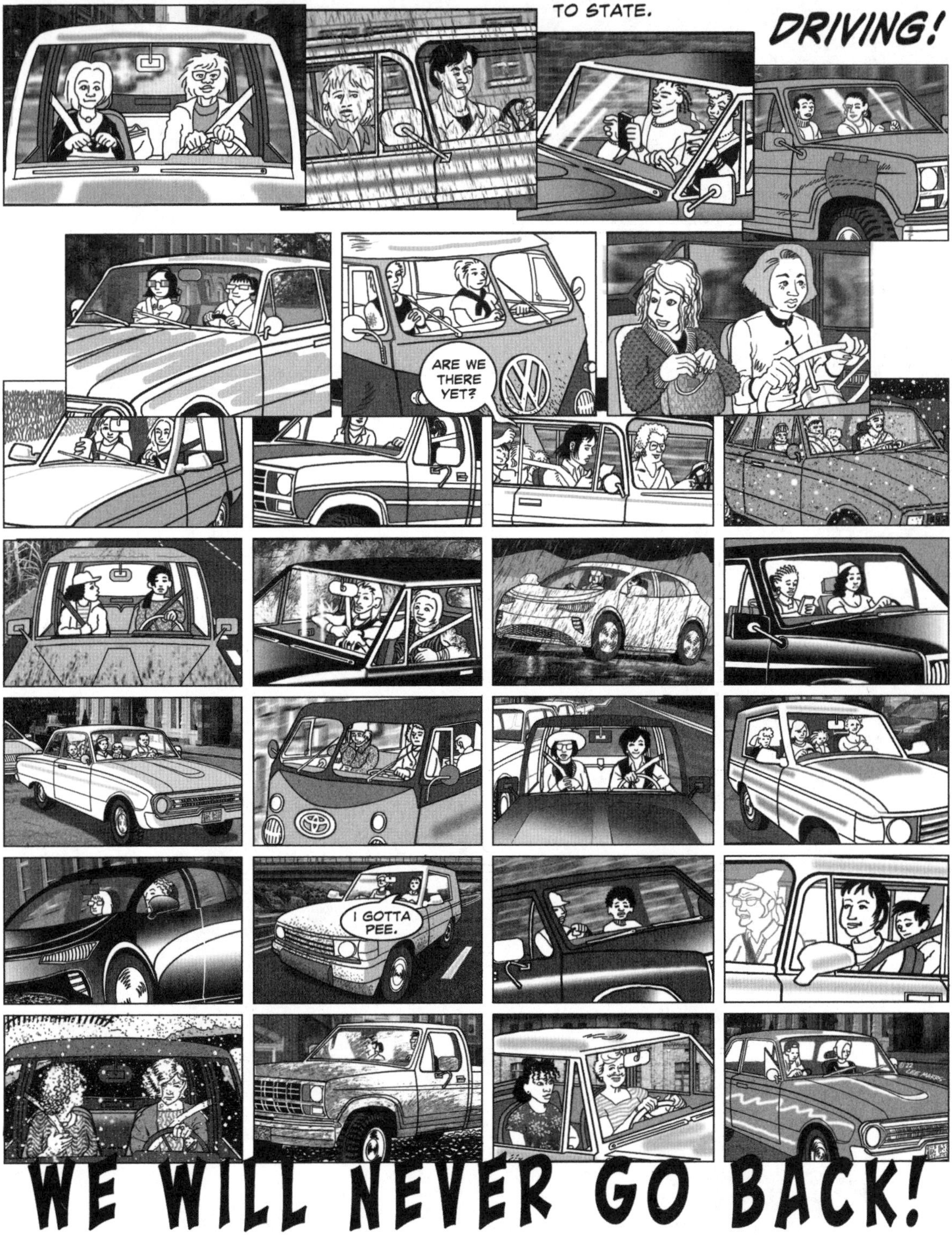
DRIVING!
ARE WE THERE YET?
I GOTTA PEE.
WE WILL NEVER GO BACK!

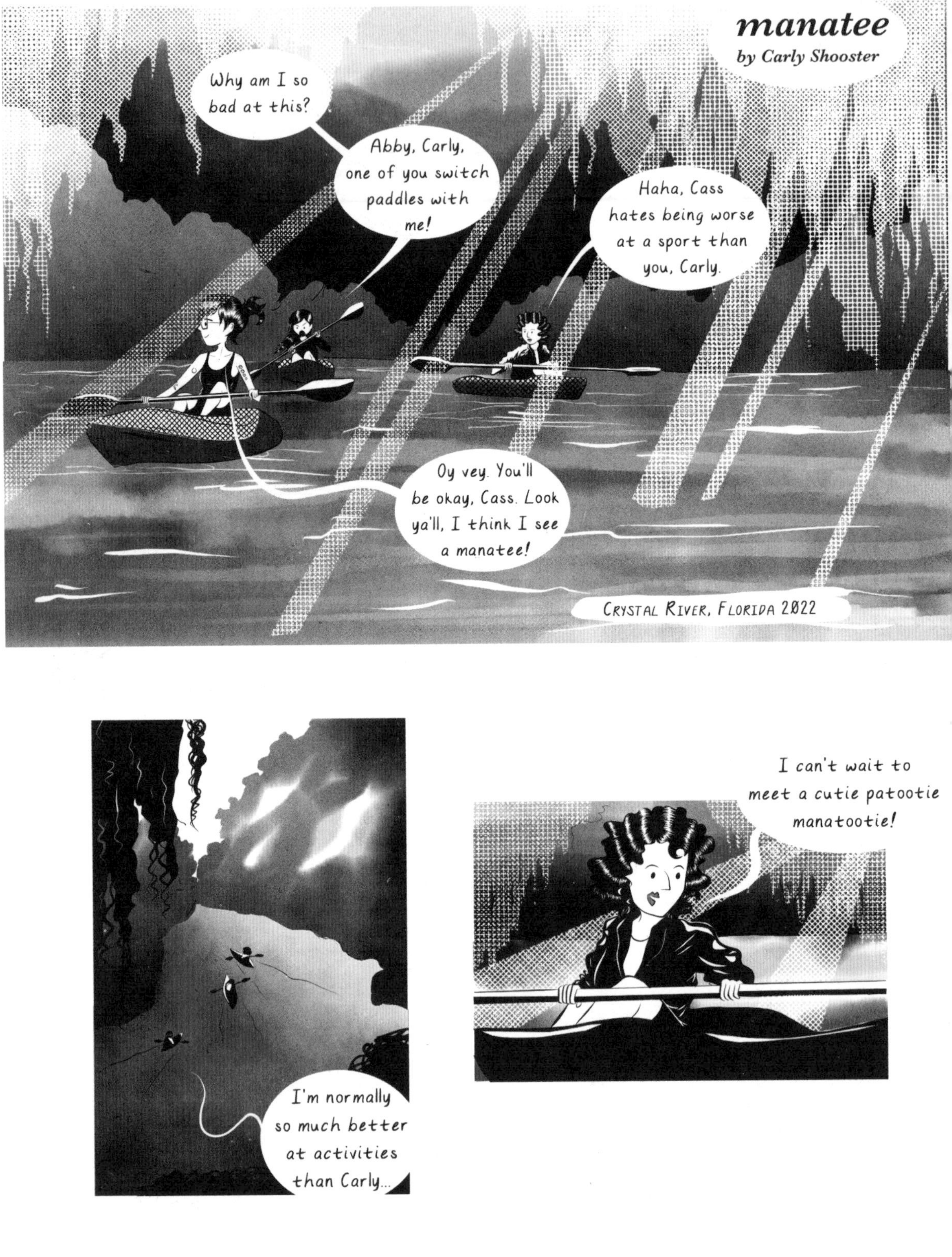
manatee
by Carly Shooster
Why am I so bad at this?
Abby, Carly, one of you switch paddles with me!
Haha, Cass hates being worse at a sport than you, Carly.
Oy vey. You'll be okay, Cass. Look ya'll, I think I see a manatee!
CRYSTAL RIVER, FLORIDA 2022
I'm normally so much better at activities than Carly...
I can't wait to meet a cutie patootie manatootie!

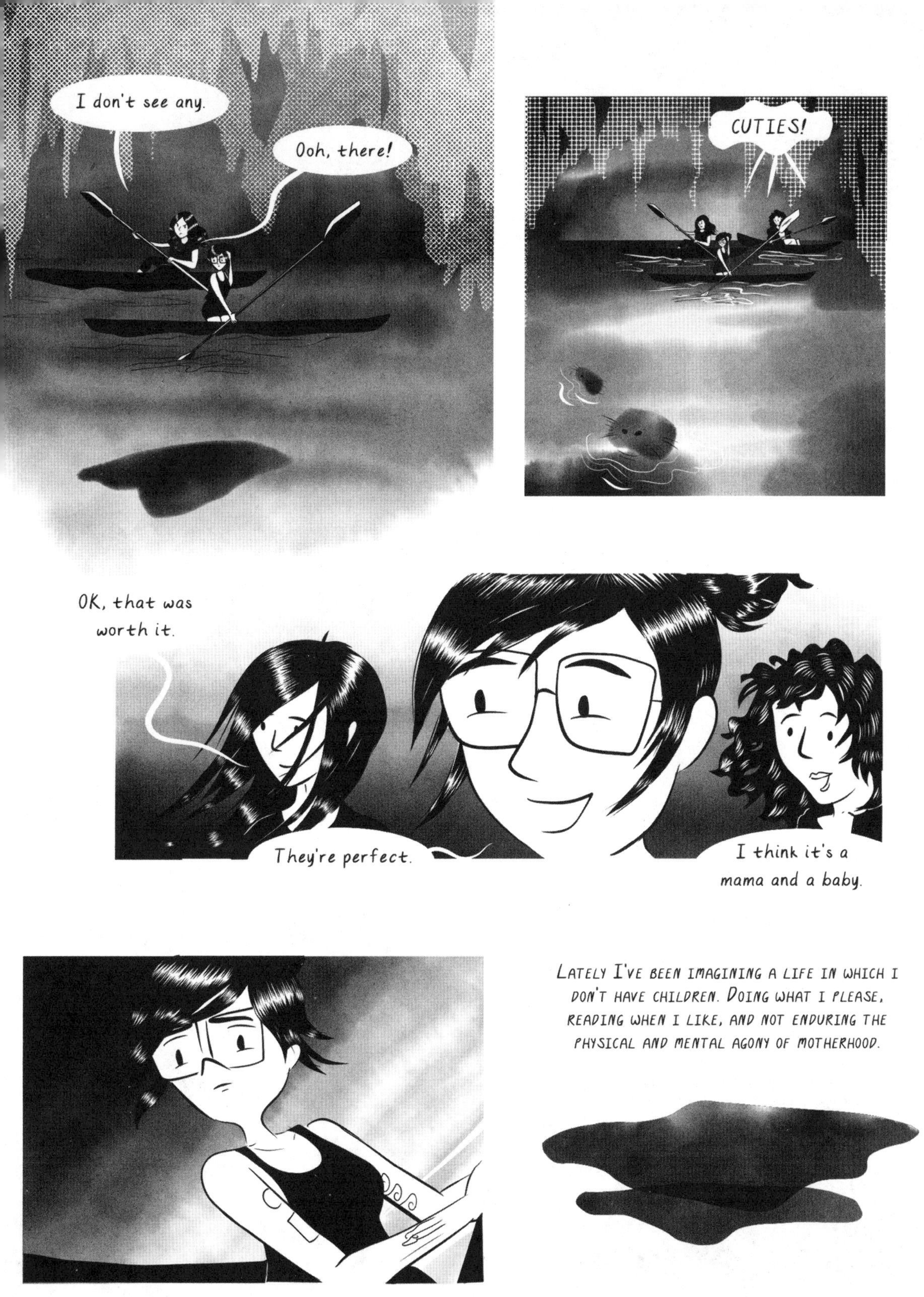

I don't see any.
Ooh, there!
CUTIES!
OK, that was worth it.
They're perfect.
I think it's a mama and a baby.
LATELY I'VE BEEN IMAGINING A LIFE IN WHICH I DON'T HAVE CHILDREN. DOING WHAT I PLEASE, READING WHEN I LIKE, AND NOT ENDURING THE PHYSICAL AND MENTAL AGONY OF MOTHERHOOD.

BUT I KNOW THE TRUTH INSIDE MY BODY.

IT CALLS FOR A FAMILY

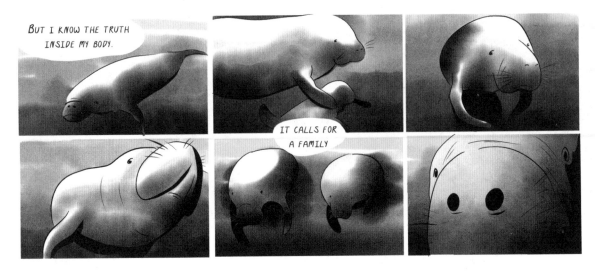

THERE'S AN UNTAPPED WELL DEEP IN THE PIT OF MY "SOUL," (OR UTERUS?) SPILLING OVER WITH MATERNAL AFFECTION.

AND SOMETIMES IT'S ALL TOO MUCH. I'M OVERWHELMED BECAUSE I KNOW I, TOO, WILL BE A MOTHER

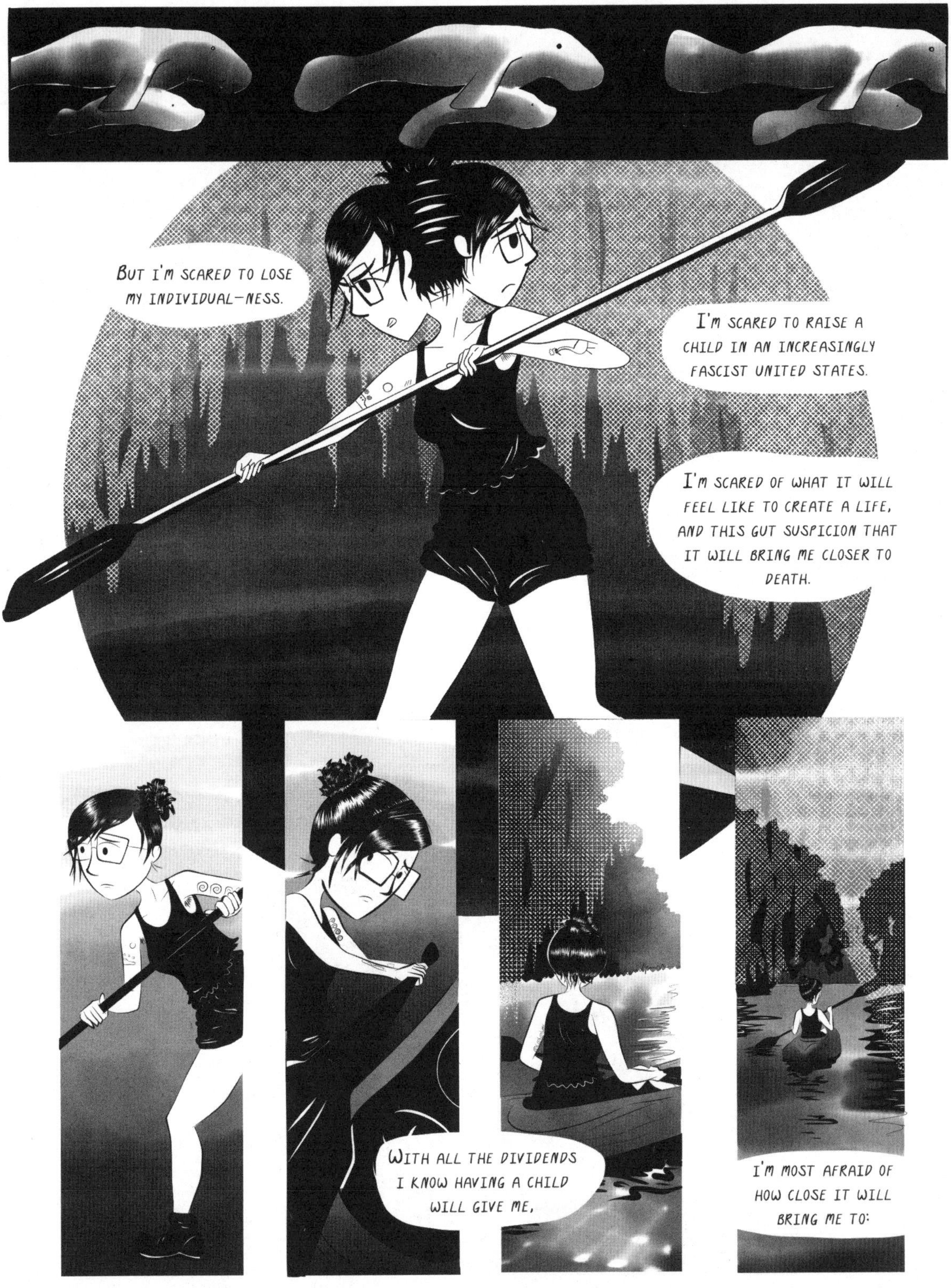
BUT I'M SCARED TO LOSE MY INDIVIDUAL-NESS.
I'M SCARED TO RAISE A CHILD IN AN INCREASINGLY FASCIST UNITED STATES.
I'M SCARED OF WHAT IT WILL FEEL LIKE TO CREATE A LIFE, AND THIS GUT SUSPICION THAT IT WILL BRING ME CLOSER TO DEATH.
WITH ALL THE DIVIDENDS I KNOW HAVING A CHILD WILL GIVE ME,
I'M MOST AFRAID OF HOW CLOSE IT WILL BRING ME TO:

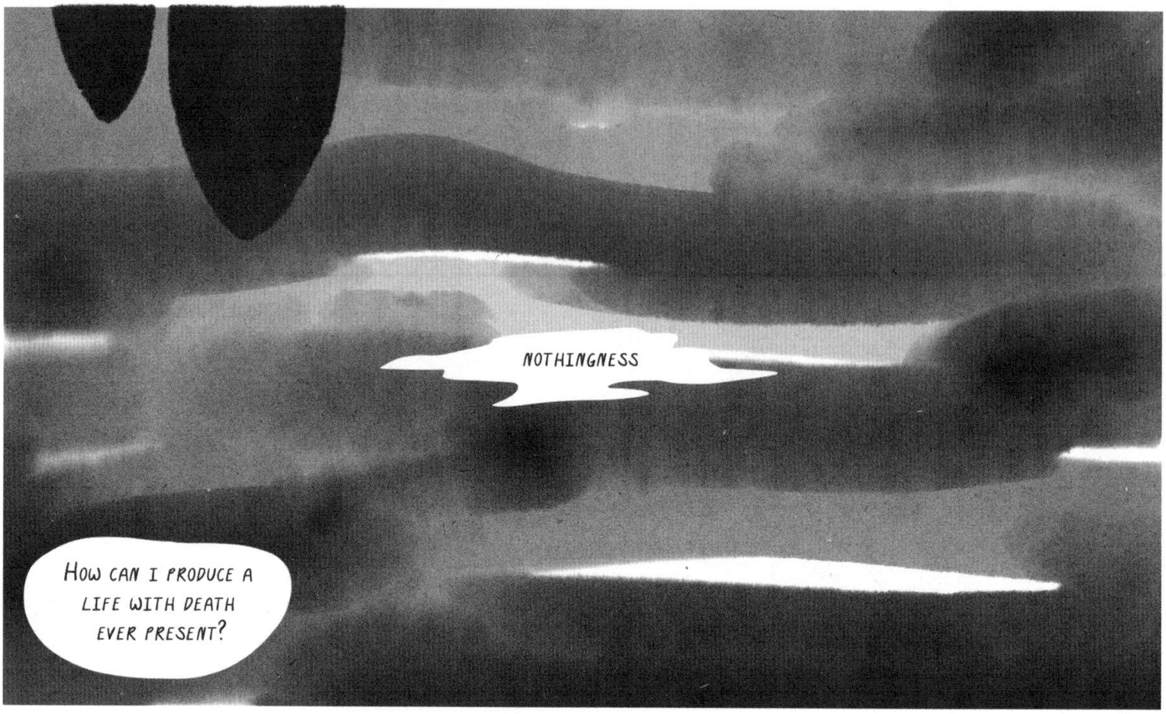
NOTHINGNESS
HOW CAN I PRODUCE A LIFE WITH DEATH EVER PRESENT?

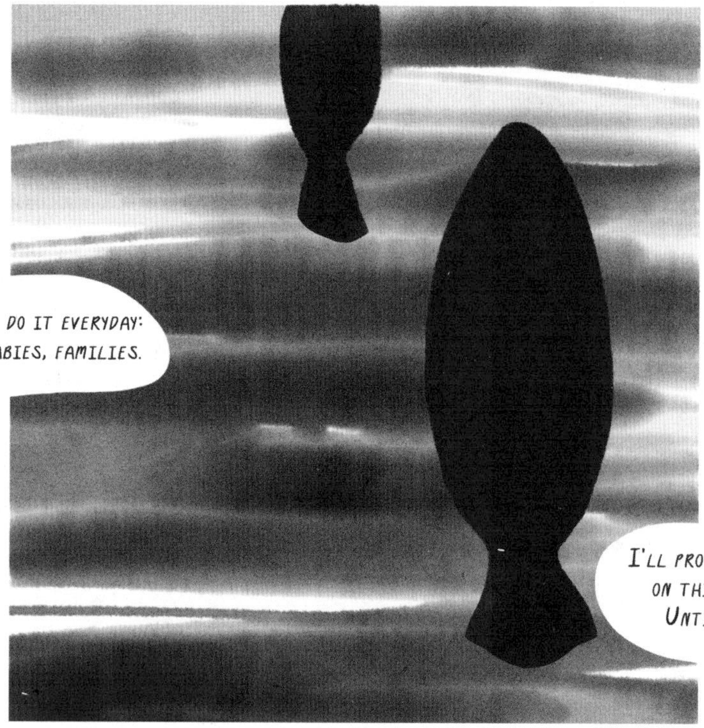
PEOPLE DO IT EVERYDAY: SEX, BABIES, FAMILIES.
I'LL PROBABLY BE TORN ON THIS FOREVER, UNTIL DEATH.

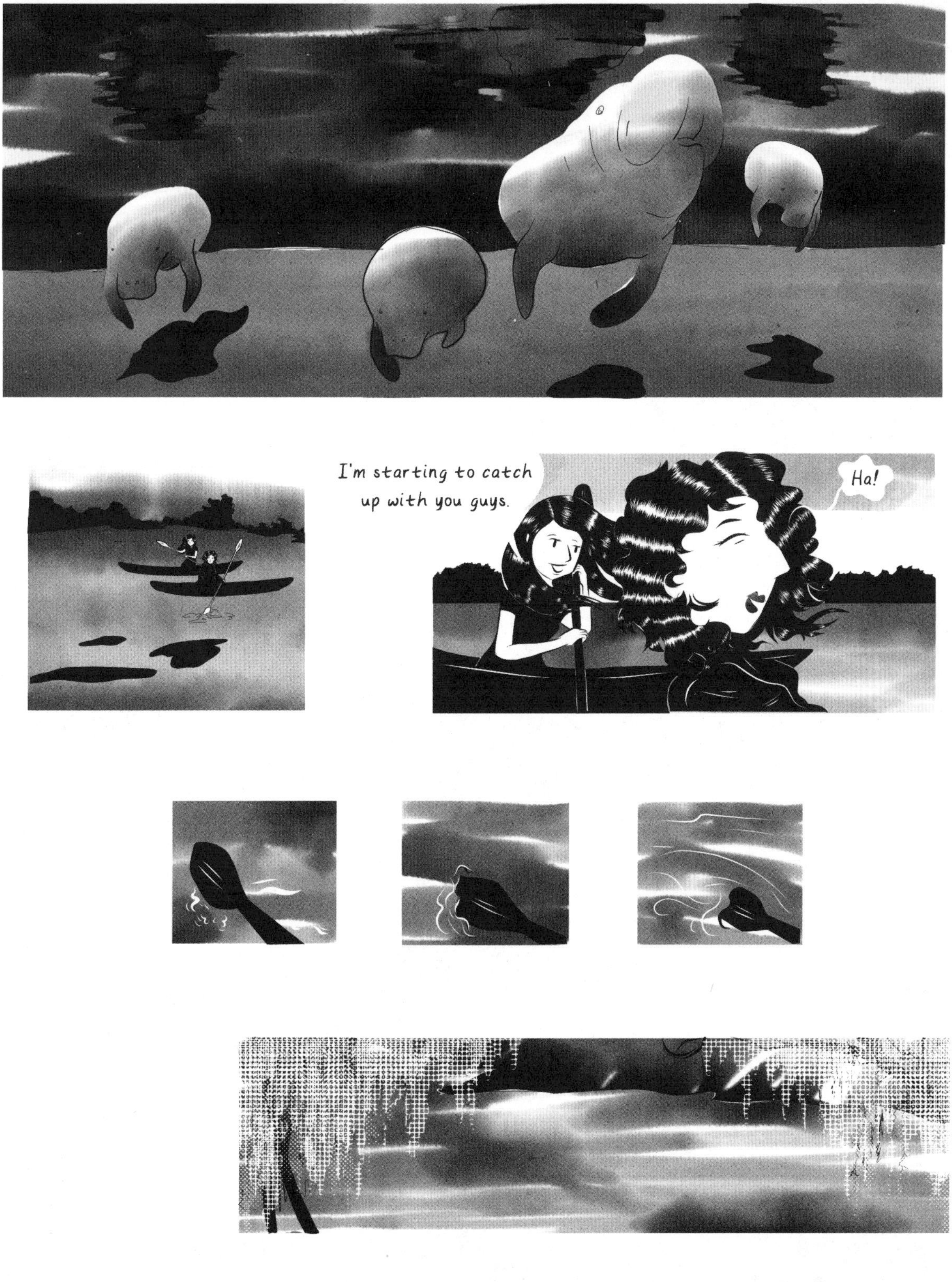
I'm starting to catch up with you guys.
Ha!

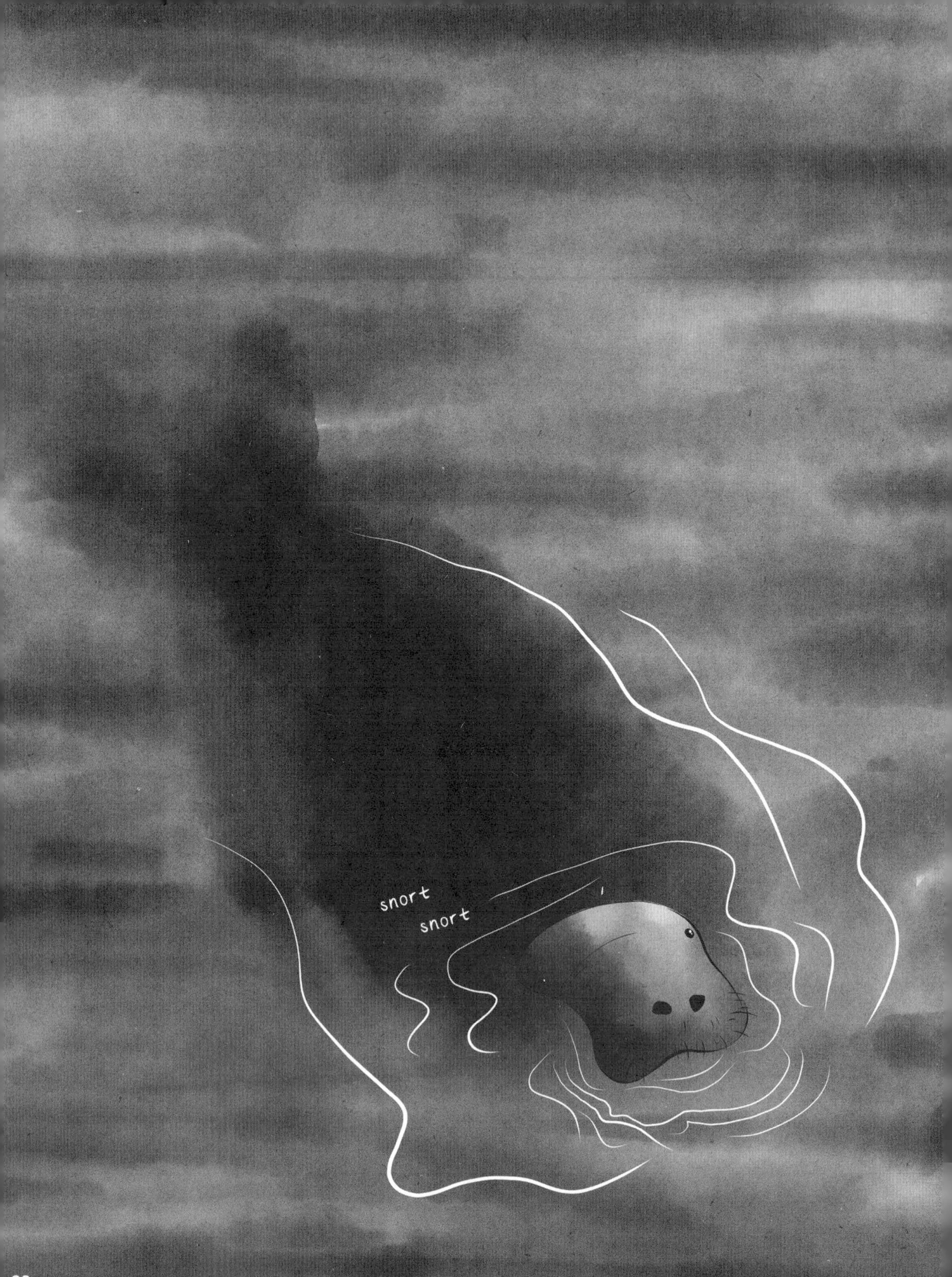
snort
snort

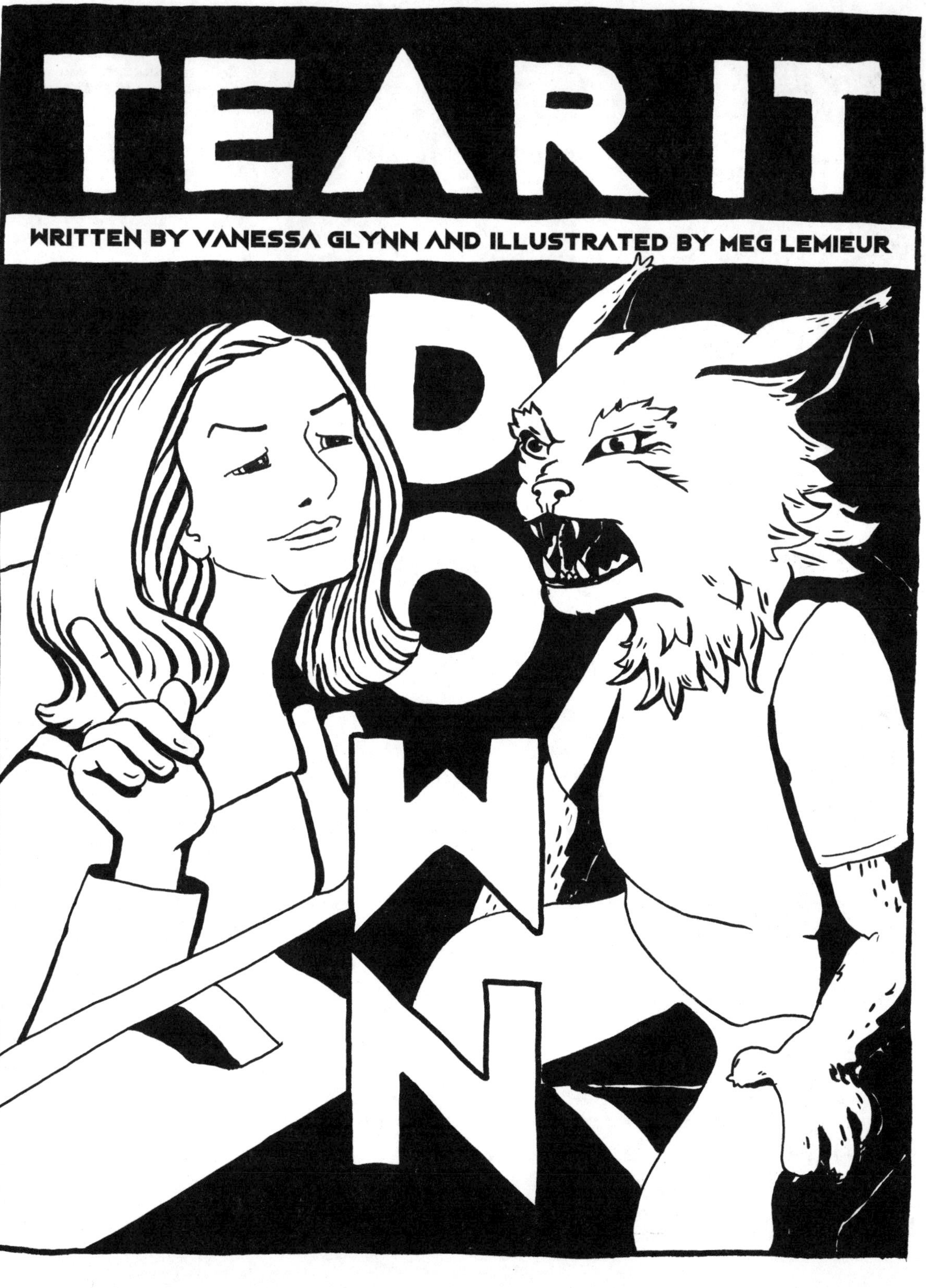
TEAR IT
WRITTEN BY VANESSA GLYNN AND ILLUSTRATED BY MEG LEMIEUR
DOWN

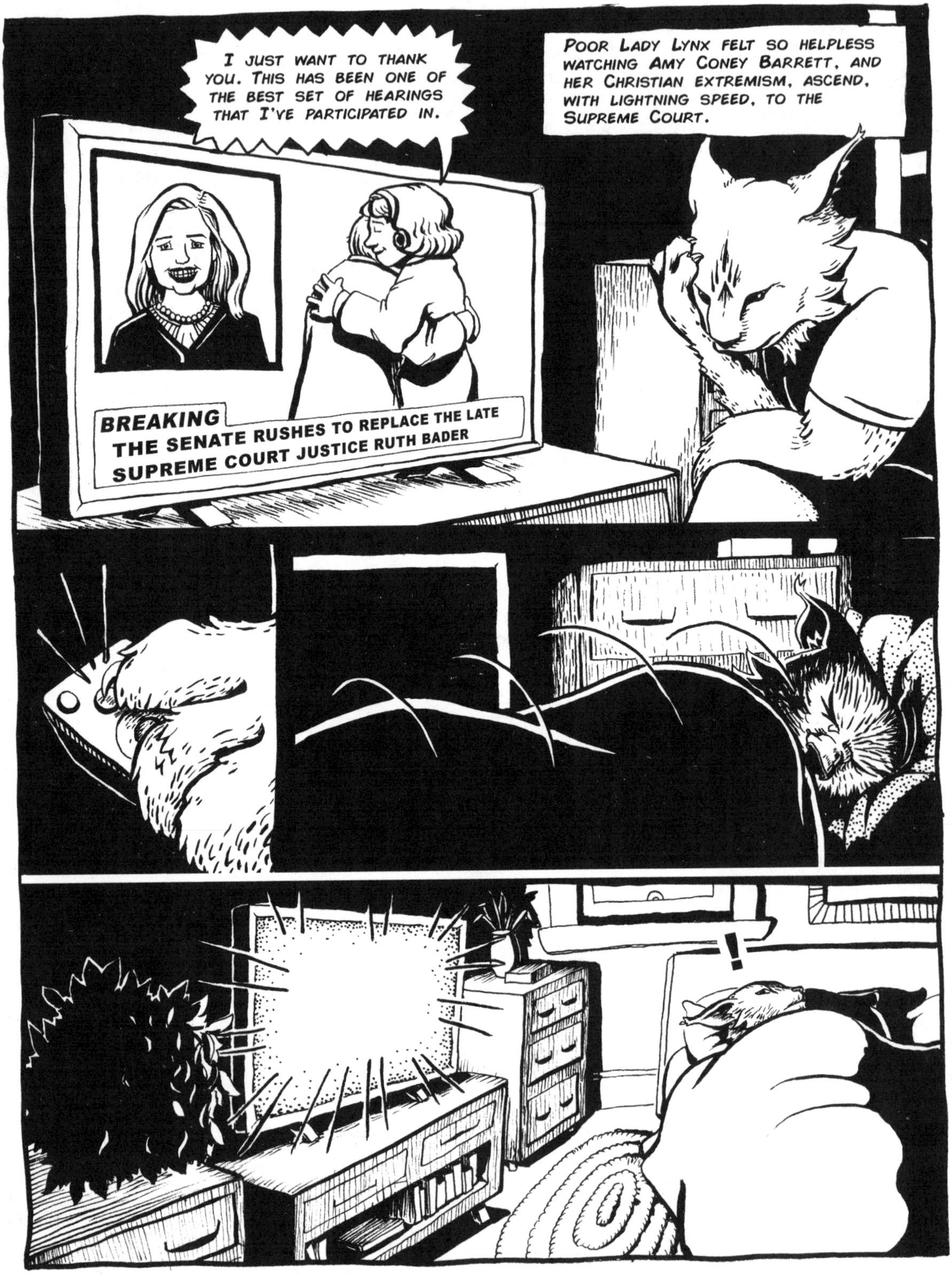
I JUST WANT TO THANK YOU. THIS HAS BEEN ONE OF THE BEST SET OF HEARINGS THAT I'VE PARTICIPATED IN.
POOR LADY LYNX FELT SO HELPLESS WATCHING AMY CONEY BARRETT, AND HER CHRISTIAN EXTREMISM, ASCEND, WITH LIGHTNING SPEED, TO THE SUPREME COURT.
BREAKING
THE SENATE RUSHES TO REPLACE THE LATE SUPREME COURT JUSTICE RUTH BADER
!

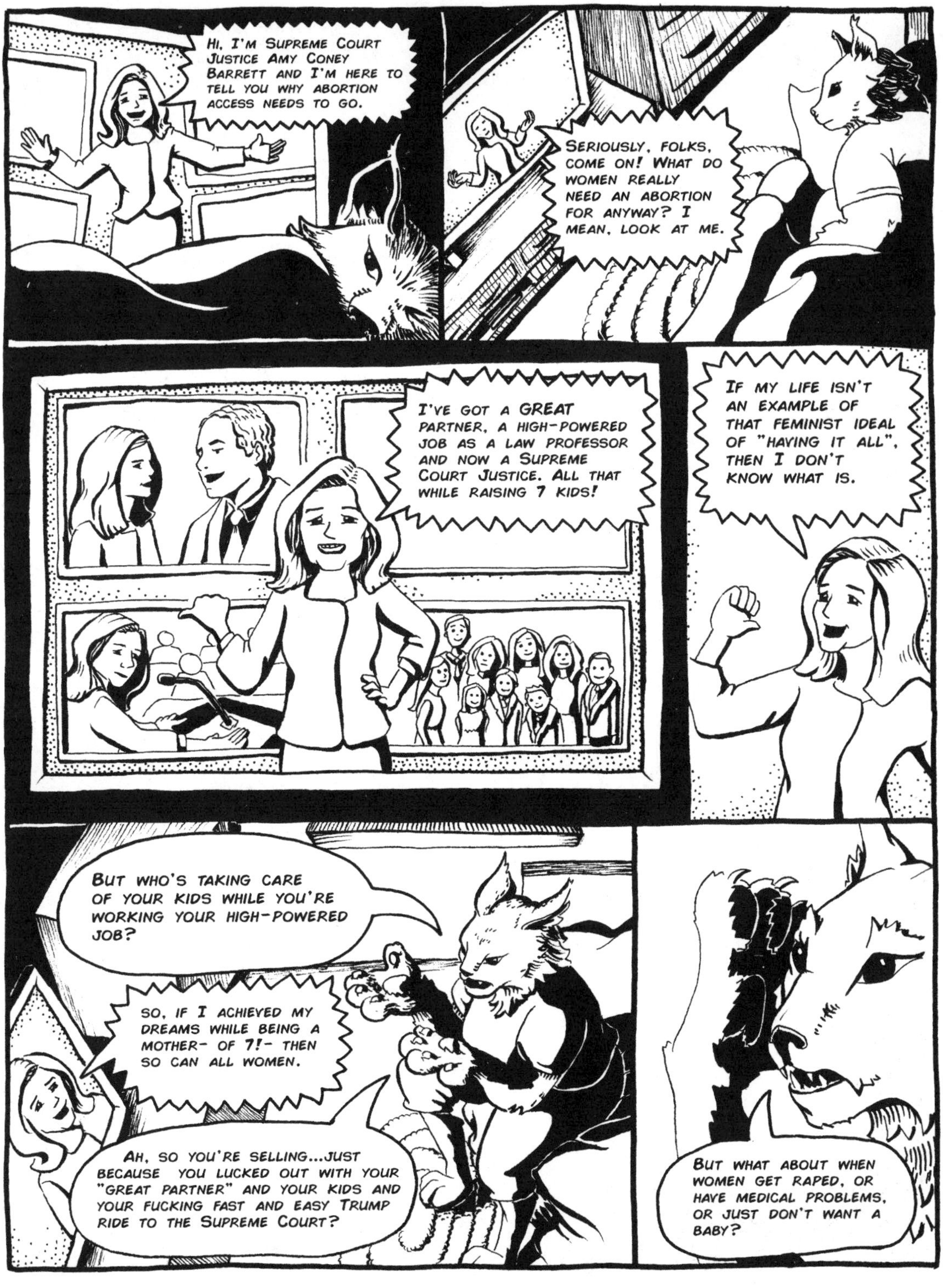
Hi, I'm Supreme Court Justice Amy Coney Barrett and I'm here to tell you why abortion access needs to go.
Seriously, folks, come on! What do women really need an abortion for anyway? I mean, look at me.
I've got a GREAT partner, a high-powered job as a law professor and now a Supreme Court Justice. All that while raising 7 kids!
If my life isn't an example of that feminist ideal of "having it all", then I don't know what is.
But who's taking care of your kids while you're working your high-powered job?
So, if I achieved my dreams while being a mother- of 7!- then so can all women.
Ah, so you're selling...just because you lucked out with your "great partner" and your kids and your fucking fast and easy Trump ride to the Supreme Court?
But what about when women get raped, or have medical problems, or just don't want a baby?

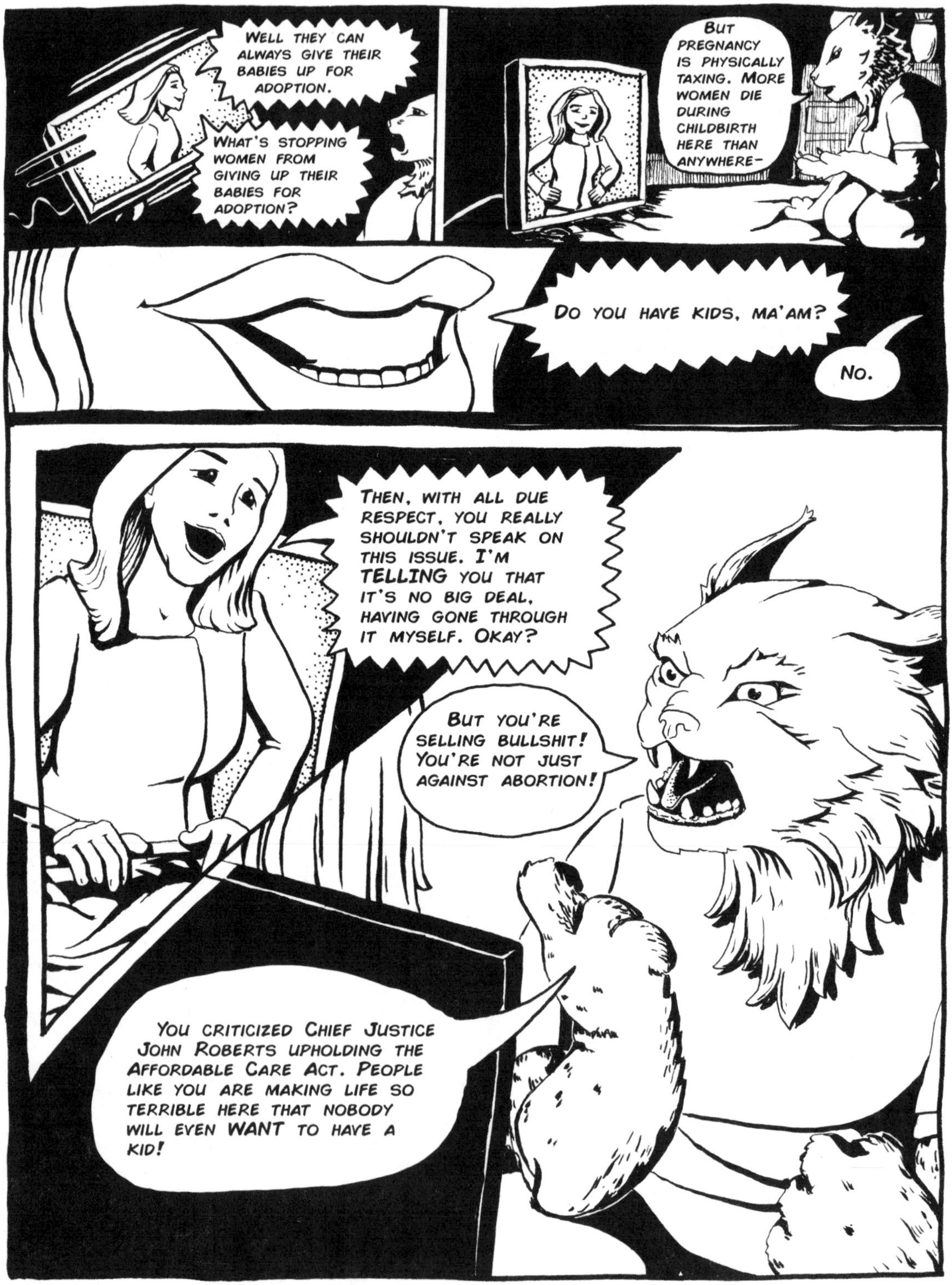
WELL THEY CAN ALWAYS GIVE THEIR BABIES UP FOR ADOPTION.
WHAT'S STOPPING WOMEN FROM GIVING UP THEIR BABIES FOR ADOPTION?
BUT PREGNANCY IS PHYSICALLY TAXING. MORE WOMEN DIE DURING CHILDBIRTH HERE THAN ANYWHERE-
DO YOU HAVE KIDS, MA'AM?
NO.
THEN, WITH ALL DUE RESPECT, YOU REALLY SHOULDN'T SPEAK ON THIS ISSUE. I'M TELLING YOU THAT IT'S NO BIG DEAL, HAVING GONE THROUGH IT MYSELF. OKAY?
BUT YOU'RE SELLING BULLSHIT! YOU'RE NOT JUST AGAINST ABORTION!
YOU CRITICIZED CHIEF JUSTICE JOHN ROBERTS UPHOLDING THE AFFORDABLE CARE ACT. PEOPLE LIKE YOU ARE MAKING LIFE SO TERRIBLE HERE THAT NOBODY WILL EVEN WANT TO HAVE A KID!

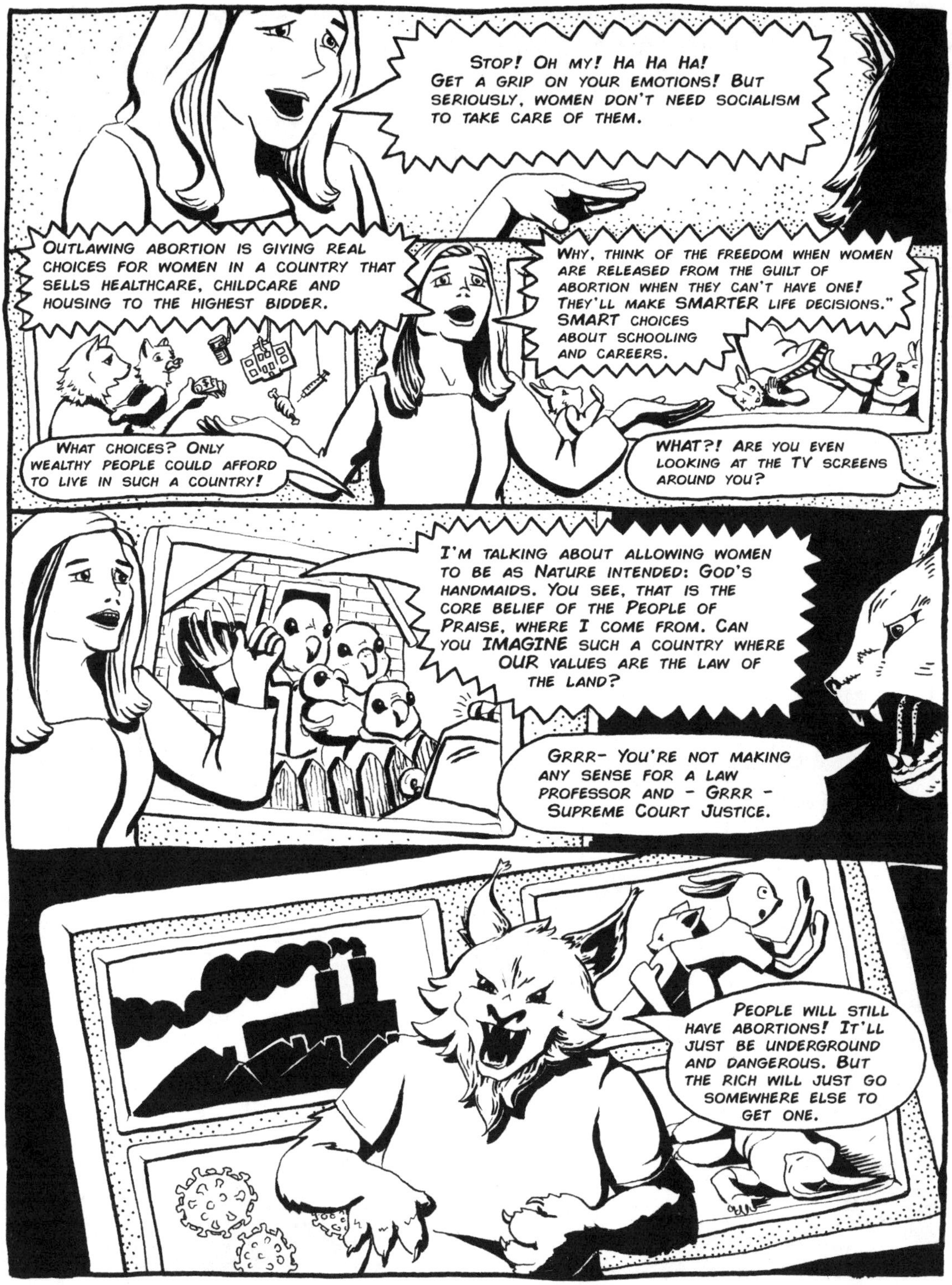

STOP! OH MY! HA HA HA! GET A GRIP ON YOUR EMOTIONS! BUT SERIOUSLY, WOMEN DON'T NEED SOCIALISM TO TAKE CARE OF THEM.
OUTLAWING ABORTION IS GIVING REAL CHOICES FOR WOMEN IN A COUNTRY THAT SELLS HEALTHCARE, CHILDCARE AND HOUSING TO THE HIGHEST BIDDER.
WHY, THINK OF THE FREEDOM WHEN WOMEN ARE RELEASED FROM THE GUILT OF ABORTION WHEN THEY CAN'T HAVE ONE! THEY'LL MAKE SMARTER LIFE DECISIONS." SMART CHOICES ABOUT SCHOOLING AND CAREERS.
WHAT CHOICES? ONLY WEALTHY PEOPLE COULD AFFORD TO LIVE IN SUCH A COUNTRY!
WHAT?! ARE YOU EVEN LOOKING AT THE TV SCREENS AROUND YOU?
I'M TALKING ABOUT ALLOWING WOMEN TO BE AS NATURE INTENDED: GOD'S HANDMAIDS. YOU SEE, THAT IS THE CORE BELIEF OF THE PEOPLE OF PRAISE, WHERE I COME FROM. CAN YOU IMAGINE SUCH A COUNTRY WHERE OUR VALUES ARE THE LAW OF THE LAND?
GRRR- YOU'RE NOT MAKING ANY SENSE FOR A LAW PROFESSOR AND - GRRR - SUPREME COURT JUSTICE.
PEOPLE WILL STILL HAVE ABORTIONS! IT'LL JUST BE UNDERGROUND AND DANGEROUS. BUT THE RICH WILL JUST GO SOMEWHERE ELSE TO GET ONE.

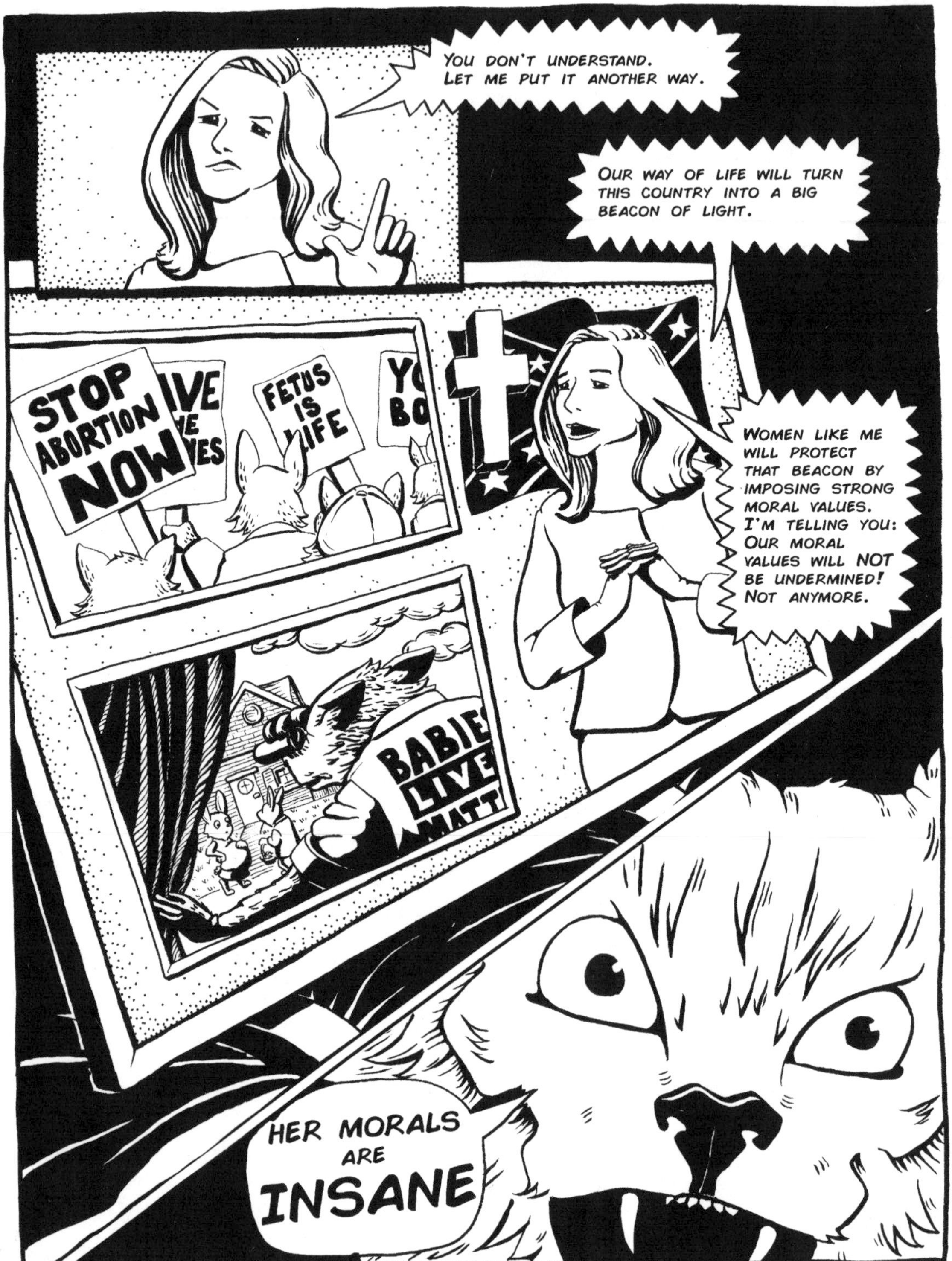
YOU DON'T UNDERSTAND.
LET ME PUT IT ANOTHER WAY.
OUR WAY OF LIFE WILL TURN THIS COUNTRY INTO A BIG BEACON OF LIGHT.
STOP ABORTION NOW
FETUS IS LIFE
WOMEN LIKE ME WILL PROTECT THAT BEACON BY IMPOSING STRONG MORAL VALUES. I'M TELLING YOU: OUR MORAL VALUES WILL NOT BE UNDERMINED! NOT ANYMORE.
HER MORALS ARE INSANE

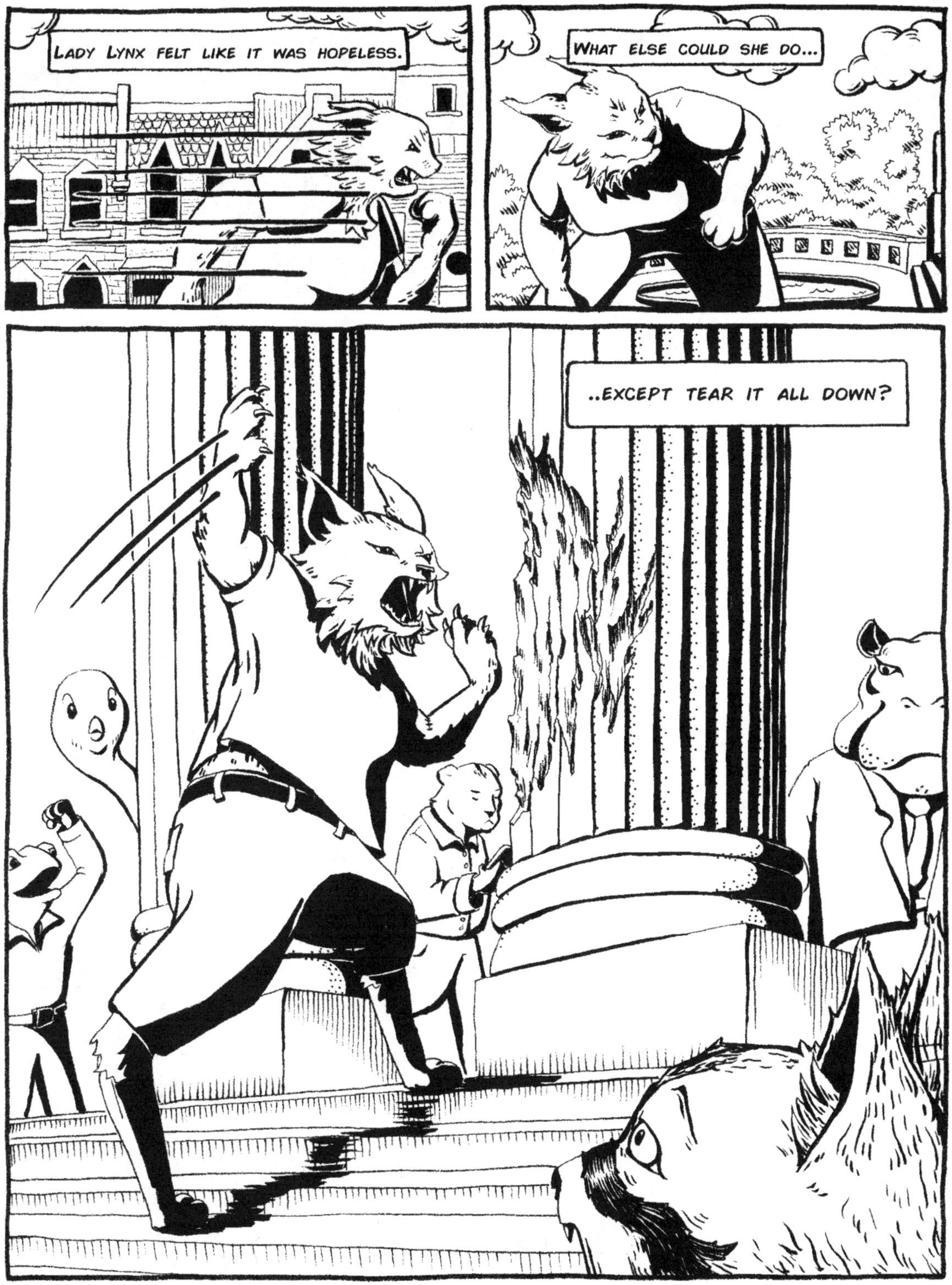

LADY LYNX FELT LIKE IT WAS HOPELESS.
WHAT ELSE COULD SHE DO...
..EXCEPT TEAR IT ALL DOWN?

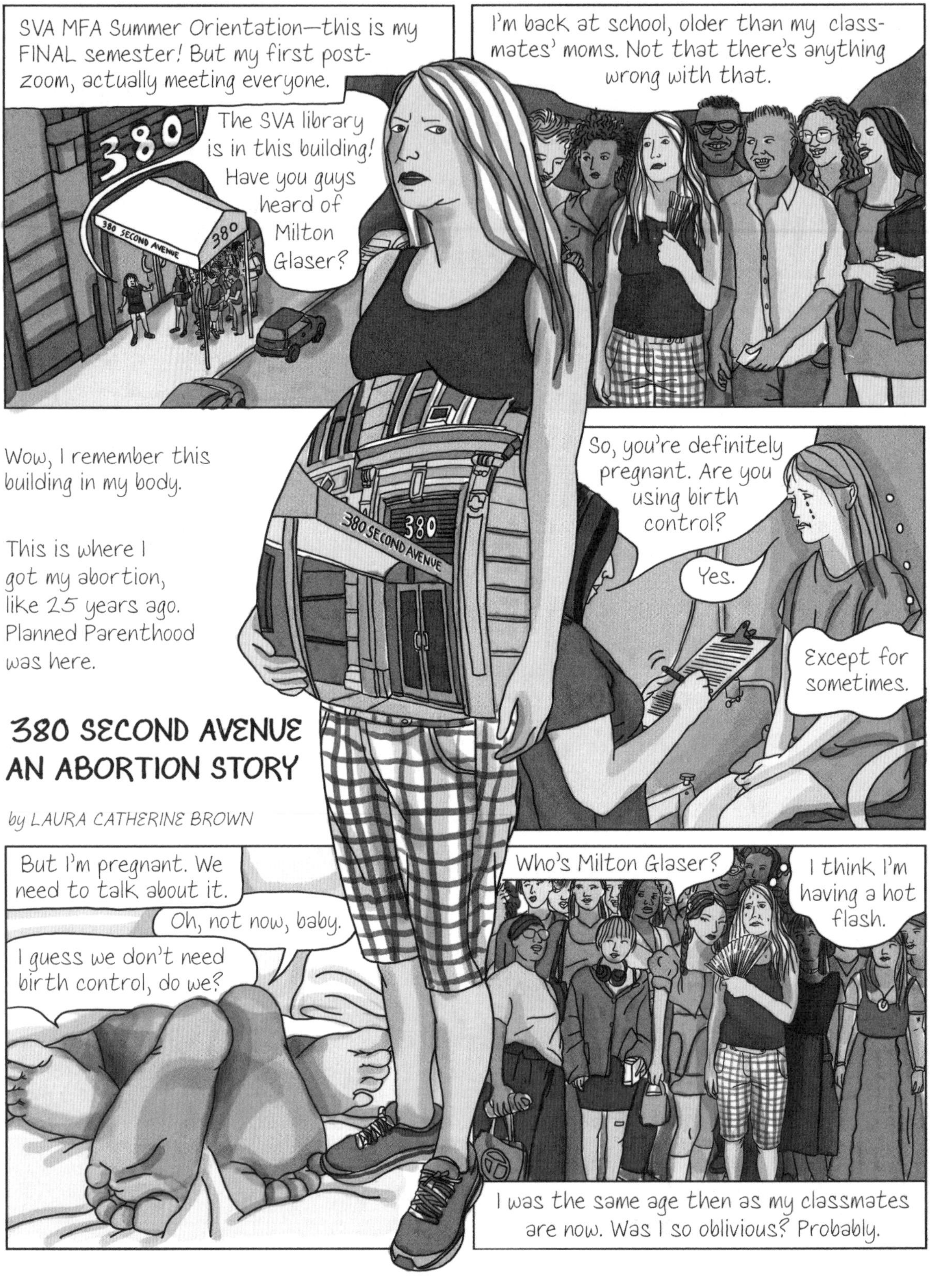

SVA MFA Summer Orientation—this is my FINAL semester! But my first post-zoom, actually meeting everyone.
380
380 SECOND AVENUE
The SVA library is in this building! Have you guys heard of Milton Glaser?
I'm back at school, older than my classmates' moms. Not that there's anything wrong with that.
Wow, I remember this building in my body.
This is where I got my abortion, like 25 years ago. Planned Parenthood was here.
380 SECOND AVENUE
So, you're definitely pregnant. Are you using birth control?
Yes.
Except for sometimes.
380 SECOND AVENUE
AN ABORTION STORY
by LAURA CATHERINE BROWN
But I'm pregnant. We need to talk about it.
Oh, not now, baby.
I guess we don't need birth control, do we?
Who's Milton Glaser?
I think I'm having a hot flash.
I was the same age then as my classmates are now. Was I so oblivious? Probably.

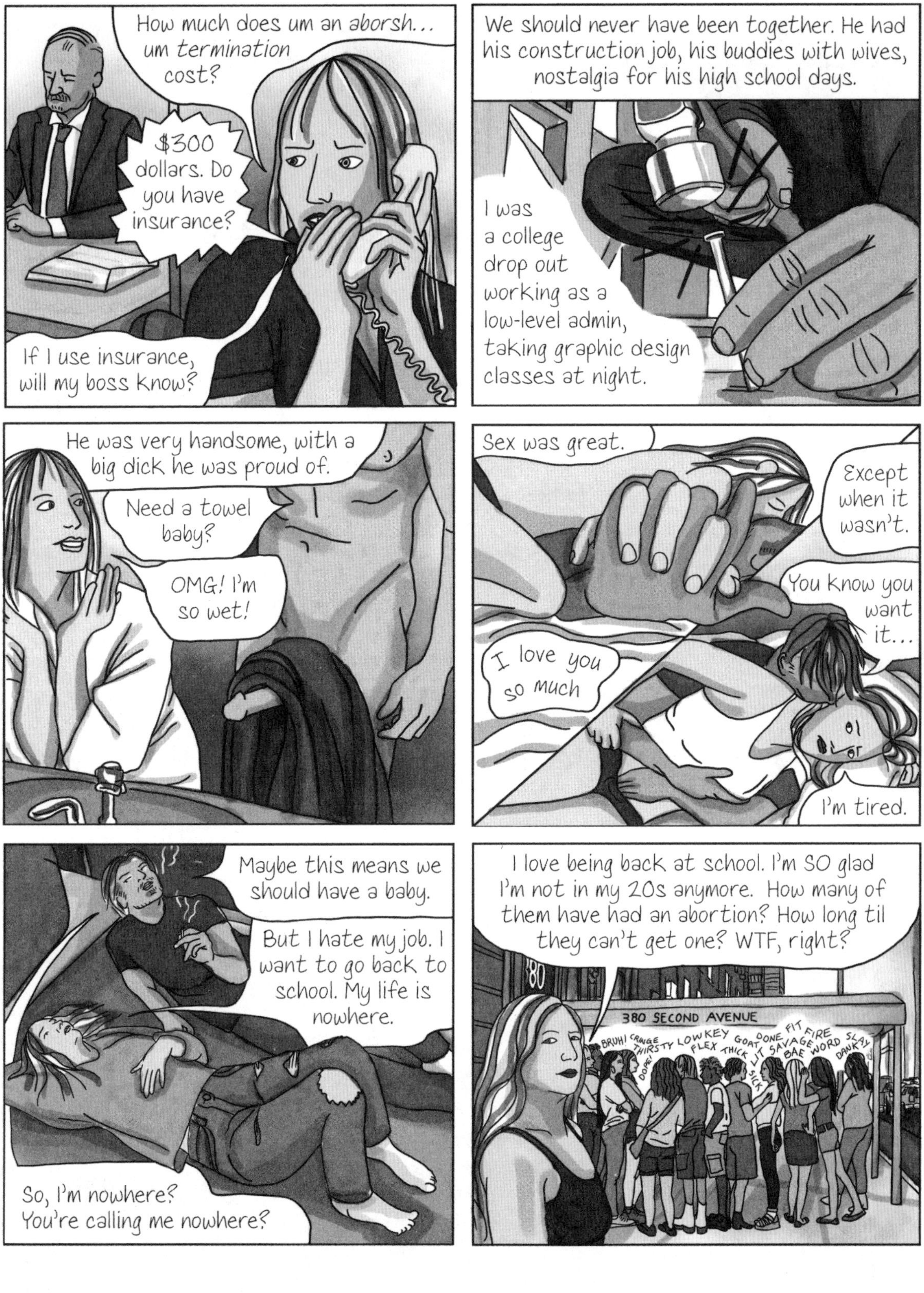
How much does um an *aborsh*... um *termination* cost?
$300 dollars. Do you have insurance?
If I use insurance, will my boss know?
We should never have been together. He had his construction job, his buddies with wives, nostalgia for his high school days.
I was a college drop out working as a low-level admin, taking graphic design classes at night.
He was very handsome, with a big dick he was proud of.
Need a towel baby?
OMG! I'm so wet!
Sex was great.
Except when it wasn't.
You know you want it...
I love you so much
I'm tired.
Maybe this means we should have a baby.
But I hate my job. I want to go back to school. My life is nowhere.
So, I'm nowhere? You're calling me nowhere?
I love being back at school. I'm SO glad I'm not in my 20s anymore. How many of them have had an abortion? How long til they can't get one? WTF, right?
380 SECOND AVENUE
BRUH! CRINGE THIRSTY LOWKEY FLEX THICK GOAT DONE LIT FIT SAVAGE FIRE BAE WORD SLAY DANK DOPE! SICK

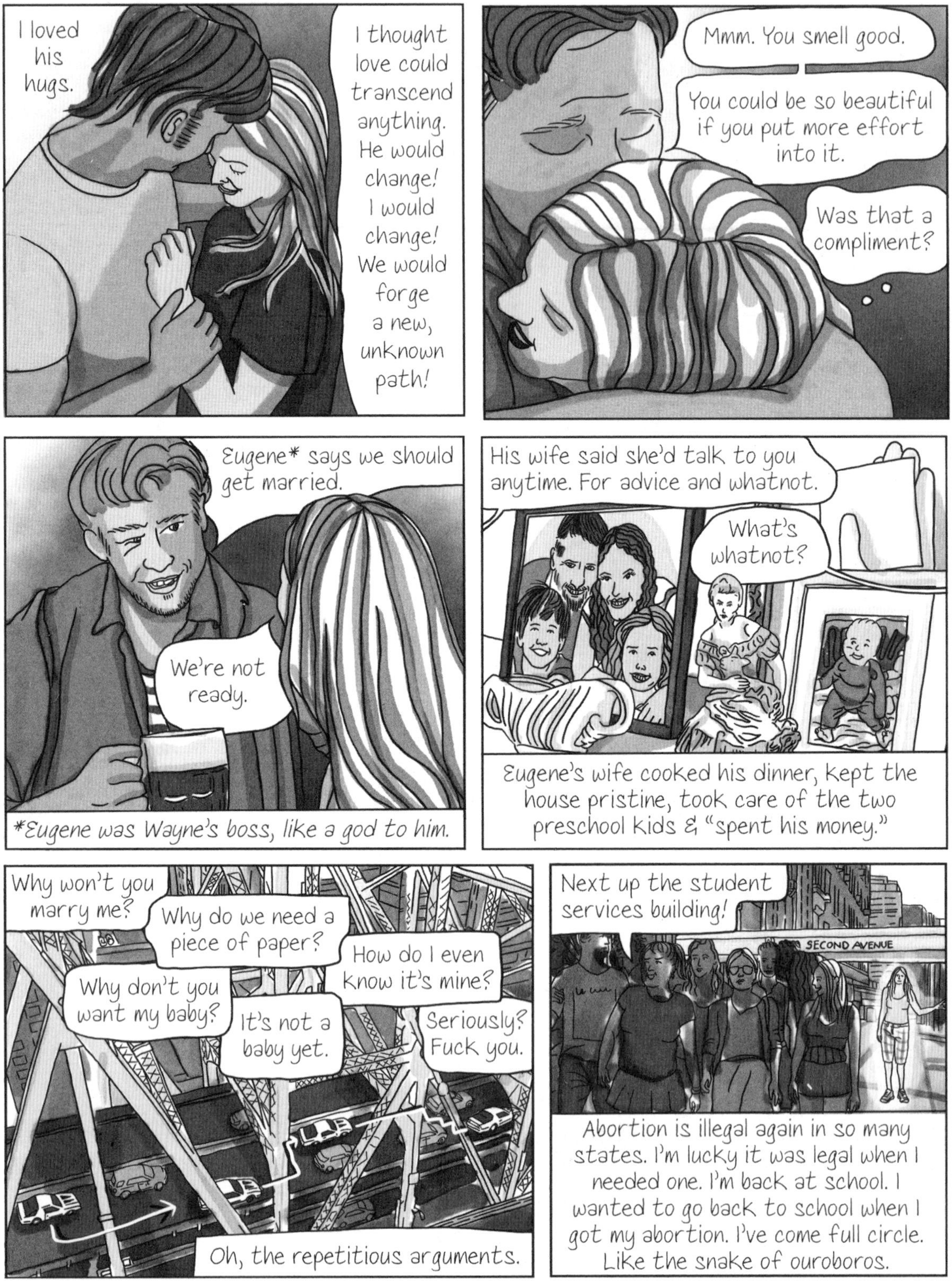

I loved his hugs.
I thought love could transcend anything. He would change! I would change! We would forge a new, unknown path!
Mmm. You smell good.
You could be so beautiful if you put more effort into it.
Was that a compliment?
Eugene* says we should get married.
We're not ready.
*Eugene was Wayne's boss, like a god to him.
His wife said she'd talk to you anytime. For advice and whatnot.
What's whatnot?
Eugene's wife cooked his dinner, kept the house pristine, took care of the two preschool kids & "spent his money."
Why won't you marry me?
Why do we need a piece of paper?
How do I even know it's mine?
Why don't you want my baby?
It's not a baby yet.
Seriously? Fuck you.
Oh, the repetitious arguments.
Next up the student services building!
SECOND AVENUE
Abortion is illegal again in so many states. I'm lucky it was legal when I needed one. I'm back at school. I wanted to go back to school when I got my abortion. I've come full circle. Like the snake of ouroboros.

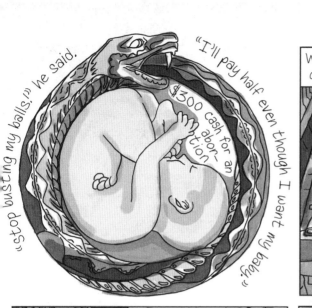

"Stop busting my balls," he said. "I'll pay half even though I want my baby."

$300 cash for an abortion

What do you mean you don't have cash? You promised to pay half!

I didn't promise shit.

You know we need cash upfront!

Keep it up and you can walk.

I'd get there faster.

You're a piece of fuckin' work.

You lied to me!

I have the money, ok psycho? I just want you to change your mind.

I know you'll be a good mother. Eugene says we're made for each other. It's like you hate being a woman. I can't be... what... so I'm glad the... this is your appointment... baby too... when... my kind of love is... self... You're acting... shit you put... put up with... me here. Can't... dog on your... world...

RAGE

Why did I think so little of myself?

Why did I stay with him for so long?

I thought he was lost.

Why didn't I see I was lost?

Why did I think I could fix him?

Why did it take me so many years to go back to school?

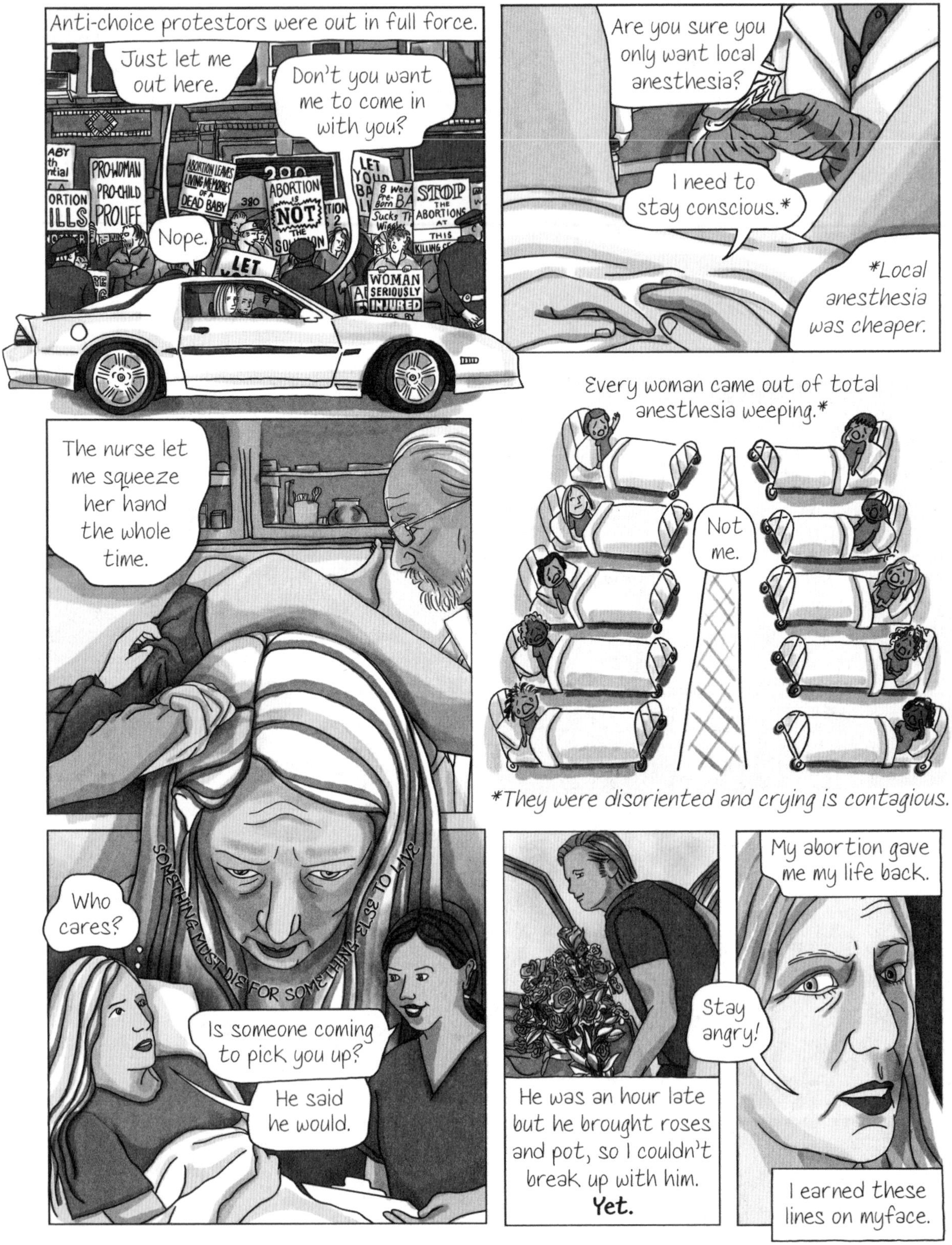

Anti-choice protestors were out in full force.
Just let me out here.
Don't you want me to come in with you?
Nope.
PRO-WOMAN PRO-CHILD PROLIFE
ABORTION LEAVES LIVING MEMORIES OF A DEAD BABY
ABORTION IS NOT THE SOLUTION
WOMAN SERIOUSLY INJURED
Are you sure you only want local anesthesia?
I need to stay conscious.*
*Local anesthesia was cheaper.
The nurse let me squeeze her hand the whole time.
Every woman came out of total anesthesia weeping.*
Not me.
*They were disoriented and crying is contagious.
Who cares?
SOMETHING MUST DIE FOR SOMETHING ELSE TO LIVE
Is someone coming to pick you up?
He said he would.
Stay angry!
He was an hour late but he brought roses and pot, so I couldn't break up with him.
Yet.
My abortion gave me my life back.
I earned these lines on myface.

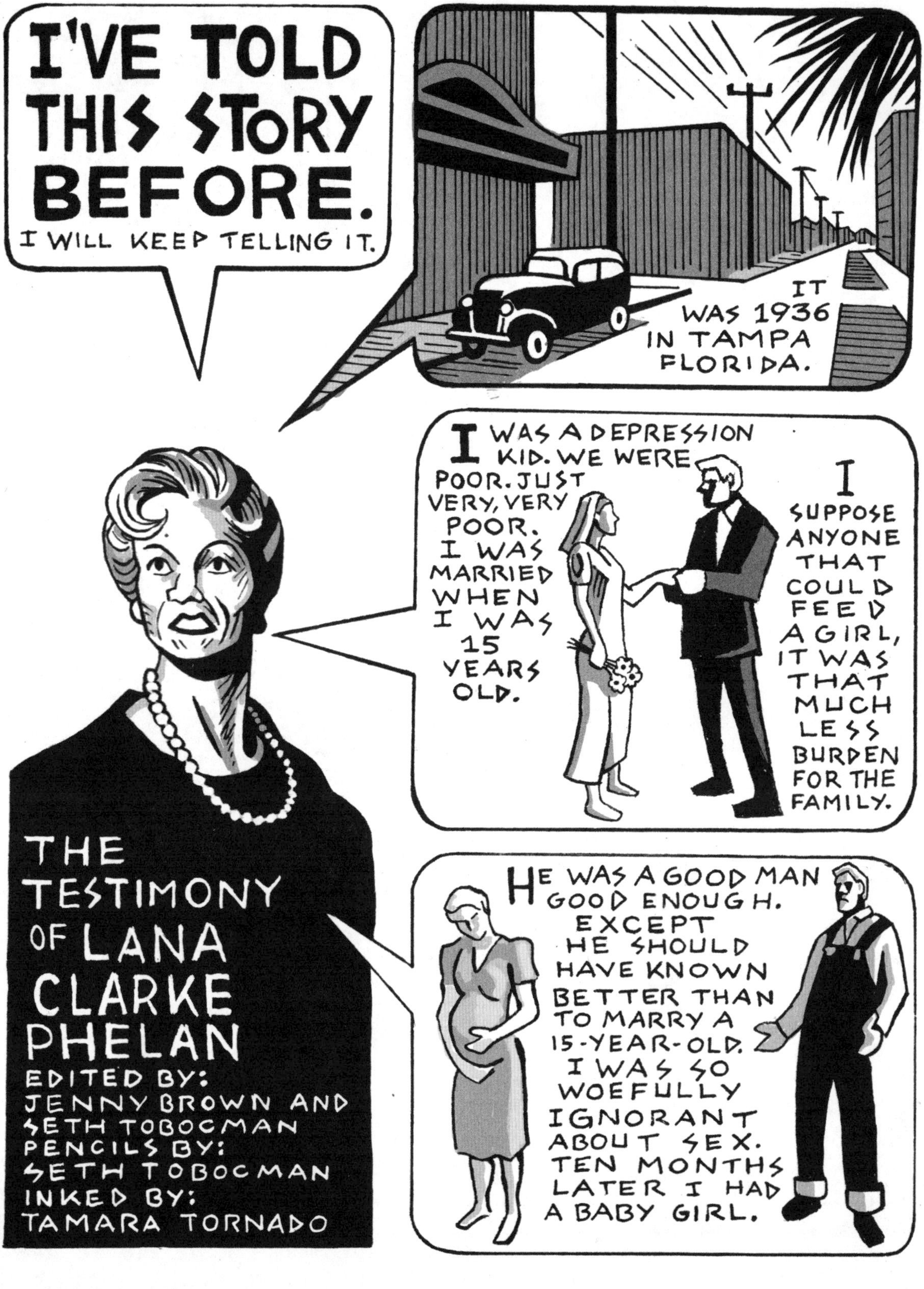
I'VE TOLD THIS STORY BEFORE.
I WILL KEEP TELLING IT.
IT WAS 1936 IN TAMPA FLORIDA.
I WAS A DEPRESSION KID. WE WERE POOR. JUST VERY, VERY POOR. I WAS MARRIED WHEN I WAS 15 YEARS OLD.
I SUPPOSE ANYONE THAT COULD FEED A GIRL, IT WAS THAT MUCH LESS BURDEN FOR THE FAMILY.
THE TESTIMONY OF LANA CLARKE PHELAN
EDITED BY: JENNY BROWN AND SETH TOBOCMAN
PENCILS BY: SETH TOBOCMAN
INKED BY: TAMARA TORNADO
HE WAS A GOOD MAN GOOD ENOUGH. EXCEPT HE SHOULD HAVE KNOWN BETTER THAN TO MARRY A 15-YEAR-OLD. I WAS SO WOEFULLY IGNORANT ABOUT SEX. TEN MONTHS LATER I HAD A BABY GIRL.

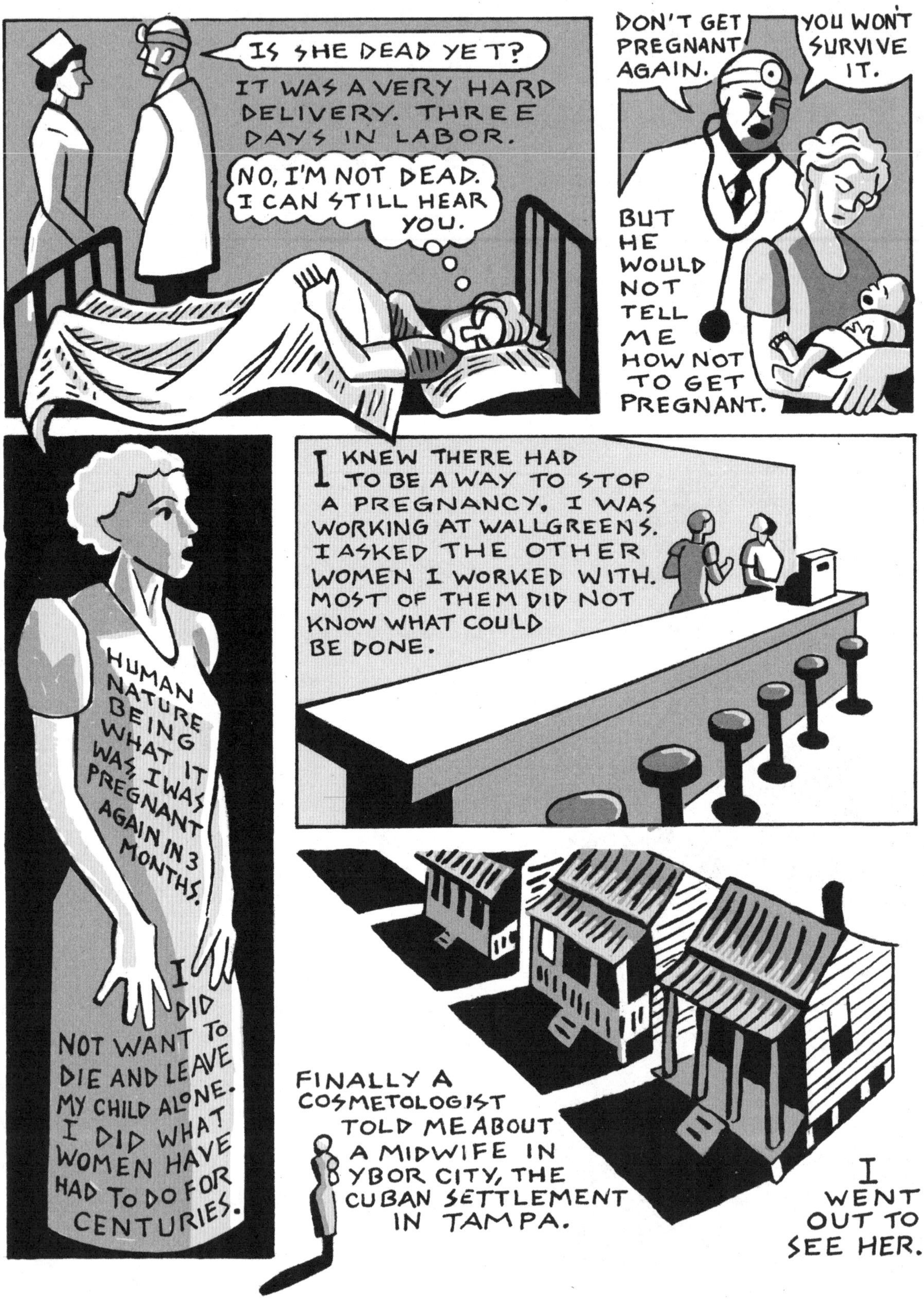
IS SHE DEAD YET?
IT WAS A VERY HARD DELIVERY. THREE DAYS IN LABOR.
NO, I'M NOT DEAD. I CAN STILL HEAR YOU.
DON'T GET PREGNANT AGAIN.
YOU WON'T SURVIVE IT.
BUT HE WOULD NOT TELL ME HOW NOT TO GET PREGNANT.
HUMAN NATURE BEING WHAT IT WAS, I WAS PREGNANT AGAIN IN 3 MONTHS.
I DID NOT WANT TO DIE AND LEAVE MY CHILD ALONE. I DID WHAT WOMEN HAVE HAD TO DO FOR CENTURIES.
I KNEW THERE HAD TO BE A WAY TO STOP A PREGNANCY. I WAS WORKING AT WALLGREENS. I ASKED THE OTHER WOMEN I WORKED WITH. MOST OF THEM DID NOT KNOW WHAT COULD BE DONE.
FINALLY A COSMETOLOGIST TOLD ME ABOUT A MIDWIFE IN YBOR CITY, THE CUBAN SETTLEMENT IN TAMPA.
I WENT OUT TO SEE HER.

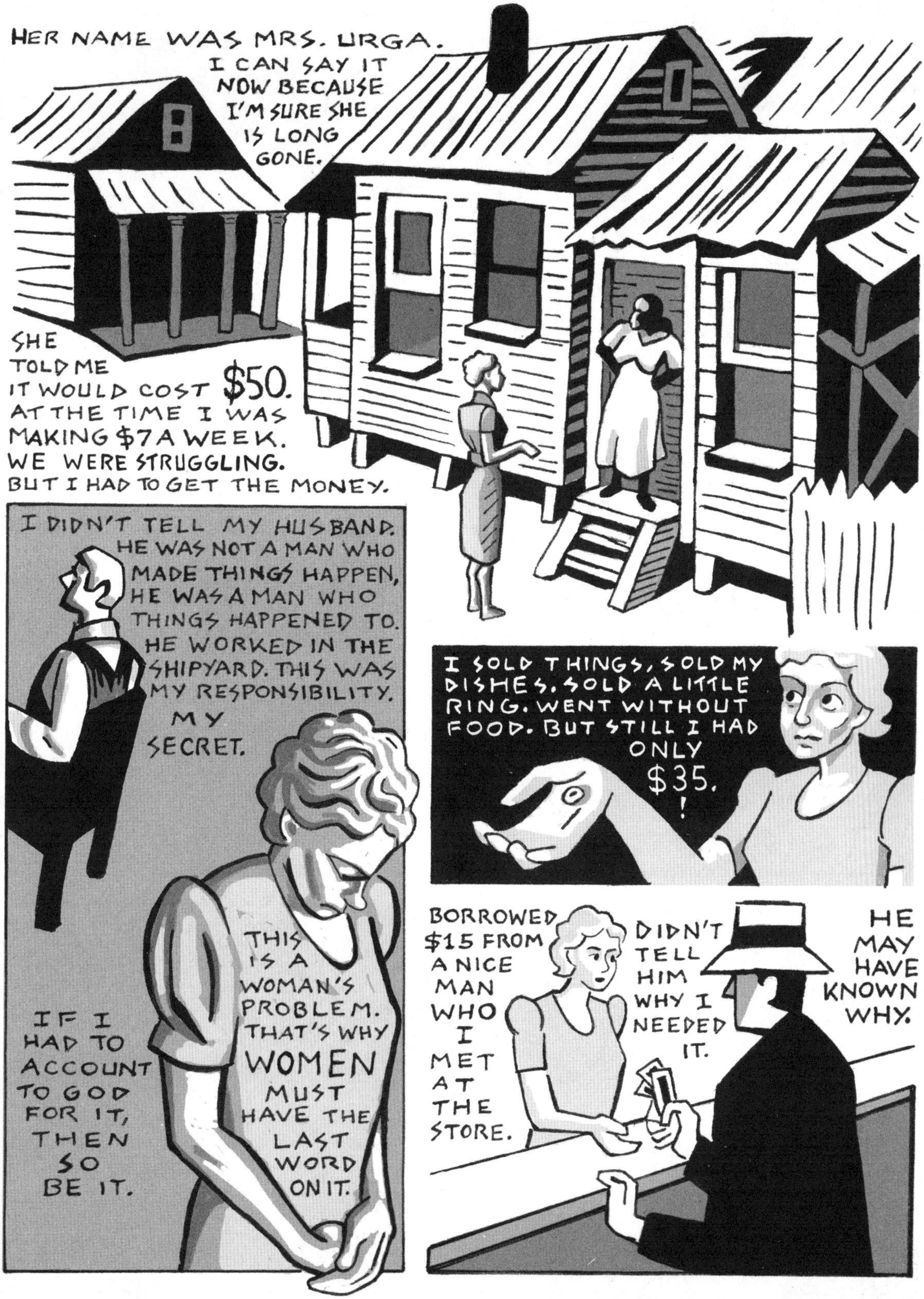
HER NAME WAS MRS. URGA.
I CAN SAY IT NOW BECAUSE I'M SURE SHE IS LONG GONE.
SHE TOLD ME IT WOULD COST $50. AT THE TIME I WAS MAKING $7 A WEEK. WE WERE STRUGGLING. BUT I HAD TO GET THE MONEY.
I DIDN'T TELL MY HUSBAND. HE WAS NOT A MAN WHO MADE THINGS HAPPEN, HE WAS A MAN WHO THINGS HAPPENED TO. HE WORKED IN THE SHIPYARD. THIS WAS MY RESPONSIBILITY. MY SECRET.
THIS IS A WOMAN'S PROBLEM. THAT'S WHY WOMEN MUST HAVE THE LAST WORD ON IT.
IF I HAD TO ACCOUNT TO GOD FOR IT, THEN SO BE IT.
I SOLD THINGS, SOLD MY DISHES. SOLD A LITTLE RING. WENT WITHOUT FOOD. BUT STILL I HAD ONLY $35. !
BORROWED $15 FROM A NICE MAN WHO I MET AT THE STORE.
DIDN'T TELL HIM WHY I NEEDED IT.
HE MAY HAVE KNOWN WHY.

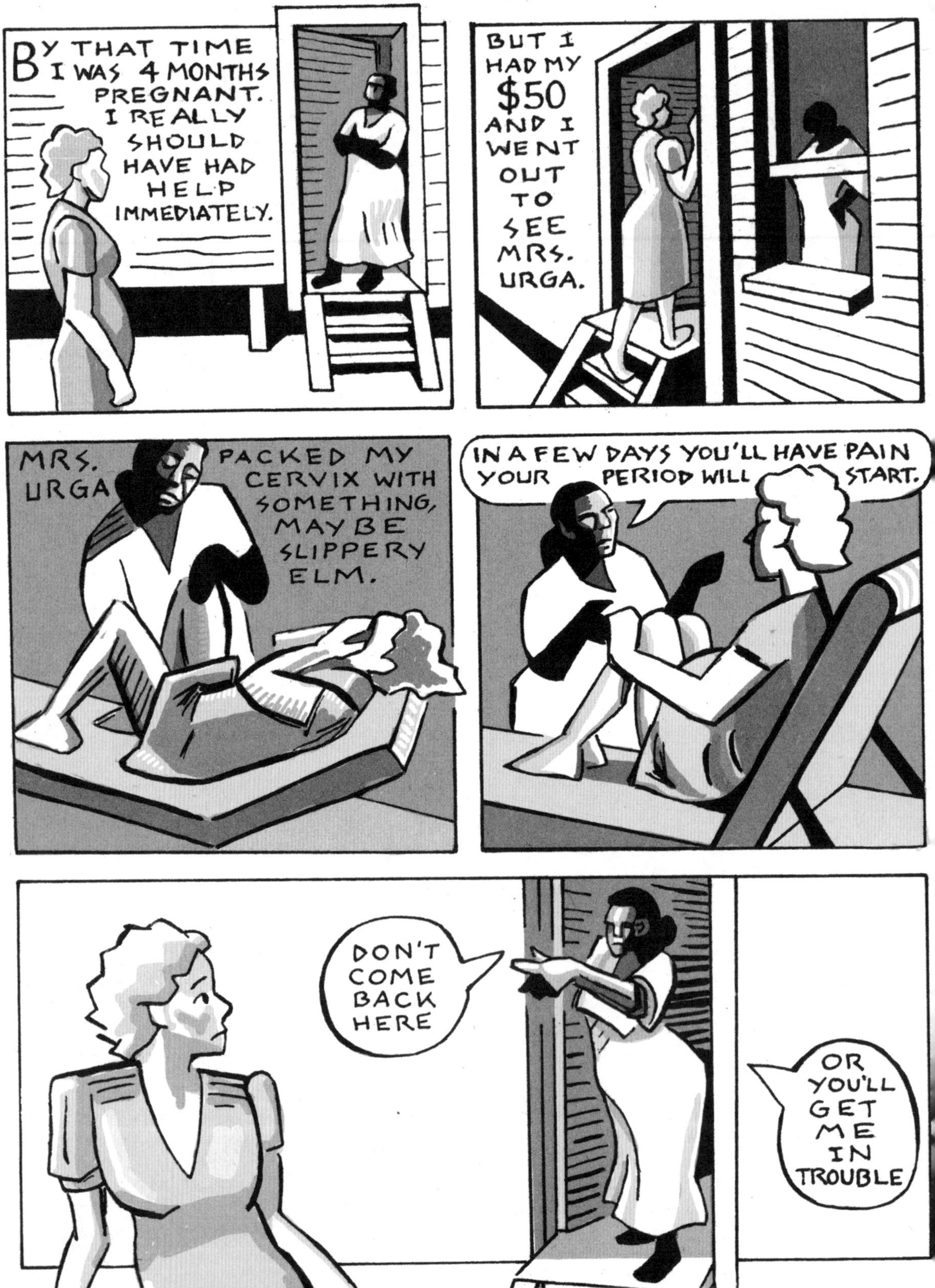
BY THAT TIME I WAS 4 MONTHS PREGNANT. I REALLY SHOULD HAVE HAD HELP IMMEDIATELY.
BUT I HAD MY $50 AND I WENT OUT TO SEE MRS. URGA.
MRS. URGA PACKED MY CERVIX WITH SOMETHING, MAYBE SLIPPERY ELM.
IN A FEW DAYS YOU'LL HAVE PAIN YOUR PERIOD WILL START.
DON'T COME BACK HERE
OR YOU'LL GET ME IN TROUBLE

I HAD PAIN AND FEVER FOR DAYS.

BUT STILL NO BLOOD, NO SPOTTING.

I WENT TO DINNER AT A RELATIVE'S HOUSE. THE WHOLE FAMILY WAS THERE.

THEY DID NOT KNOW WHAT WAS GOING ON WITH ME. I COULDN'T TELL THEM.

AT THE TABLE I COULD NO LONGER CONTAIN THE PAIN. I EXCUSED MYSELF.

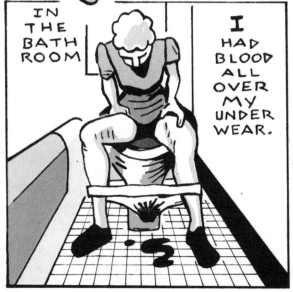

IN THE BATH ROOM

I HAD BLOOD ALL OVER MY UNDER WEAR.

THEN I SAW A TINY LITTLE LIMB... STICKING OUT OF MY VAGINA.

I WAS HORRIFIED!

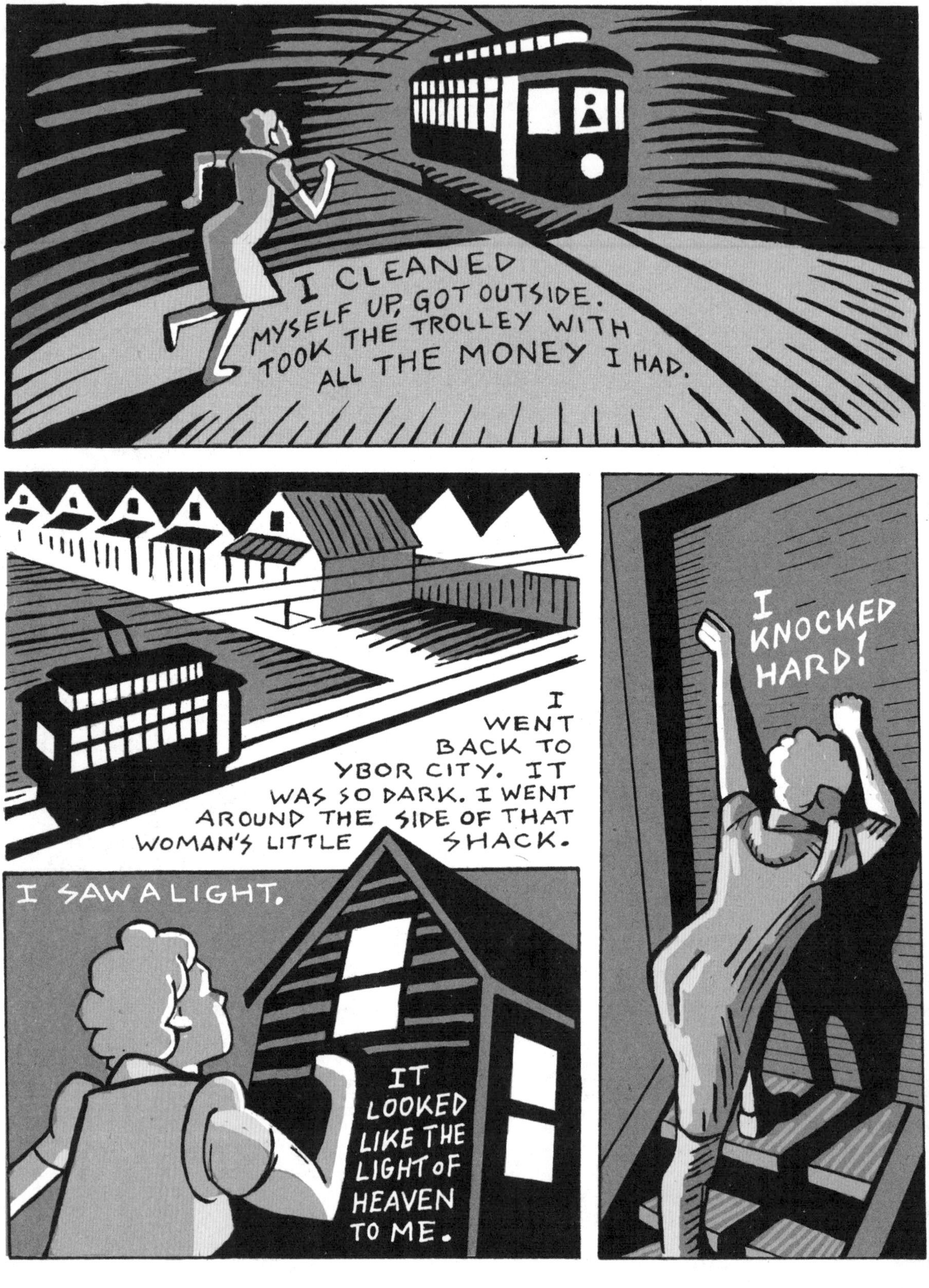
I CLEANED MYSELF UP, GOT OUTSIDE. TOOK THE TROLLEY WITH ALL THE MONEY I HAD.
I WENT BACK TO YBOR CITY. IT WAS SO DARK. I WENT AROUND THE SIDE OF THAT WOMAN'S LITTLE SHACK.
I SAW A LIGHT.
IT LOOKED LIKE THE LIGHT OF HEAVEN TO ME.
I KNOCKED HARD!

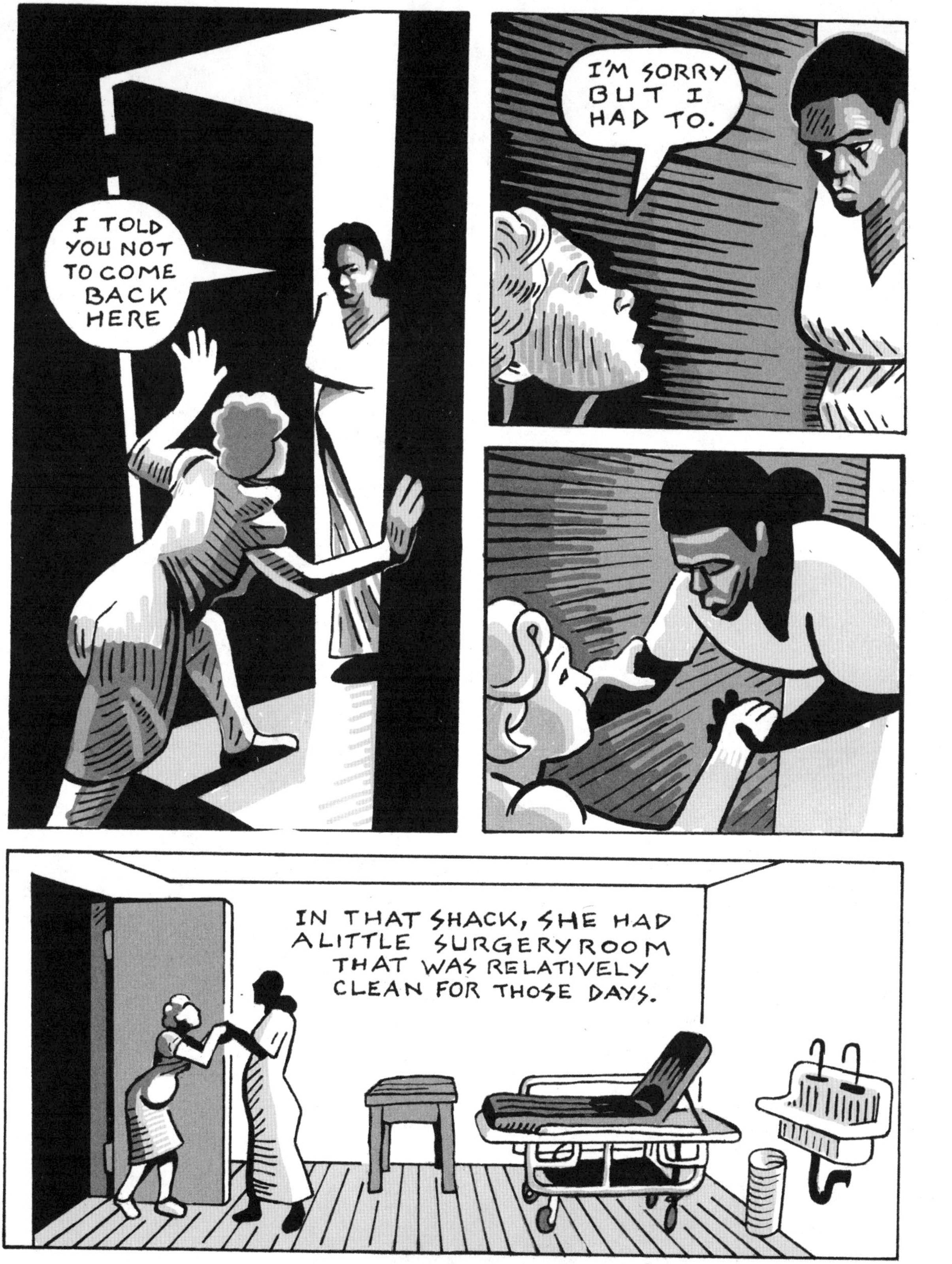
I TOLD YOU NOT TO COME BACK HERE
I'M SORRY BUT I HAD TO.
IN THAT SHACK, SHE HAD A LITTLE SURGERY ROOM THAT WAS RELATIVELY CLEAN FOR THOSE DAYS.

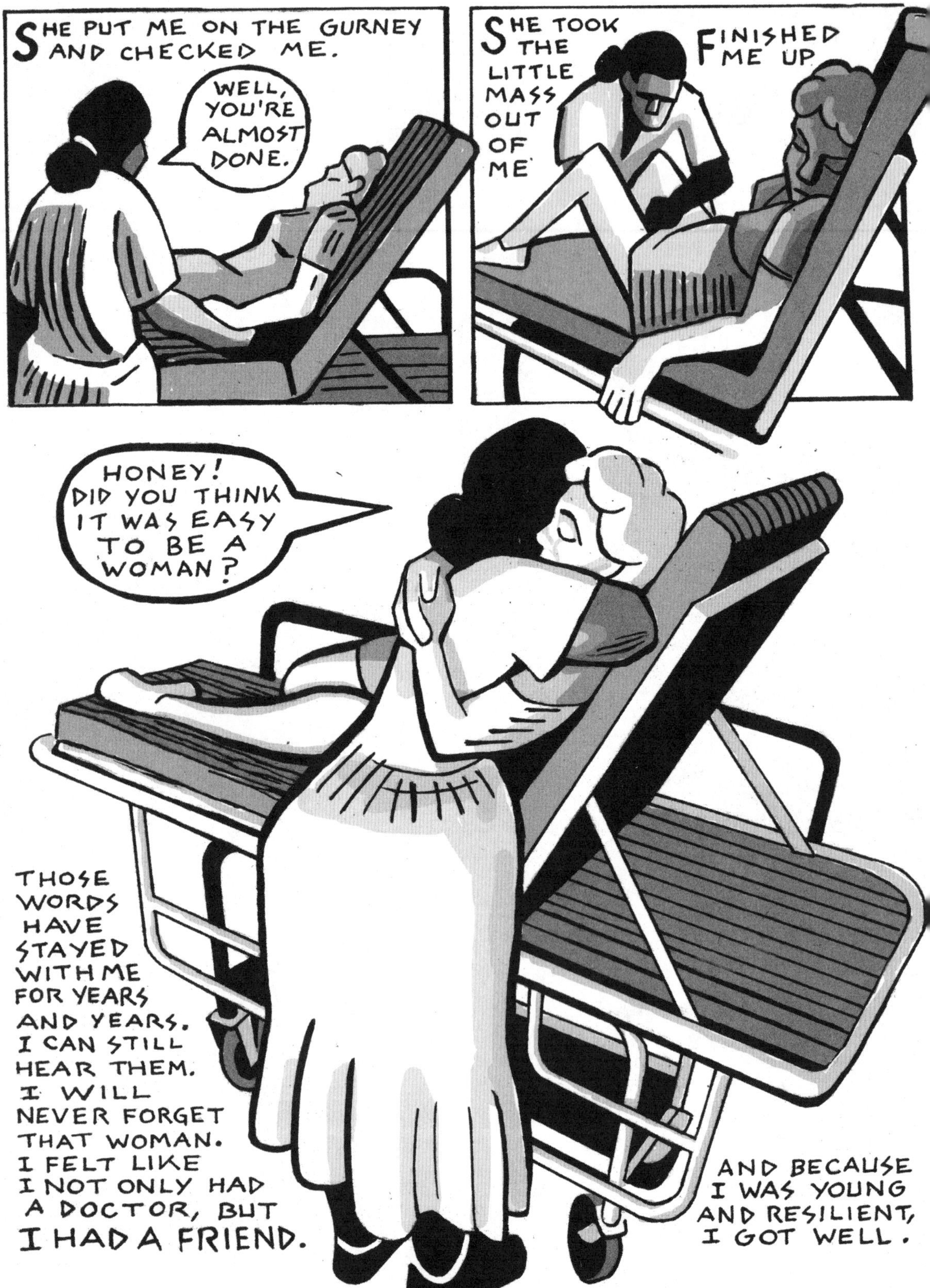
SHE PUT ME ON THE GURNEY AND CHECKED ME.
WELL, YOU'RE ALMOST DONE.
SHE TOOK THE LITTLE MASS OUT OF ME
FINISHED ME UP
HONEY! DID YOU THINK IT WAS EASY TO BE A WOMAN?
THOSE WORDS HAVE STAYED WITH ME FOR YEARS AND YEARS. I CAN STILL HEAR THEM. I WILL NEVER FORGET THAT WOMAN. I FELT LIKE I NOT ONLY HAD A DOCTOR, BUT I HAD A FRIEND.
AND BECAUSE I WAS YOUNG AND RESILIENT, I GOT WELL.

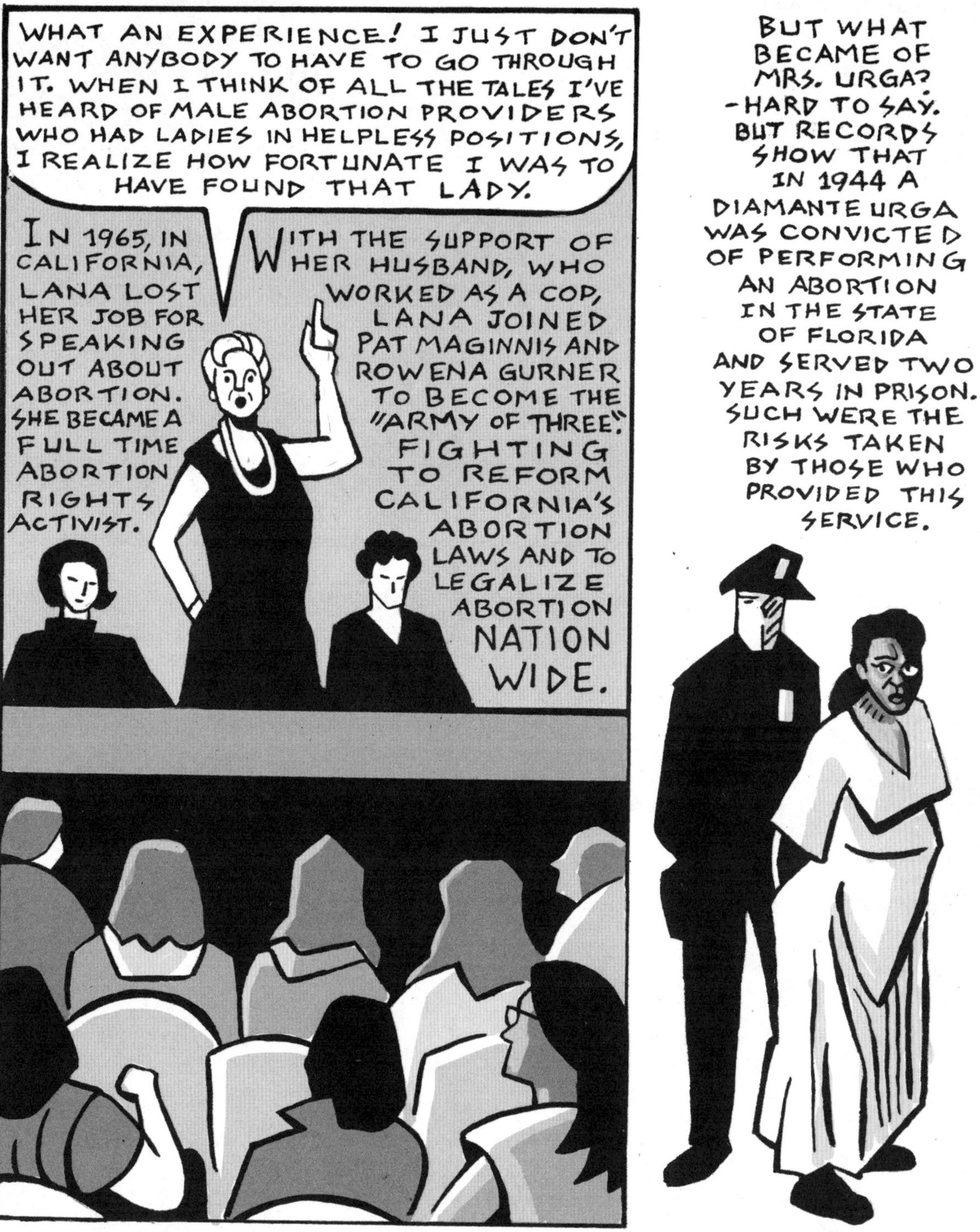
WHAT AN EXPERIENCE! I JUST DON'T WANT ANYBODY TO HAVE TO GO THROUGH IT. WHEN I THINK OF ALL THE TALES I'VE HEARD OF MALE ABORTION PROVIDERS WHO HAD LADIES IN HELPLESS POSITIONS, I REALIZE HOW FORTUNATE I WAS TO HAVE FOUND THAT LADY.
IN 1965, IN CALIFORNIA, LANA LOST HER JOB FOR SPEAKING OUT ABOUT ABORTION. SHE BECAME A FULL TIME ABORTION RIGHTS ACTIVIST.
WITH THE SUPPORT OF HER HUSBAND, WHO WORKED AS A COP, LANA JOINED PAT MAGINNIS AND ROWENA GURNER TO BECOME THE "ARMY OF THREE", FIGHTING TO REFORM CALIFORNIA'S ABORTION LAWS AND TO LEGALIZE ABORTION NATION WIDE.
BUT WHAT BECAME OF MRS. URGA? -HARD TO SAY. BUT RECORDS SHOW THAT IN 1944 A DIAMANTE URGA WAS CONVICTED OF PERFORMING AN ABORTION IN THE STATE OF FLORIDA AND SERVED TWO YEARS IN PRISON. SUCH WERE THE RISKS TAKEN BY THOSE WHO PROVIDED THIS SERVICE.

Based on 2 interviews with Lana Clarke Phelan, one on ***patmaginnis.org***, the other from ***Abortion Without Apology, A radical history for the 1990s*** by Nina Baehr.
Art models: Joan Conklin, Barbara Lee, Spike Polite, Louisa Krupp, Tamara Tornado props: Eclectic Props, Delivery: Flash Messenger, Big thanks to the Earth Church

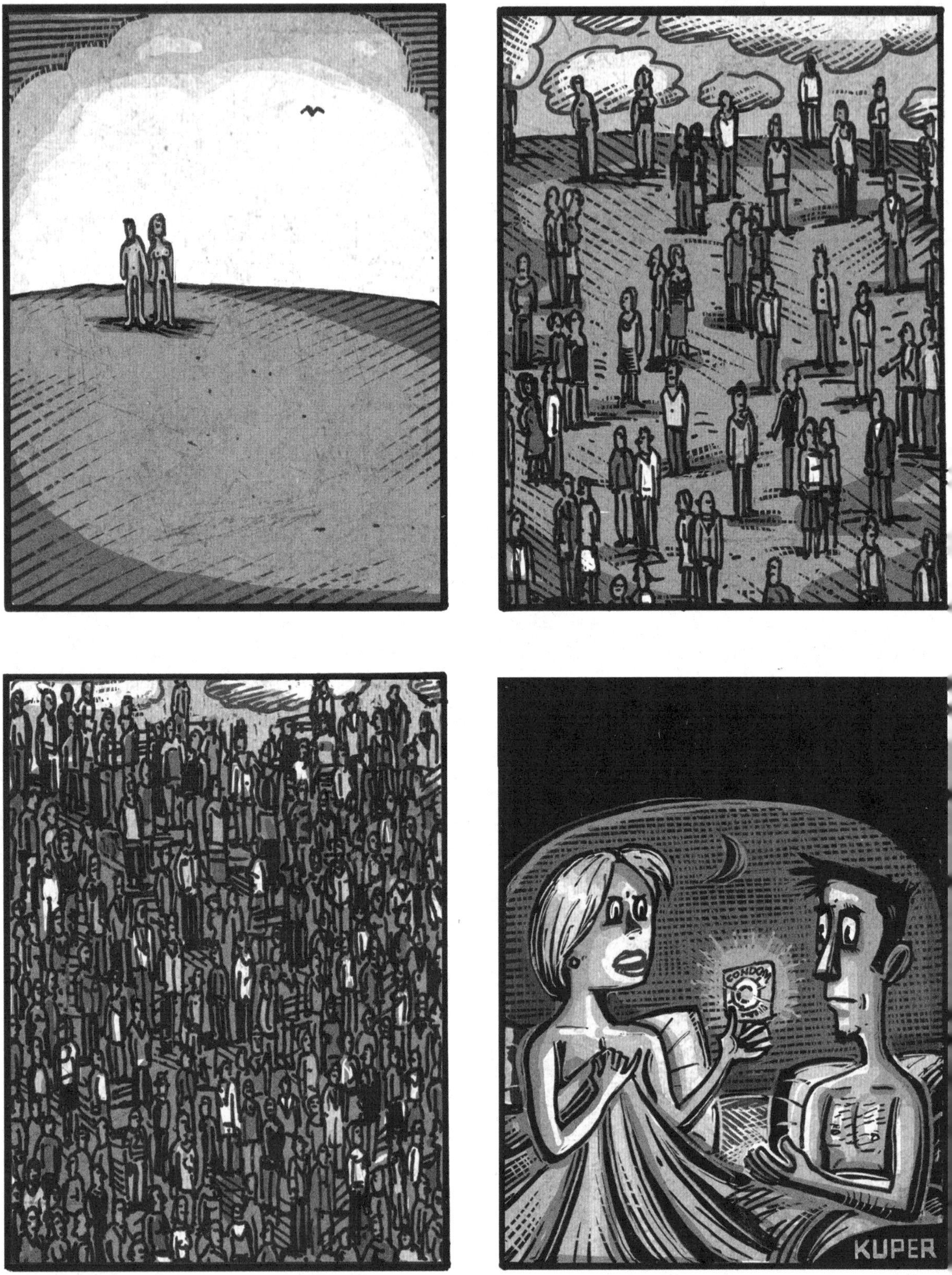
CONDOM
KUPER

For all he cares, you could be a broom!

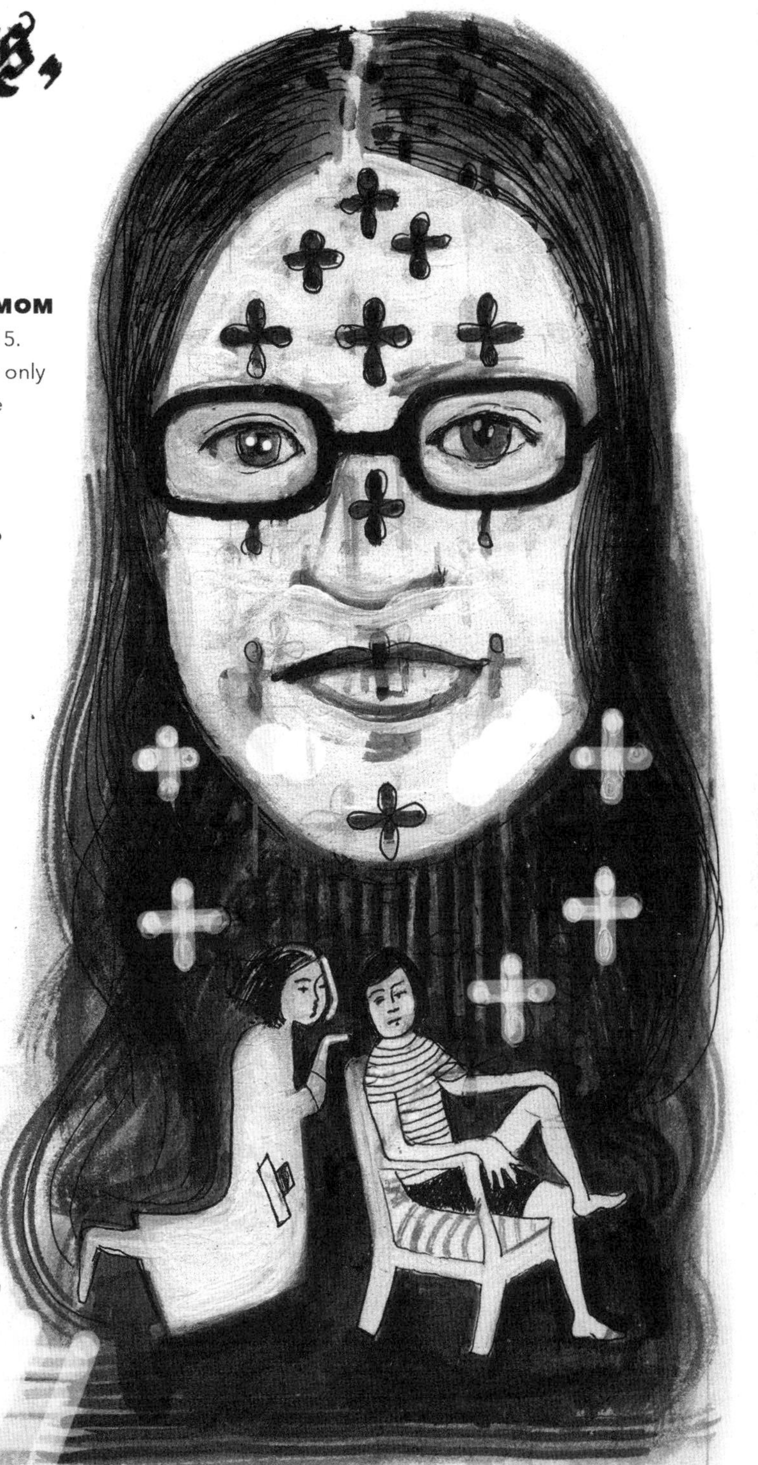

THE WORDS OF ADVICE FROM MY MOM as I wait for my date to pick me up. I was 15. I was the seventh of nine children and the only one to date while living at home. We were Catholics. We went to Catholic schools. Everyone I knew was Catholic and came from a large family. We were cursed with Original Sin and it would be hard for us to get into heaven.

Our neighbors had children with physical and mental disabilities. My mom would often say, "Well, Bobby and Jeannie are blessed because when they die, they will go straight to heaven because they, unlike you, can't commit sins on earth.

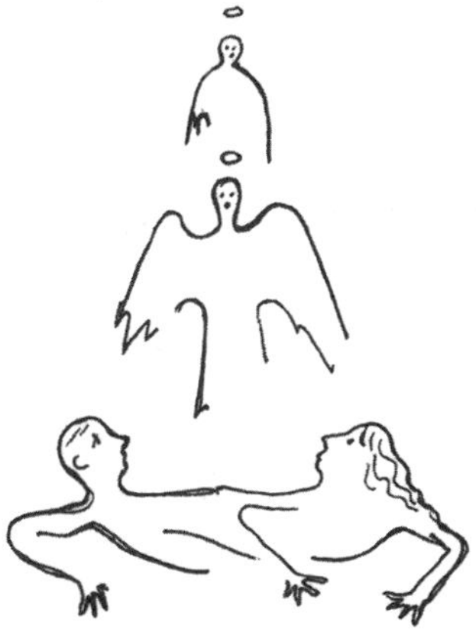

Why was I doubly cursed with Original Sin and a healthy body? What is the body? Who does it belong to? Does the body even matter? This was 1972.

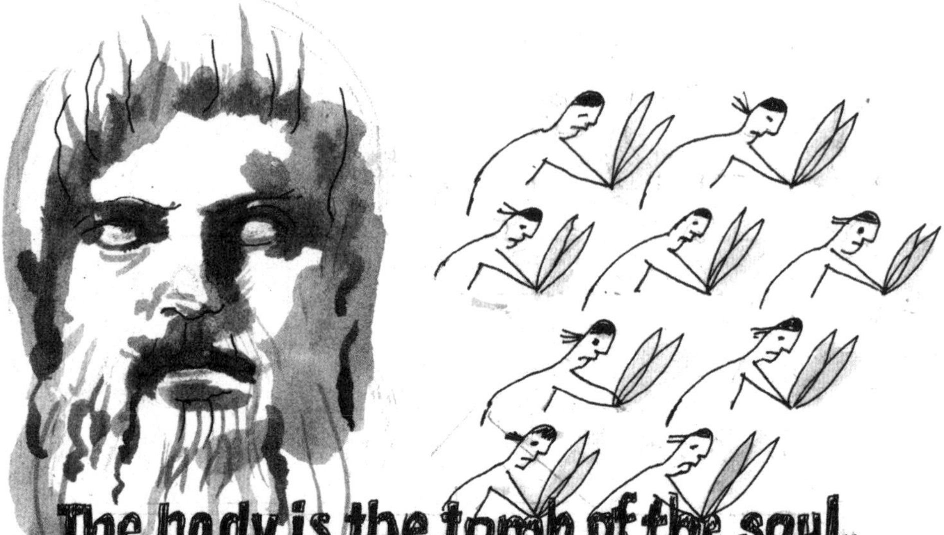

The body is the tomb of the soul.

—PLATO

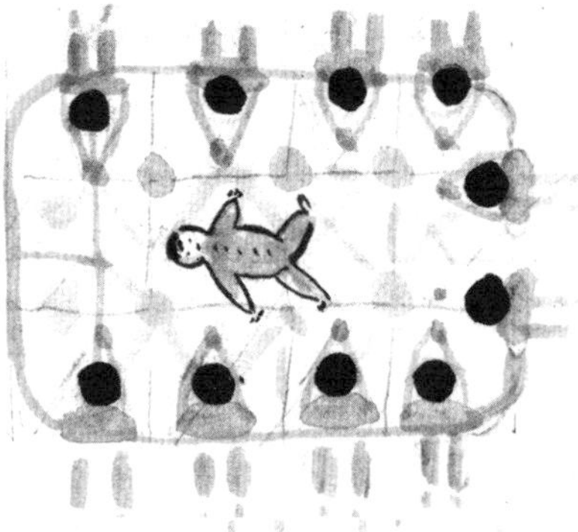

~~WE WEREN'T SUPPOSED TO THINK~~ or care about our bodies. The body housed the soul. But on earth, the body has to eat and work. We were put to work early; making meals, cleaning house, picking weeds, baling hay, grinding feed for pigs and steer, shoveling corn, shoveling snow, and watching the younger kids.

Sex Education was about multiplication!

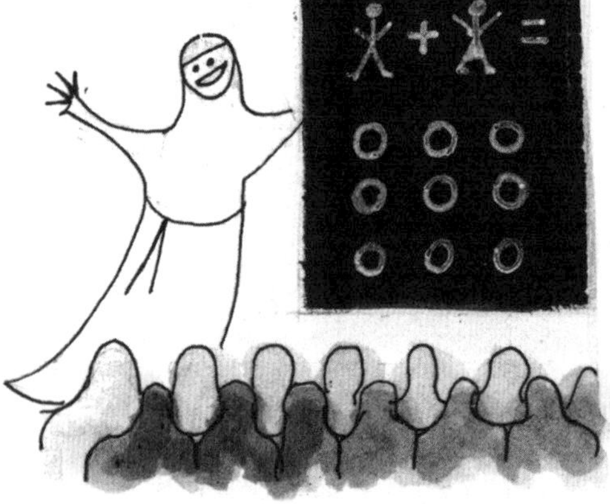

Catholics were very silent about sex and reproduction. They just had kids and more kids. Our mother never told us about menstruation. I wondered what that box of Kotex was in her closet. What was the first day? Why was it heavier and what did that even mean?

In fourth or fifth grade, Sheila Z. started bleeding in gym class. She was quickly whisked out of gym by a nun. This started a whirlwind of whispering. "What happened?" Some girls gave each other knowing looks while others stared with mouths open.

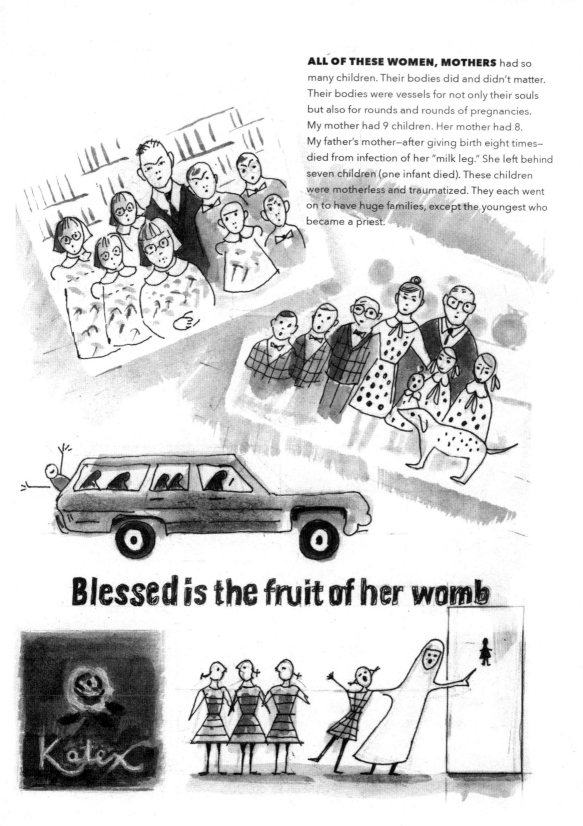

ALL OF THESE WOMEN, MOTHERS had so many children. Their bodies did and didn't matter. Their bodies were vessels for not only their souls but also for rounds and rounds of pregnancies. My mother had 9 children. Her mother had 8. My father's mother—after giving birth eight times—died from infection of her "milk leg." She left behind seven children (one infant died). These children were motherless and traumatized. They each went on to have huge families, except the youngest who became a priest.

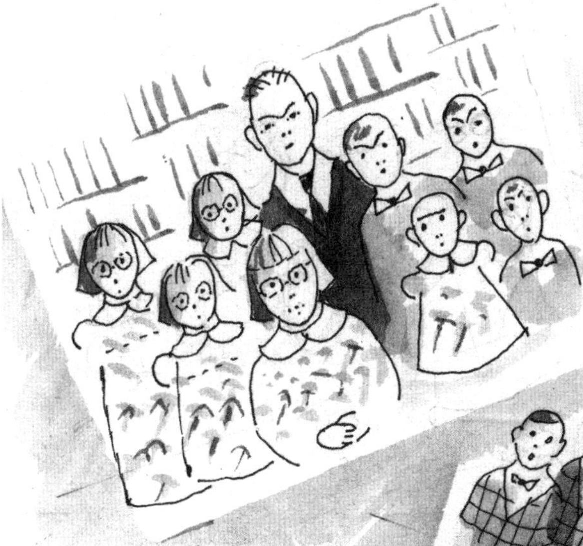

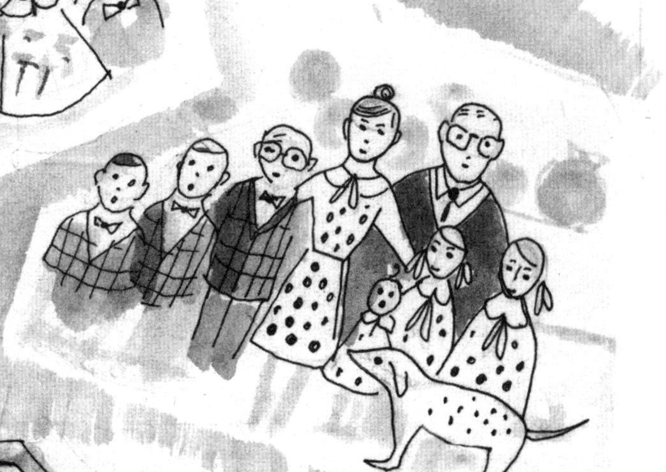

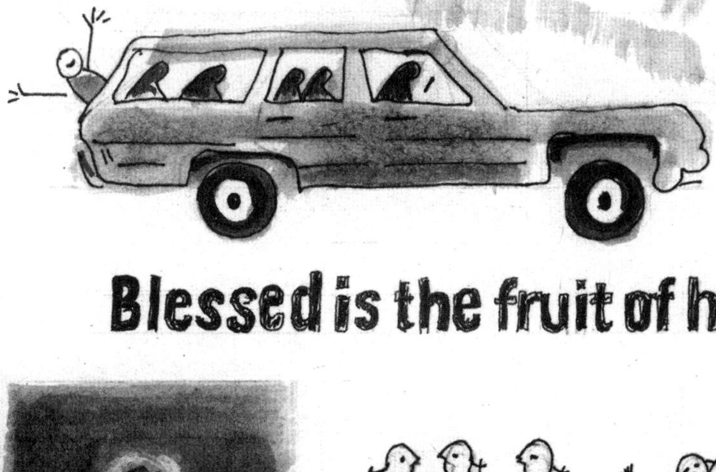

Blessed is the fruit of her womb

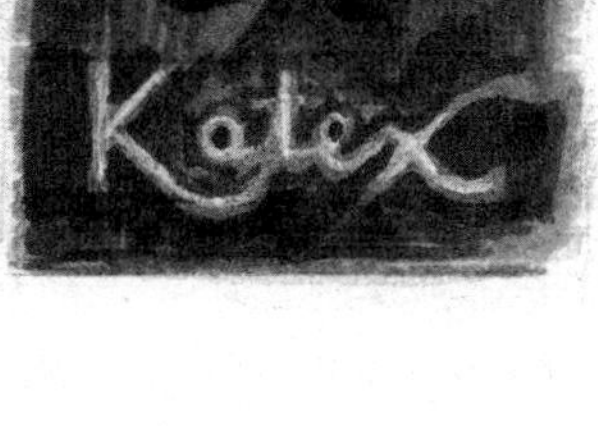
Kotex

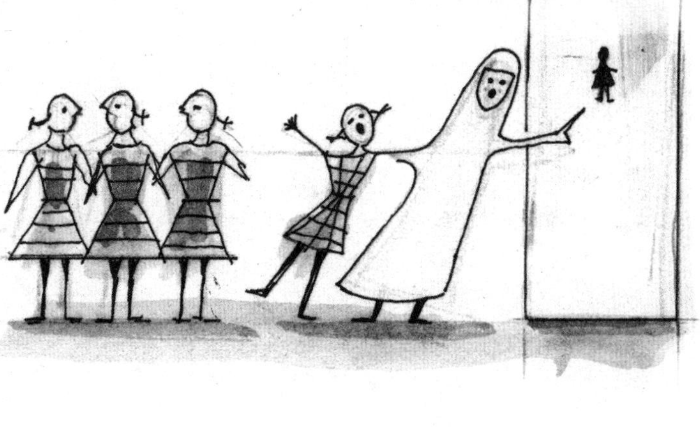

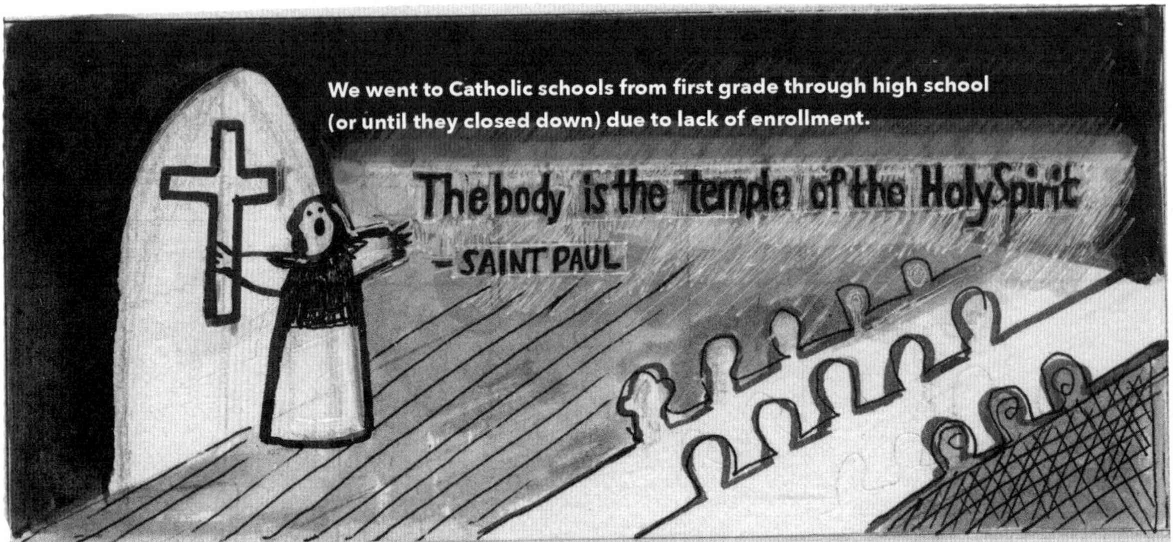
We went to Catholic schools from first grade through high school (or until they closed down) due to lack of enrollment.
The body is the temple of the Holy Spirit
- SAINT PAUL

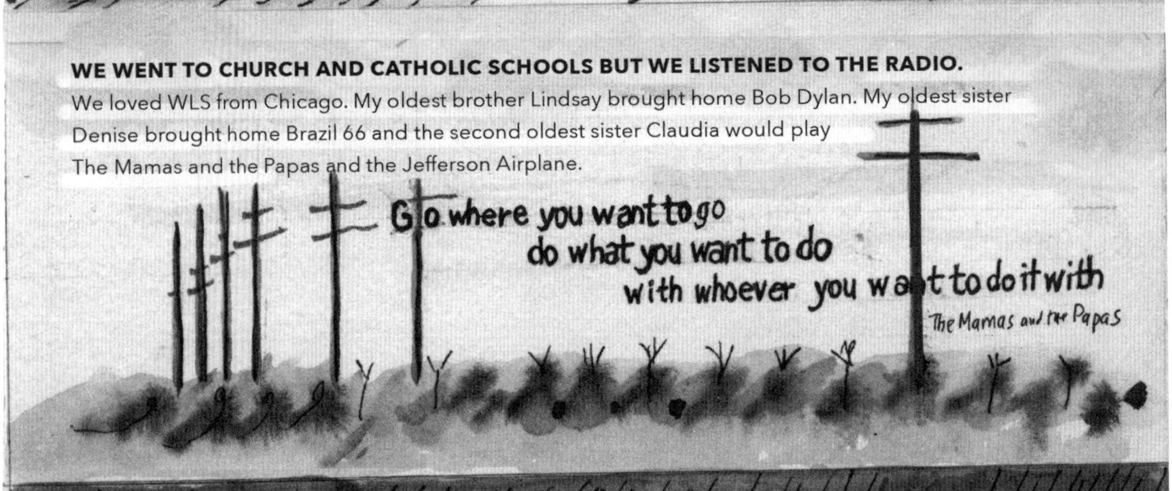
WE WENT TO CHURCH AND CATHOLIC SCHOOLS BUT WE LISTENED TO THE RADIO.
We loved WLS from Chicago. My oldest brother Lindsay brought home Bob Dylan. My oldest sister Denise brought home Brazil 66 and the second oldest sister Claudia would play The Mamas and the Papas and the Jefferson Airplane.
Go where you want to go
do what you want to do
with whoever you want to do it with
The Mamas and the Papas

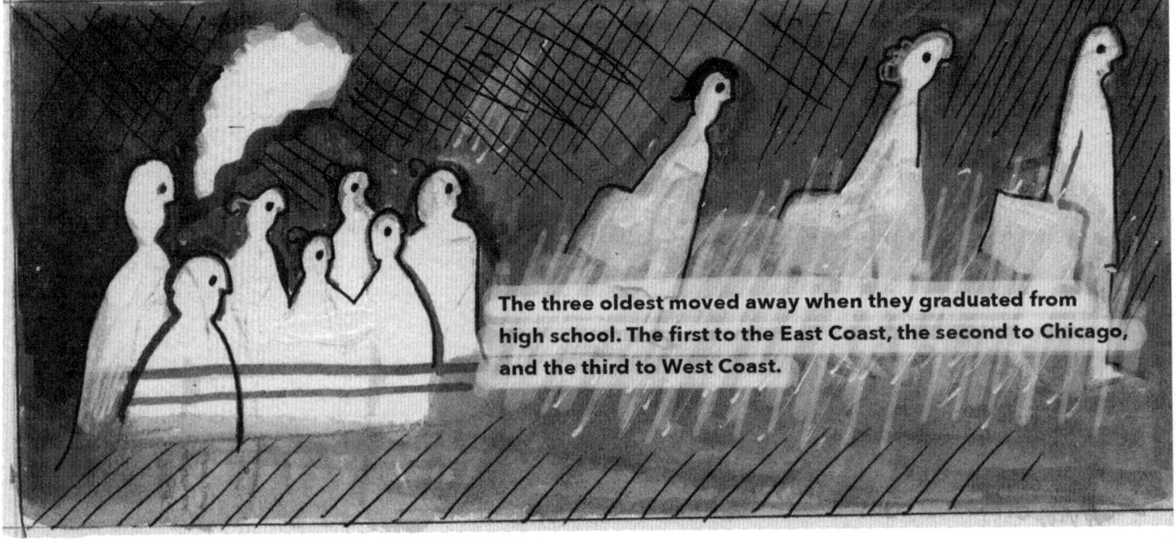
The three oldest moved away when they graduated from high school. The first to the East Coast, the second to Chicago, and the third to West Coast.

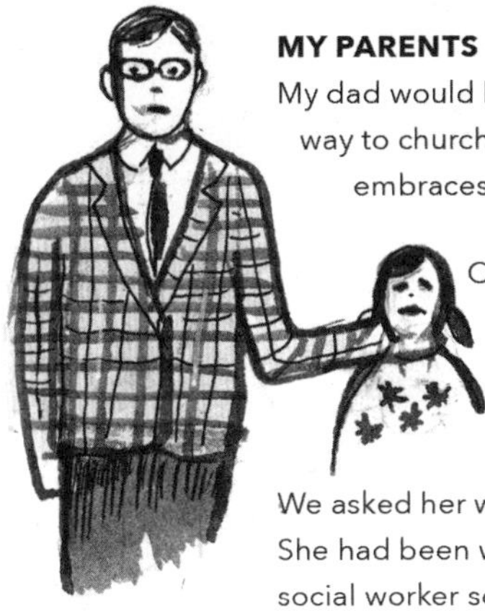

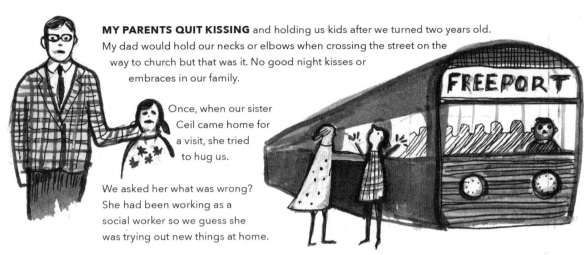

MY PARENTS QUIT KISSING and holding us kids after we turned two years old. My dad would hold our necks or elbows when crossing the street on the way to church but that was it. No good night kisses or embraces in our family.

Once, when our sister Ceil came home for a visit, she tried to hug us.

We asked her what was wrong? She had been working as a social worker so we guess she was trying out new things at home.

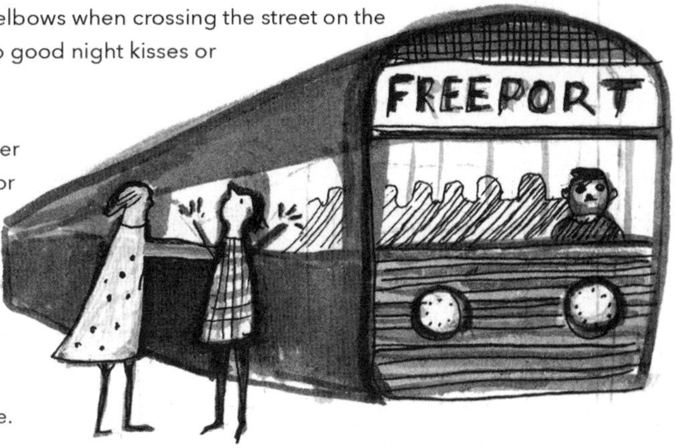
FREEPORT

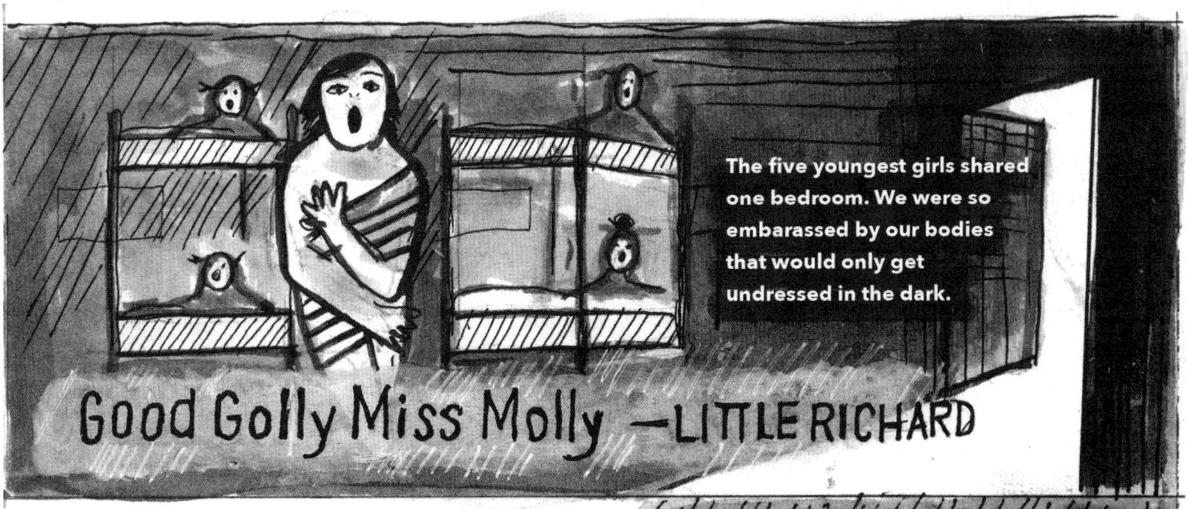
The five youngest girls shared one bedroom. We were so embarassed by our bodies that would only get undressed in the dark.
Good Golly Miss Molly —LITTLE RICHARD

My second brother, Kevin wasn't obedient. He didn't want to work on the farm. He wanted to play sports and ride horses. He got thrown out of the Catholic military academy and all of the other local schools. He and my father fought all of the time. My dad tried to beat the sense into him. He'd run away and get picked up by the police. After my father broke his nose, a cop advised him to find another place to live if he didn't want to get killed. He left home at 14, first to Mexico, then to Colorado, and then the streets of California. He did eventually return ten years later. By that time our parents had moved to Florida.

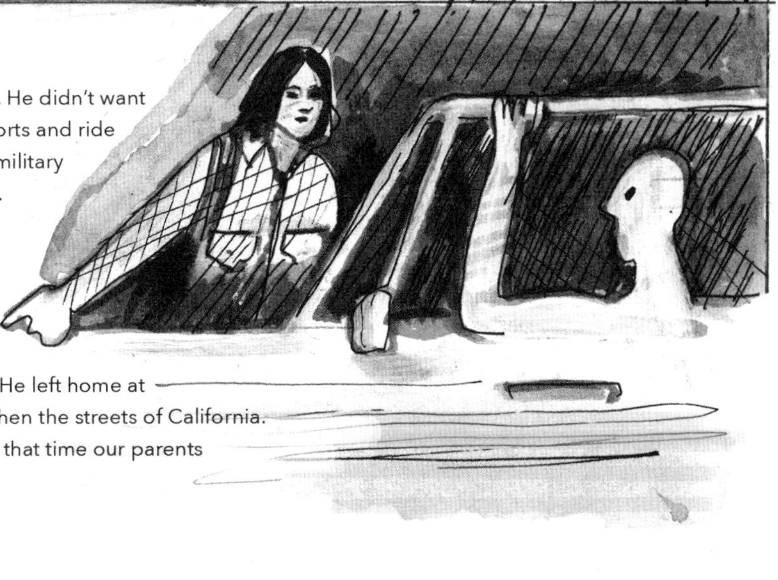

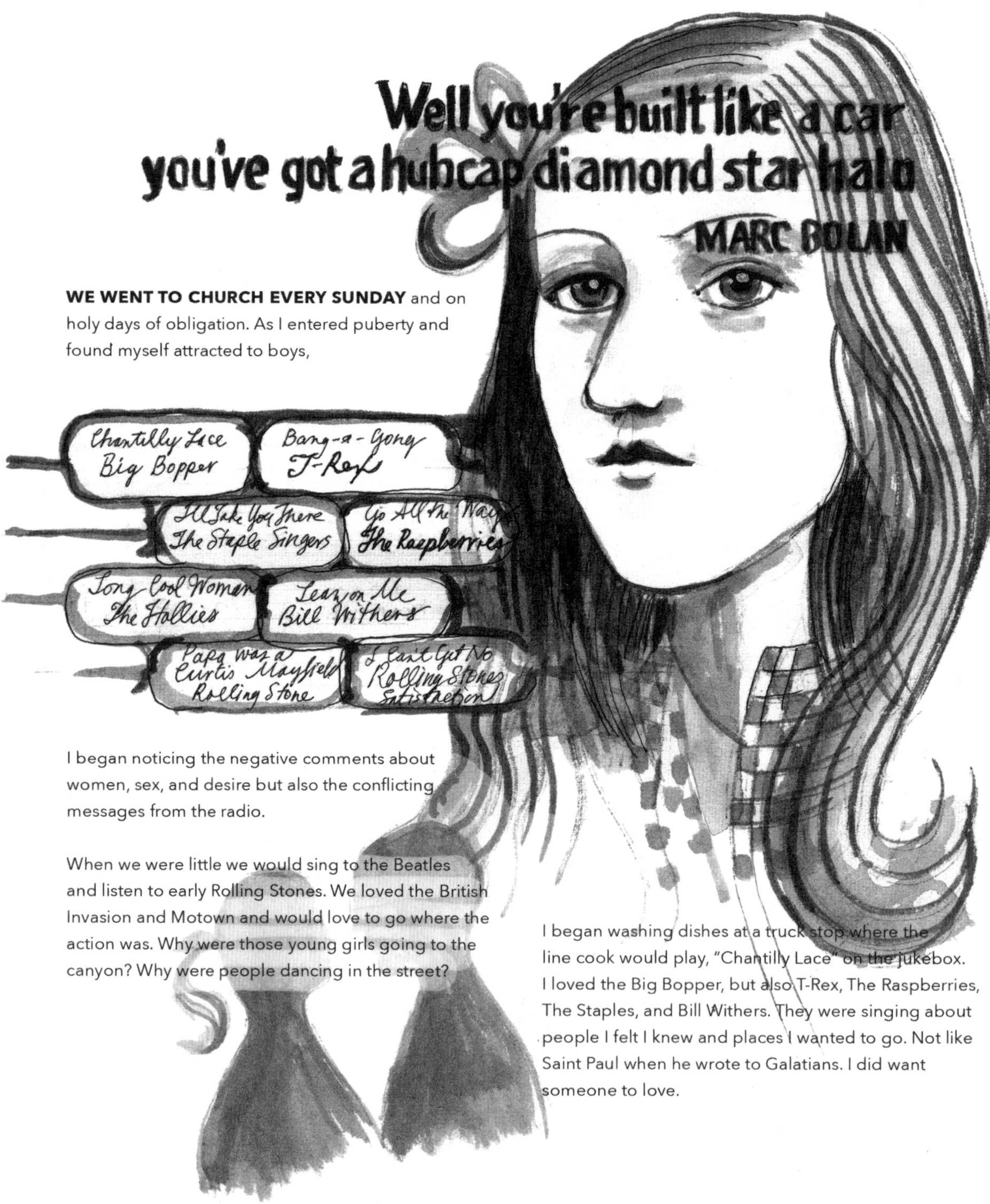
Well you're built like a car
you've got a hubcap diamond star halo
MARC BOLAN
Chantilly Lace
Big Bopper
Bang-a-Gong
T-Rex
I'll Take You There
The Staple Singers
Go All the Way
The Raspberries
Long Cool Woman
The Hollies
Lean on Me
Bill Withers
Papa was a
Curtis Mayfield
Rolling Stone
I Can't Get No
Rolling Stones
Satisfaction

WE WENT TO CHURCH EVERY SUNDAY and on holy days of obligation. As I entered puberty and found myself attracted to boys,

I began noticing the negative comments about women, sex, and desire but also the conflicting messages from the radio.

When we were little we would sing to the Beatles and listen to early Rolling Stones. We loved the British Invasion and Motown and would love to go where the action was. Why were those young girls going to the canyon? Why were people dancing in the street?

I began washing dishes at a truck stop where the line cook would play, "Chantilly Lace" on the jukebox. I loved the Big Bopper, but also T-Rex, The Raspberries, The Staples, and Bill Withers. They were singing about people I felt I knew and places I wanted to go. Not like Saint Paul when he wrote to Galatians. I did want someone to love.

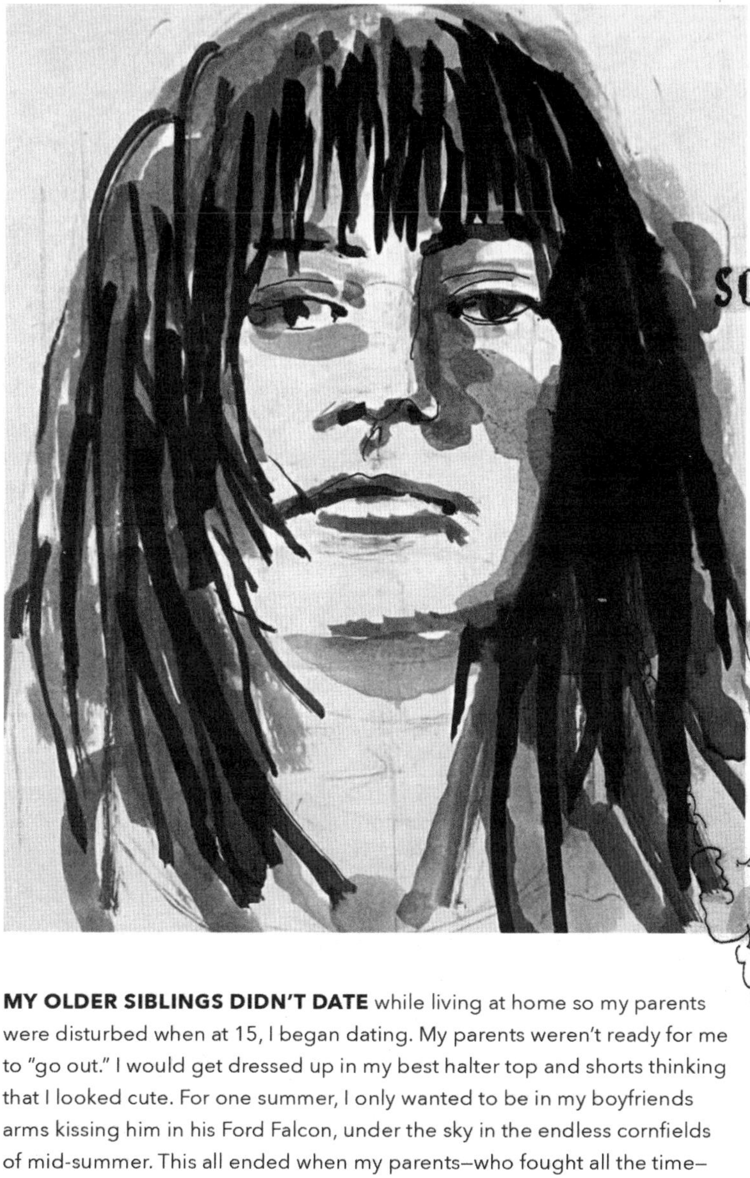

Jesus died for somebody's sins but not mine
— PATTI SMITH

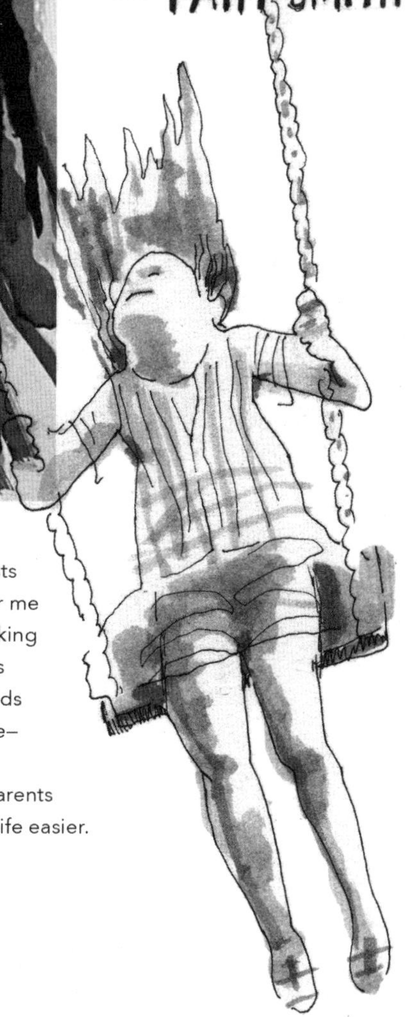

MY OLDER SIBLINGS DIDN'T DATE while living at home so my parents were disturbed when at 15, I began dating. My parents weren't ready for me to "go out." I would get dressed up in my best halter top and shorts thinking that I looked cute. For one summer, I only wanted to be in my boyfriends arms kissing him in his Ford Falcon, under the sky in the endless cornfields of mid-summer. This all ended when my parents—who fought all the time—said that we had to leave this small town. Sometimes I think that it was because I was becoming "so wild." The remaining three lived with our parents until they moved to Florida to make my emphysema suffering mother's life easier.

Our home left us. We younger ones were dropped into our freedoms.
Were we ready to claim ourselves, our minds and our bodies?
Who to listen to? Where to go? Who to follow? What to be?

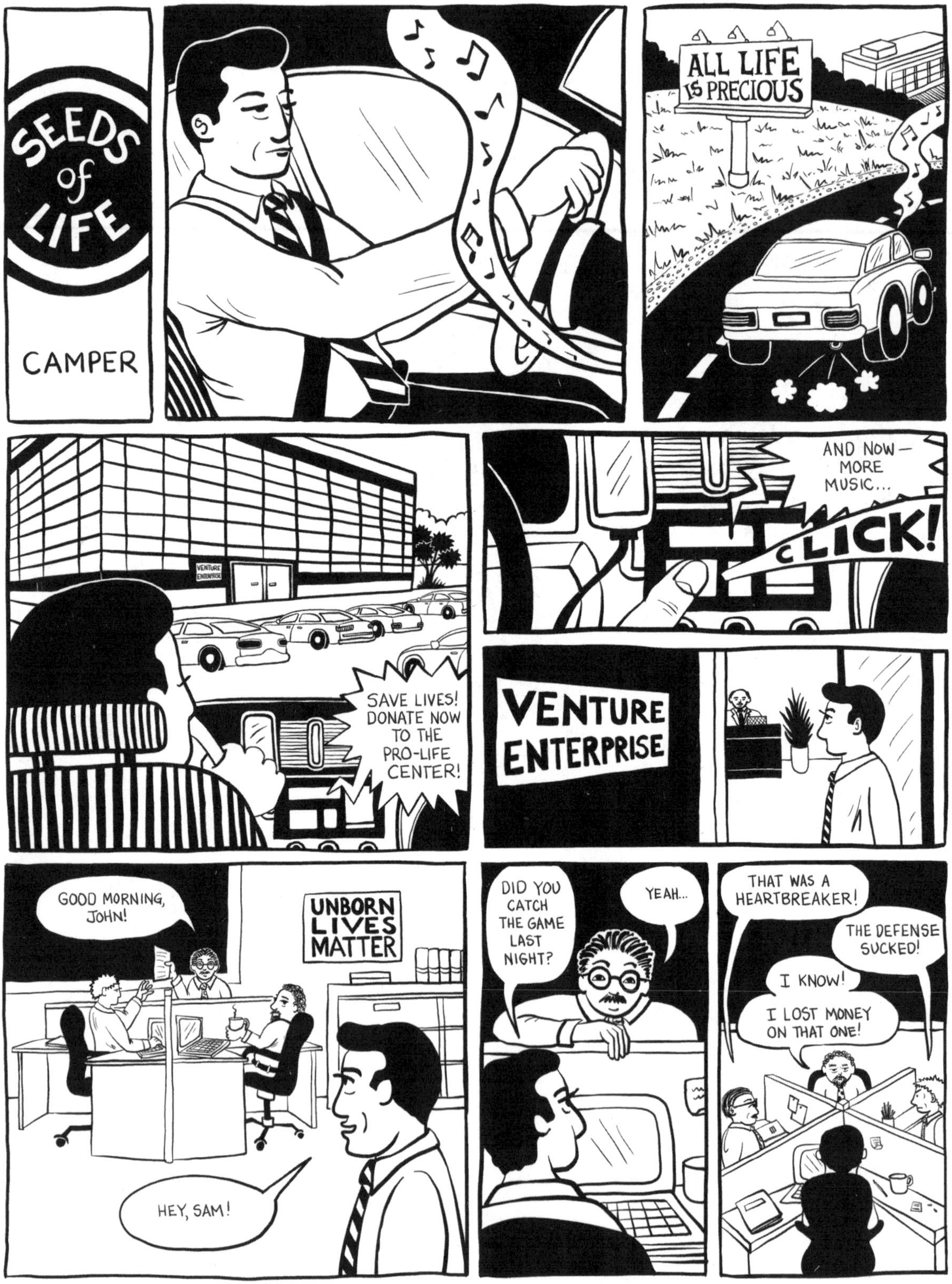
SEEDS of LIFE
CAMPER
ALL LIFE IS PRECIOUS
VENTURE ENTERPRISE
SAVE LIVES! DONATE NOW TO THE PRO-LIFE CENTER!
AND NOW— MORE MUSIC...
CLICK!
VENTURE ENTERPRISE
GOOD MORNING, JOHN!
UNBORN LIVES MATTER
HEY, SAM!
DID YOU CATCH THE GAME LAST NIGHT?
YEAH...
THAT WAS A HEARTBREAKER!
THE DEFENSE SUCKED!
I KNOW!
I LOST MONEY ON THAT ONE!

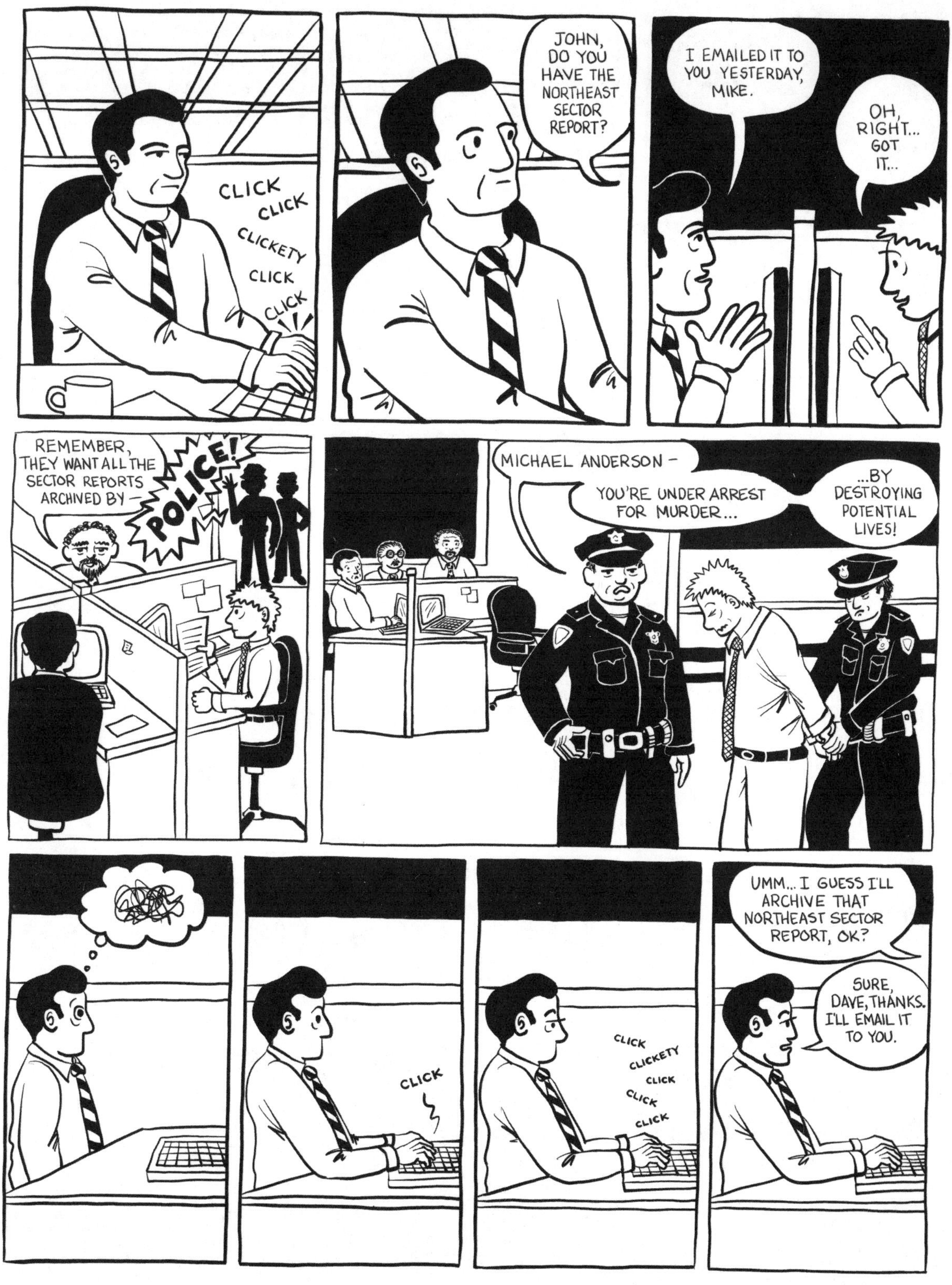
CLICK
CLICK
CLICKETY
CLICK
CLICK
JOHN, DO YOU HAVE THE NORTHEAST SECTOR REPORT?
I EMAILED IT TO YOU YESTERDAY, MIKE.
OH, RIGHT... GOT IT...
REMEMBER, THEY WANT ALL THE SECTOR REPORTS ARCHIVED BY—
POLICE!
MICHAEL ANDERSON—
YOU'RE UNDER ARREST FOR MURDER...
...BY DESTROYING POTENTIAL LIVES!
CLICK
CLICK
CLICKETY
CLICK
CLICK
CLICK
UMM... I GUESS I'LL ARCHIVE THAT NORTHEAST SECTOR REPORT, OK?
SURE, DAVE, THANKS. I'LL EMAIL IT TO YOU.

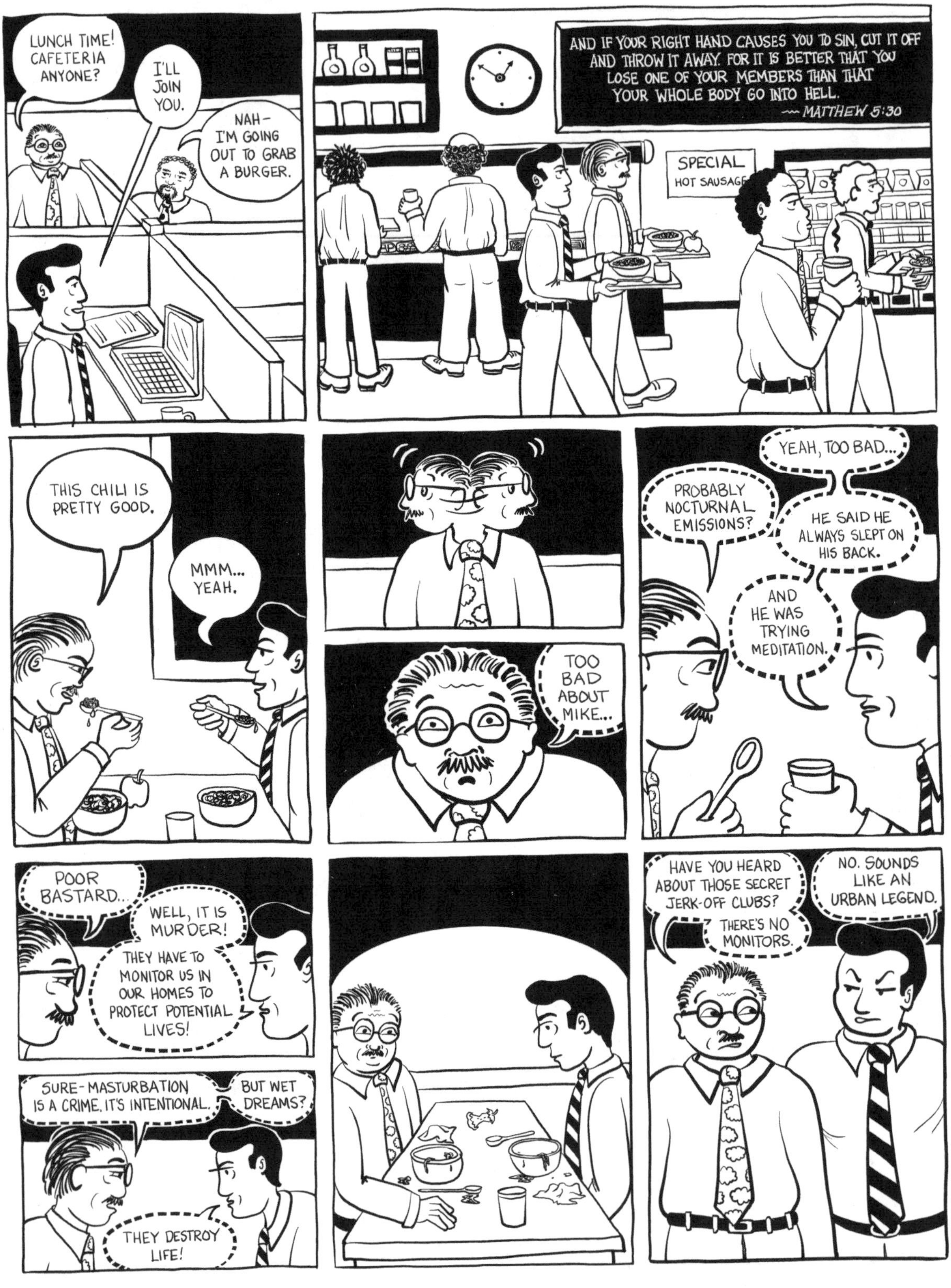
LUNCH TIME! CAFETERIA ANYONE?
I'LL JOIN YOU.
NAH- I'M GOING OUT TO GRAB A BURGER.
AND IF YOUR RIGHT HAND CAUSES YOU TO SIN, CUT IT OFF AND THROW IT AWAY. FOR IT IS BETTER THAT YOU LOSE ONE OF YOUR MEMBERS THAN THAT YOUR WHOLE BODY GO INTO HELL.
— MATTHEW 5:30
SPECIAL
HOT SAUSAGE
THIS CHILI IS PRETTY GOOD.
MMM... YEAH.
TOO BAD ABOUT MIKE...
YEAH, TOO BAD...
PROBABLY NOCTURNAL EMISSIONS?
HE SAID HE ALWAYS SLEPT ON HIS BACK.
AND HE WAS TRYING MEDITATION.
POOR BASTARD...
WELL, IT IS MURDER!
THEY HAVE TO MONITOR US IN OUR HOMES TO PROTECT POTENTIAL LIVES!
SURE- MASTURBATION IS A CRIME. IT'S INTENTIONAL.
BUT WET DREAMS?
THEY DESTROY LIFE!
HAVE YOU HEARD ABOUT THOSE SECRET JERK-OFF CLUBS?
THERE'S NO MONITORS.
NO. SOUNDS LIKE AN URBAN LEGEND.

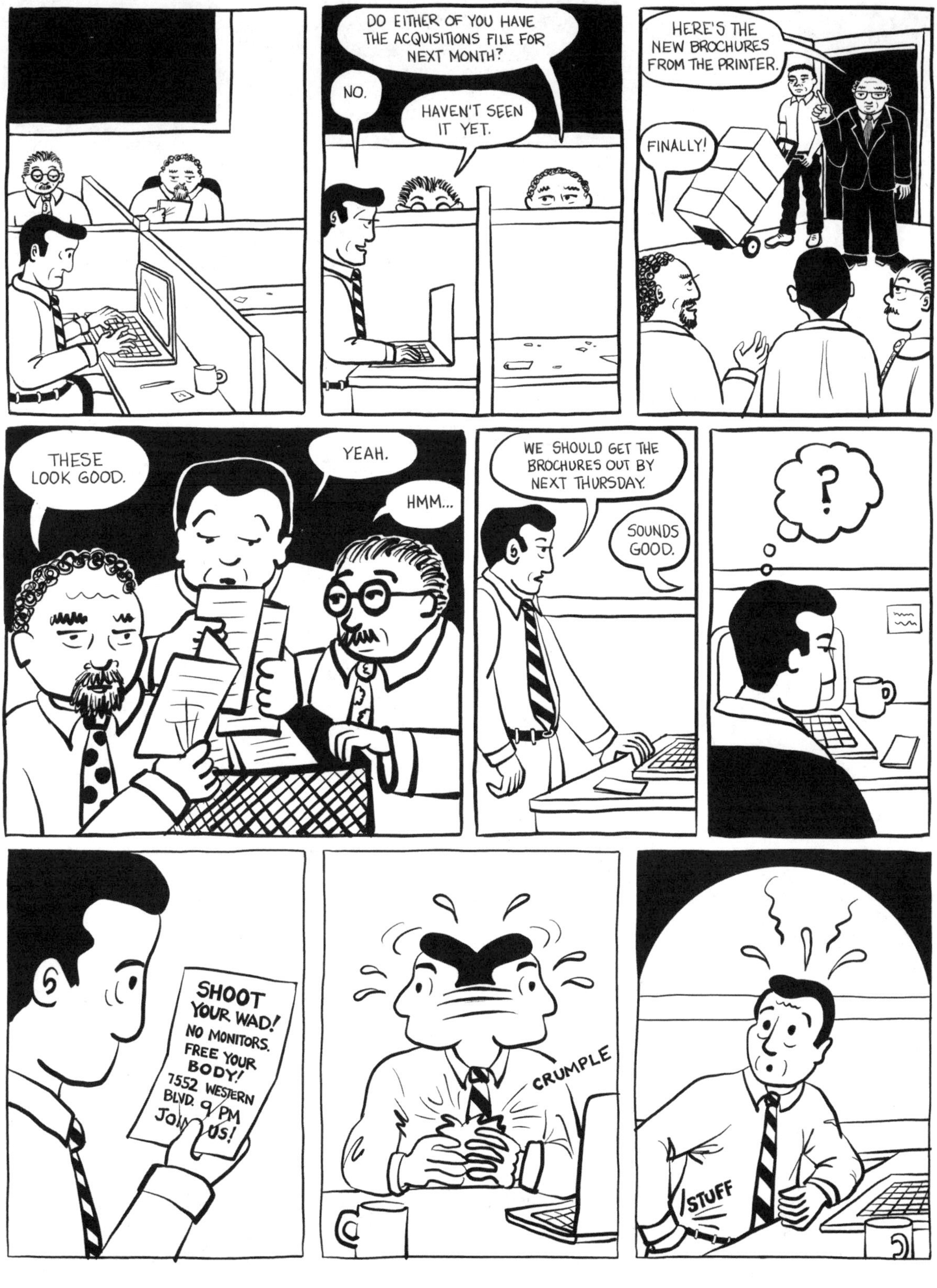
DO EITHER OF YOU HAVE THE ACQUISITIONS FILE FOR NEXT MONTH?
NO.
HAVEN'T SEEN IT YET.
HERE'S THE NEW BROCHURES FROM THE PRINTER.
FINALLY!
THESE LOOK GOOD.
YEAH.
HMM...
WE SHOULD GET THE BROCHURES OUT BY NEXT THURSDAY.
SOUNDS GOOD.
?
SHOOT YOUR WAD! NO MONITORS. FREE YOUR BODY! 7552 WESTERN BLVD. 9 PM JOIN US!
CRUMPLE
STUFF

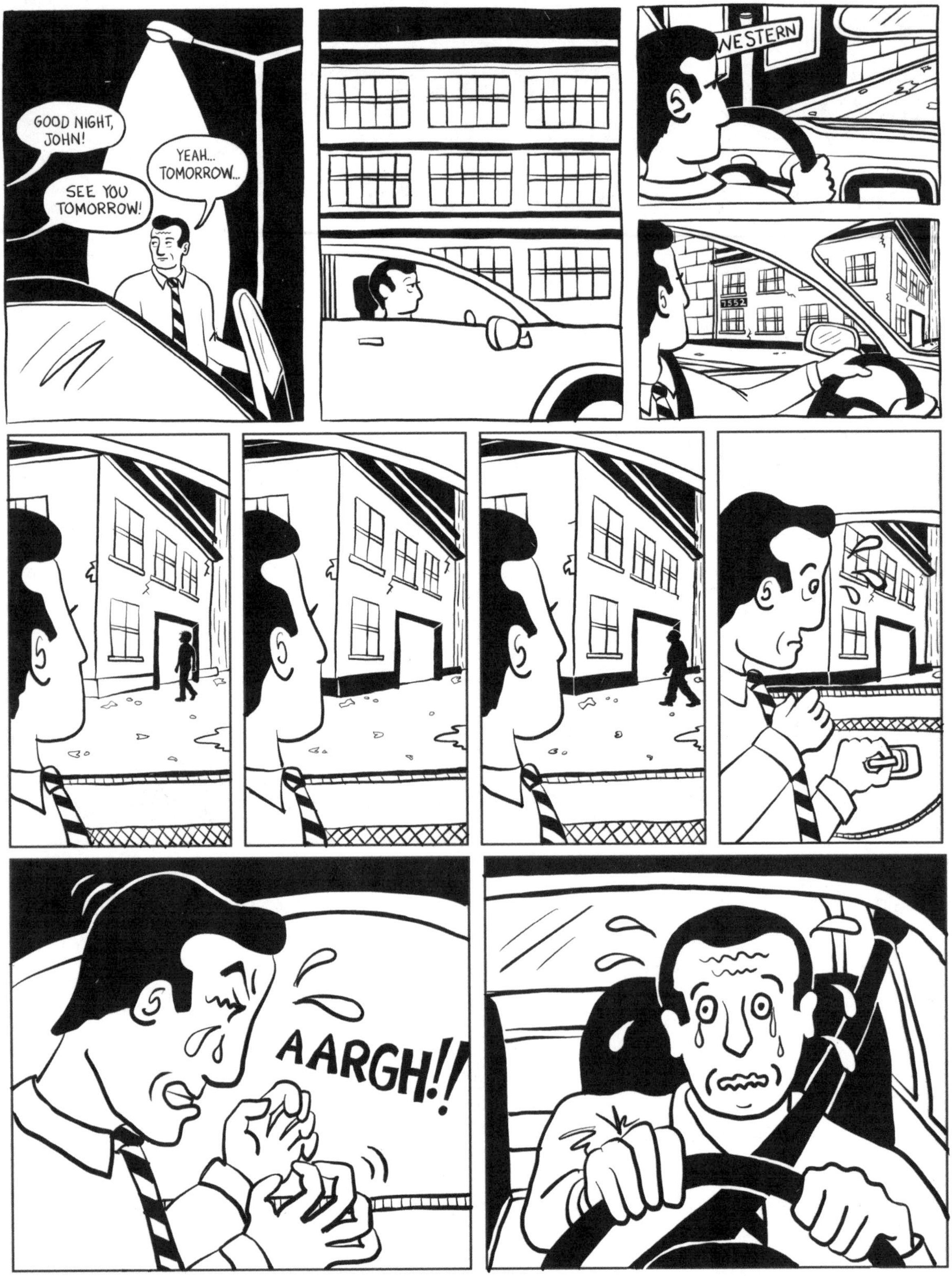
GOOD NIGHT, JOHN!
SEE YOU TOMORROW!
YEAH... TOMORROW...
WESTERN
7552
AARGH!!

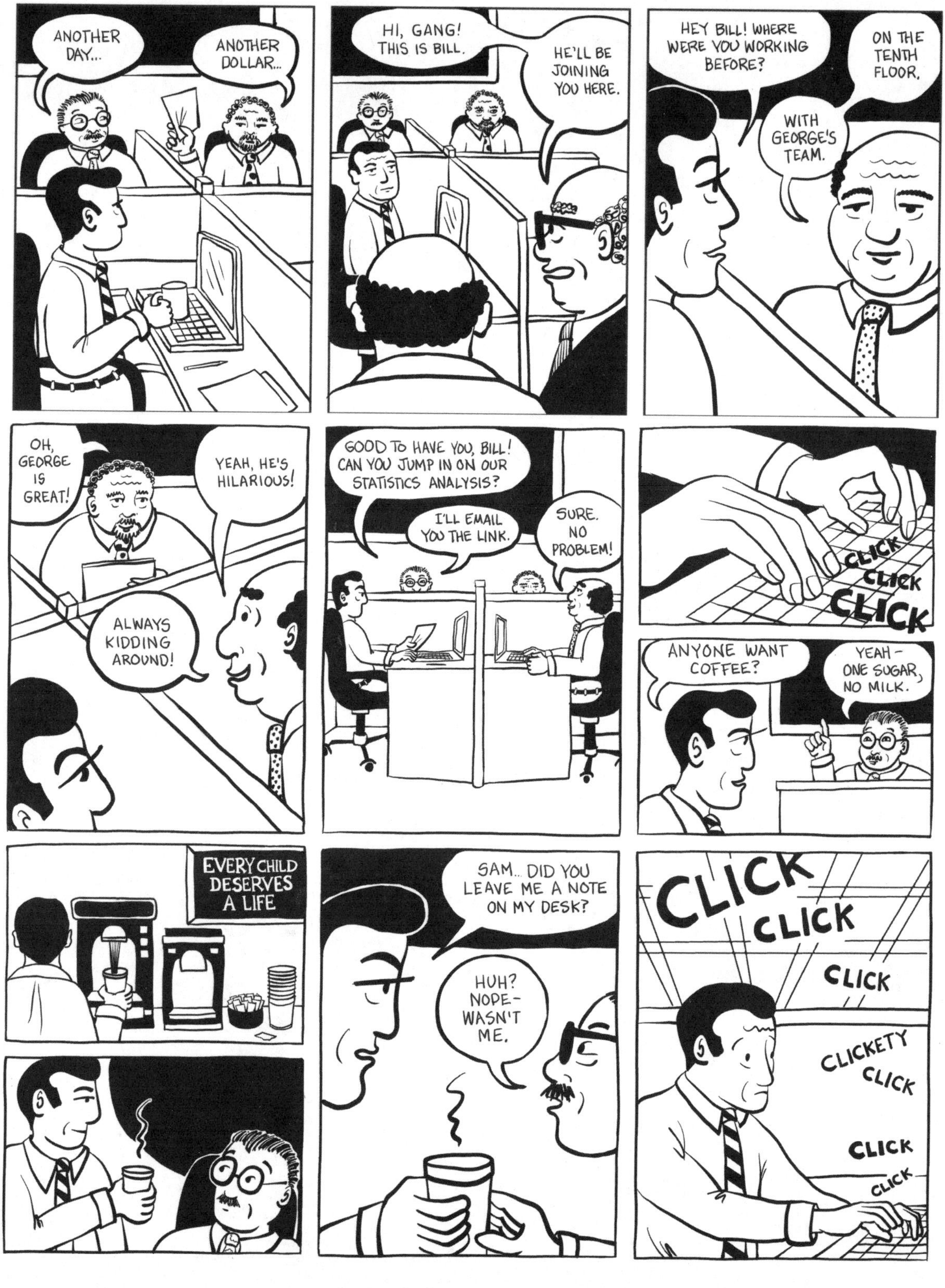
ANOTHER DAY...
ANOTHER DOLLAR...
HI, GANG! THIS IS BILL.
HE'LL BE JOINING YOU HERE.
HEY BILL! WHERE WERE YOU WORKING BEFORE?
ON THE TENTH FLOOR.
WITH GEORGE'S TEAM.
OH, GEORGE IS GREAT!
YEAH, HE'S HILARIOUS!
ALWAYS KIDDING AROUND!
GOOD TO HAVE YOU, BILL! CAN YOU JUMP IN ON OUR STATISTICS ANALYSIS?
I'LL EMAIL YOU THE LINK.
SURE. NO PROBLEM!
CLICK
CLICK
CLICK
ANYONE WANT COFFEE?
YEAH - ONE SUGAR, NO MILK.
EVERY CHILD DESERVES A LIFE
SAM... DID YOU LEAVE ME A NOTE ON MY DESK?
HUH? NOPE- WASN'T ME.
CLICK
CLICK
CLICK
CLICKETY CLICK
CLICK
CLICK

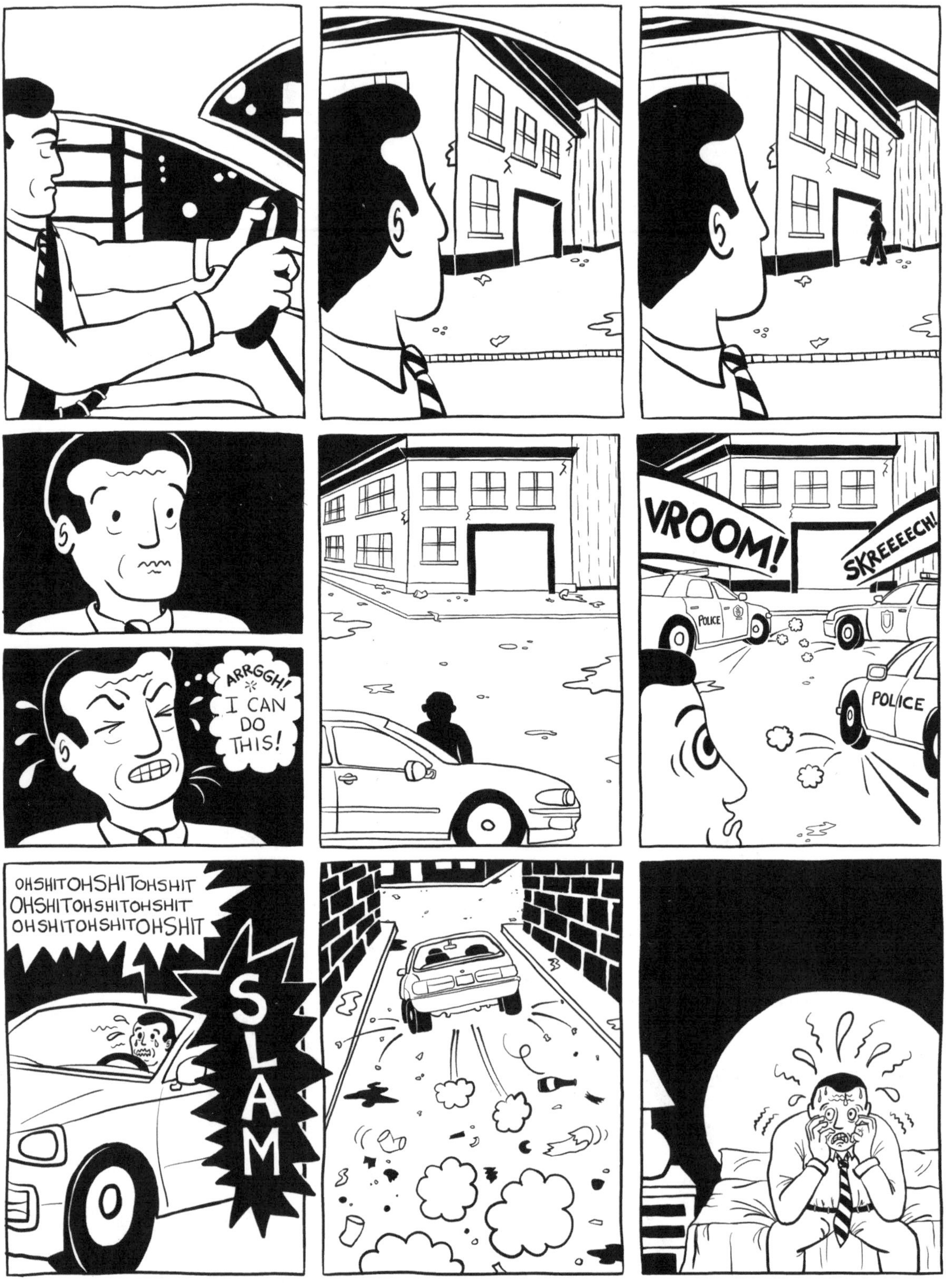
ARRGGH! I CAN DO THIS!
VROOM!
SKREEEECH!
POLICE
POLICE
OHSHITOHSHITOHSHIT
OHSHITOHSHITOHSHIT
OHSHITOHSHITOHSHIT
SLAM

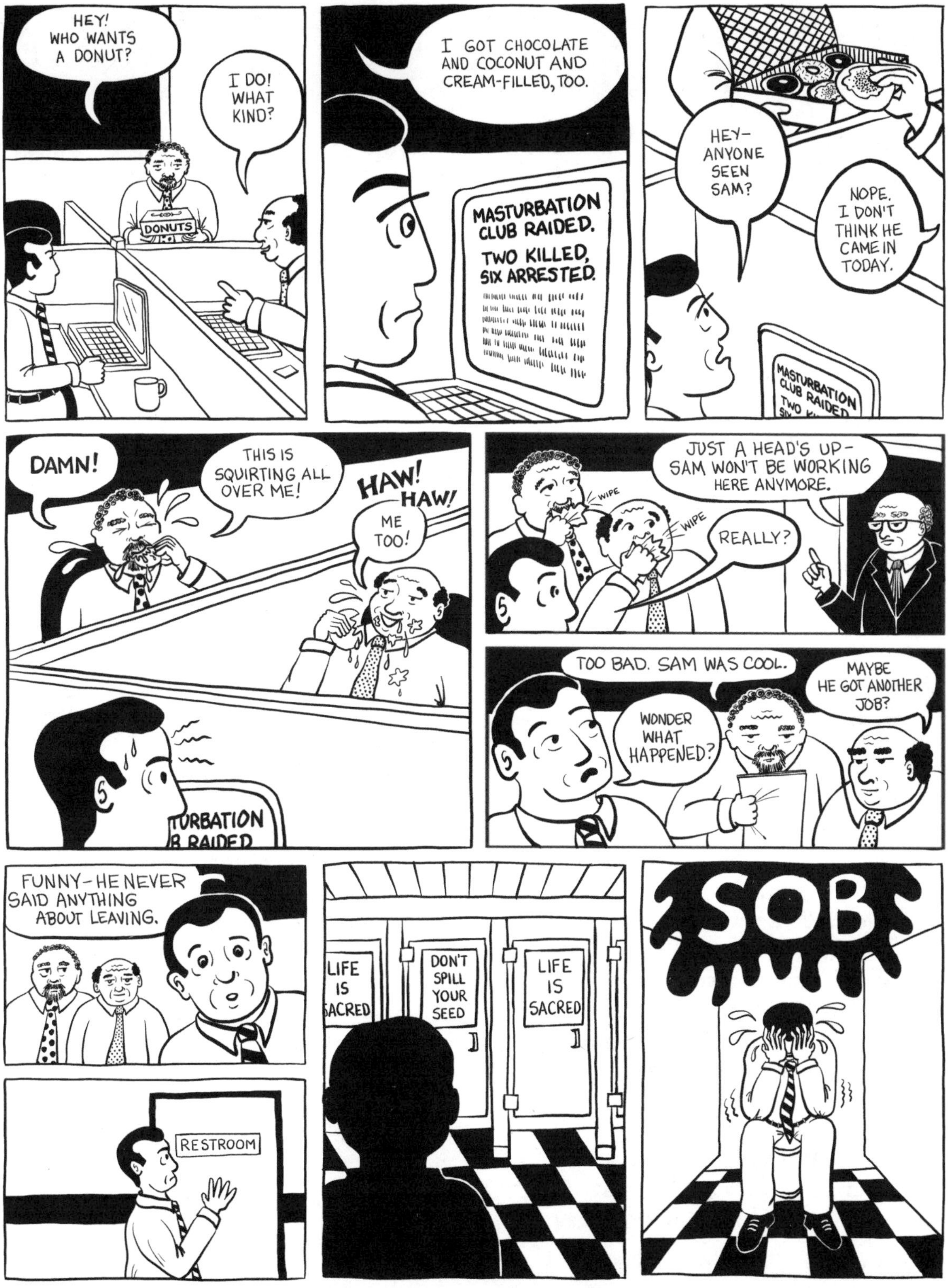

HEY! WHO WANTS A DONUT?
I DO! WHAT KIND?
DONUTS
I GOT CHOCOLATE AND COCONUT AND CREAM-FILLED, TOO.
MASTURBATION CLUB RAIDED. TWO KILLED, SIX ARRESTED.
HEY- ANYONE SEEN SAM?
NOPE. I DON'T THINK HE CAME IN TODAY.
MASTURBATION CLUB RAIDED
DAMN!
THIS IS SQUIRTING ALL OVER ME!
HAW! HAW!
ME TOO!
TURBATION B RAIDED
JUST A HEAD'S UP- SAM WON'T BE WORKING HERE ANYMORE.
WIPE
WIPE
REALLY?
TOO BAD. SAM WAS COOL.
MAYBE HE GOT ANOTHER JOB?
WONDER WHAT HAPPENED?
FUNNY- HE NEVER SAID ANYTHING ABOUT LEAVING.
RESTROOM
LIFE IS SACRED
DON'T SPILL YOUR SEED
LIFE IS SACRED
SOB

GODDESS ARISE

AN INCANTATION TO HEAL THE FEMININE · BY REBECCA MIGDAL

The Mother Goddess is an ancient image, a primal reflection of the qualities which make us human. She is an archetype of strength, creative power, sacrifice, transcendence, compassion, wisdom, loyalty, life, beauty, and inspiration. Above all, she champions the autonomy of the feminine principle, which is the essnce of loving consciousness. Sadly, due to the rise of the self-perpetuating cultural forces of violence and war, and the resultant economies based on rape and slavery, the feminine divine has long been eclipsed. The attributes of the Goddess, and her life-changing powers, have over time become the domain of masculine gods, gods who have presided over a global crisis for both humanity and nature.

In this historical context, the controversy over abortion rights is revealed as the product of unresolved intergenerational trauma, expressing a widespread alienation from, and toxic attitude toward the Mother. Requiring unwilling women to become mothers keeps the cycle of trauma alive. If we want healthy, happy families, we must empower women to have agency. As poet and scholar Adrienne Rich wrote, modern women and men are called upon to "release the creation and sustenance of life into the same realm of decision, struggle, surprise, imagination, and conscious intelligence, as any other difficult, but freely chosen work." *

Goddess Arise is an incantation for revealing and healing the feminine aspect of our humanity. The images on these pages appeared to me in dreams. The circular paintings are designs for the petals of The Motherflower, a performance piece which plays a part in my research for a doctoral dissertation in Jungian Psychology. It will be an enfolding flower constructed in mixed-media fibers and beads, part of a multisensory journey of return to the womb of the Great Mother, of transformation and rebirth.

I believe that in order to heal humanity, we must allow the feminine divine to rise again within us all. We need the Goddess near us so we can be fully human. When we have a vessel for the feminine divine, we free human women from expectations of perfection, and from our fearful projections of darkness and mortality. We free our feminine, nurturing qualities from the prison of gender. We can see females as persons with the same rights, needs, doubts and failings as men. And maybe we can finally forgive our mothers, and ourselves, for being human.

The Mother is our first teacher, helping us develop consciousness and understand our own humanity. Her qualities are necessary, but our images of the divine feminine have been erased or distorted. Lost as we are, cut off from the source of our highest human aspirations and our deepest human needs, the time has come to turn toward Her voice, and find our way home.

— Rebecca Migdal, November 2022

* Rich, A., *Of Woman Born* 1976

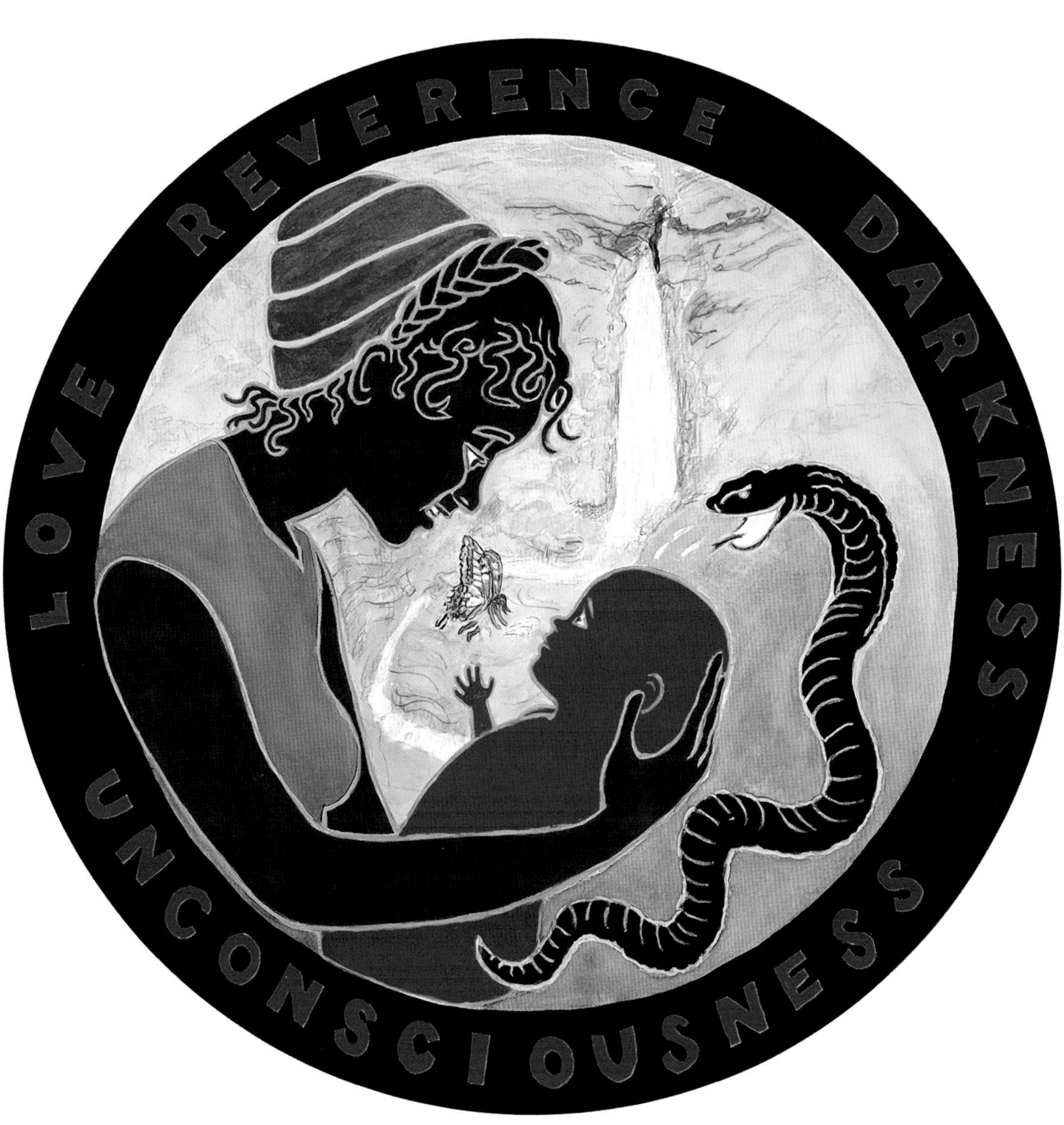
LOVE
REVERENCE
DARKNESS
UNCONSCIOUSNESS

Durga / Isis

Born out of the female body
Born out of the deep unconscious
Love and reverence has a shadow
Needing mother, hungry, angry
Born unconscious

Expelled, resenting
Love and reverence, guilt and shame
From the darkness, growing conscious
From the darkness, growing conscious
Let it go, open up, and be loved.

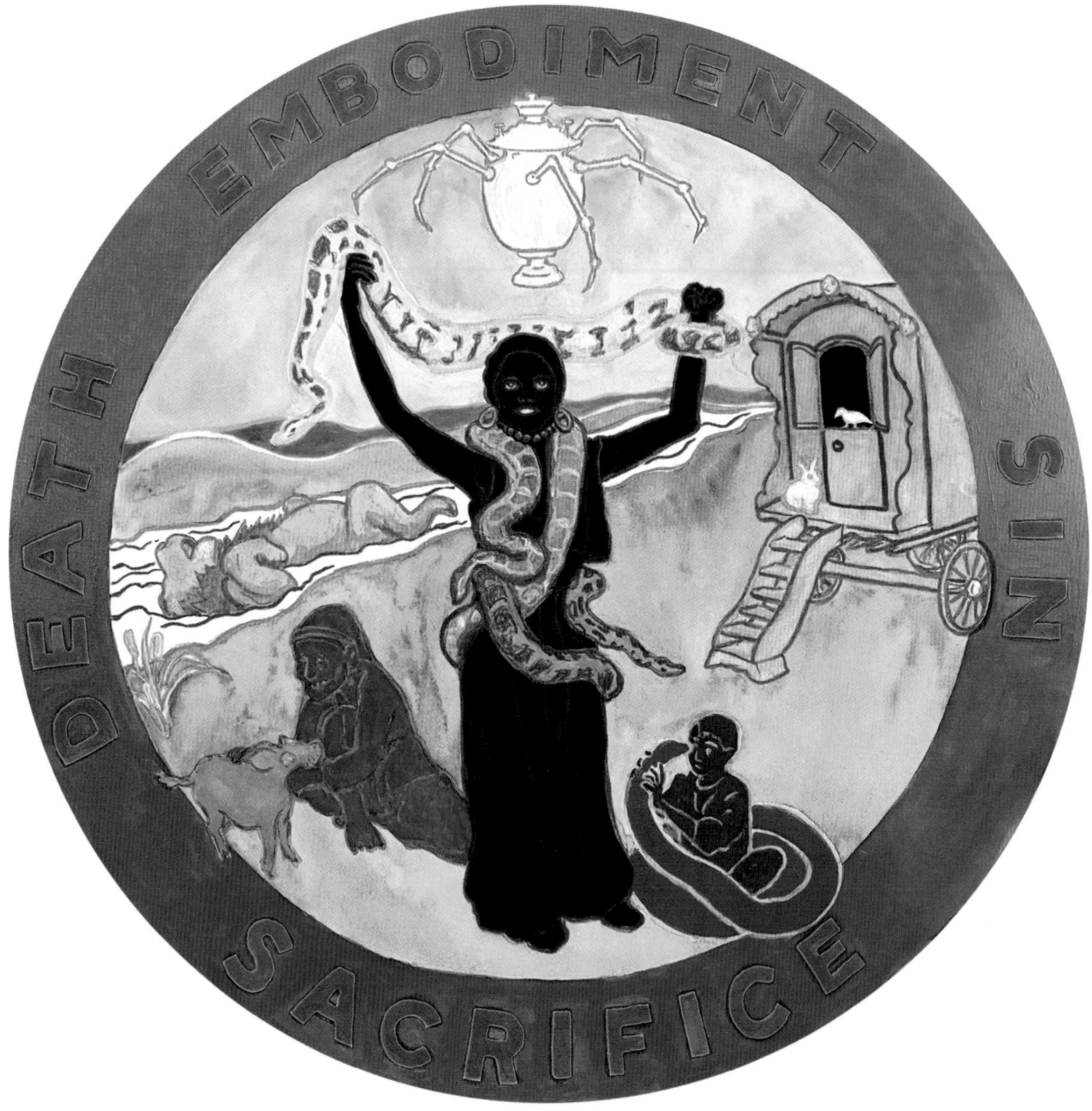
EMBODIMENT
DEATH
SIN
SACRIFICE

Cybele

Born into this needy body
Made of shit and made of mud
Born into this sinful body
Made of meat and made of blood
I cannot control this body
Violent with dark desire
Mother I was born of darkness
Mother burns me with her fire
Mother death, I need control!
Let it go, open out, and be loved.

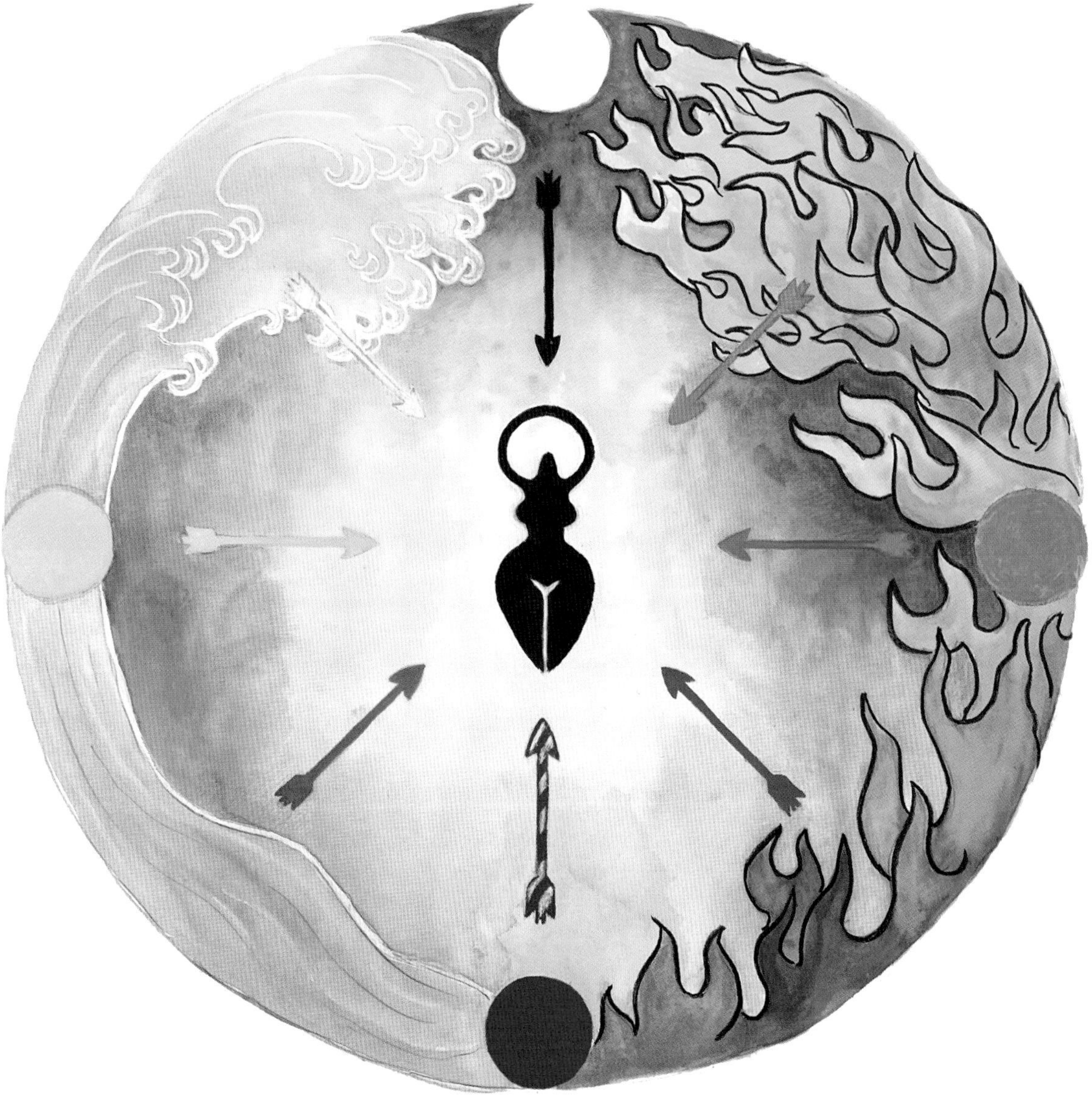

Venus

Woman's body is the source
Of feelings that take us by force
Willy-nilly hot desire
Tossed by waves and burned by fire
For our wrongs you bear the blame
We cover mother with our shame
It is your strength that makes me weak
Mother's love is what I seek
Let it go, be free, and be loved.

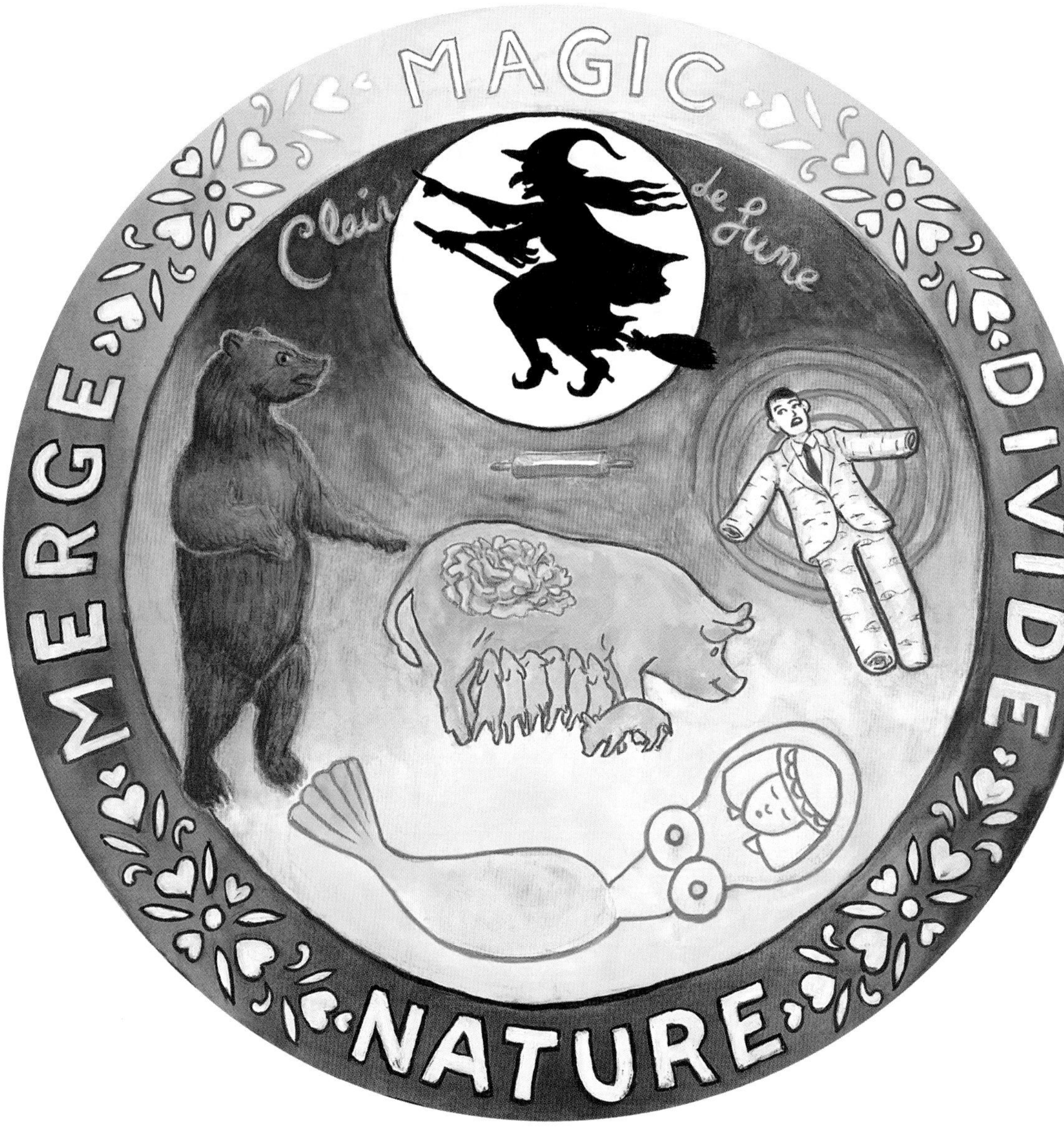
MAGIC
Clair de Lune
MERGE
DIVIDE
NATURE

Hecate

Emerge and split from Hecate
Nature cannot conquer me
Join and suck upon the teat
Mother's milk is good and sweet
Beast of instinct lives within
Unaware that he can sin
Cut adrift and floating free
Lonely, helpless, scarecrow me
Magic, Nature, Merge, Divide
Let it go, open in, and be loved.

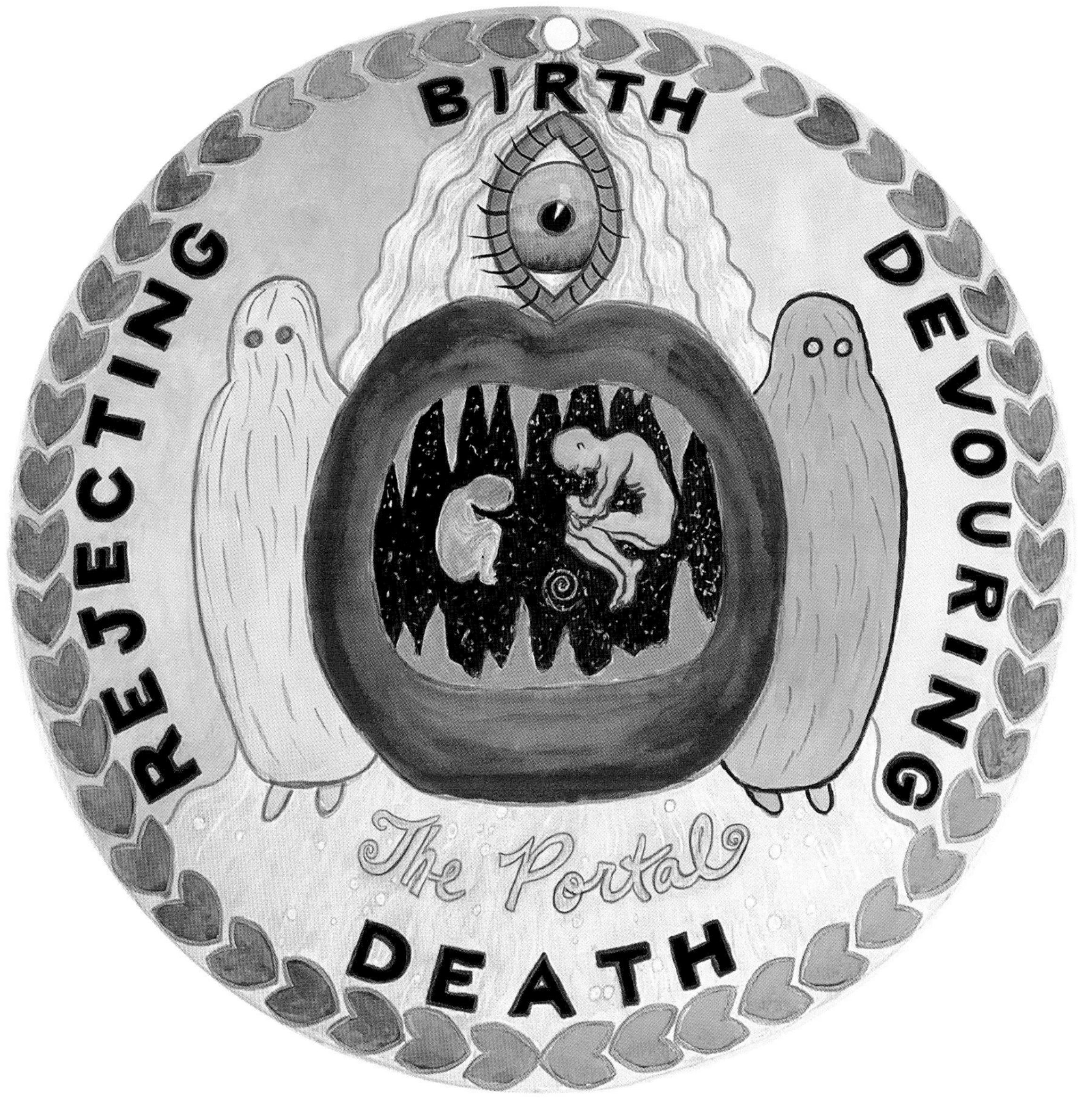
BIRTH
REJECTING
DEVOURING
The Portal
DEATH

Kali

Deep inside the earthly womb
Lies a portal and a tomb
No more ego, no more pride
Leave them at the door outside
Enter now the gate of life
Leave behind all need, all strife

There is no call to be afraid
By Kali you will be unmade
Do not fear the sacred cave
For life commands us to be brave
Let it go, pass through, and be loved.

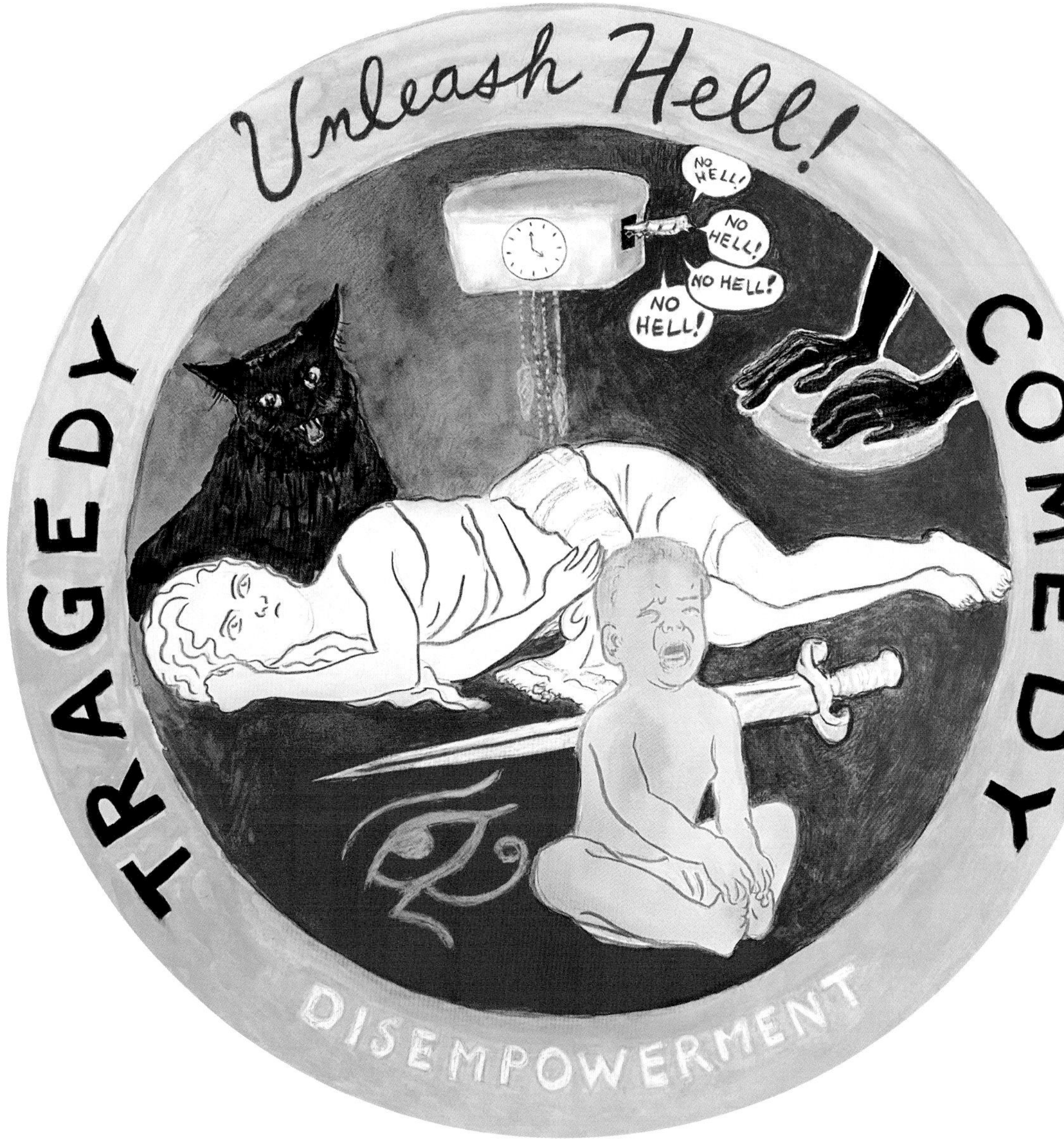
Unleash Hell!
NO HELL!
NO HELL!
NO HELL!
NO HELL!
TRAGEDY
COMEDY
DISEMPOWERMENT

Hera

Unleash hell! If I only had the power
I would unleash hell!
It's a comedy of hours
When the bread is rising
and the cuckoo's calling:
No hell! No hell!
No hell no hell no hell no hell no hell!

Unleash hell!
If you only would adore me
I would unleash hell!
And the world would bow before me
It's a tragedy of errors
I'm a ticking bomb in a hall of mirrors!
Let it go, let it pass, and be loved.

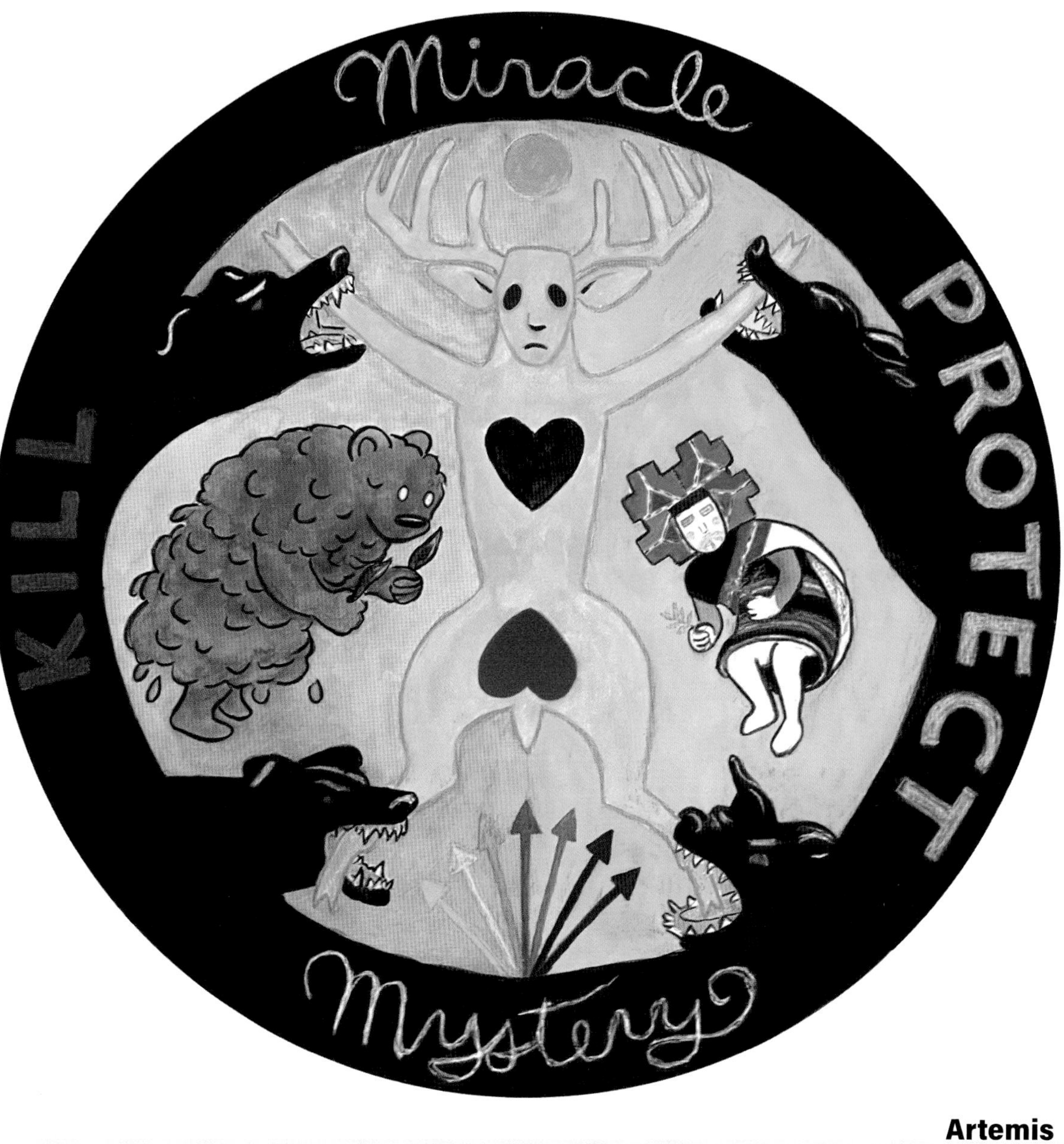
Miracle
KILL
PROTECT
Mystery

Artemis

Meet me where the road meets the river
I've got a bow and arrow that never miss
a gigantic, fierce bear is following me
I am willing to make that sacrifice,
that sacrifice

mysterious purpose, transformation
reach out your hand, distract the bear
are you willing to make that sacrifice?
Dancing in geometric figures
Let it go, let it be, and be loved.

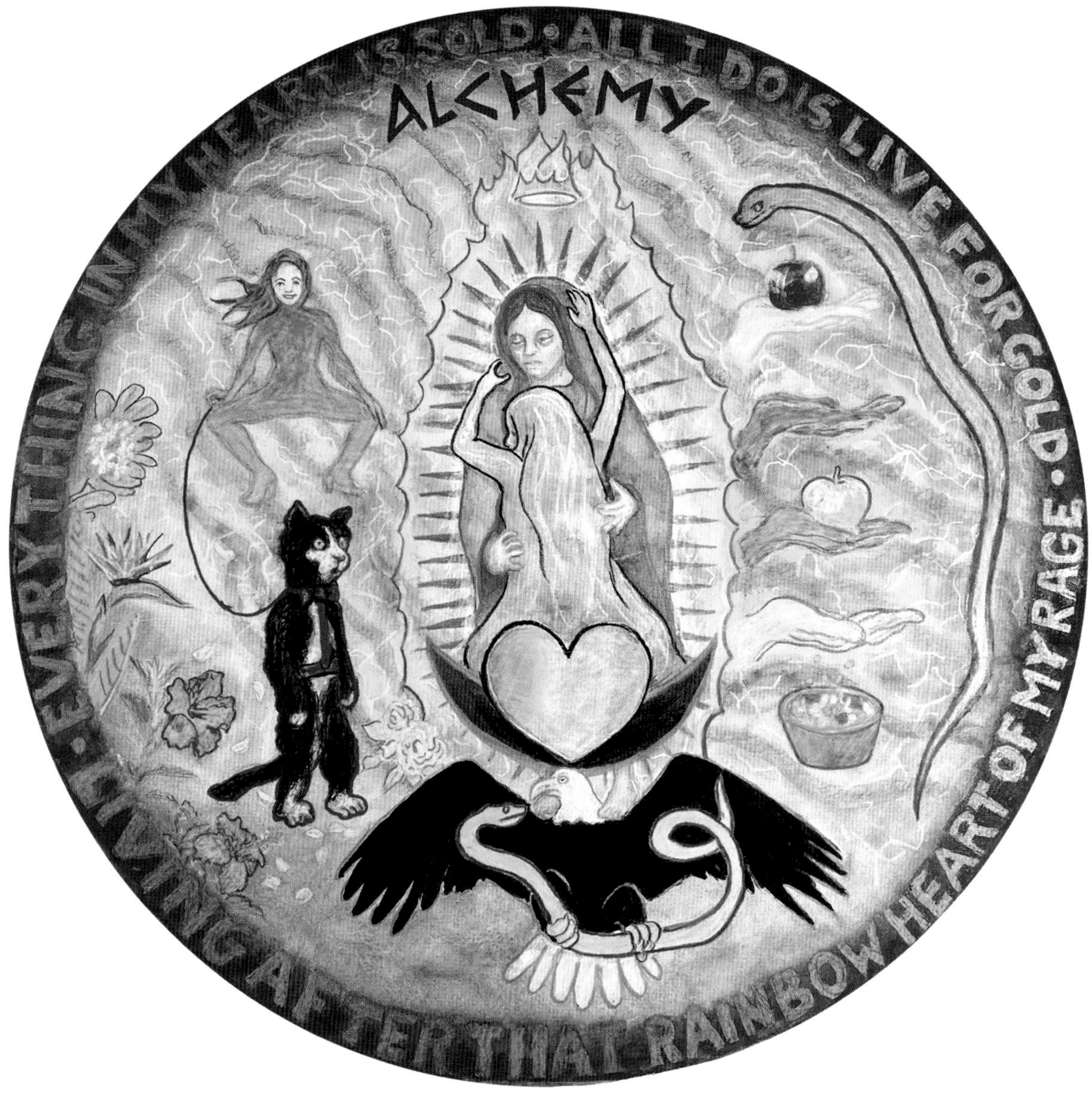
ALCHEMY
EVERYTHING IN MY HEART IS SOLD • ALL I DO IS LIVE FOR GOLD •
LIVING AFTER THAT RAINBOW HEART OF MY RAGE

Sophia

Something is missing:
the sacredness of the body.
In this garden of tropical flowers
we know
what is harmless from what is toxic.
Blessed be, divine virgin from the dawn of
time.

The power of darkness is woven into your
light.

Everything in my heart is sold,
All I do is live for gold
Living after that rainbow heart of my rage.

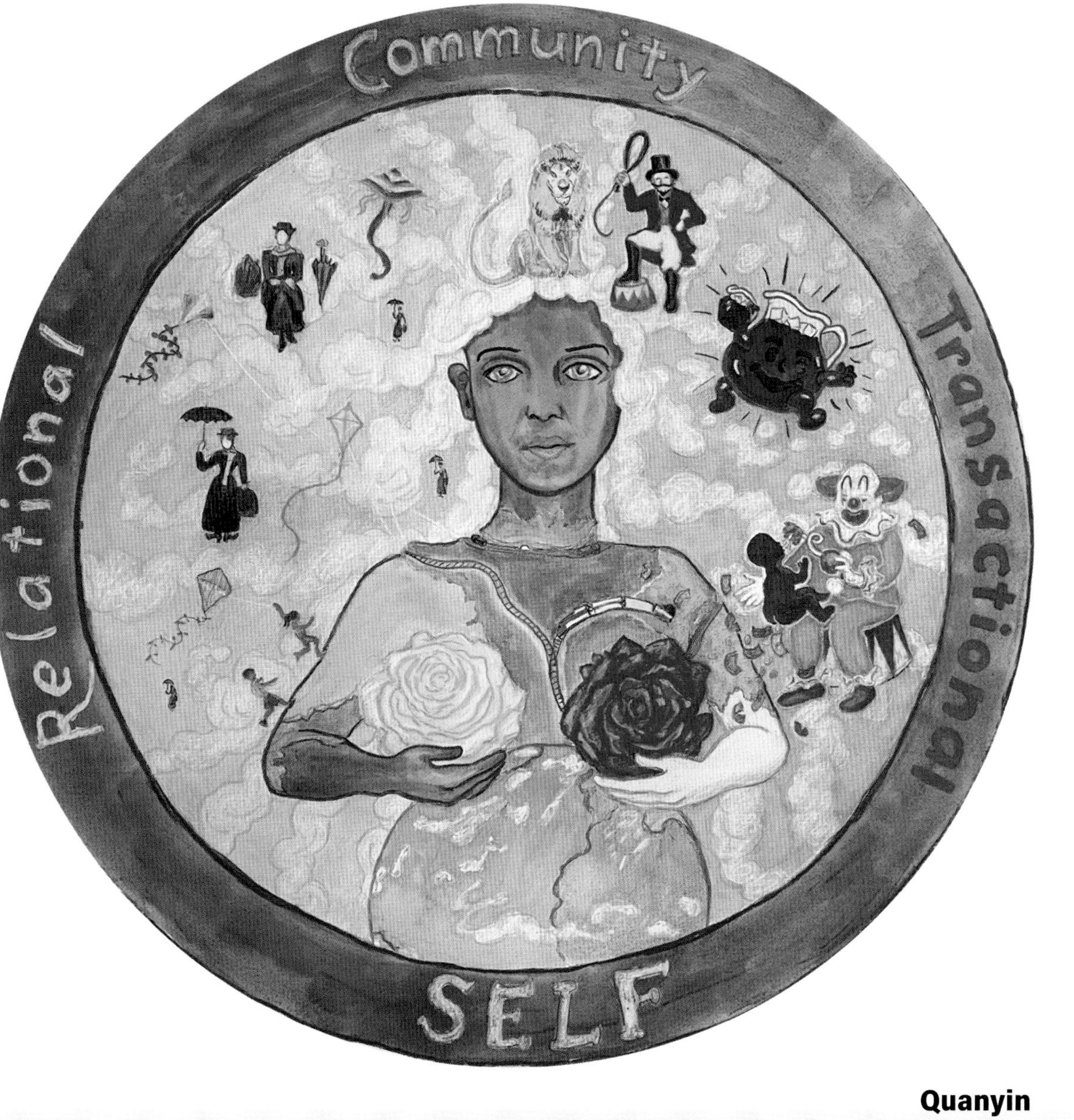
Community
Transactional
SELF
Relational

Quanyin

Long ago we had a goddess
Source of comfort, meaning, love.
Where did she go?
Our constant gardener
Path of Nature, path of Life
Instinctively we know her truth

She is our world personified
Safely in her web we rock
A tiny cell of everything
Nature sacred, body sacred,
Joy and sorrow, taking wing
Let it go, surrender, and be loved.

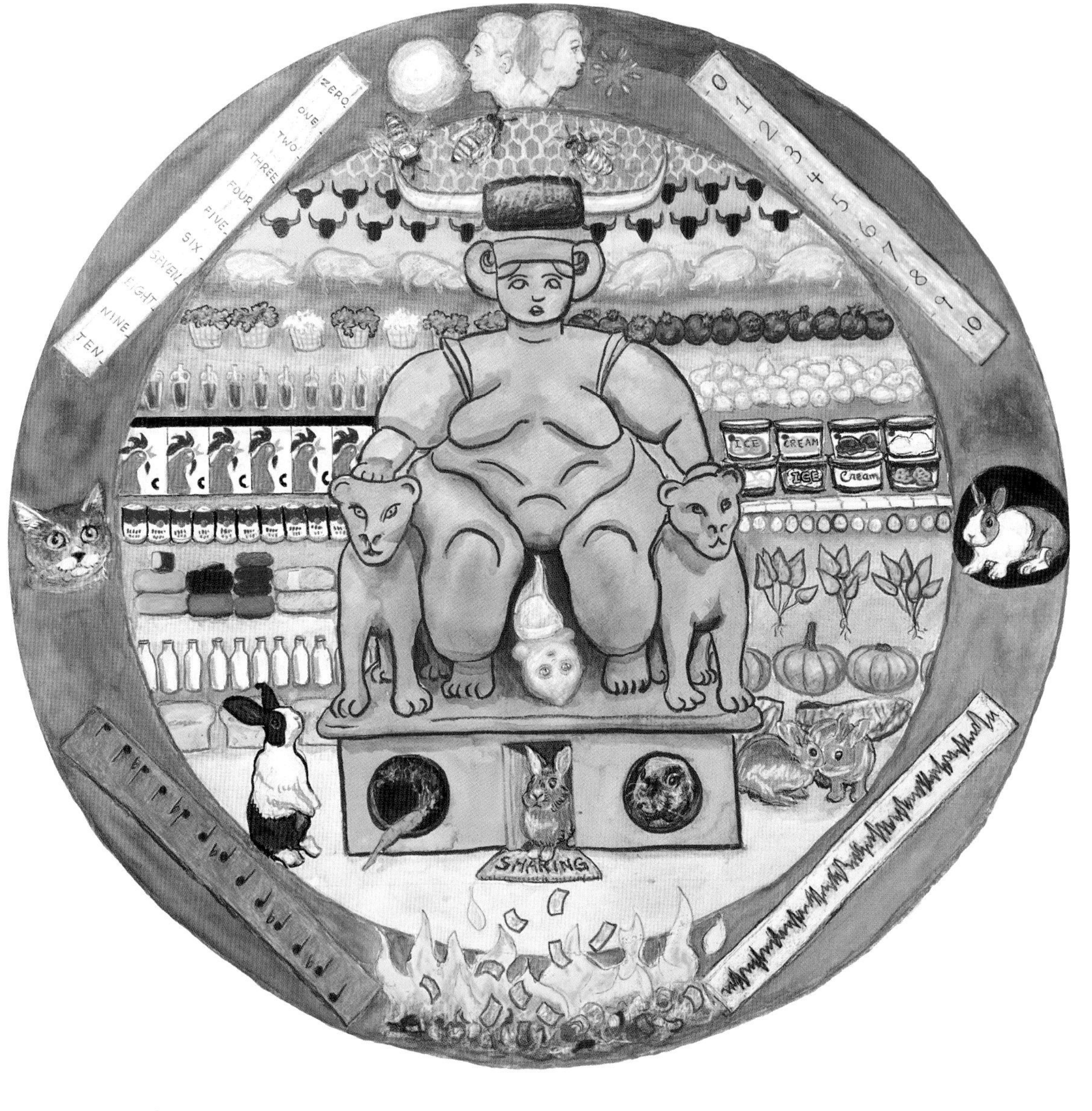
ZERO
ONE
TWO
THREE
FOUR
FIVE
SIX
SEVEN
EIGHT
NINE
TEN
0 1 2 3 4 5 6 7 8 9 10
ICE
CREAM
ICE
Cream
SHARING

Great Mother

From her nipples splendor streaming
In her bowels volcanoes rumbling
Mother's body is our world.
Mother's body is our world.
Bacon, cornflakes, cheese and wine
On her body we will dine
Blood and bone, we are her brood
As she is mine, I am her food
Mother's body is our world.
Sacred body is our world.
Let it go, enjoy, and be loved.

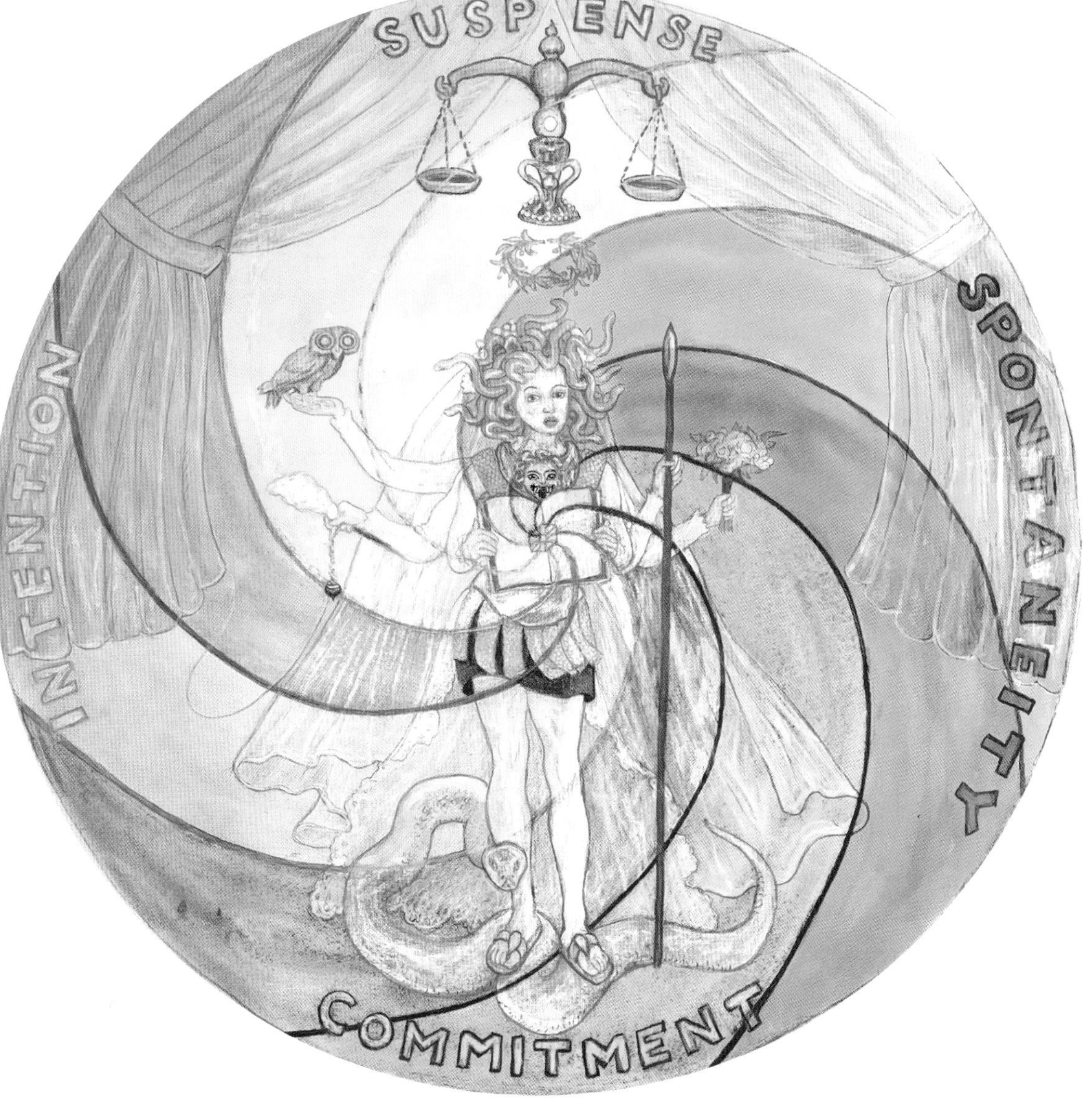
SUSPENSE
SPONTANEITY
COMMITMENT
INTENTION

Athena

What is reason? What is wisdom?
Wisdom does not have the answers.
Thou kaleidoscope of love!
Beauty dances in the wind
Ecstasy in proper proportion
Goddess finger on the bowstring

Pulling, waiting, yearning, acting
Every moment fractal blossom
Feel her gyrate in your sternum!
Thou kaleidoscope of love!
Let it go, be in flow, and be loved.

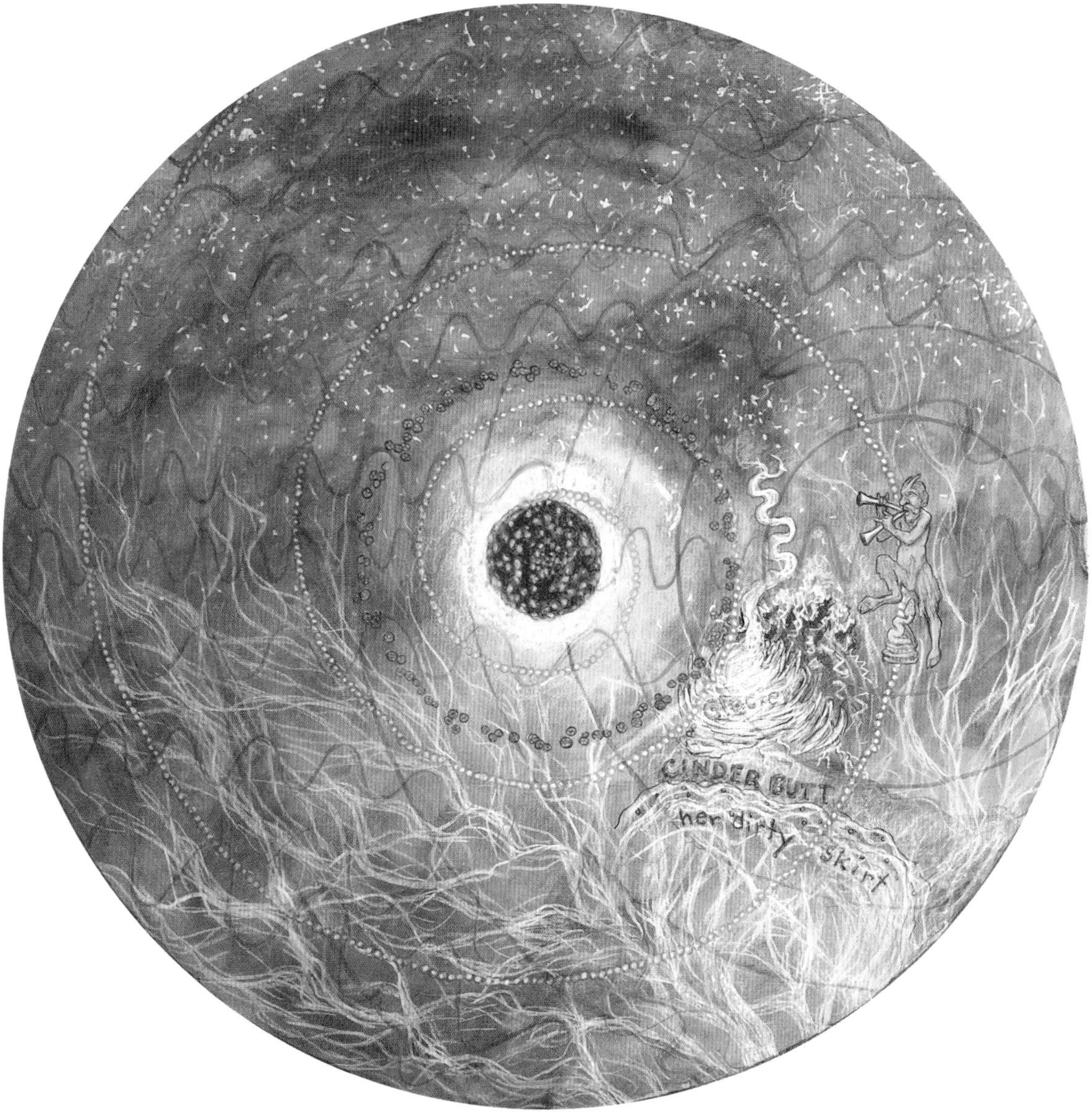
CINDER BUTT
her dirty skirt

Gaia / Cosmos

At the heart of the conscious cosmos
Life is messy,
She cannot be defined
She cannot be contained
Cinder Butt sits in the dirt
the mud of melting glaciers
on the hem of her skirt

She hears the music of the haunted
spheres
Pan piping to awaken the Cosmic Egg.
Play on, Piper, let your wild voice be
heard
For She is the Song, for She is All—
Let it in, let it go, and be loved.

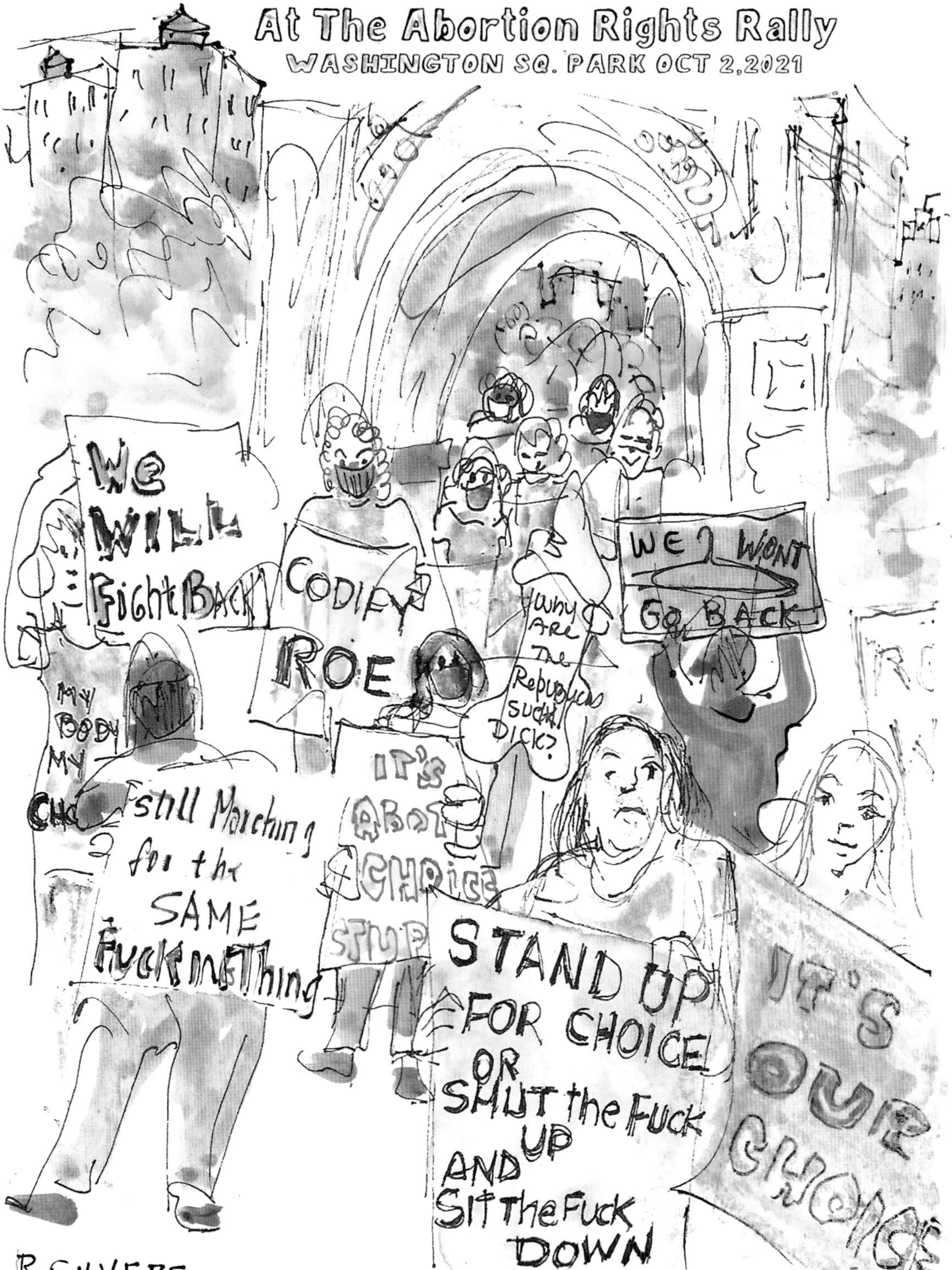
At The Abortion Rights Rally
WASHINGTON SQ. PARK OCT 2,2021
WE WILL FIGHT BACK
CODIFY ROE
WE WONT GO BACK
WHY ARE THE REPUBLICANS SUCH DICKS?
MY BODY MY CHO
Still Marching for the SAME Fucking Thing
IT'S ABORT CHOICE STUP
STAND UP FOR CHOICE OR SHUT the FUCK UP AND SIT The Fuck DOWN
IT'S OUR CHOICE
R. SILVERS

At The Abortion Rights Rally

WASHINGTON SQ. PARK, OCT 2, 2021

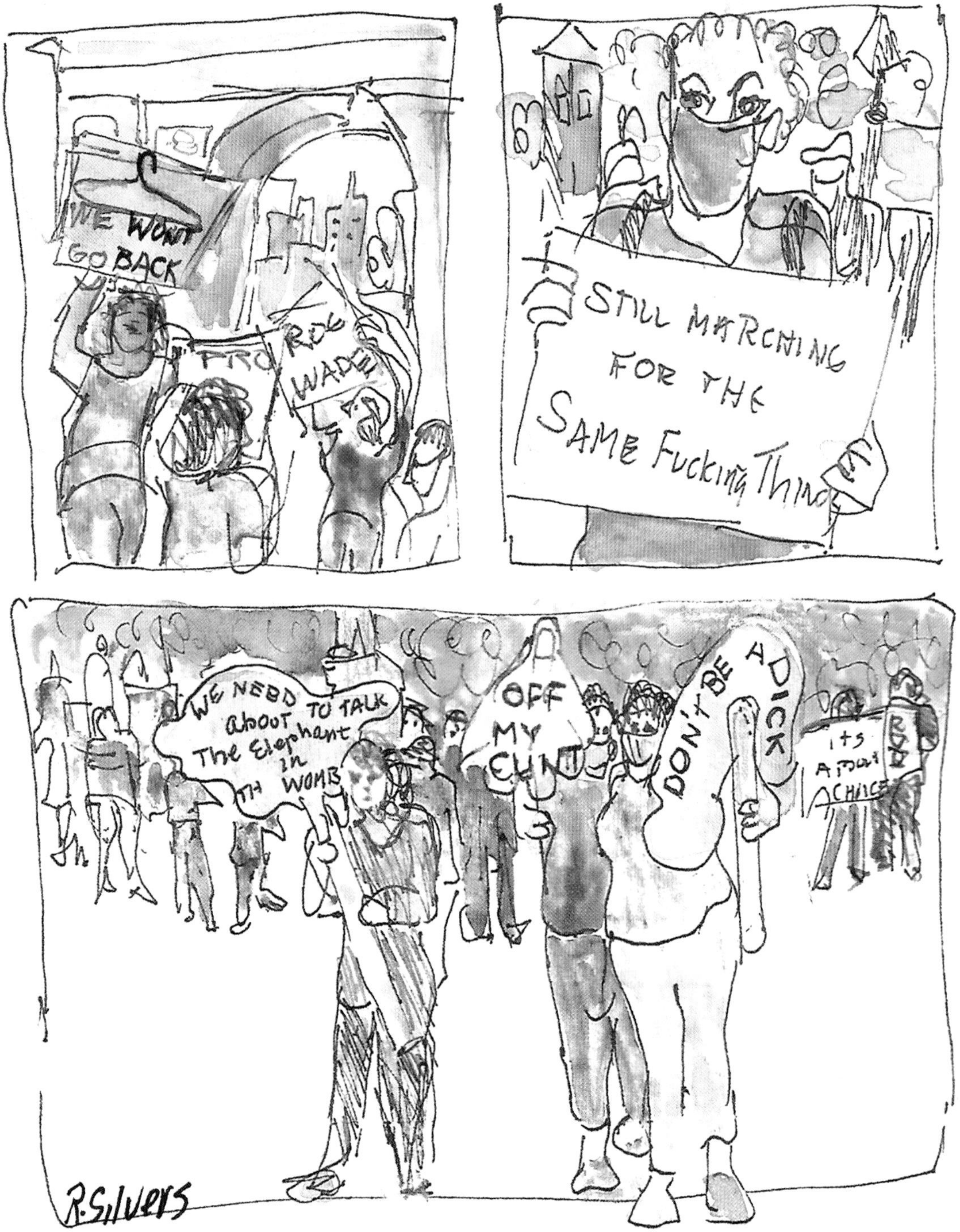

WE WONT GO BACK
PRO
ROE WADE
STILL MARCHING FOR THE SAME FUCKING THING
WE NEED TO TALK about The Elephant in TH WOMB
OFF MY CUNT
DON'T BE A DICK
its ABOUT A CHOICE
R. Silvers

Seen at the Abortion Rights Rally

WASHINGTON SQ. PARK OCT 2 2021

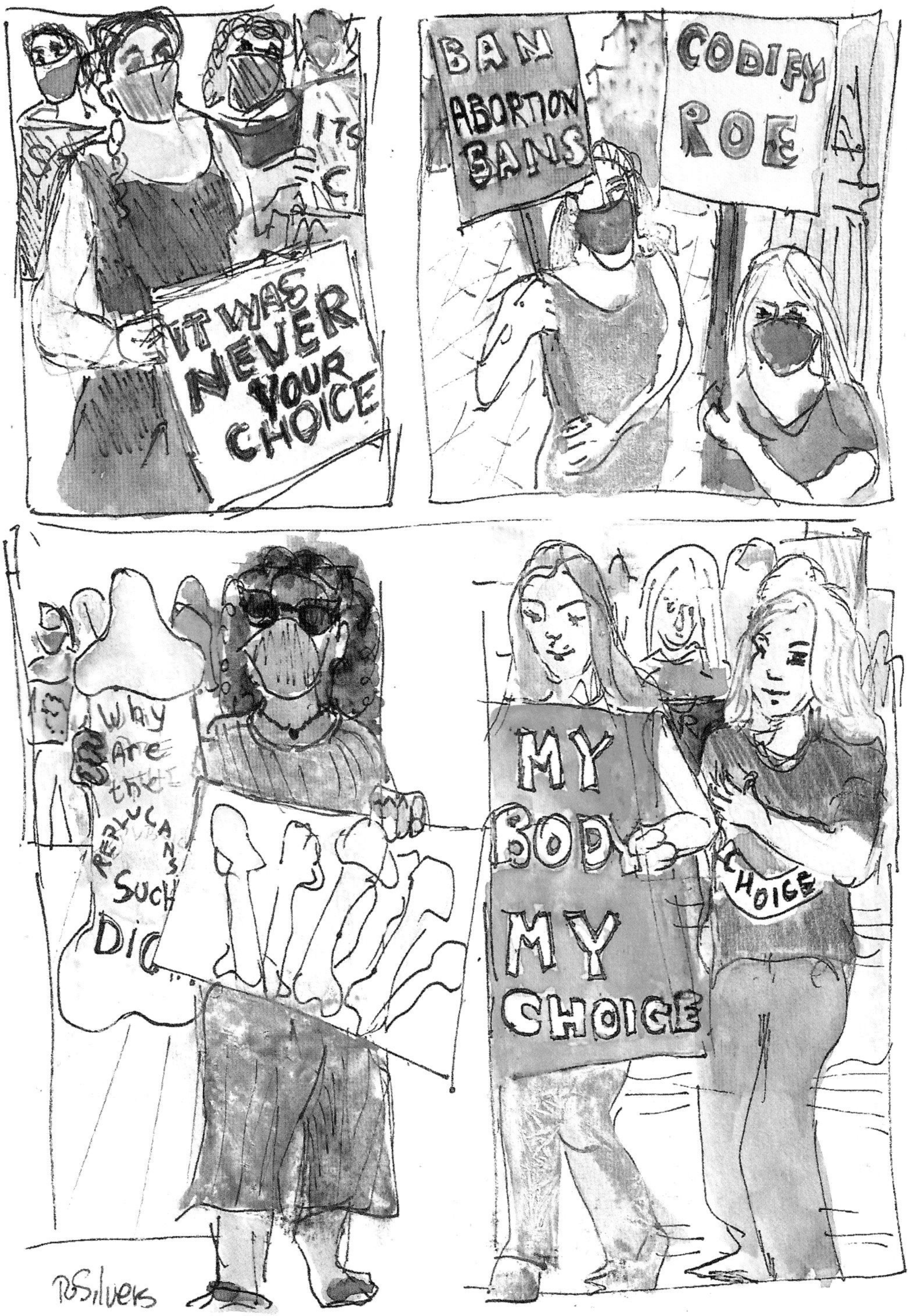
ITS
IT WAS NEVER YOUR CHOICE
BAN ABORTION BANS
CODIFY ROE
Why Are the
REPLUCANS
SUCH
DIC
MY BOD
MY CHOICE
CHOICE
RSilvers

MEET THE CREEPS

Brett Kavanaugh
Had a tantrum and cried at his SCOTUS hearing after multiple women accused him of sexual assault & a college roommate described him as a "black out drunk." Believes Catholic adoption agencies can reject same sex couples.

WHO STRIPPED AWAY OUR ABORTION RIGHTS

Samuel Alito
Claims women's rights derive from the 13th century, when women were kept illiterate, were hburned at the stake if outspoken, could be legally beaten & raped by their husbands & the earth was flat.

Clarence Thomas
Accused the Senate of trying to lynch him in order to cover up his sexual harassment of an employee & his obsession with pornography. Married to a women who supports the violent overthrow of the US government.

Neil Gorsuch
Preppy classmate of Kavanaugh. Considers the Constitution, with no mention of slavery or abortion, perfect – except for the separation of church & state. Doesn't seem to give a fu*k about women, since they're not mentioned in the Constitution, either.

Amy Coney Barrett
Believes her law career will build "The Kingdom of God," where even a child in a high-risk pregnancy, raped by her father, living in poverty, would be forced to endure the dangers of childbirth & then the trauma of giving up the baby instead of having a safe, legal abortion.

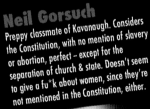

A MESSAGE FROM THE GUERRILLA GIRLS

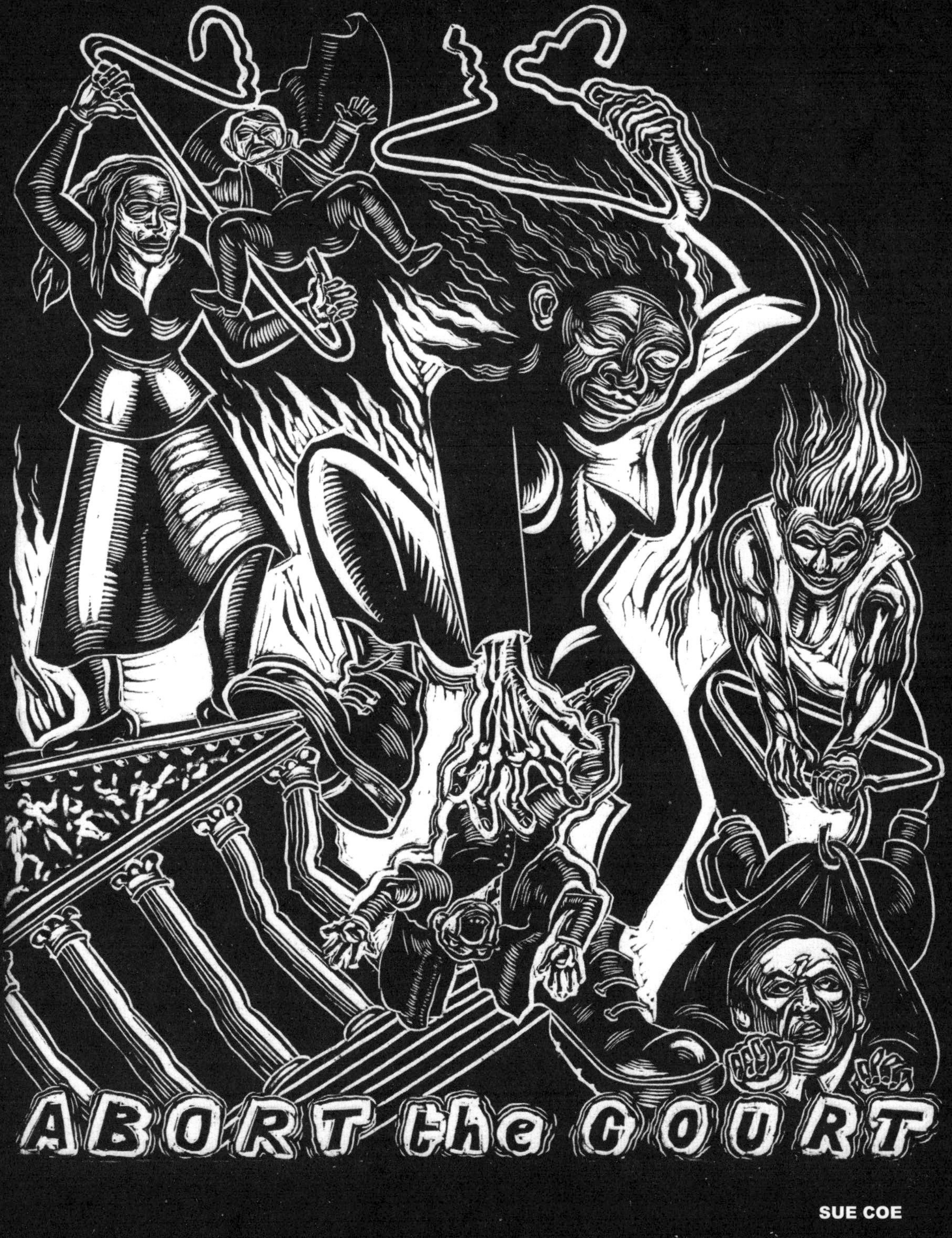
ABORT the COURT

SUE COE

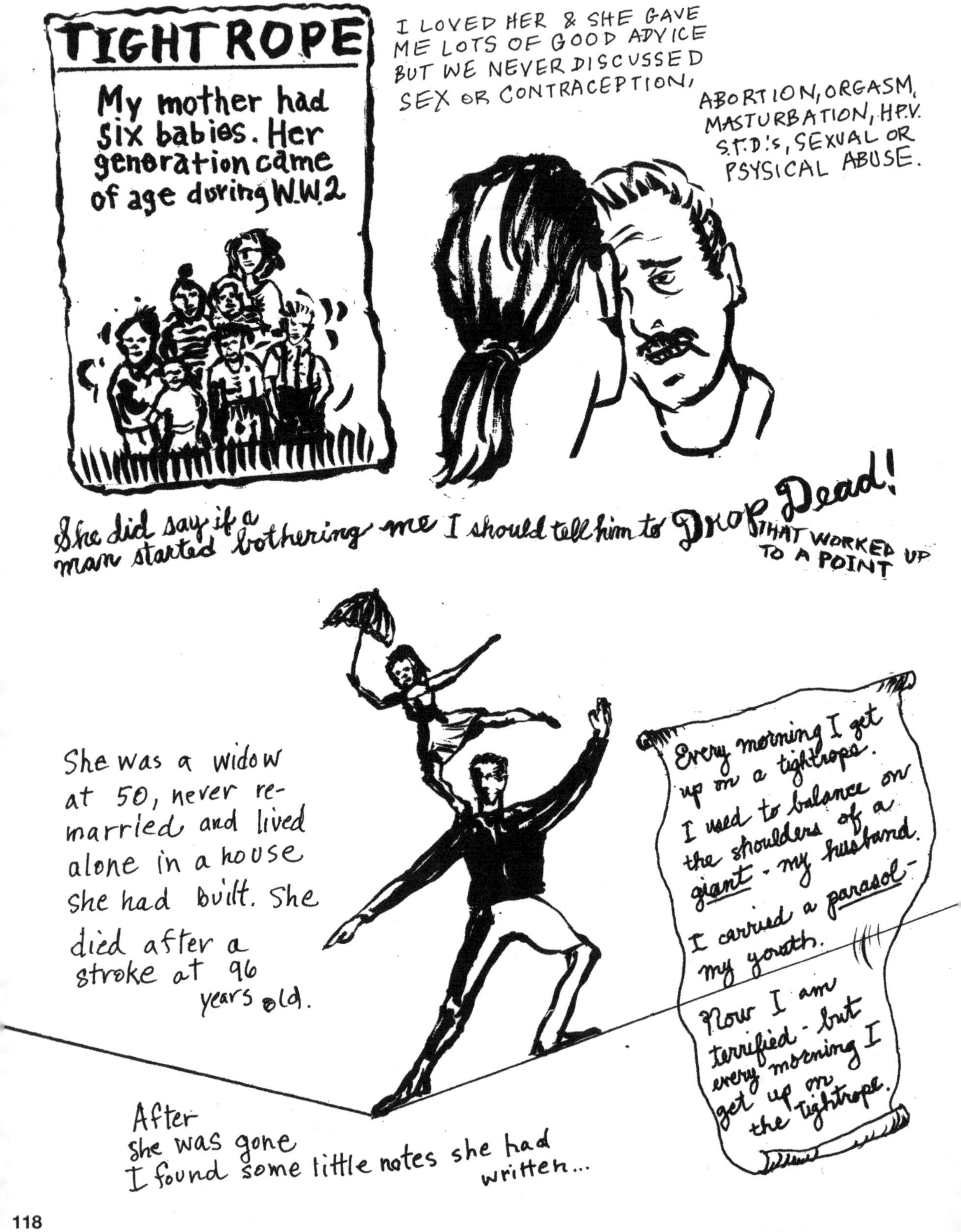

TIGHTROPE
My mother had six babies. Her generation came of age during W.W.2
I LOVED HER & SHE GAVE ME LOTS OF GOOD ADVICE BUT WE NEVER DISCUSSED SEX OR CONTRACEPTION,
ABORTION, ORGASM, MASTURBATION, H.P.V. S.T.D.'s, SEXUAL OR PSYSICAL ABUSE.
She did say if a man started bothering me I should tell him to Drop Dead!
THAT WORKED UP TO A POINT
She was a widow at 50, never re-married and lived alone in a house she had built. She died after a stroke at 96 years old.
Every morning I get up on a tightrope. I used to balance on the shoulders of a giant - my husband. I carried a parasol - my youth. Now I am terrified - but every morning I get up on the tightrope.
After she was gone I found some little notes she had written...

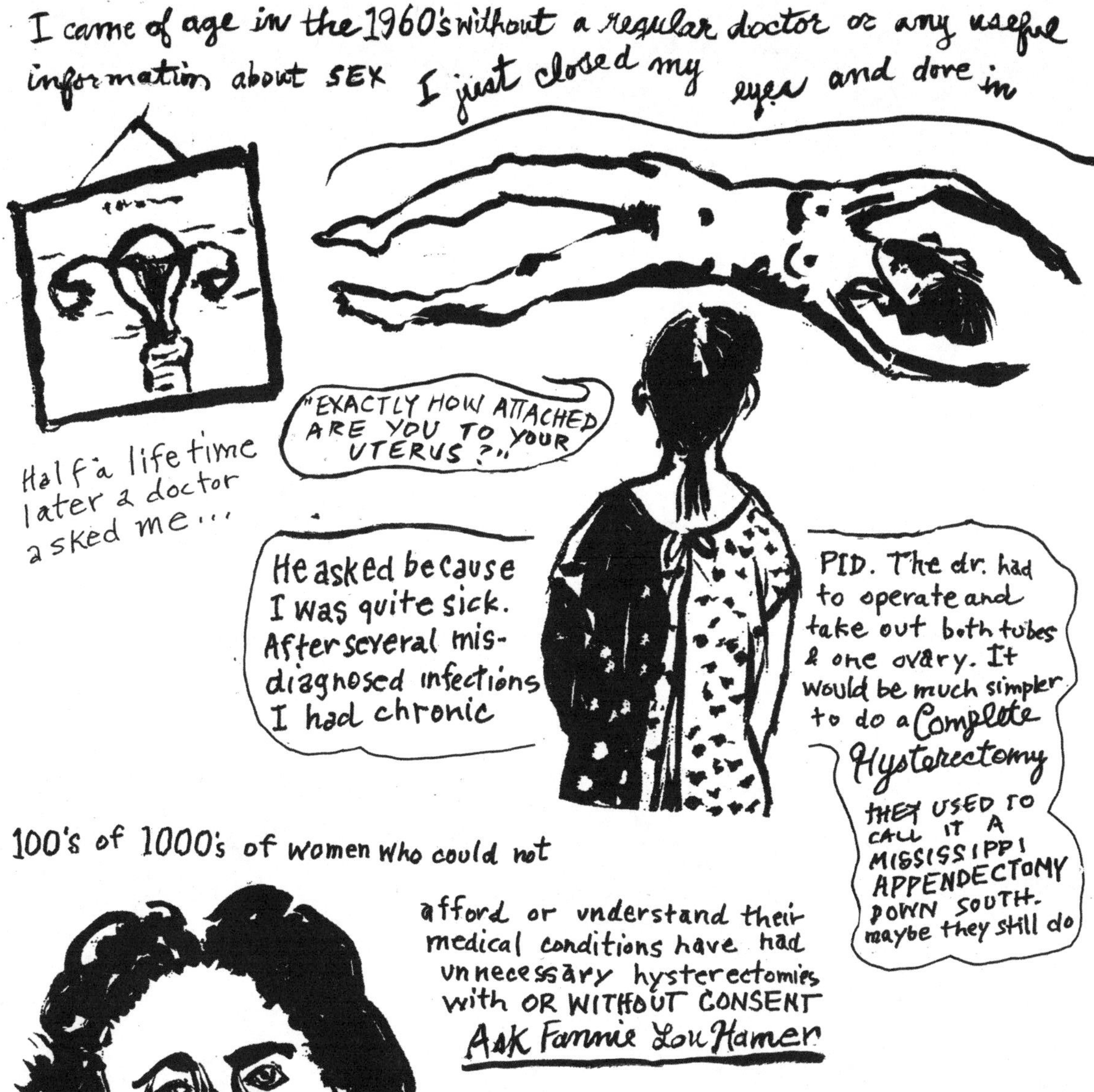
I came of age in the 1960's without a regular doctor or any useful information about SEX
I just closed my eyes and dove in
Half a life time later a doctor asked me...
"EXACTLY HOW ATTACHED ARE YOU TO YOUR UTERUS?"
He asked because I was quite sick. After several mis-diagnosed infections I had chronic
PID. The dr. had to operate and take out both tubes & one ovary. It would be much simpler to do a Complete Hysterectomy
THEY USED TO CALL IT A MISSISSIPPI APPENDECTOMY DOWN SOUTH. maybe they still do
100's of 1000's of women who could not
afford or understand their medical conditions have had unnecessary hysterectomies with OR WITHOUT CONSENT
Ask Fannie Lou Hamer

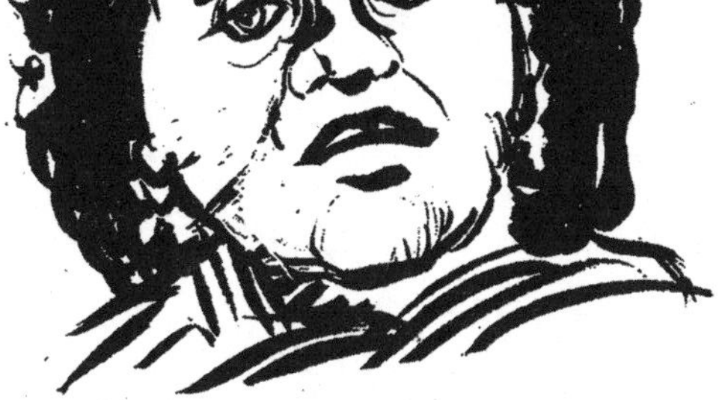

I was fond of my uterus and I was very lucky.
My doctor knew how to fix what was wrong
and I had a job with health insurance to pay for it.
I was given enough information in time to make
my own medical decision about my body.
I can't rely on permission from the government,
the state, the court. It's an ongoing battle.

Help others if you can:
apiaryps.org or donations4abortion.com/funds-by-state

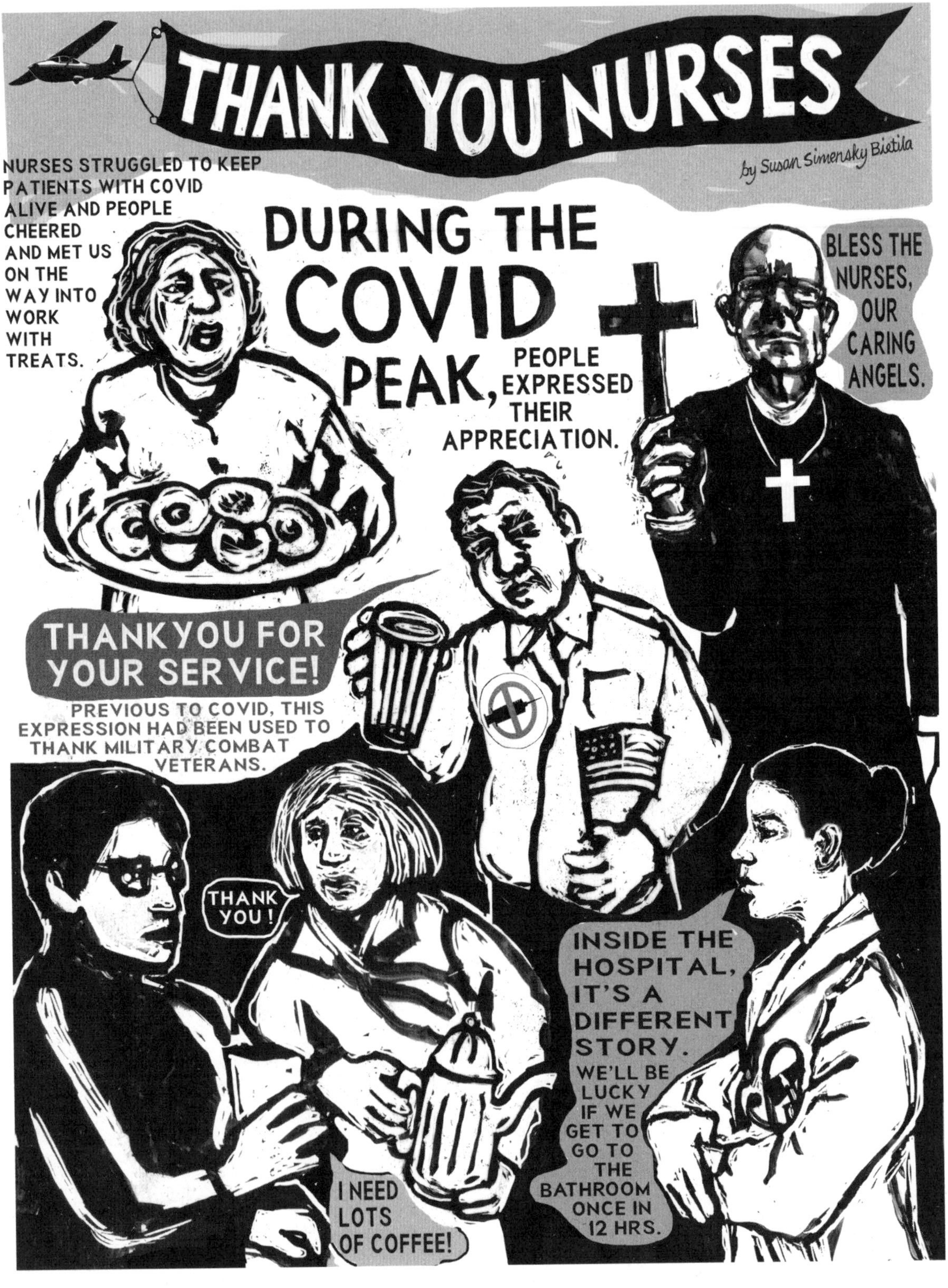
THANK YOU NURSES
by Susan Simensky Bietila
NURSES STRUGGLED TO KEEP PATIENTS WITH COVID ALIVE AND PEOPLE CHEERED AND MET US ON THE WAY INTO WORK WITH TREATS.
DURING THE COVID PEAK, PEOPLE EXPRESSED THEIR APPRECIATION.
BLESS THE NURSES, OUR CARING ANGELS.
THANK YOU FOR YOUR SERVICE!
PREVIOUS TO COVID, THIS EXPRESSION HAD BEEN USED TO THANK MILITARY COMBAT VETERANS.
THANK YOU!
INSIDE THE HOSPITAL, IT'S A DIFFERENT STORY.
WE'LL BE LUCKY IF WE GET TO GO TO THE BATHROOM ONCE IN 12 HRS.
I NEED LOTS OF COFFEE!

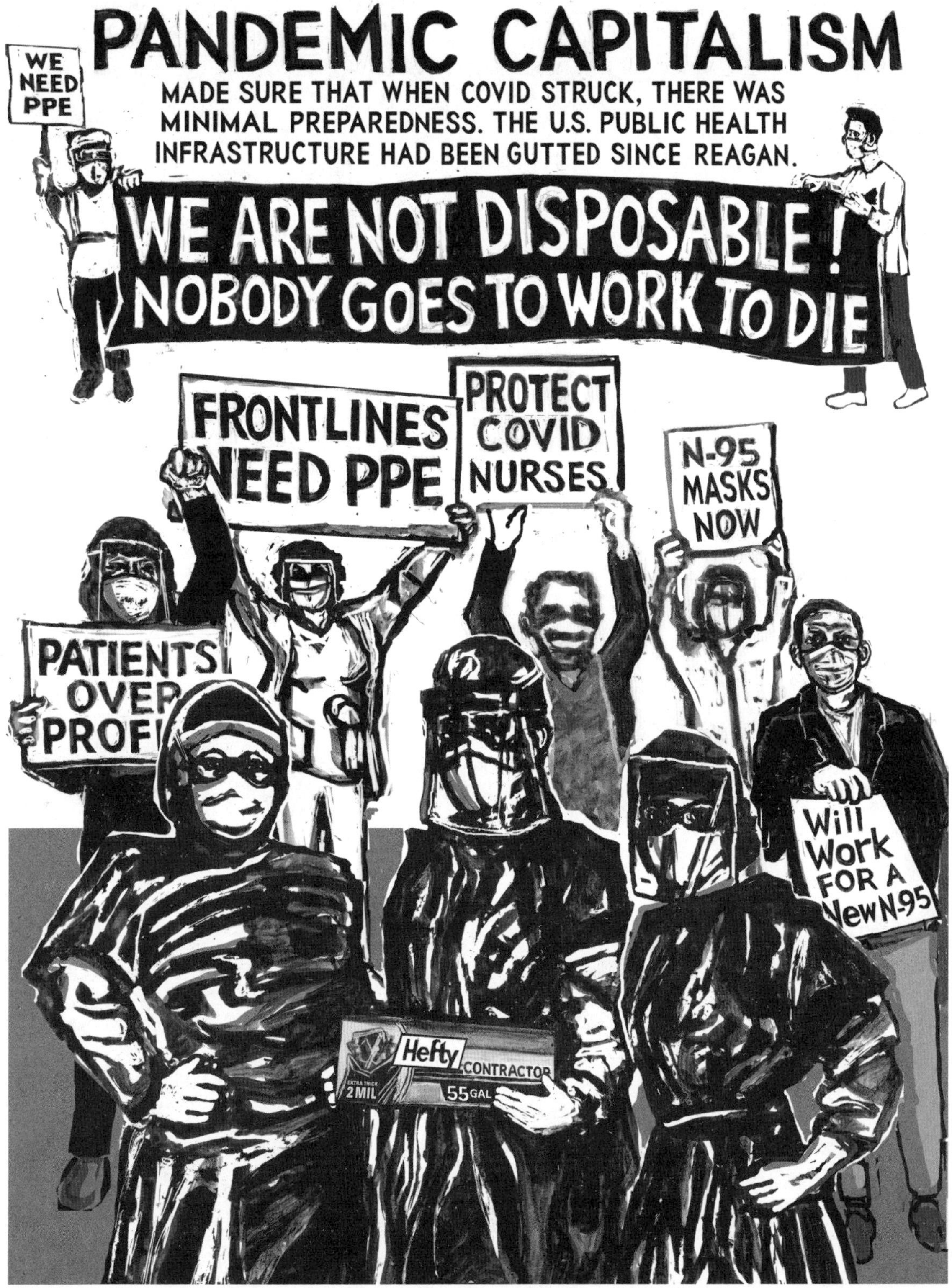
PANDEMIC CAPITALISM
MADE SURE THAT WHEN COVID STRUCK, THERE WAS MINIMAL PREPAREDNESS. THE U.S. PUBLIC HEALTH INFRASTRUCTURE HAD BEEN GUTTED SINCE REAGAN.
WE NEED PPE
WE ARE NOT DISPOSABLE! NOBODY GOES TO WORK TO DIE
FRONTLINES NEED PPE
PROTECT COVID NURSES
N-95 MASKS NOW
PATIENTS OVER PROFI
Will Work FOR A New N-95
Hefty CONTRACTOR
EXTRA THICK 2 MIL
55 GAL

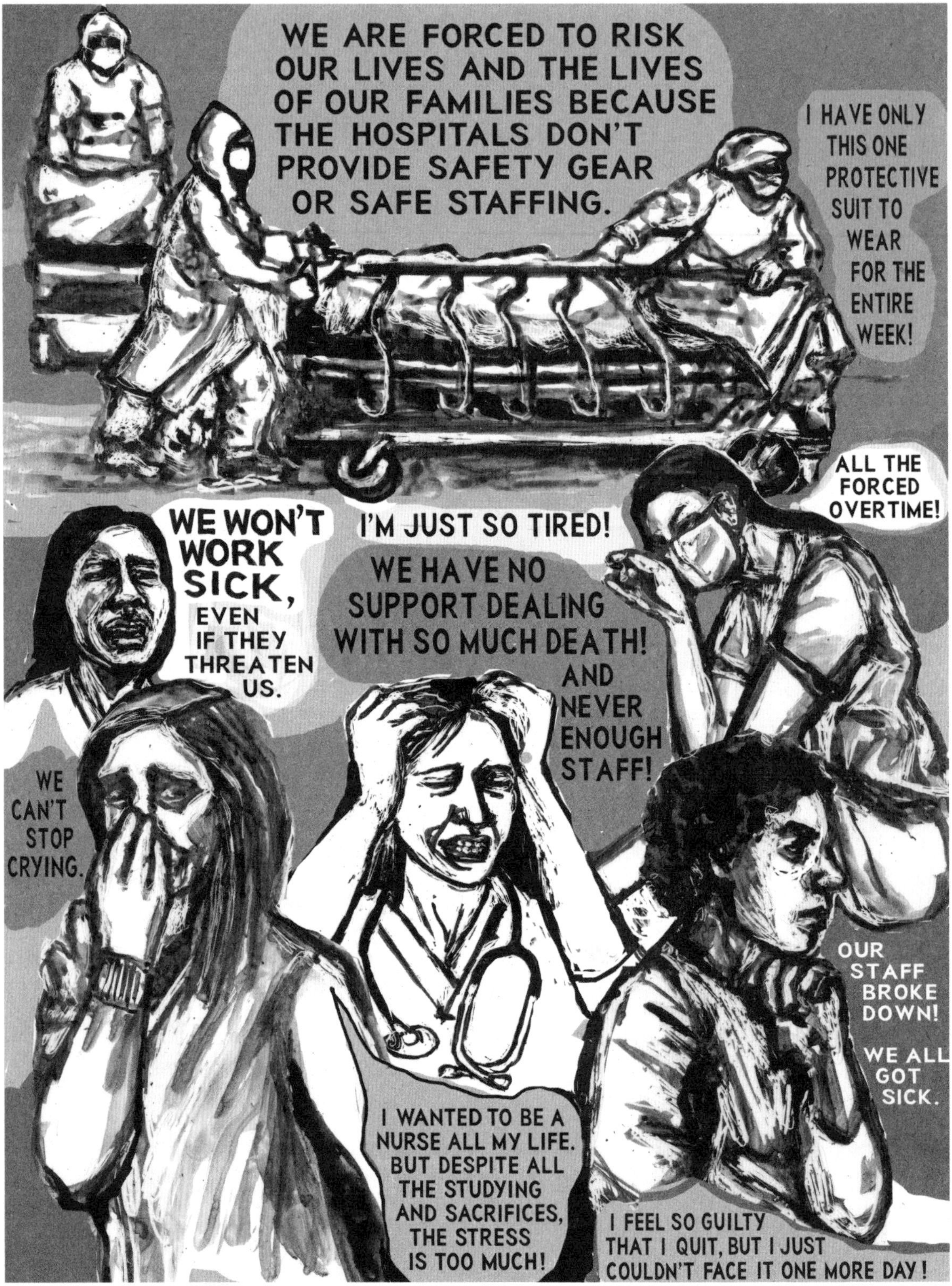

WE ARE FORCED TO RISK OUR LIVES AND THE LIVES OF OUR FAMILIES BECAUSE THE HOSPITALS DON'T PROVIDE SAFETY GEAR OR SAFE STAFFING.
I HAVE ONLY THIS ONE PROTECTIVE SUIT TO WEAR FOR THE ENTIRE WEEK!
ALL THE FORCED OVERTIME!
WE WON'T WORK SICK, EVEN IF THEY THREATEN US.
I'M JUST SO TIRED!
WE HAVE NO SUPPORT DEALING WITH SO MUCH DEATH!
AND NEVER ENOUGH STAFF!
WE CAN'T STOP CRYING.
OUR STAFF BROKE DOWN!
WE ALL GOT SICK.
I WANTED TO BE A NURSE ALL MY LIFE. BUT DESPITE ALL THE STUDYING AND SACRIFICES, THE STRESS IS TOO MUCH!
I FEEL SO GUILTY THAT I QUIT, BUT I JUST COULDN'T FACE IT ONE MORE DAY!

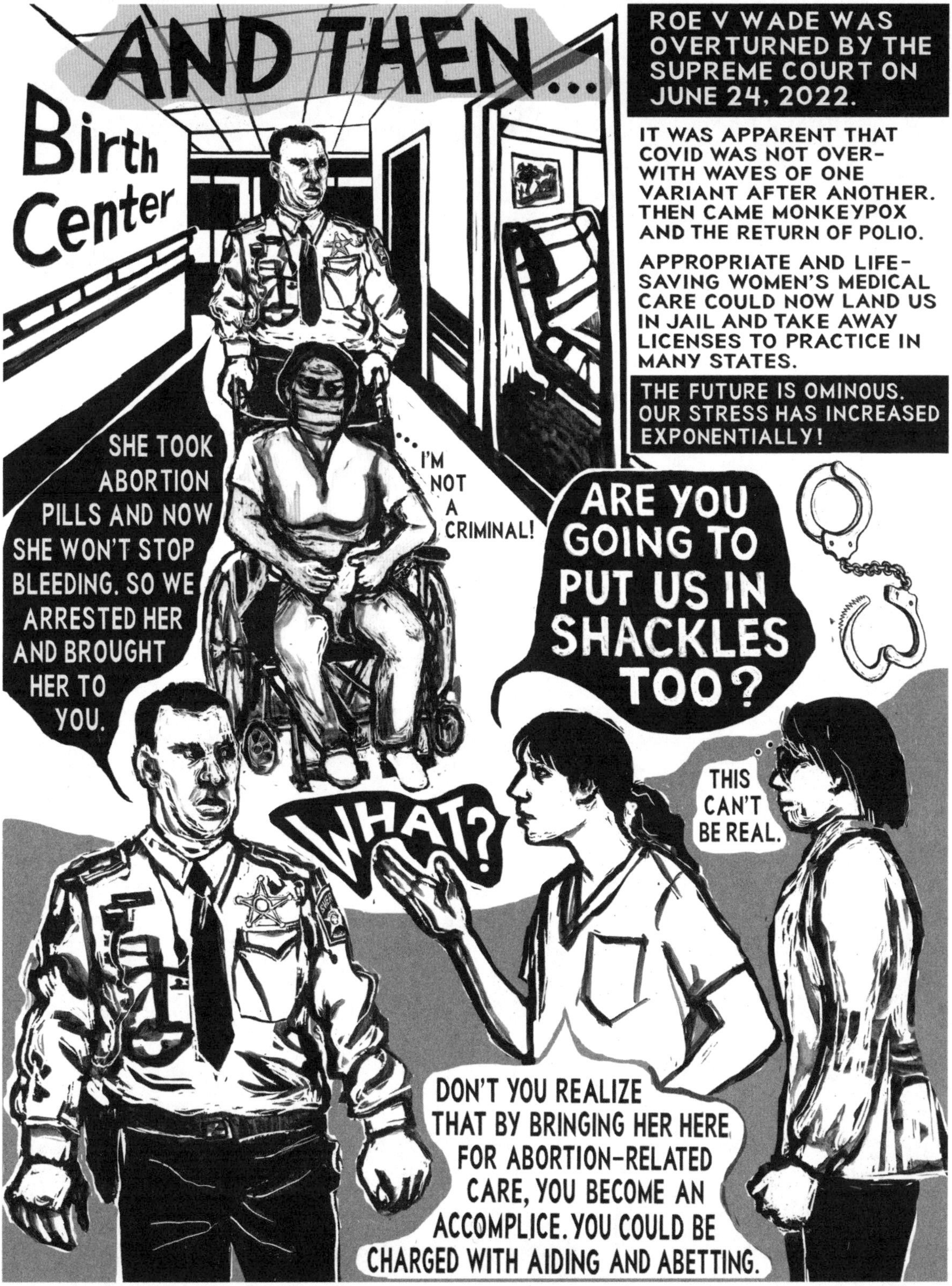
AND THEN...
Birth Center
ROE V WADE WAS OVERTURNED BY THE SUPREME COURT ON JUNE 24, 2022.
IT WAS APPARENT THAT COVID WAS NOT OVER- WITH WAVES OF ONE VARIANT AFTER ANOTHER. THEN CAME MONKEYPOX AND THE RETURN OF POLIO.
APPROPRIATE AND LIFE-SAVING WOMEN'S MEDICAL CARE COULD NOW LAND US IN JAIL AND TAKE AWAY LICENSES TO PRACTICE IN MANY STATES.
THE FUTURE IS OMINOUS. OUR STRESS HAS INCREASED EXPONENTIALLY!
SHE TOOK ABORTION PILLS AND NOW SHE WON'T STOP BLEEDING. SO WE ARRESTED HER AND BROUGHT HER TO YOU.
...I'M NOT A CRIMINAL!
ARE YOU GOING TO PUT US IN SHACKLES TOO?
WHAT?
THIS CAN'T BE REAL.
DON'T YOU REALIZE THAT BY BRINGING HER HERE FOR ABORTION-RELATED CARE, YOU BECOME AN ACCOMPLICE. YOU COULD BE CHARGED WITH AIDING AND ABETTING.

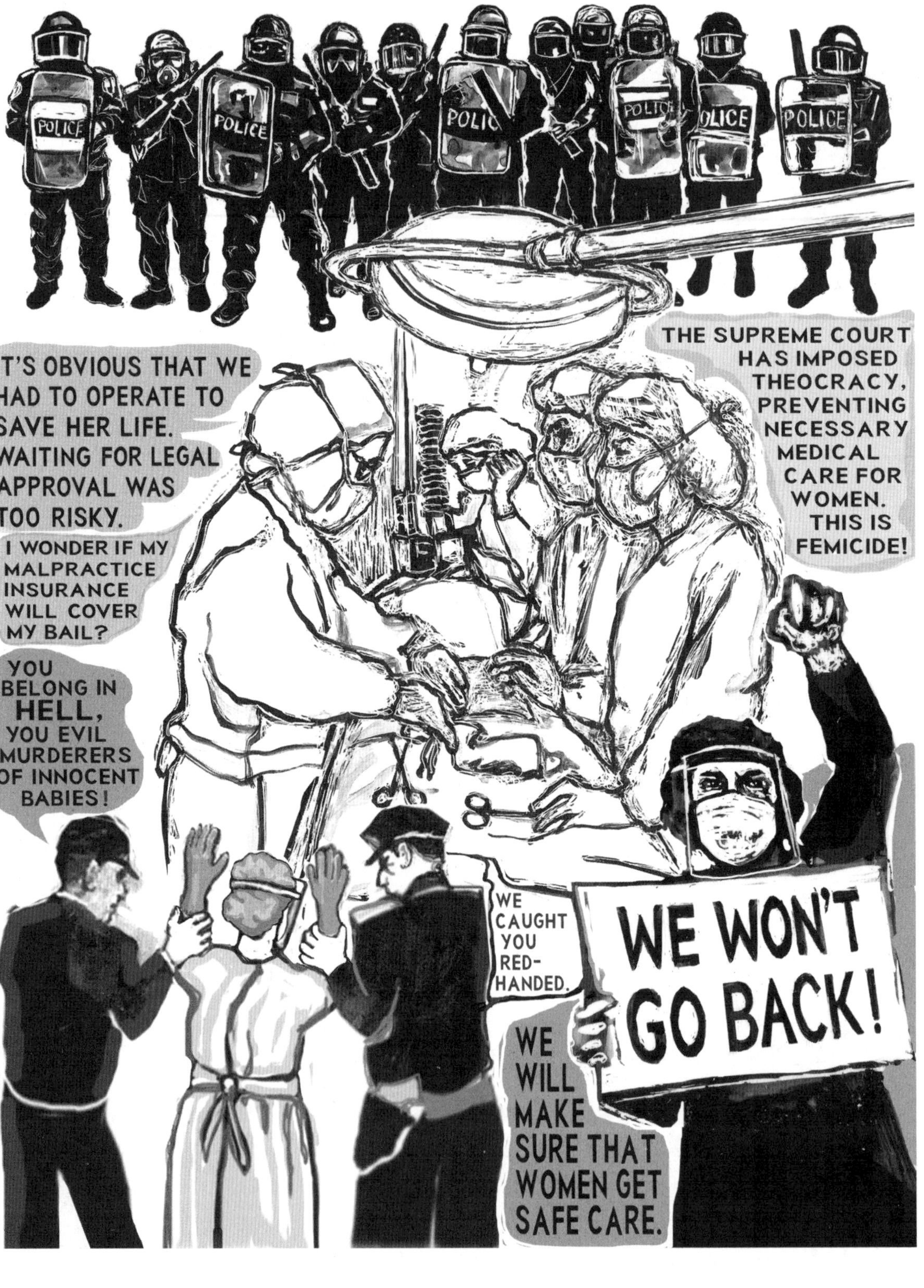
POLICE
POLICE
POLICE
POLICE
POLICE
POLICE
IT'S OBVIOUS THAT WE HAD TO OPERATE TO SAVE HER LIFE. WAITING FOR LEGAL APPROVAL WAS TOO RISKY.
I WONDER IF MY MALPRACTICE INSURANCE WILL COVER MY BAIL?
THE SUPREME COURT HAS IMPOSED THEOCRACY, PREVENTING NECESSARY MEDICAL CARE FOR WOMEN. THIS IS FEMICIDE!
YOU BELONG IN HELL, YOU EVIL MURDERERS OF INNOCENT BABIES!
WE CAUGHT YOU RED-HANDED.
WE WON'T GO BACK!
WE WILL MAKE SURE THAT WOMEN GET SAFE CARE.

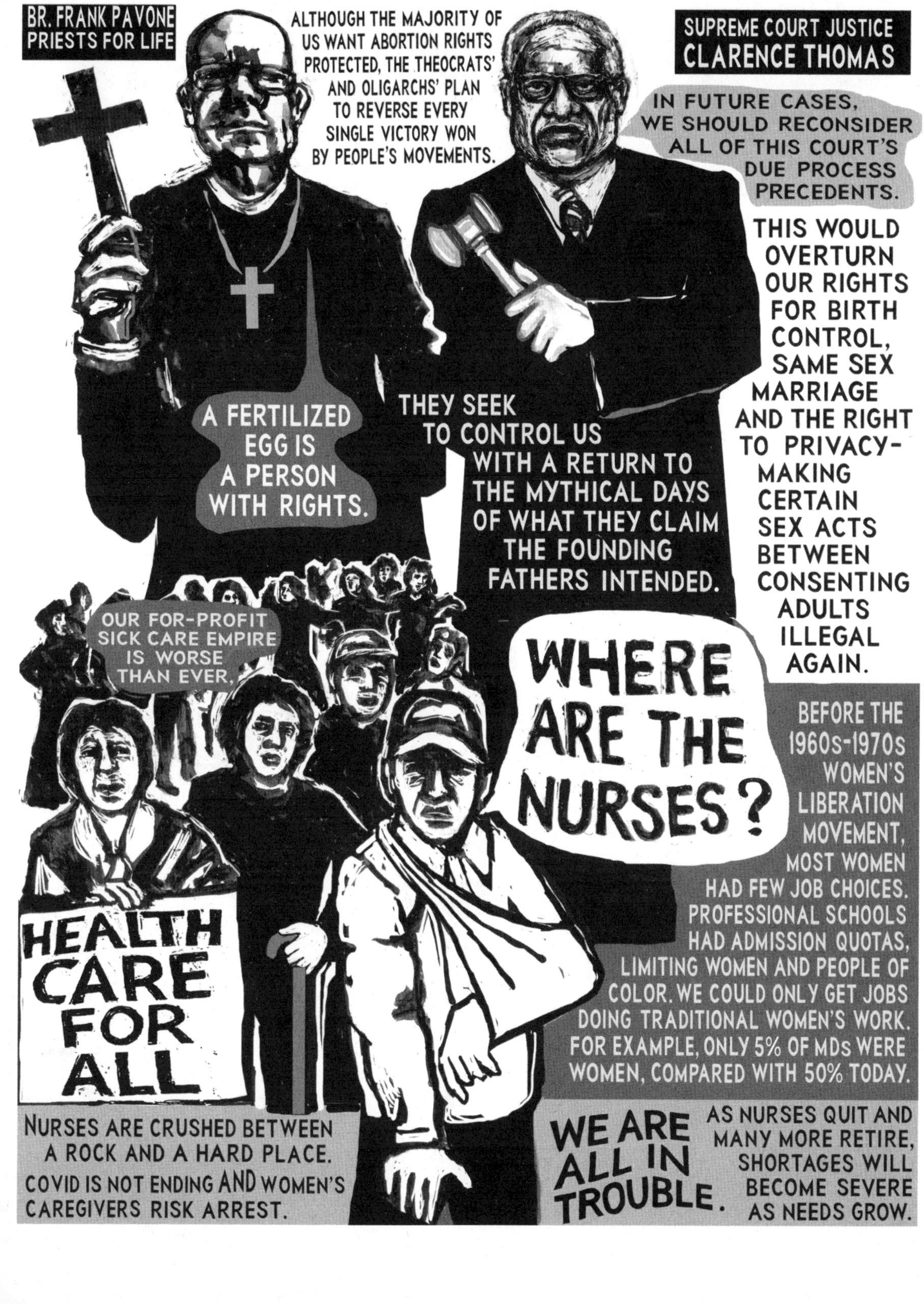
BR. FRANK PAVONE
PRIESTS FOR LIFE
ALTHOUGH THE MAJORITY OF US WANT ABORTION RIGHTS PROTECTED, THE THEOCRATS' AND OLIGARCHS' PLAN TO REVERSE EVERY SINGLE VICTORY WON BY PEOPLE'S MOVEMENTS.
SUPREME COURT JUSTICE
CLARENCE THOMAS
IN FUTURE CASES, WE SHOULD RECONSIDER ALL OF THIS COURT'S DUE PROCESS PRECEDENTS.
THIS WOULD OVERTURN OUR RIGHTS FOR BIRTH CONTROL, SAME SEX MARRIAGE AND THE RIGHT TO PRIVACY- MAKING CERTAIN SEX ACTS BETWEEN CONSENTING ADULTS ILLEGAL AGAIN.
A FERTILIZED EGG IS A PERSON WITH RIGHTS.
THEY SEEK TO CONTROL US WITH A RETURN TO THE MYTHICAL DAYS OF WHAT THEY CLAIM THE FOUNDING FATHERS INTENDED.
OUR FOR-PROFIT SICK CARE EMPIRE IS WORSE THAN EVER,
WHERE ARE THE NURSES?
BEFORE THE 1960s-1970s WOMEN'S LIBERATION MOVEMENT, MOST WOMEN HAD FEW JOB CHOICES. PROFESSIONAL SCHOOLS HAD ADMISSION QUOTAS, LIMITING WOMEN AND PEOPLE OF COLOR. WE COULD ONLY GET JOBS DOING TRADITIONAL WOMEN'S WORK. FOR EXAMPLE, ONLY 5% OF MDs WERE WOMEN, COMPARED WITH 50% TODAY.
HEALTH CARE FOR ALL
NURSES ARE CRUSHED BETWEEN A ROCK AND A HARD PLACE.
COVID IS NOT ENDING AND WOMEN'S CAREGIVERS RISK ARREST.
WE ARE ALL IN TROUBLE.
AS NURSES QUIT AND MANY MORE RETIRE, SHORTAGES WILL BECOME SEVERE AS NEEDS GROW.

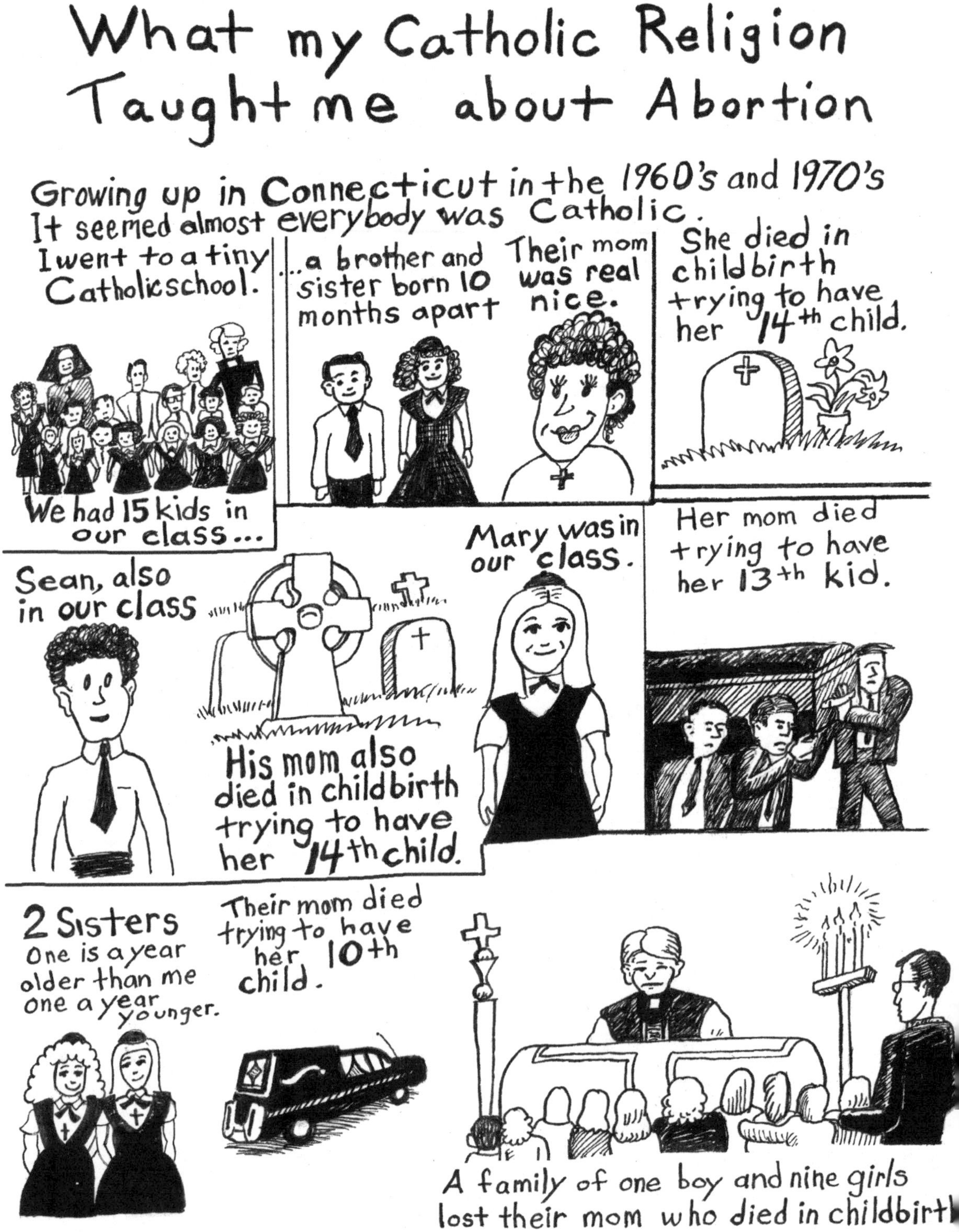
What my Catholic Religion Taught me about Abortion
Growing up in Connecticut in the 1960's and 1970's It seemed almost everybody was Catholic.
I went to a tiny Catholic school.
We had 15 kids in our class...
...a brother and sister born 10 months apart
Their mom was real nice.
She died in childbirth trying to have her 14th child.
Sean, also in our class
His mom also died in childbirth trying to have her 14th child.
Mary was in our class.
Her mom died trying to have her 13th kid.
2 Sisters
One is a year older than me one a year younger.
Their mom died trying to have her 10th child.
A family of one boy and nine girls lost their mom who died in childbirt

Tom Keough

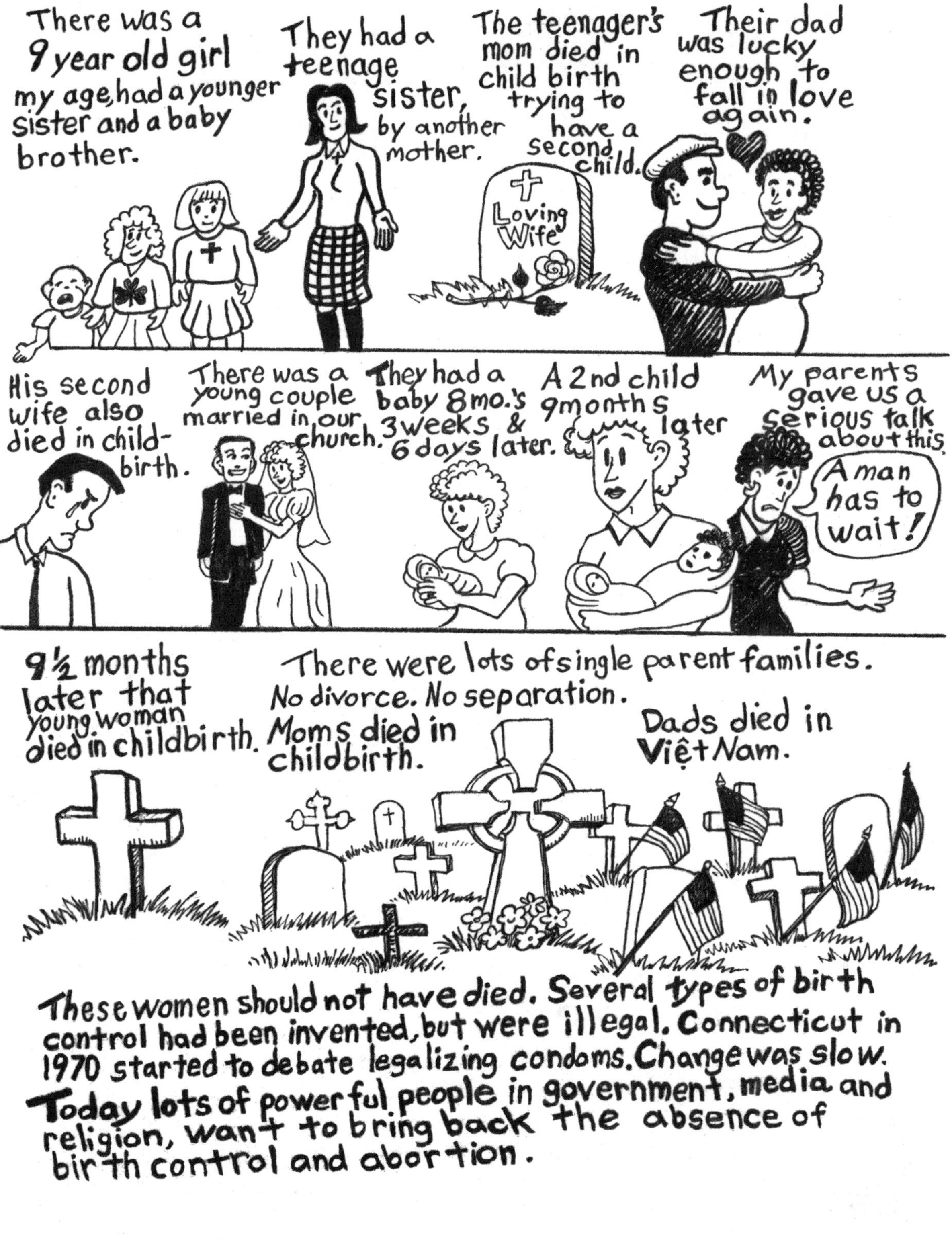
There was a 9 year old girl my age, had a younger sister and a baby brother.
They had a teenage sister, by another mother.
The teenager's mom died in child birth trying to have a second child.
Loving Wife
Their dad was lucky enough to fall in love again.
His second wife also died in child-birth.
There was a young couple married in our church.
They had a baby 8 mo.'s 3 weeks & 6 days later.
A 2nd child 9 months later
My parents gave us a serious talk about this.
A man has to wait!
9½ months later that young woman died in childbirth.
There were lots of single parent families. No divorce. No separation.
Moms died in childbirth.
Dads died in Việt Nam.
These women should not have died. Several types of birth control had been invented, but were illegal. Connecticut in 1970 started to debate legalizing condoms. Change was slow.
Today lots of powerful people in government, media and religion, want to bring back the absence of birth control and abortion.

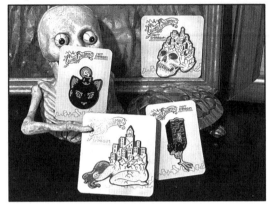

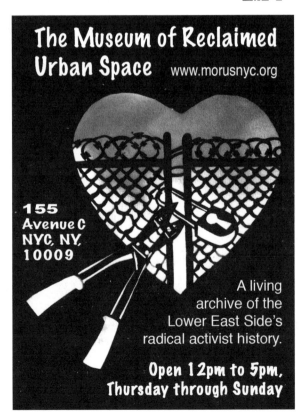

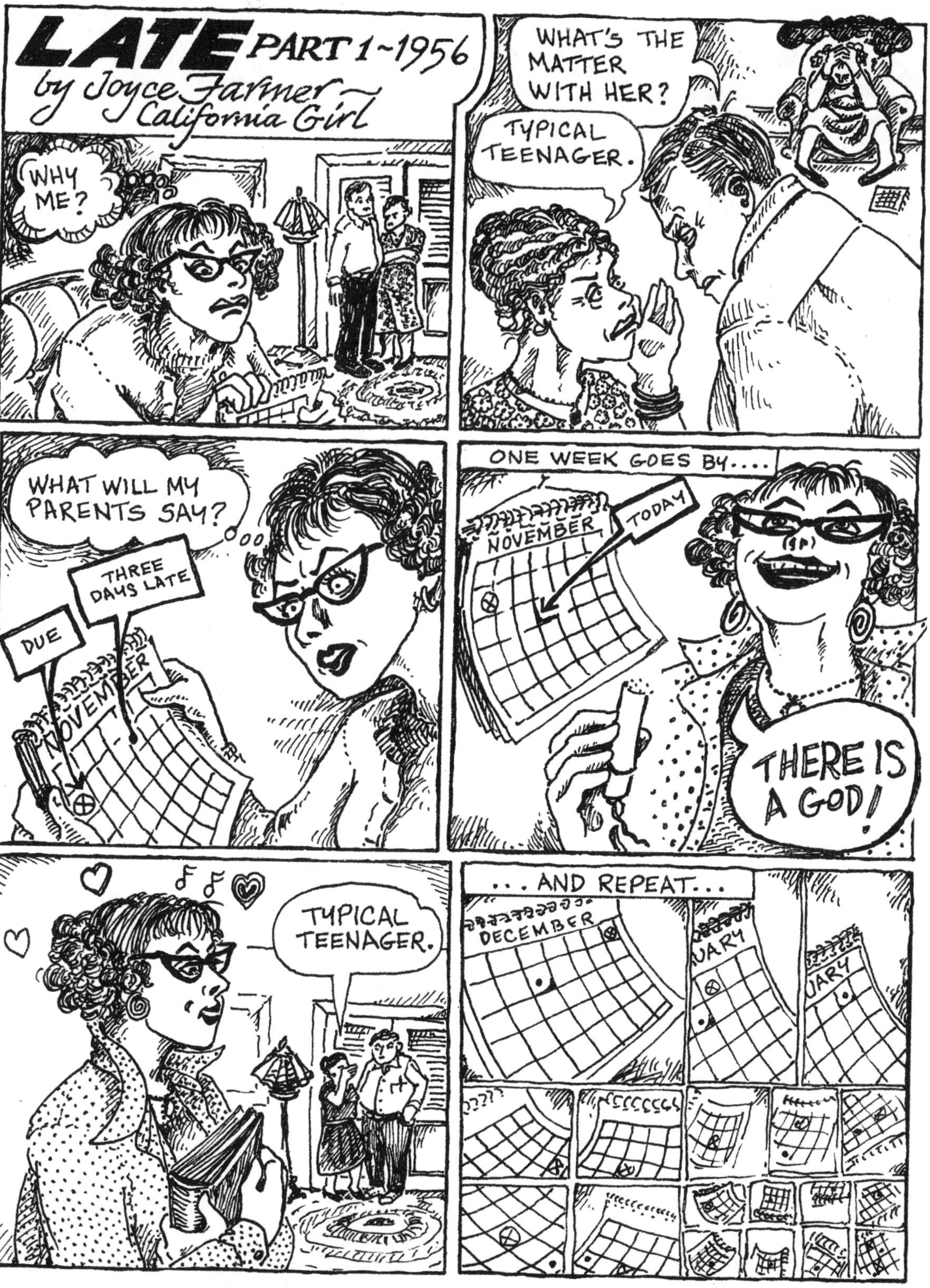

LATE PART 1~1956
by Joyce Farmer ~ California Girl
WHY ME?
WHAT'S THE MATTER WITH HER?
TYPICAL TEENAGER.
WHAT WILL MY PARENTS SAY?
THREE DAYS LATE
DUE
NOVEMBER
ONE WEEK GOES BY....
NOVEMBER
TODAY
THERE IS A GOD!
TYPICAL TEENAGER.
...AND REPEAT...
DECEMBER

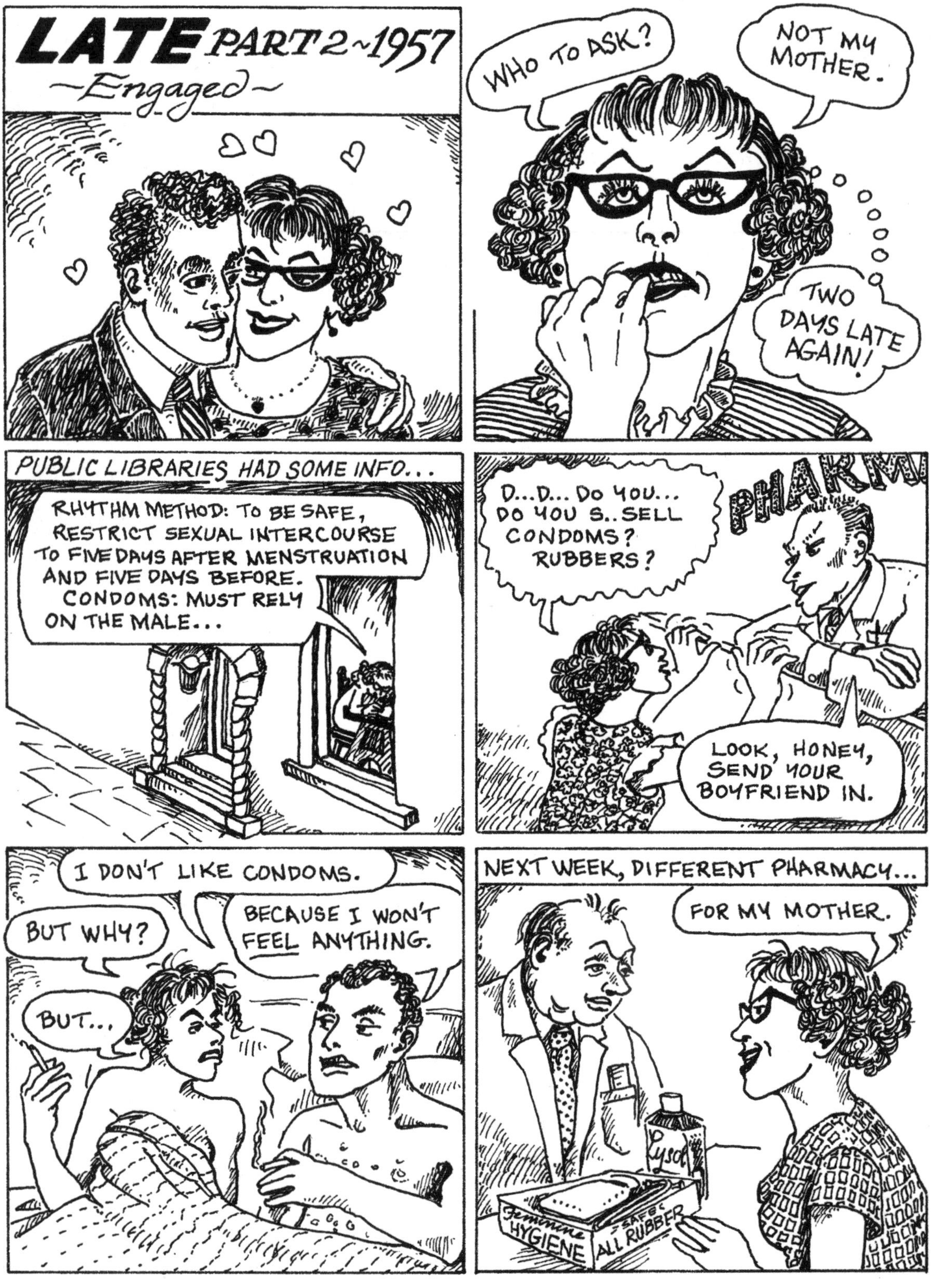
LATE PART 2 ~ 1957
~Engaged~
WHO TO ASK?
NOT MY MOTHER.
TWO DAYS LATE AGAIN!
PUBLIC LIBRARIES HAD SOME INFO...
RHYTHM METHOD: TO BE SAFE, RESTRICT SEXUAL INTERCOURSE TO FIVE DAYS AFTER MENSTRUATION AND FIVE DAYS BEFORE. CONDOMS: MUST RELY ON THE MALE...
D...D... DO YOU... DO YOU S..SELL CONDOMS? RUBBERS?
PHARM
LOOK, HONEY, SEND YOUR BOYFRIEND IN.
I DON'T LIKE CONDOMS.
BUT WHY?
BECAUSE I WON'T FEEL ANYTHING.
BUT...
NEXT WEEK, DIFFERENT PHARMACY...
FOR MY MOTHER.
Lysol
Feminine HYGIENE
SAFE ALL RUBBER

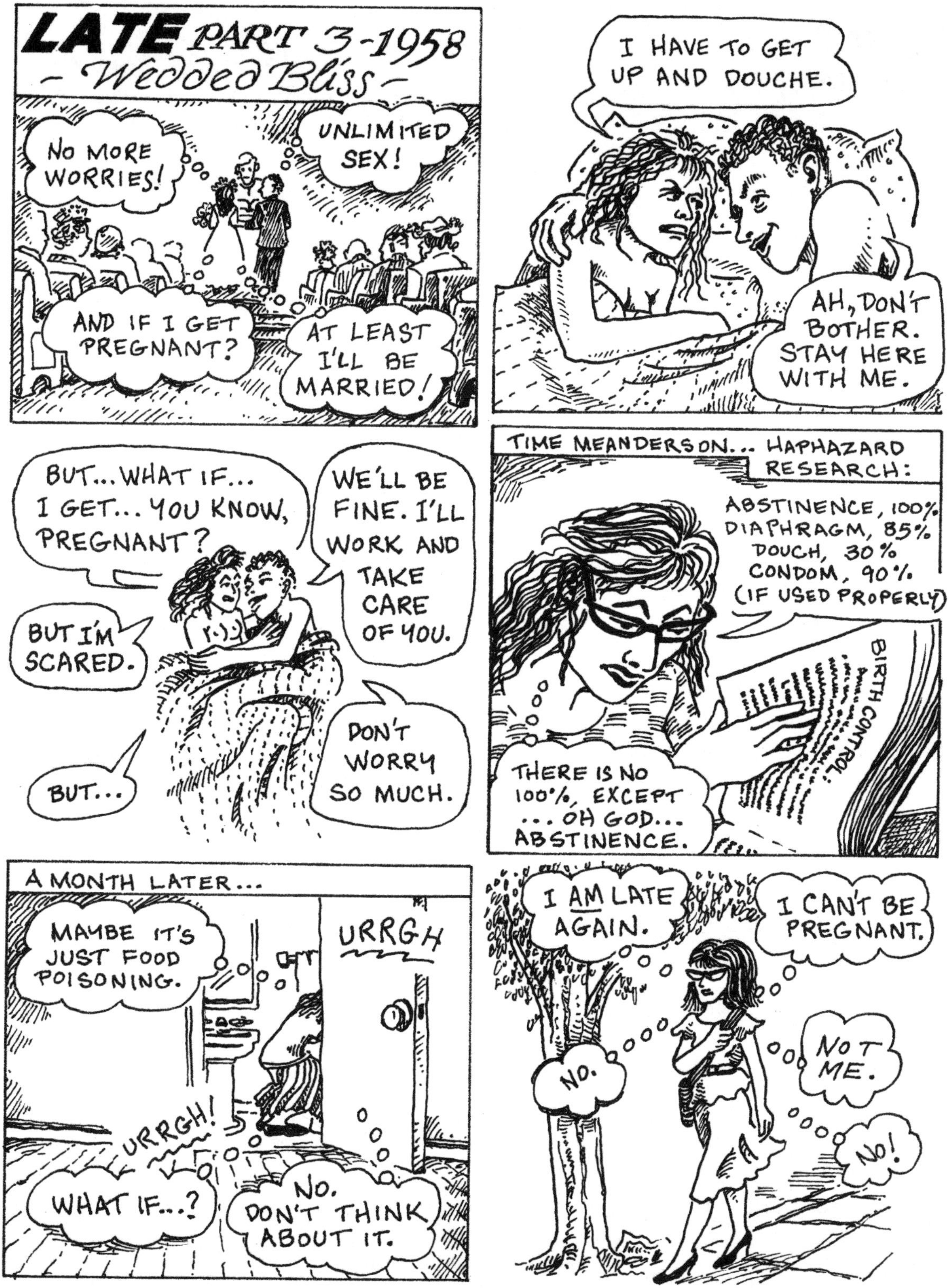
LATE PART 3-1958
- Wedded Bliss -
NO MORE WORRIES!
UNLIMITED SEX!
AND IF I GET PREGNANT?
AT LEAST I'LL BE MARRIED!
I HAVE TO GET UP AND DOUCHE.
AH, DON'T BOTHER. STAY HERE WITH ME.
BUT... WHAT IF... I GET... YOU KNOW, PREGNANT?
WE'LL BE FINE. I'LL WORK AND TAKE CARE OF YOU.
BUT I'M SCARED.
BUT...
DON'T WORRY SO MUCH.
TIME MEANDERS ON... HAPHAZARD RESEARCH:
ABSTINENCE, 100%
DIAPHRAGM, 85%
DOUCH, 30%
CONDOM, 90%
(IF USED PROPERLY)
BIRTH CONTROL
THERE IS NO 100%, EXCEPT ... OH GOD... ABSTINENCE.
A MONTH LATER...
MAYBE IT'S JUST FOOD POISONING.
URRGH
URRGH!
WHAT IF...?
NO. DON'T THINK ABOUT IT.
I AM LATE AGAIN.
I CAN'T BE PREGNANT.
NO.
NOT ME.
NO!

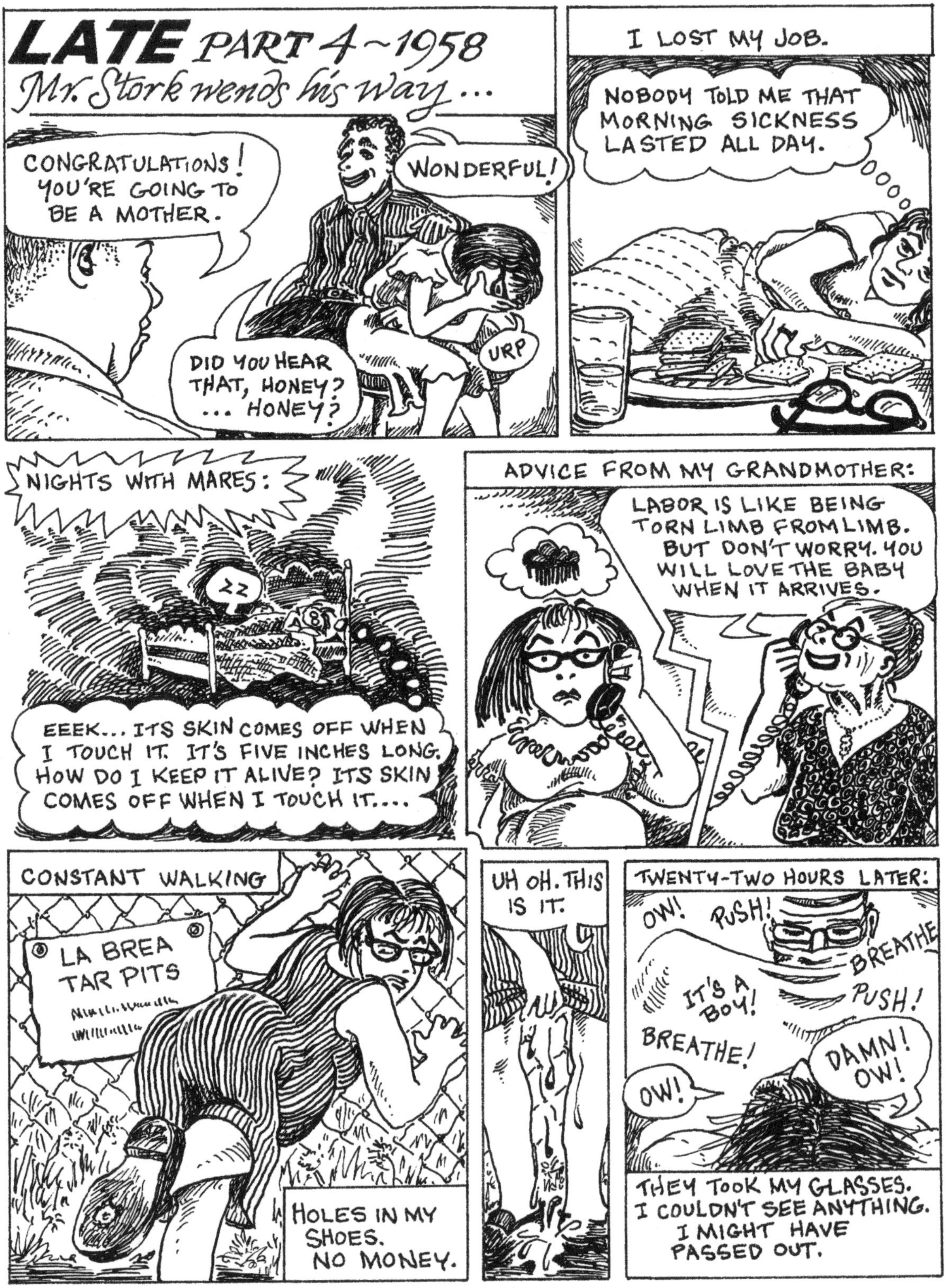
LATE PART 4 ~ 1958
Mr. Stork wends his way...
CONGRATULATIONS! YOU'RE GOING TO BE A MOTHER.
WONDERFUL!
DID YOU HEAR THAT, HONEY? ... HONEY?
URP
I LOST MY JOB.
NOBODY TOLD ME THAT MORNING SICKNESS LASTED ALL DAY.
NIGHTS WITH MARES:
ZZ
EEEK... ITS SKIN COMES OFF WHEN I TOUCH IT. IT'S FIVE INCHES LONG. HOW DO I KEEP IT ALIVE? ITS SKIN COMES OFF WHEN I TOUCH IT....
ADVICE FROM MY GRANDMOTHER:
LABOR IS LIKE BEING TORN LIMB FROM LIMB. BUT DON'T WORRY. YOU WILL LOVE THE BABY WHEN IT ARRIVES.
CONSTANT WALKING
LA BREA TAR PITS
HOLES IN MY SHOES. NO MONEY.
UH OH. THIS IS IT.
TWENTY-TWO HOURS LATER:
OW!
PUSH!
BREATHE
IT'S A BOY!
PUSH!
BREATHE!
DAMN! OW!
OW!
THEY TOOK MY GLASSES. I COULDN'T SEE ANYTHING. I MIGHT HAVE PASSED OUT.

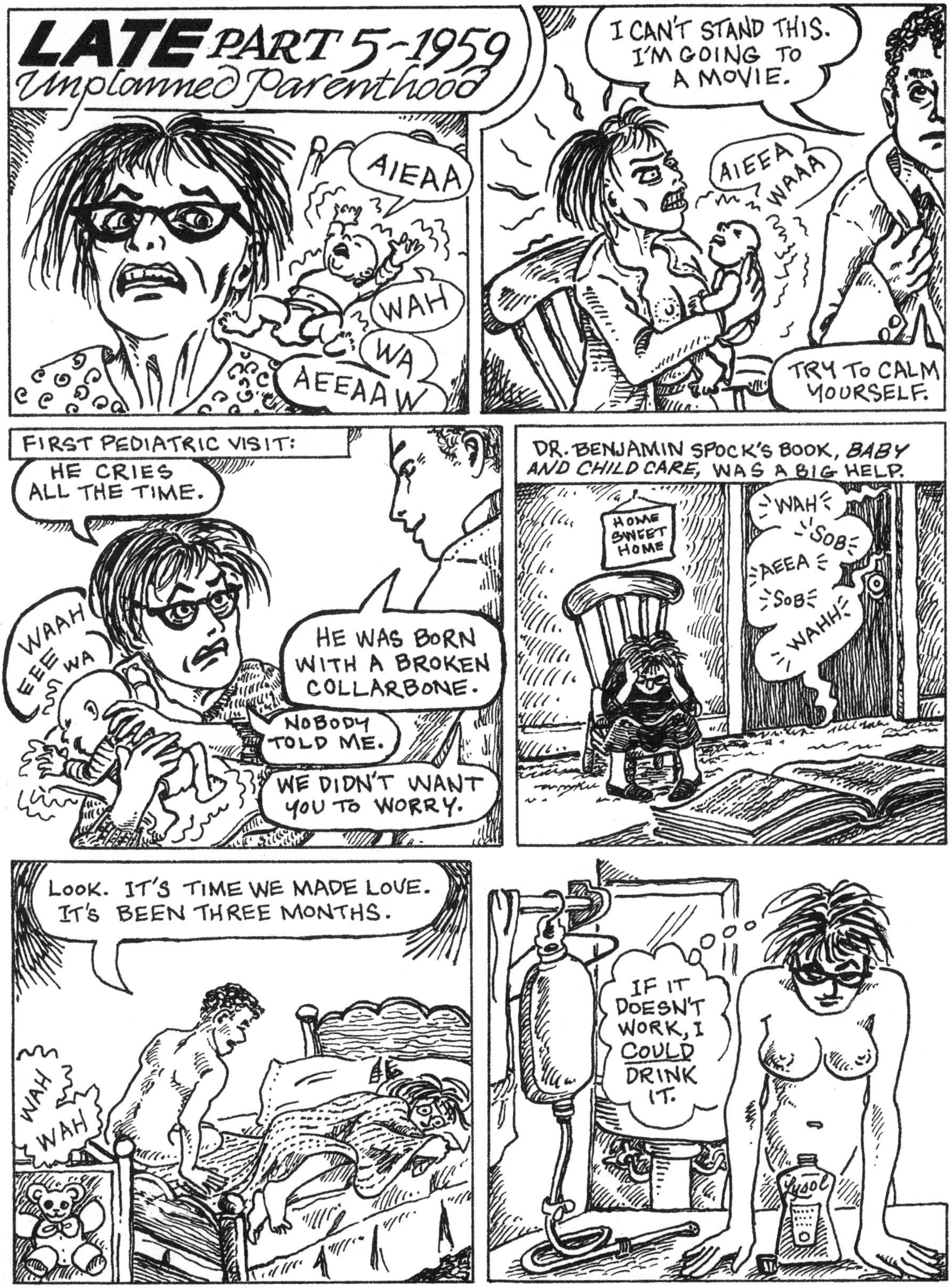
LATE PART 5 - 1959
Unplanned Parenthood
AIEAA
WAH
WA
AEEAAW
I CAN'T STAND THIS. I'M GOING TO A MOVIE.
AIEEA
WAAA
TRY TO CALM YOURSELF.
FIRST PEDIATRIC VISIT:
HE CRIES ALL THE TIME.
WAAH
EEE WA
HE WAS BORN WITH A BROKEN COLLARBONE.
NOBODY TOLD ME.
WE DIDN'T WANT YOU TO WORRY.
DR. BENJAMIN SPOCK'S BOOK, *BABY AND CHILD CARE,* WAS A BIG HELP.
HOME SWEET HOME
WAH
SOB
AEEA
SOB
WAHH
LOOK. IT'S TIME WE MADE LOVE. IT'S BEEN THREE MONTHS.
WAH
WAH
IF IT DOESN'T WORK, I COULD DRINK IT.
Lysol

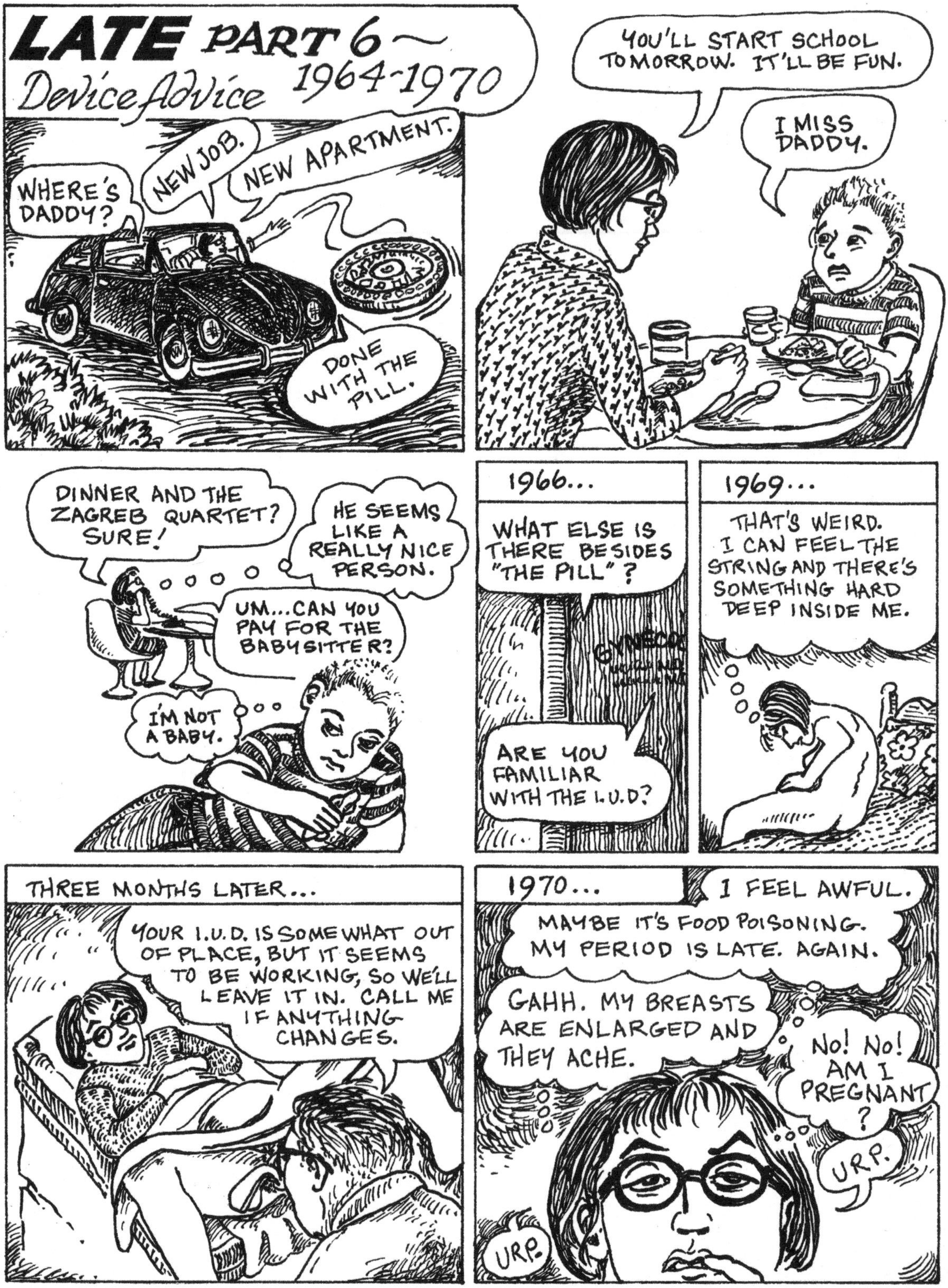
LATE PART 6 ~
Device Advice 1964-1970
WHERE'S DADDY?
NEW JOB.
NEW APARTMENT.
DONE WITH THE PILL.
YOU'LL START SCHOOL TOMORROW. IT'LL BE FUN.
I MISS DADDY.
DINNER AND THE ZAGREB QUARTET? SURE!
HE SEEMS LIKE A REALLY NICE PERSON.
UM...CAN YOU PAY FOR THE BABYSITTER?
I'M NOT A BABY.
1966...
WHAT ELSE IS THERE BESIDES "THE PILL"?
ARE YOU FAMILIAR WITH THE I.U.D?
1969...
THAT'S WEIRD. I CAN FEEL THE STRING AND THERE'S SOMETHING HARD DEEP INSIDE ME.
THREE MONTHS LATER...
YOUR I.U.D. IS SOMEWHAT OUT OF PLACE, BUT IT SEEMS TO BE WORKING, SO WE'LL LEAVE IT IN. CALL ME IF ANYTHING CHANGES.
1970...
I FEEL AWFUL.
MAYBE IT'S FOOD POISONING. MY PERIOD IS LATE. AGAIN.
GAHH. MY BREASTS ARE ENLARGED AND THEY ACHE.
No! No! AM I PREGNANT?
URP.
URP.

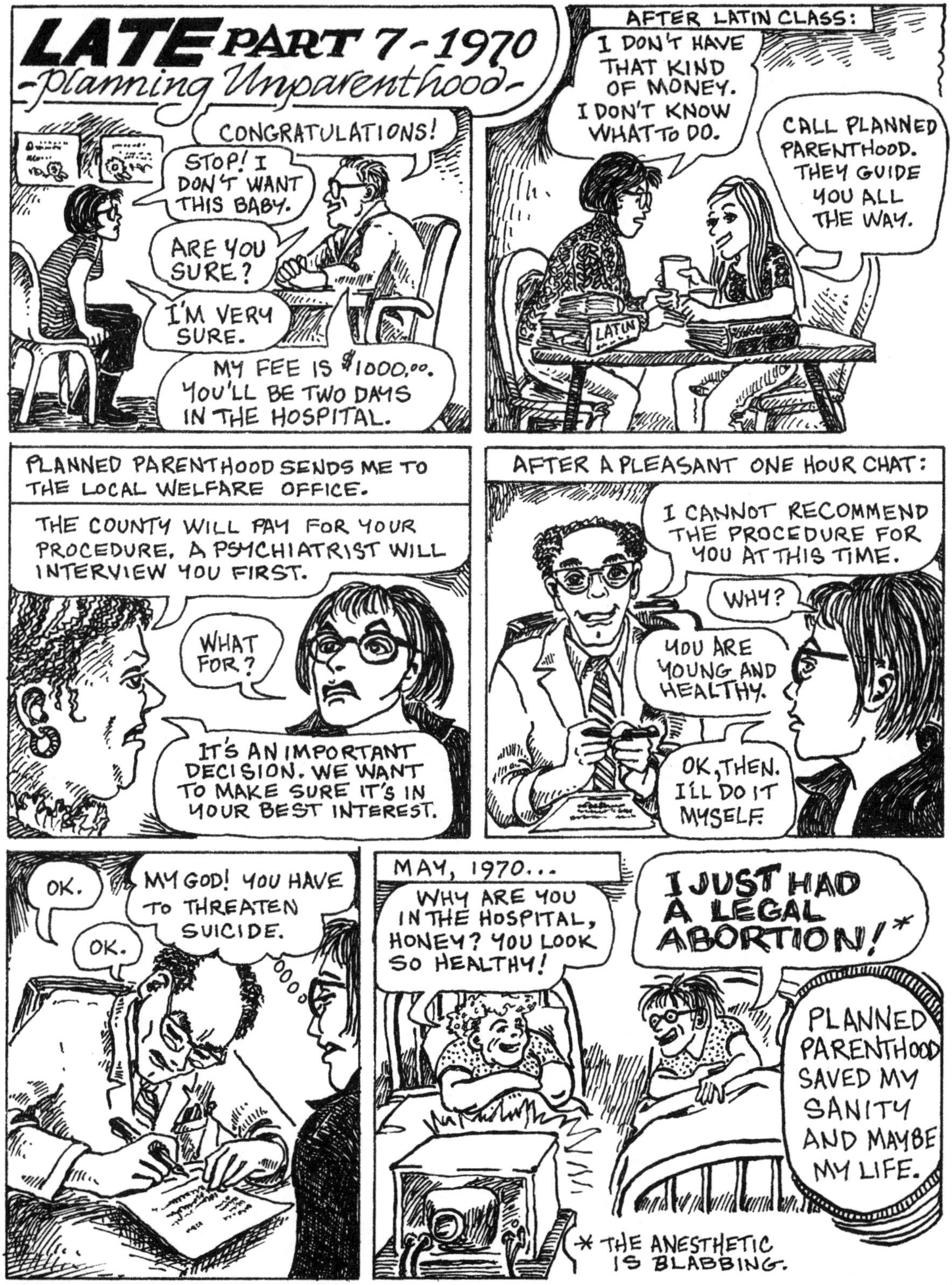
LATE PART 7 - 1970
-Planning Unparenthood-
CONGRATULATIONS!
STOP! I DON'T WANT THIS BABY.
ARE YOU SURE?
I'M VERY SURE.
MY FEE IS $1000.00. YOU'LL BE TWO DAYS IN THE HOSPITAL.
AFTER LATIN CLASS:
I DON'T HAVE THAT KIND OF MONEY. I DON'T KNOW WHAT TO DO.
CALL PLANNED PARENTHOOD. THEY GUIDE YOU ALL THE WAY.
LATIN
PLANNED PARENTHOOD SENDS ME TO THE LOCAL WELFARE OFFICE.
THE COUNTY WILL PAY FOR YOUR PROCEDURE. A PSYCHIATRIST WILL INTERVIEW YOU FIRST.
WHAT FOR?
IT'S AN IMPORTANT DECISION. WE WANT TO MAKE SURE IT'S IN YOUR BEST INTEREST.
AFTER A PLEASANT ONE HOUR CHAT:
I CANNOT RECOMMEND THE PROCEDURE FOR YOU AT THIS TIME.
WHY?
YOU ARE YOUNG AND HEALTHY.
OK, THEN. I'LL DO IT MYSELF.
OK.
OK.
MY GOD! YOU HAVE TO THREATEN SUICIDE.
MAY, 1970...
WHY ARE YOU IN THE HOSPITAL, HONEY? YOU LOOK SO HEALTHY!
I JUST HAD A LEGAL ABORTION!*
PLANNED PARENTHOOD SAVED MY SANITY AND MAYBE MY LIFE.
* THE ANESTHETIC IS BLABBING.

Keeping it to Yourself

by Ali Solomon

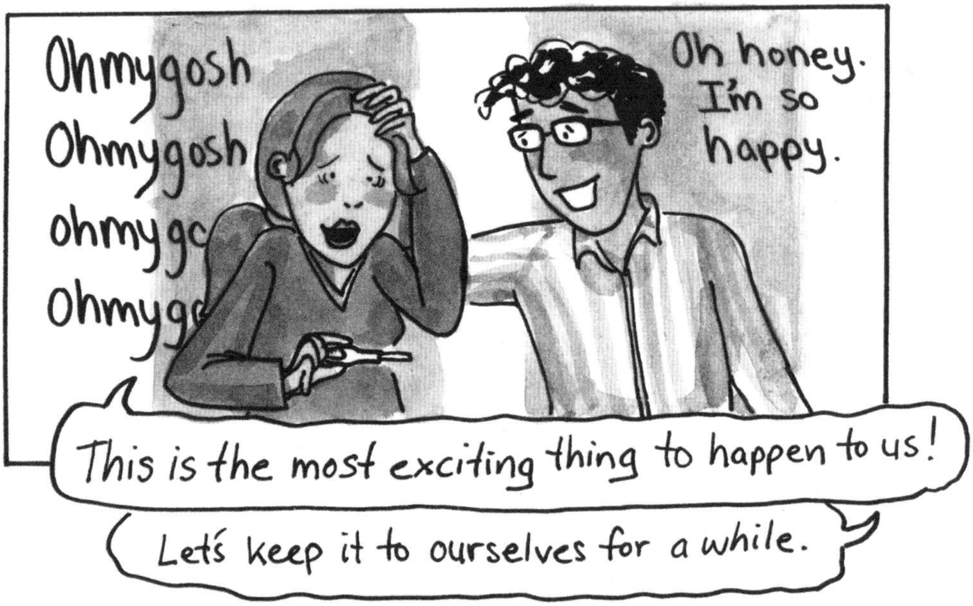
Ohmygosh
Ohmygosh
ohmyg
Ohmyg
Oh honey. I'm so happy.
This is the most exciting thing to happen to us!
Let's keep it to ourselves for a while.

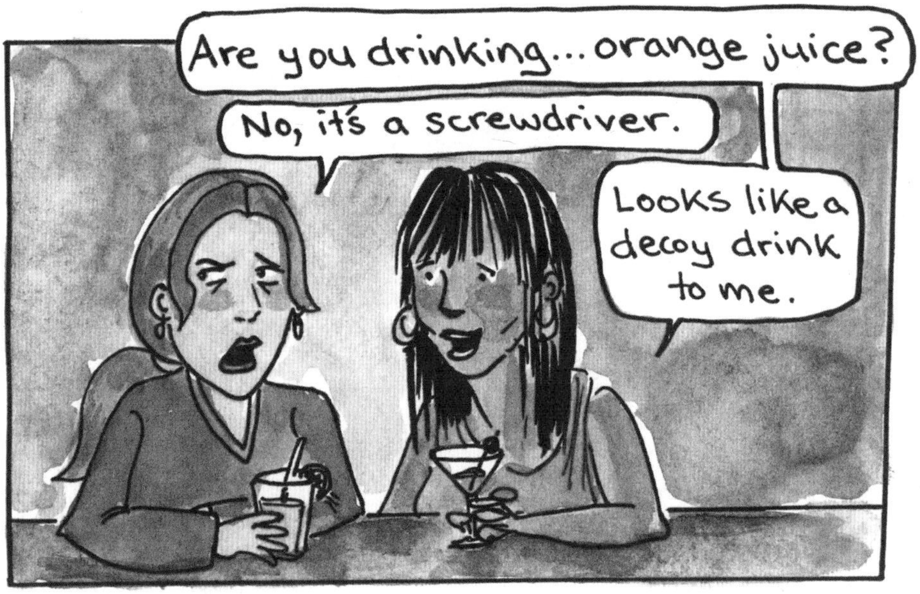
Are you drinking... orange juice?
No, it's a screwdriver.
Looks like a decoy drink to me.

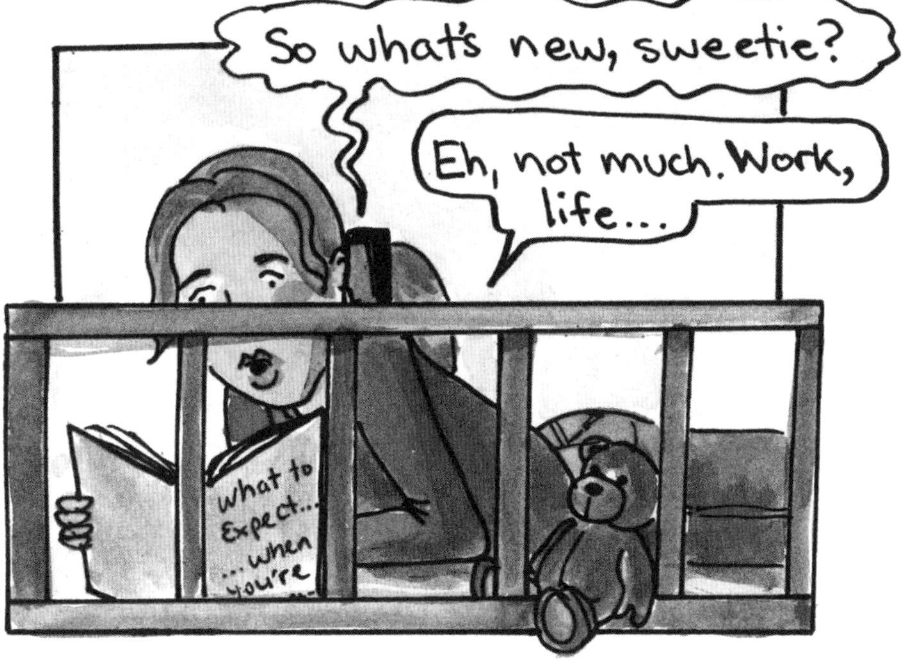
So what's new, sweetie?
Eh, not much. Work, life...
What to Expect... ...when you're

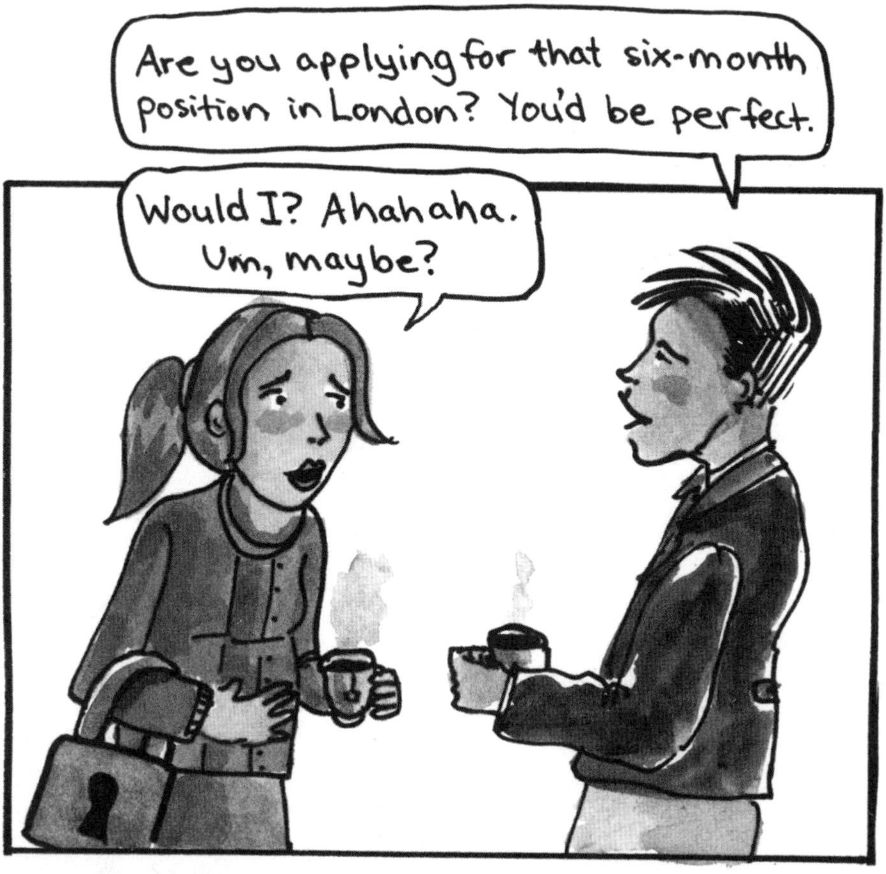
Are you applying for that six-month position in London? You'd be perfect.
Would I? Ahahaha. Um, maybe?

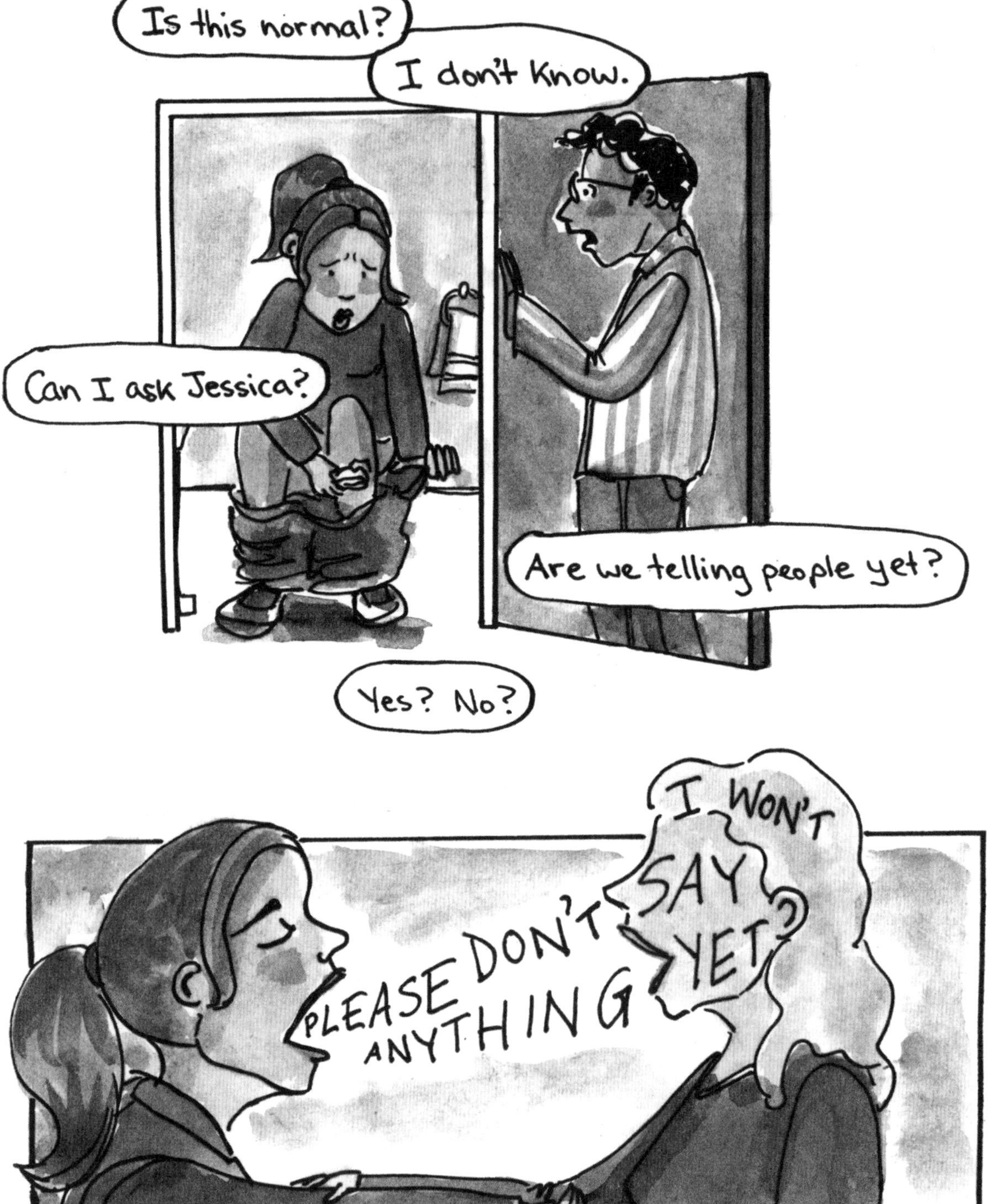
Is this normal?
I don't know.
Can I ask Jessica?
Are we telling people yet?
Yes? No?
PLEASE DON'T ANYTHING
I WON'T SAY YET

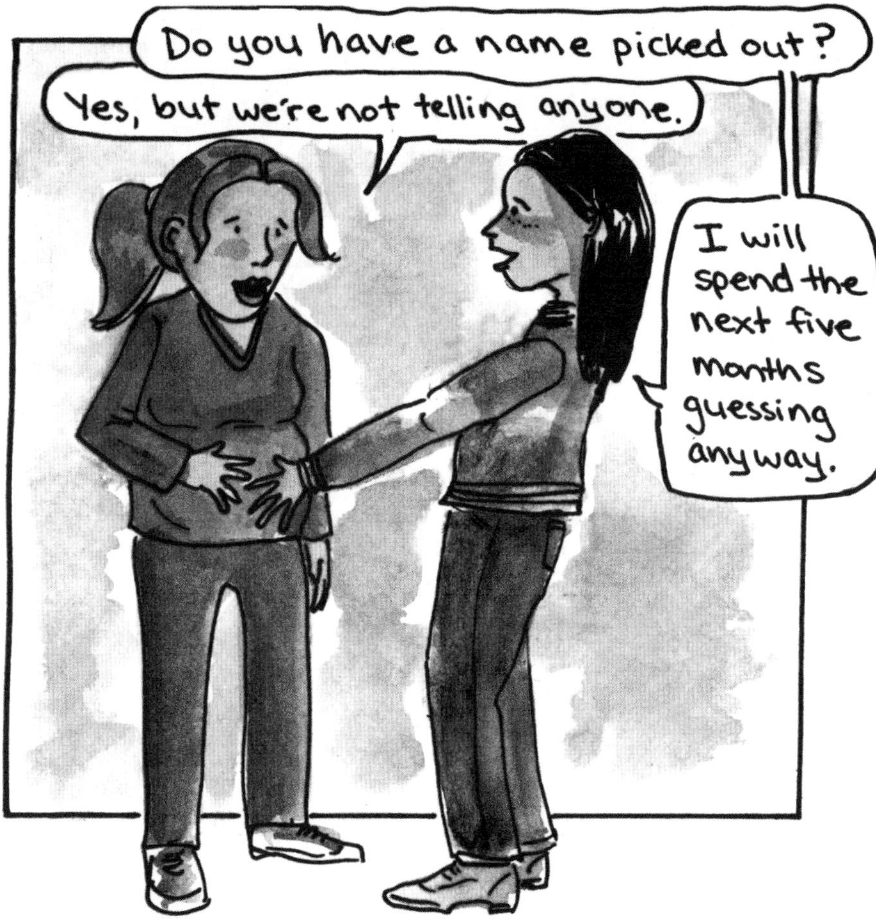
Do you have a name picked out?
Yes, but we're not telling anyone.
I will spend the next five months guessing anyway.

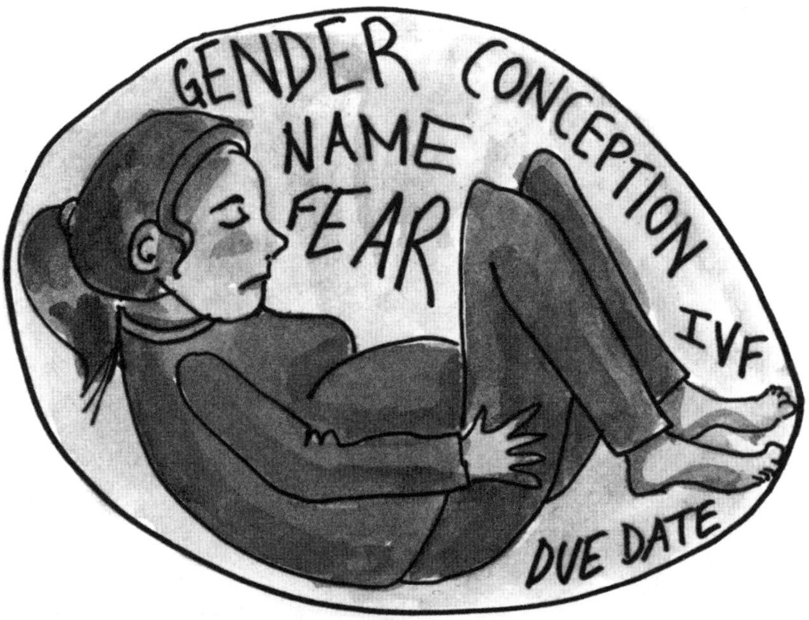
GENDER
CONCEPTION
NAME
FEAR
IVF
DUE DATE

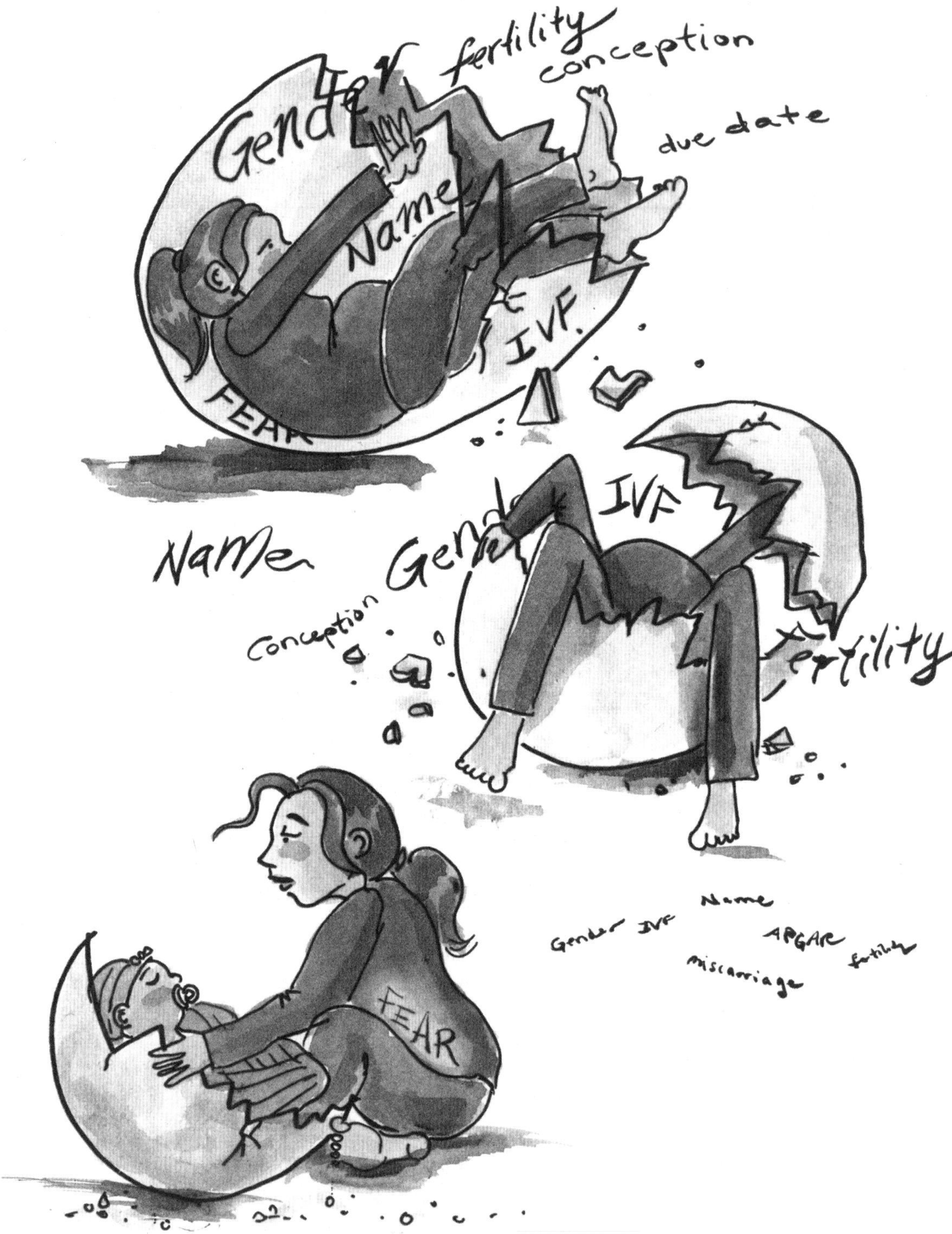
Gender
fertility
conception
due date
Name
IVF
FEAR
Name
Gend
IVF
Conception
fertility
FEAR
Name
Gender IVF
APGAR
miscarriage

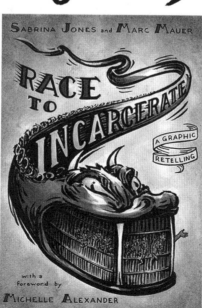

My name is Nancy Davis and I am 36 years old. My significant other and I have three children and live a very fulfilling life in Baton Rouge, Louisiana. Recently we decided we wanted to have another child. We successfully conceived and began the process of another birth journey. We learned some weeks into the pregnancy our baby was diagnosed with Acrania, which refers to the absence of a fetal skull with freely exposed brain tissue to amniotic fluid. Acrania often results in anencephaly, and some believe it is a precursor to all cases of anencephaly. Both can be seen on ultrasound in the first trimester. Unfortunately, the prognosis is uniformly dismal as these are lethal disorders.

We were told by a doctor at Woman's Hospital our baby would probably not survive if I carried the baby the full term; as over 90% of fetuses with Acrania as a diagnoses do not make it. The doctor recommended we terminate the pregnancy to avoid the physical and emotional trauma. The doctor initially agreed to perform the procedure and told us it would be $5000 (which we believe to be really high). They then told us at the direction of the hospital administrator he could not perform the procedure as a result of the recent reversal of Roe vs. Wade and the strict baby termination laws in the state of Louisiana. I would need to travel out of state, and started a gofundme to help pay for travel to have this very challenging procedure.

'I'm carrying it to bury it'

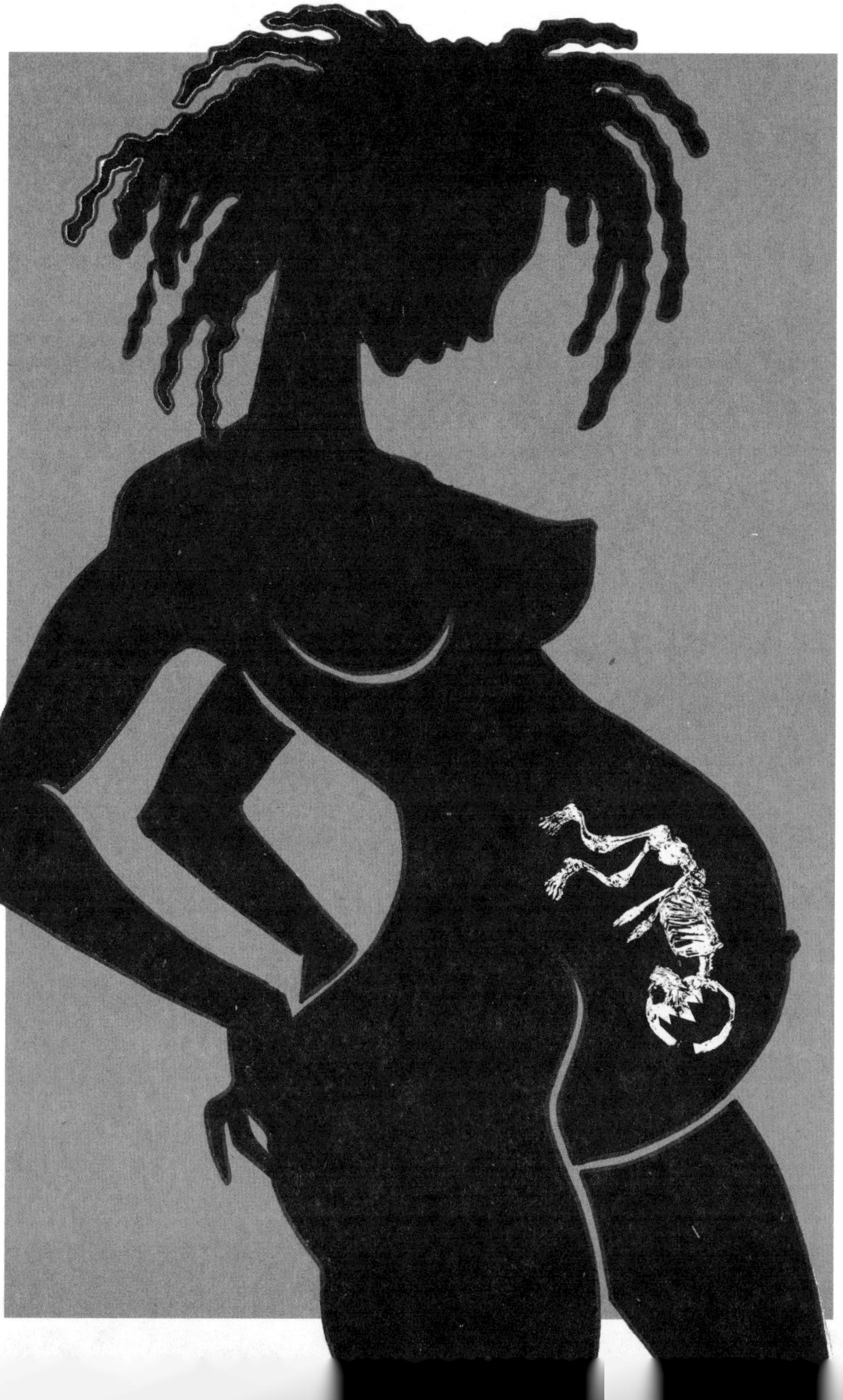

A pregnant Louisiana woman faced with either carrying a skull-less fetus to term – for the baby to probably die within hours – or traveling several states away to obtain an abortion has hired a prominent civil rights attorney as she weighs how to move forward.

Nancy Davis embodies the gut-wrenching decisions some women are being forced to make after the US supreme court's decision in June to strip away nationwide abortion rights.

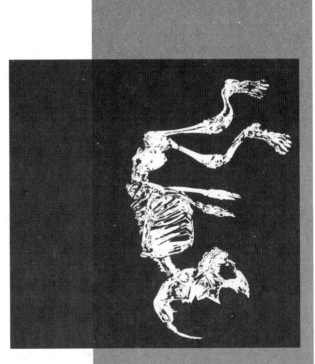

"There's nothing I wanted more than this child," she told told The New York Times.
But she also explained to CBS affiliate WAFB in Baton Rouge that it was excruciating to think that she was "carrying it to bury it."

Davis' attorney David Crump said in a statement Friday that "Ms. Nancy Davis was put in a horrifically cruel position."
She "has had to endure unthinkable emotional pain and mounting physical risk," Crump said.

The state senator who authored Louisiana's abortion ban, Katrina Jackson, insisted to WAFB that the hospital should have authorized the termination of Davis' pregnancy. Jackson said the statute includes exceptions for fetuses that are not viable outside a mother's womb.

But Crump indicated in his statement that the law is confusing and intimidating to hospitals fearful of performing an illegal abortion.

Without commenting on Davis' case, because of medical privacy laws, a hospital spokesperson told CNN that unviable pregnancies are difficult to navigate within Louisiana's confusing, complex abortion ban.

"Even if a specific diagnosis falls under medically futile exceptions provided by [the Louisiana Department of Health], the laws addressing treatment methods are much more complex and seemingly contradictory," said Caroline Isemann, spokesperson for Woman's Hospital in Baton Rouge.

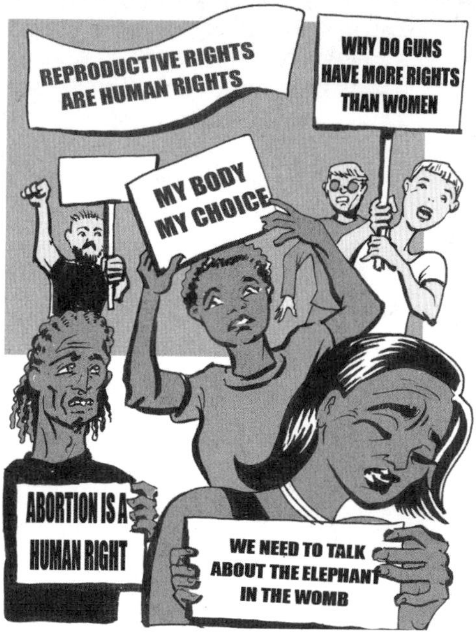
REPRODUCTIVE RIGHTS ARE HUMAN RIGHTS
WHY DO GUNS HAVE MORE RIGHTS THAN WOMEN
MY BODY MY CHOICE
ABORTION IS A HUMAN RIGHT
WE NEED TO TALK ABOUT THE ELEPHANT IN THE WOMB

Davis' situation is one of a mounting series of tragedies amid a wave of abortion bans in states in the wake of the Supreme Court's repeal of Roe v. Wade. Other clients of Attorney Crump have included relatives of George Floyd, who was murdered by Minneapolis police; Trayvon Martin, an unarmed teen who was shot dead by a neighborhood watch captain; and Breonna Taylor, who was killed by Kentucky police while they searched her home. Crump's office helped the families of Floyd, Martin and Taylor secure tens of millions of dollars in settlement money.

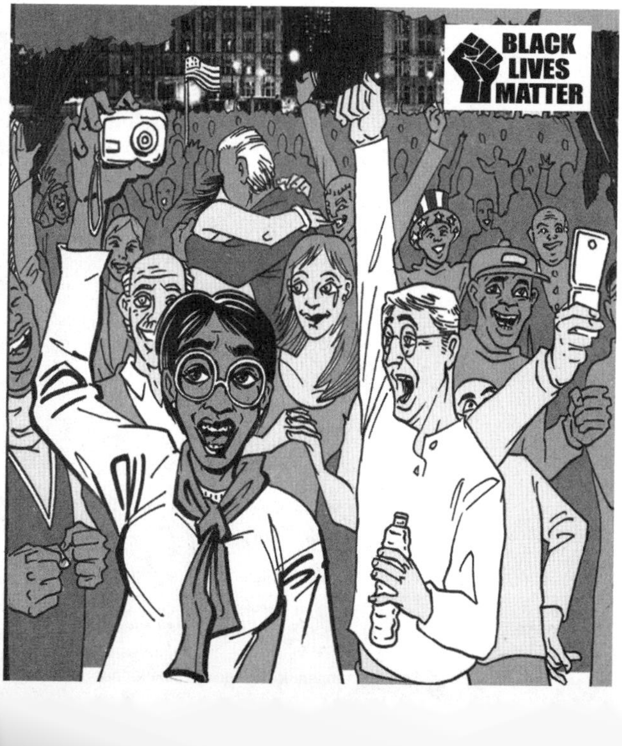
BLACK LIVES MATTER

Word of Davis's plight emerged almost at the same time that a Florida court blocked a pregnant 16-year-old girl from having an abortion. The court found the girl was too immature to decide whether or not she should have an abortion and therefore must instead give birth to a child.

Meanwhile, earlier in the summer, a 10-year-old Ohio girl who was raped and impregnated had to travel to neighboring Indiana to terminate her pregnancy because of her state's ban on most abortions. Though some media outlets and rightwing politicians baselessly questioned whether the girl existed or was instead a liberal hoax to stoke support for abortion rights, authorities have since charged a man in connection with the girl's rape, a crime to which he has purportedly confessed.

The medical center, Woman's hospital in Baton Rouge, directed Davis to an abortion clinic, saying her Medicaid insurance would not cover the procedure. But Louisiana's abortion clinics have announced plans to leave the state amid legal battles over the ban's enforcement, the New Orleans news outlet Gambit reported.

Nancy Davis was planning to travel to North Carolina – which allows abortions up to 20 weeks – rather than give birth to a child, which she would lose immediately.

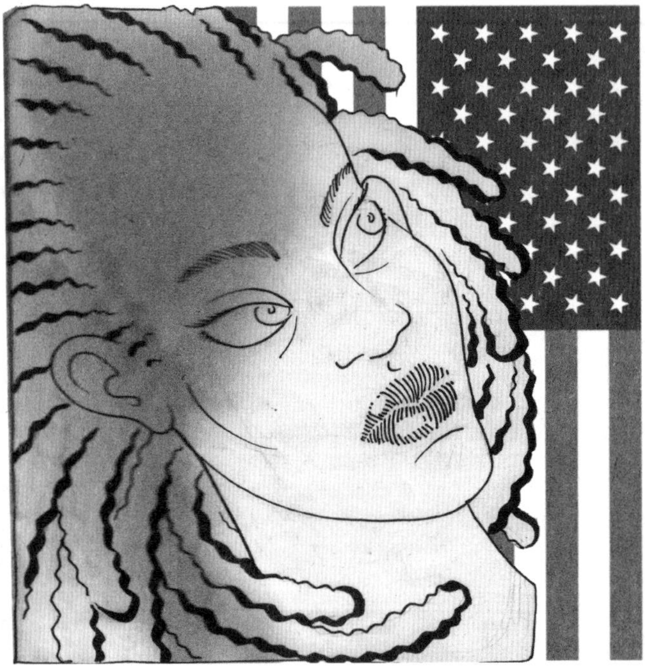

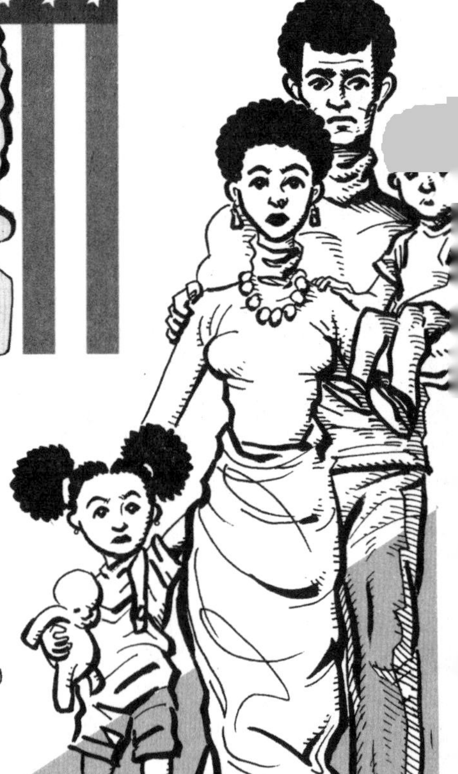

The challenge is under Louisiana law. Nancy qualifies for a termination of the pregnancy, but the hospital is refusing to do it for fear of prosecution by the federal and or state government. The mother shouldn't have to carry a fetus full term with a definite diagnosis of death. She may suffer severe trauma having to go through the process which could cause severe harm to her. One has to consider the irreversible damage this is going to cause along with the long term PTSD. All of this has been mentally exhausting . Whether she realizes it or not. And we feel Nancy is in need of therapy to ensure she is mentally stable to properly care for her other children.

Sources - the guardian, huffpost, latimes, wwno.org, gofundme.com, nola.com

Jenny Gonzalez-Blitz

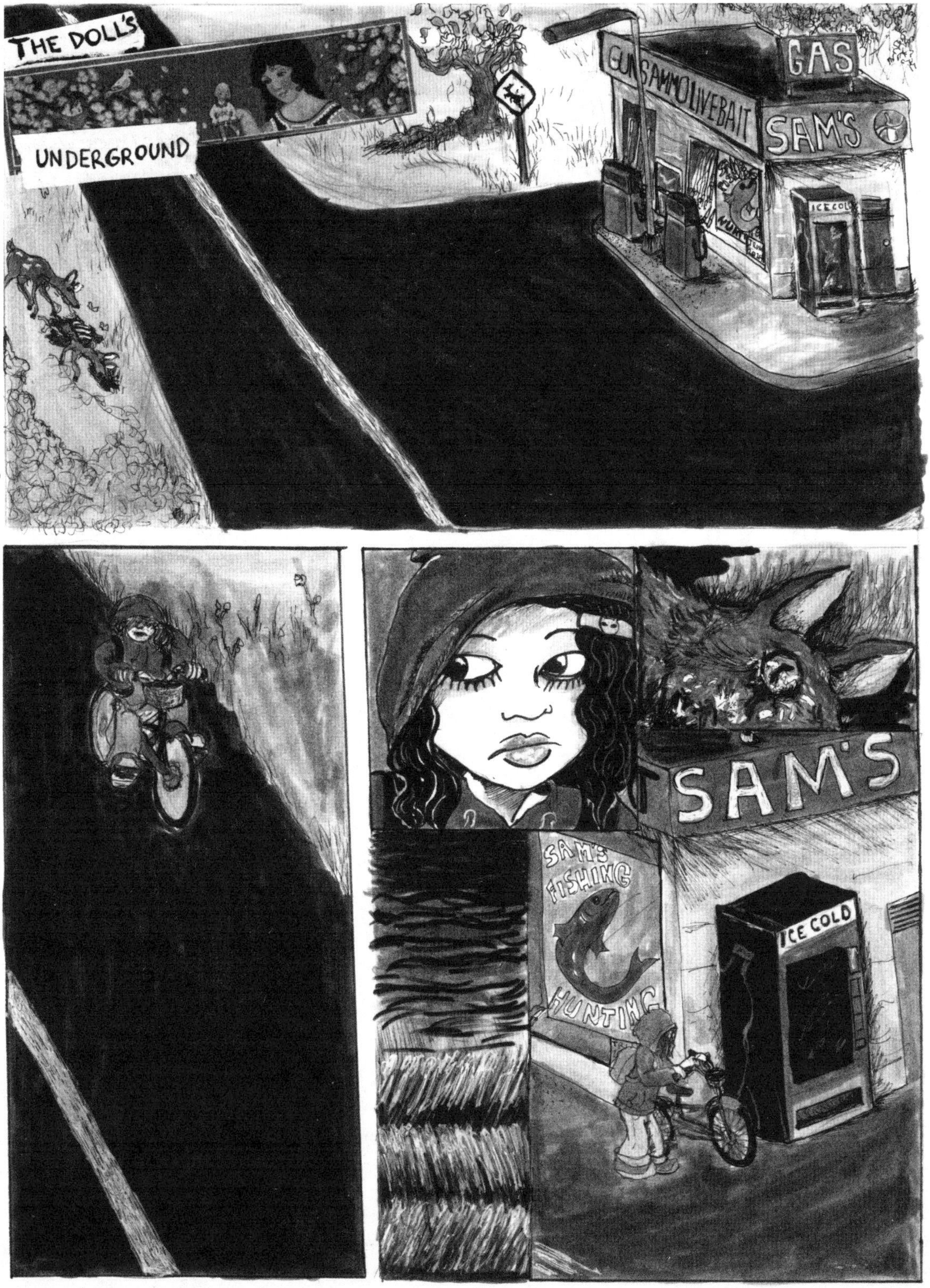
THE DOLL'S
UNDERGROUND
GAS
GUNSAMMOLIVEBAIT
SAM'S
SAM'S
SAM'S FISHING
HUNTING
ICE COLD

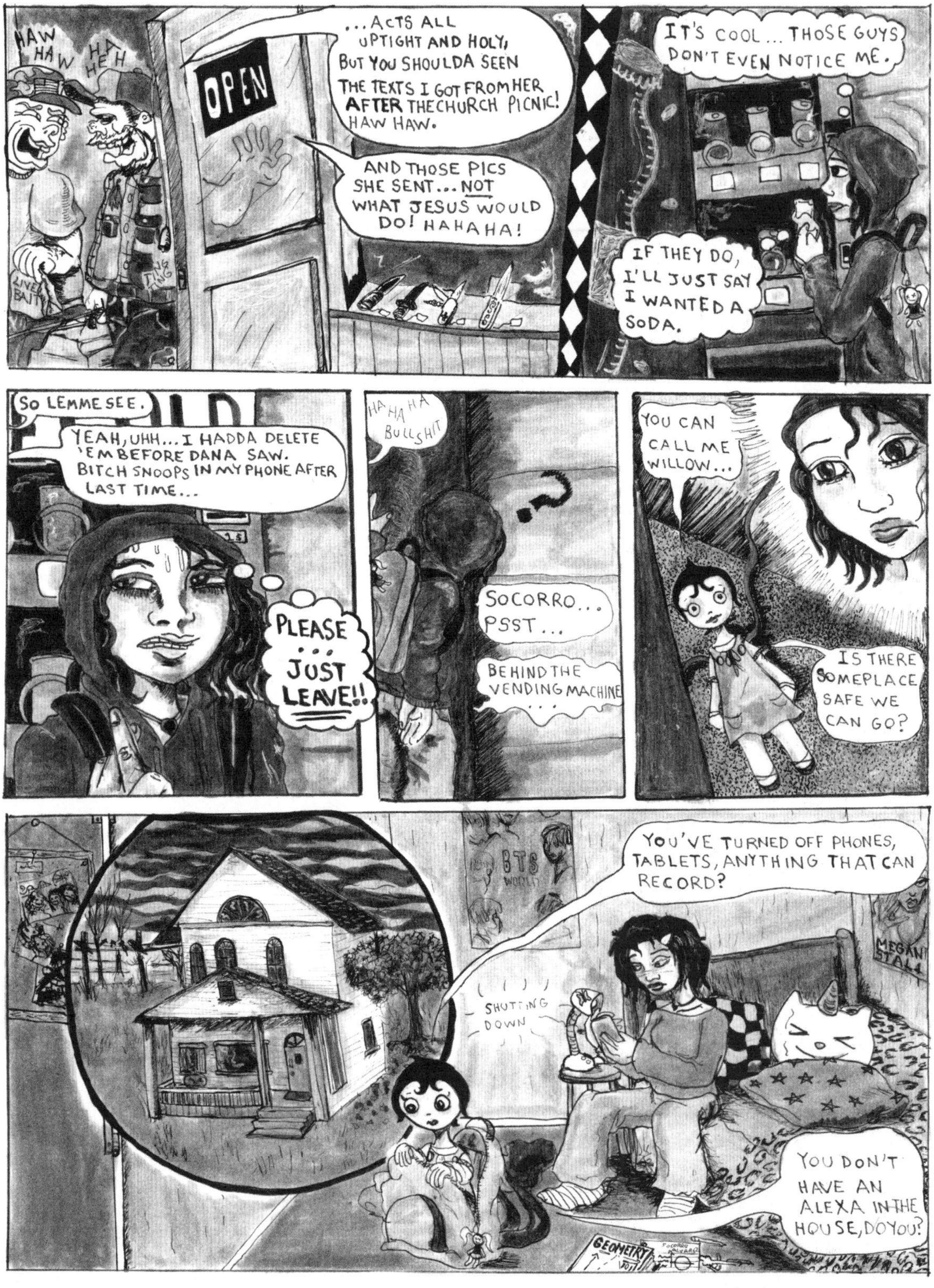
HAW HAW
HEH HEH
...ACTS ALL UPTIGHT AND HOLY, BUT YOU SHOULDA SEEN THE TEXTS I GOT FROM HER AFTER THE CHURCH PICNIC! HAW HAW.
AND THOSE PICS SHE SENT... NOT WHAT JESUS WOULD DO! HAHAHA!
OPEN
LIVE BAIT
IT'S COOL... THOSE GUYS DON'T EVEN NOTICE ME.
IF THEY DO, I'LL JUST SAY I WANTED A SODA.
SO LEMME SEE.
YEAH, UHH... I HADDA DELETE 'EM BEFORE DANA SAW. BITCH SNOOPS IN MY PHONE AFTER LAST TIME...
PLEASE... JUST LEAVE!!
HA HA HA BULLSHIT
SOCORRO... PSST...
BEHIND THE VENDING MACHINE...
YOU CAN CALL ME WILLOW...
IS THERE SOMEPLACE SAFE WE CAN GO?
YOU'VE TURNED OFF PHONES, TABLETS, ANYTHING THAT CAN RECORD?
BTS
SHUTTING DOWN
MEGAN STAL
GEOMETRY
YOU DON'T HAVE AN ALEXA IN THE HOUSE, DO YOU?

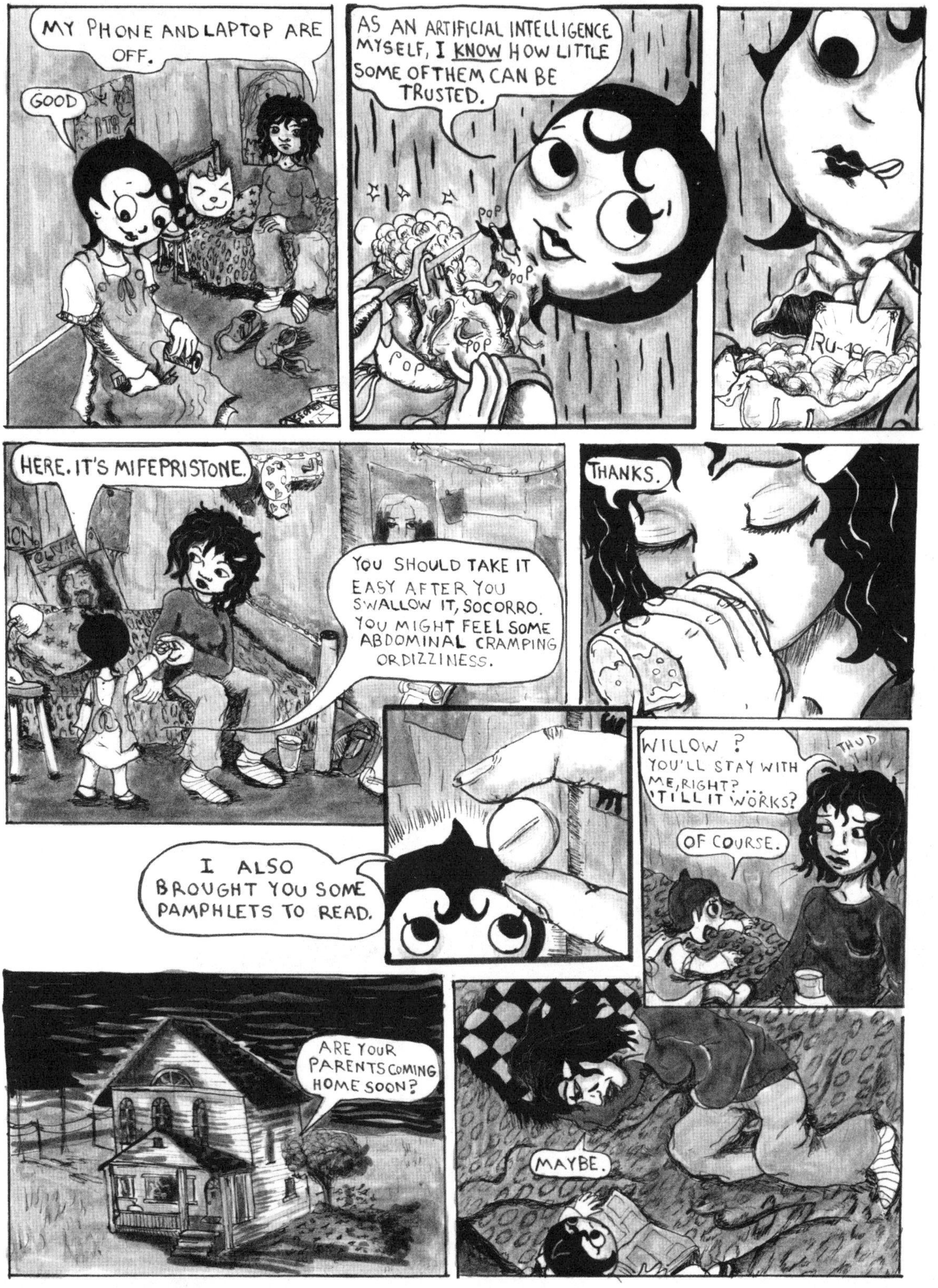
MY PHONE AND LAPTOP ARE OFF.
GOOD
AS AN ARTIFICIAL INTELLIGENCE MYSELF, I KNOW HOW LITTLE SOME OF THEM CAN BE TRUSTED.
POP
POP
POP
POP
POP
RU-486
HERE. IT'S MIFEPRISTONE.
YOU SHOULD TAKE IT EASY AFTER YOU SWALLOW IT, SOCORRO. YOU MIGHT FEEL SOME ABDOMINAL CRAMPING OR DIZZINESS.
THANKS.
I ALSO BROUGHT YOU SOME PAMPHLETS TO READ.
WILLOW? YOU'LL STAY WITH ME, RIGHT?... 'TILL IT WORKS?
THUD
OF COURSE.
ARE YOUR PARENTS COMING HOME SOON?
MAYBE.

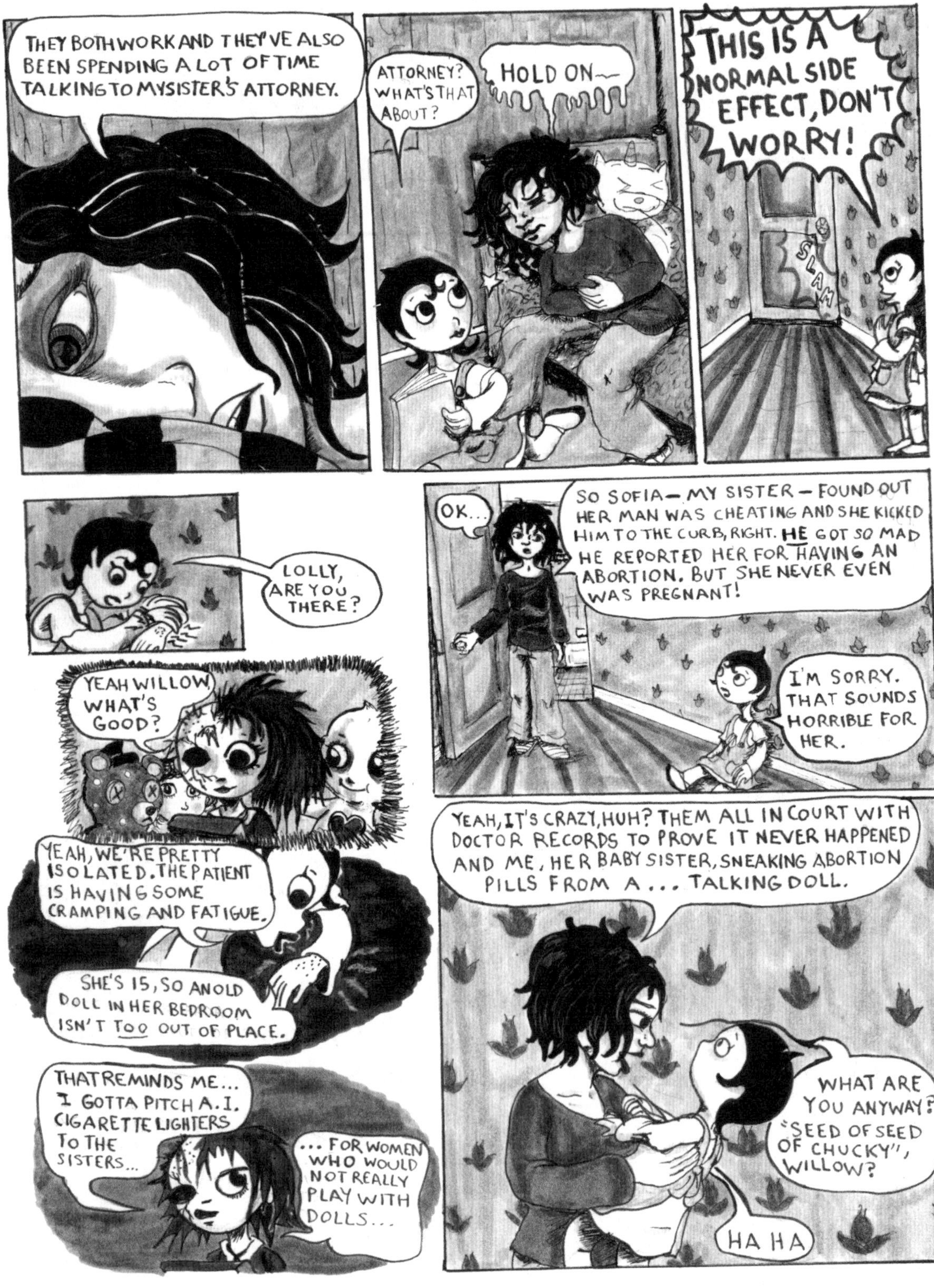

THEY BOTH WORK AND THEY'VE ALSO BEEN SPENDING A LOT OF TIME TALKING TO MY SISTER'S ATTORNEY.
ATTORNEY? WHAT'S THAT ABOUT?
HOLD ON—
THIS IS A NORMAL SIDE EFFECT, DON'T WORRY!
SLAM
LOLLY, ARE YOU THERE?
YEAH WILLOW, WHAT'S GOOD?
YEAH, WE'RE PRETTY ISOLATED. THE PATIENT IS HAVING SOME CRAMPING AND FATIGUE.
SHE'S 15, SO AN OLD DOLL IN HER BEDROOM ISN'T TOO OUT OF PLACE.
THAT REMINDS ME... I GOTTA PITCH A.I. CIGARETTE LIGHTERS TO THE SISTERS...
...FOR WOMEN WHO WOULD NOT REALLY PLAY WITH DOLLS...
OK...
SO SOFIA — MY SISTER — FOUND OUT HER MAN WAS CHEATING AND SHE KICKED HIM TO THE CURB, RIGHT. HE GOT SO MAD HE REPORTED HER FOR HAVING AN ABORTION. BUT SHE NEVER EVEN WAS PREGNANT!
I'M SORRY. THAT SOUNDS HORRIBLE FOR HER.
YEAH, IT'S CRAZY, HUH? THEM ALL IN COURT WITH DOCTOR RECORDS TO PROVE IT NEVER HAPPENED AND ME, HER BABY SISTER, SNEAKING ABORTION PILLS FROM A... TALKING DOLL.
WHAT ARE YOU ANYWAY? "SEED OF SEED OF CHUCKY", WILLOW?
HA HA

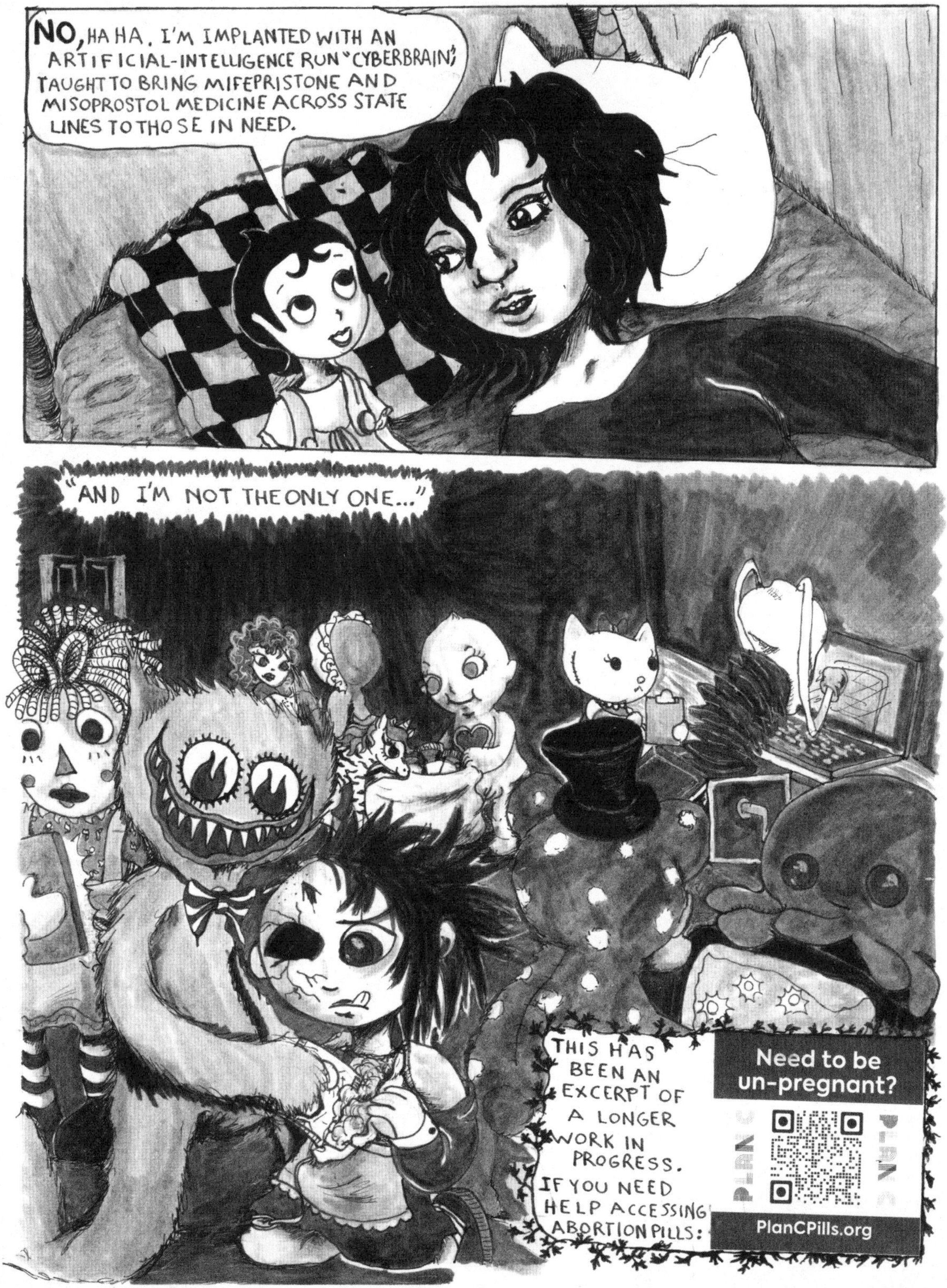

NO, HA HA. I'M IMPLANTED WITH AN ARTIFICIAL-INTELLIGENCE RUN "CYBERBRAIN," TAUGHT TO BRING MIFEPRISTONE AND MISOPROSTOL MEDICINE ACROSS STATE LINES TO THOSE IN NEED.
"AND I'M NOT THE ONLY ONE..."
THIS HAS BEEN AN EXCERPT OF A LONGER WORK IN PROGRESS. IF YOU NEED HELP ACCESSING ABORTION PILLS:
Need to be un-pregnant?
PLAN C
PlanCPills.org

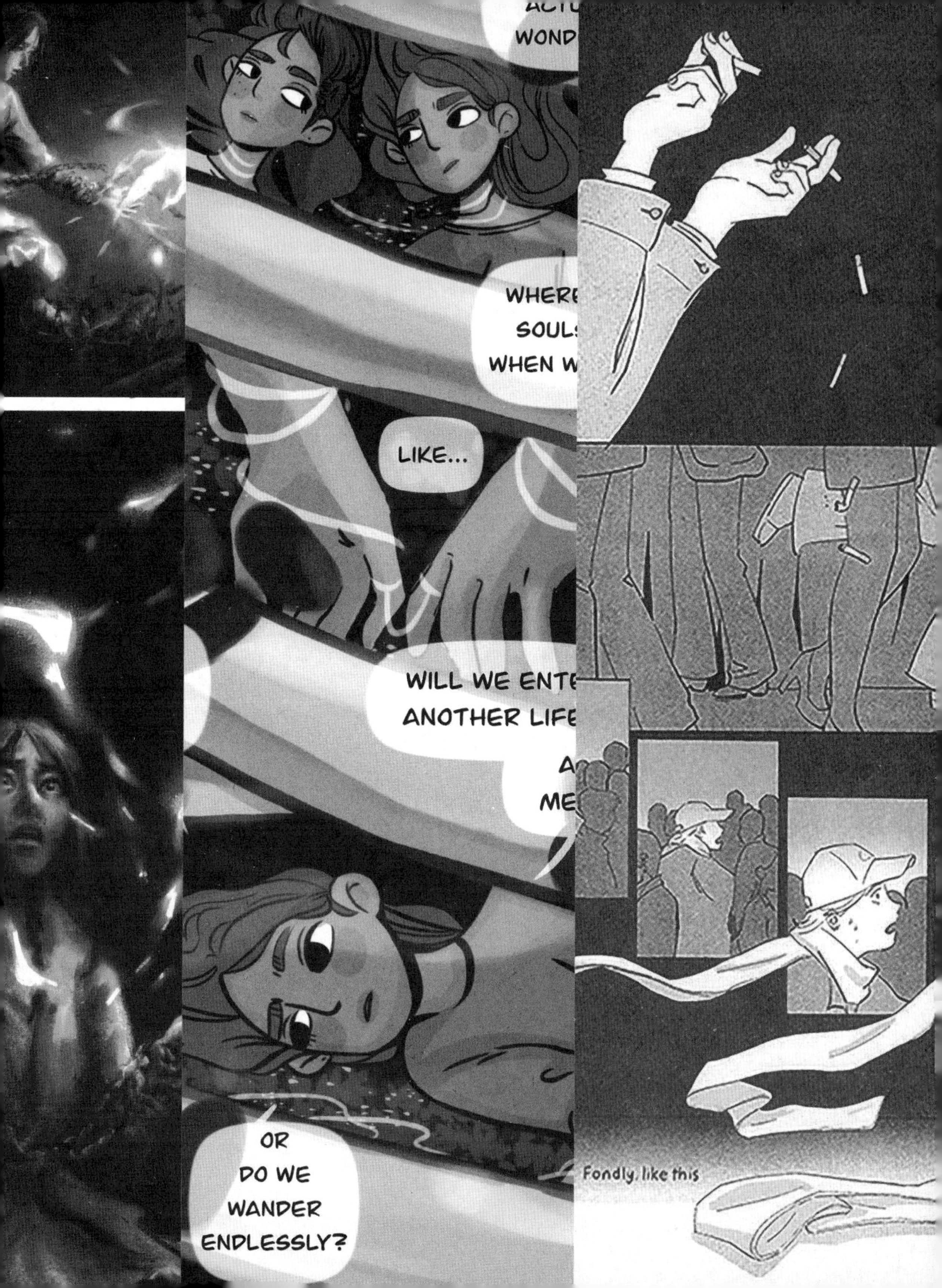

ACTU
WOND
WHERE
SOUL
WHEN W
LIKE...
WILL WE ENTE
ANOTHER LIFE
A
ME
OR
DO WE
WANDER
ENDLESSLY?
Fondly, like this

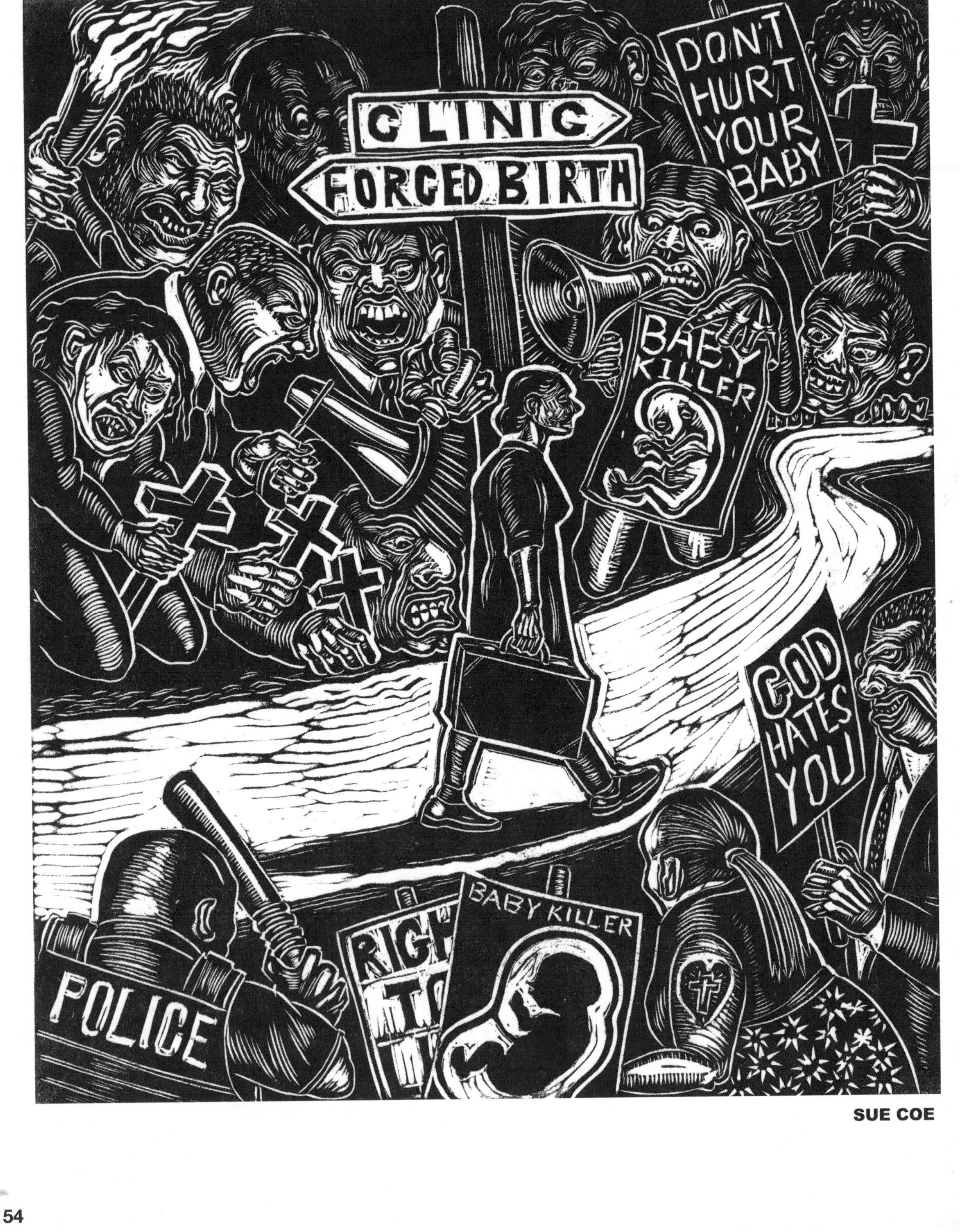
CLINIC
FORCED BIRTH
DON'T HURT YOUR BABY
BABY KILLER
GOD HATES YOU
BABY KILLER
POLICE

SUE COE

THE BEST OFFENSE IS MORE CLINIC DEFENSE

An abortion provider discusses the tactic of clinic defense, and why it's necessary to defend abortion rights.

by Anonymous

A version of this article previously appeared in The Tempest in February, 2022.

On December 1, 2022 The U.S. Supreme Court began hearing oral arguments in Dobbs v. Jackson Women's Health Organization, a case that seeks to overturn Roe v. Wade. The case is set to determine the so-called constitutionality of a 15-week Mississippi abortion ban. Most observers suspect that SCOTUS will rule in favor of the ban, ending abortion rights in the U.S. as currently conceived, which are already alarmingly limited.

This looming crisis has been forecasted by those fighting hardest for safe and legal abortion for decades. Unfortunately, liberal organizations that position themselves as being "on the front lines" of abortion access have disempowered some of those most willing to fight for abortion rights. In this piece, I will argue that the corporate dismissal of abortion clinic defenders has contributed to the precarity—and in some cases, absence—of abortion rights. I will make the case that abortion providers and advocates need to end their complicity with law enforcement and other oppressive institutions and, instead, engage in campaigns of active resistance and civil disobedience to defend abortion access.

THE BATTLE OUTSIDE ABORTION CLINICS

Since the legalization of Roe, abortion has been marginalized in medicine, forcing the majority of abortion care to be provided in freestanding abortion clinics. And for the entirety of their existence, abortion clinics have been on the receiving end of right-wing extremist terror. In 1977, only four years after Roe v. Wade, an abortion clinic in Long Island, NY was attacked by anti-choice arsonists. After that event, clinics began seeing more regular attacks, with bombings and arsons occurring almost quarterly over the next six years (29 total). In the mid-eighties, the Right began formalizing, escalating, and becoming more efficient and effective in their violent organizing.

Often overlooked when we consider violent clinic terror is the day-to-day presence of anti-abortion extremists in front of clinics. Forced-birth advocates routinely show up to abortion clinics to intimidate patients through performative prayer, the sharing of religious handouts littered with disinformation, offensive signage, and so-called "sidewalk counseling" in which they attempt to coerce patients to continue their pregnancies. In some cases, these efforts lead to the blocking of clinic entrances or the invasion of clinics.

Anti-abortion extremists' ongoing attacks and routine presence at the site of health care delivery have contributed to the success of the anti-abortion movement. First, the oft-unchallenged voices in front of clinics have normalized extremist positions and increased abortion shame. These activists have claimed the moral high ground in their obstruction of health care. Their rhetoric, persistent and unchallenged, has defined the grounds on which the battle over abortion has been waged.

Many people to the left of center have come to accept that abortion is evil or distasteful and should be avoided. We were, famously, to keep abortion "safe, legal, and rare." The rare part was entirely driven by a loud minority of anti-abortion extremists, and adopted by centrist feminists. Then, Democrats made an

WE FACE OFF BEHIND POLICE LINES.
Mommy don't do it! Save your baby!
Dad! Be a man
Not the Church Not the State WOMEN will decide our FATE!
CLINIC
15'
POLICE
POLICE
FIFTEEN FEET FROM THE ENTRANCE, AS PER THE CITY'S BUFFER ZONE LAW.

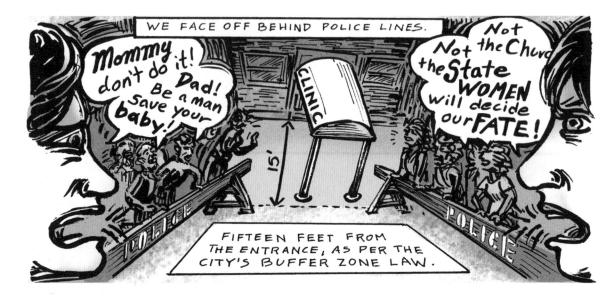

argument about political expediency, claiming that progressives would never find a broad class coalition unless they dropped abortion rights as a "litmus test" for determining support. And just like that, coalitions formed based on the denial of fundamental human rights.

THE "MAINSTREAM" PLAN TO COUNTER CLINIC HARASSMENT AND VIOLENCE

Another effect of the regular, unopposed presence of anti-choice zealots showing up in the streets week after week is the opportunities it has provided for anti-abortion organizing and coalition building. Clinic protests offer opportunities for growth of people-powered, decentralized anti-abortion action. Foot soldiers have been putting anti-abortion ideology into practice week after week, month after month for decades. They recruit, build, reflect, and learn how to be more effective.

By contrast, the so-called "pro-choice" establishment encourages supporters to respond to these attacks on abortion rights primarily through institutionalized channels: donating and voting. If there are concerns about "safety," given the escalation of violent attacks at clinics, establishment institutions encourage supporters to rely on the police for protection.

In some cases, establishment liberals have ignored the need to protect clinics. Take Mississippi: as a result of right-wing terrorist violence, the number of these clinics shrunk to eight in 1992 and eventually to one by 2006. Mississippi-based reproductive justice activists have argued that abortion rights advocates in other parts of the country have ignored the crisis there, characterizing the state as "backwards" or disposable. They argued that what was happening in Mississippi, and in the South more generally, could happen anywhere and that what happened in Mississippi could impact the entire country. They were right, of course: Jackson Women's Health Organization, the one remaining abortion clinic in the state, is the clinic involved in the Supreme Court case upon which Roe currently depends.

Perhaps the strongest evidence of the success of right-wing tactics, and the concomitant failure of the liberal establishment's approach, is that despite overwhelming public support for legal abortion, there is no mass movement organized to take to the streets to protect abortion rights in the face of the potential fall of Roe.

CLINIC DEFENSE

As long as there have been clinic protesters, there have been people willing to challenge them. Over the years, clinic defense has taken a variety of forms, from clinic-employed or volunteer patient escorts to counter-protesters who engage rhetorically with anti-choice zealots to clinic defenders who put their bodies between terrorists and patients. In many cases, clinic administrators and/or clinic owners discourage clinic defense. They claim that the presence of clinic defenders creates chaos and causes patients confusion. Some have argued that clinic defense more intensely activates anti-abortion protesters and brings larger and larger crowds to the clinic. Many clinics opt for hiring private–oftentimes armed–security guards, or they call the police on protesters, relying on racist, misogynist, violent institutions to "protect" patients.

Clinic defense is a grassroots, often militant tactic of interrupting radical anti-abortion extremists from harassing abortion clinics, staff, and patients. In spite of success stories all around the country, clinic defense and clinic defenders have been marginalized, scolded, and shamed by large, mainstream abortion providers.

But, in recent years, clinic defense has reappeared in pockets across the U.S. In New York City, NYC for Abortion Rights (NYC4AR) has been working to counter the protesters from a local church who harass patients at a busy clinic in Manhattan. The defenders wield signs with supportive messages, sing songs of

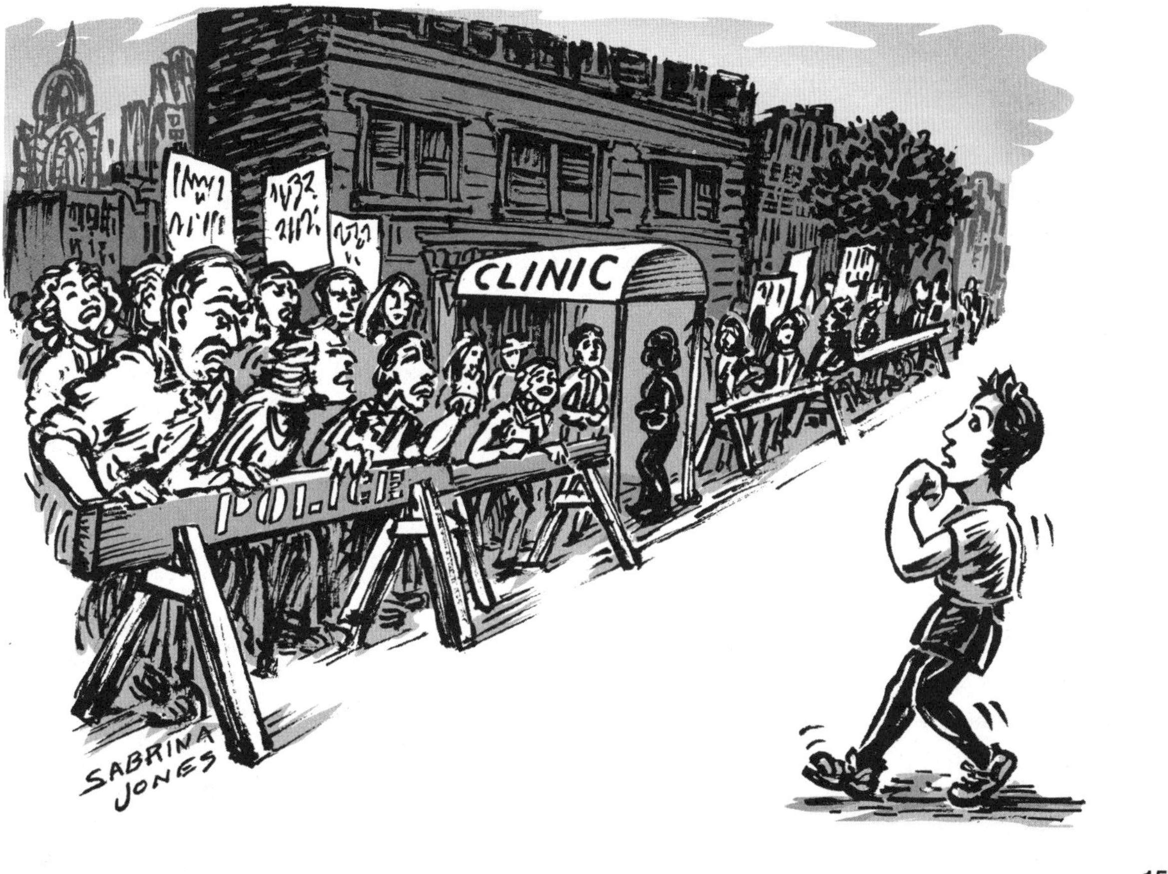
CLINIC
POLICE
SABRINA JONES

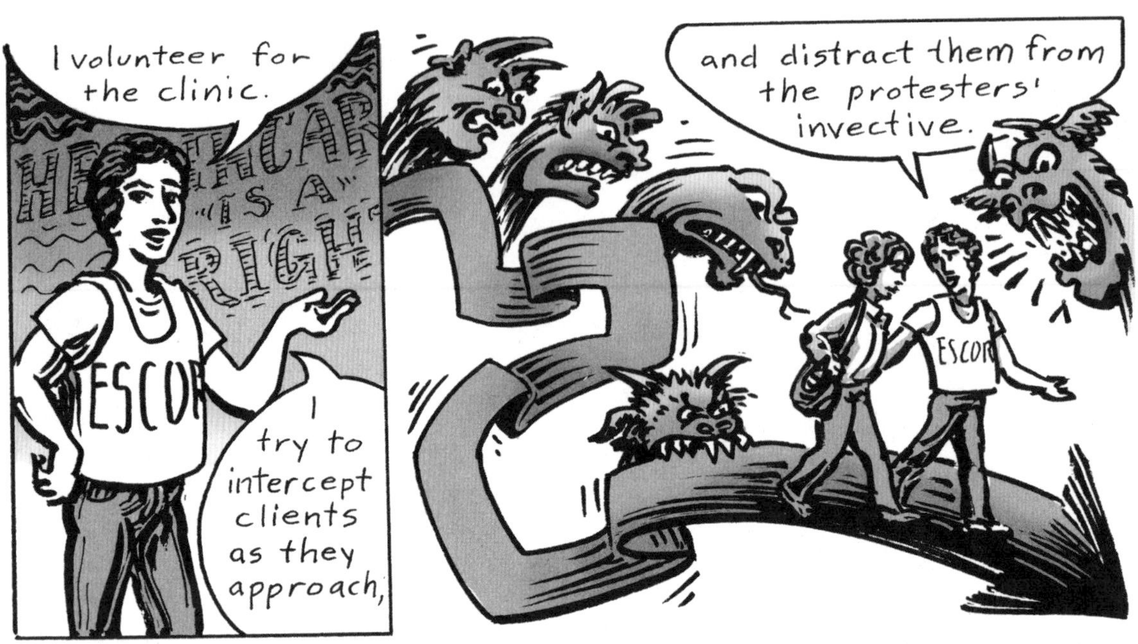
I volunteer for the clinic.
HEALTHCARE "IS A" RIGHT
ESCORT
I try to intercept clients as they approach,
and distract them from the protesters' invective.
ESCORT

liberation, and chant pro-abortion messages while slowing the harassers' procession from the church to the clinic. Typically, NYC4AR defenders are wildly outnumbered: there are sometimes hundreds of forced-birthers compared to dozens of clinic defenders. NYC4AR's presence in the street has offered an opportunity not only to protect patients and staff, but also to learn about the systems which uphold and perpetuate clinic and street harassment.

A SUCCESSFUL DEFENSE CAMPAIGN

NYC4AR's campaign to protect NYC abortion clinics from protestors escalated last May, when clinic invader Fidelis Moscinski, announced he would expand his harassment to Brooklyn. Over the course of the next few months, NYC4AR counter-protested there, forcing the procession to slow and delaying their arrival to the clinic (sometimes by hours), using tactics learned from years of defending the Manhattan-based clinic. In August, after the Archdiocese of NYC launched a PR campaign and lobbied the NYPD publicly to come down hard on the (wildly outnumbered and nonviolent) counter-protesters, the cops showed up in full militarized gear and arrested two members of NYC4AR, charging them with disorderly conduct, resisting arrest, and obstruction of pedestrian traffic. NYC4AR vowed that they would continue to show up to defend clinics. The next month, the church announced, "Due to the 20th Anniversary of 9/11, the police who normally accompany us during our prayerful Witness for Life in Brooklyn on the second Saturdays of the month will be unable to join us, and so the Brooklyn Witness has been suspended this Saturday…."

The counter-protesters showed up on the day of the canceled protest, flyered the neighborhood with information about how the church harasses patients, and collected signatures for a petition to have the church stop hosting the events. Less than two months later, Fidelis Moscinski announced they would no longer dedicate efforts to harassing patients at the Brooklyn-based clinic. An NYC4AR email announcement explains, "we were told that the church got tired of all the attention."

This short example of a clinic defense victory highlights the police's alignment with the Right in working to control reproductive lives and reproductive labor. The state cannot be relied upon to protect reproductive autonomy. On the contrary, the state has proven concretely harmful. When clinic administrators and spokespeople tell clinic defenders to stay home and that the police will provide safety, they fail to acknowledge that police pose a threat to the well being of their Black, Brown, immigrant, queer, and/or poor patients and staff. It is far more likely that police will be activated against a patient of color or a disabled person who becomes agitated in a waiting room or against a clinic defender than to interrupt street harassment or clinic attacks. And, when they are called, it is more likely that the police will use the tools of the state against a patient than against an anti-choice harasser.

CREATING OUR OWN SAFETY

Clinic defense offers a strategic alternative to the failing liberal approach to protecting reproductive autonomy. With the explicit goal of guarding clinics against the Right and taking back the space in front of abortion-providing health centers, clinic defense also allows an opportunity to reclaim the moral high ground and to reject, in word and deed, the shame assigned to abortion. Perhaps most importantly, the infrastructure required to build clinic defense networks could be the basis upon which our movement might activate abortion supporters, providing opportunities for the kind of community-building and praxis-based political education required to mobilize masses.

I originally wrote this piece for Tempest in February, 2022. Four months later, as expected, the Supreme Court overturned Roe vs. Wade. I was working at a Planned Parenthood clinic in a "safe" state the day Roe fell.

When the news came in, my colleagues cried and hugged. One senior doctor told me that she was grateful to be near the end of her career. She wanted to exit the field, to retire and "sell socks." She reflected on how sad it was that younger doctors would not be able to build a career around abortion.

No patients mentioned the decision, and none of the doctors said anything about it to the patients either. As for the bosses, they ordered cookies and demanded that staff stay for a breathing and stretching exercise after the patients had left.

Most of my colleagues went home after that, despite the fact that a massive protest was gathering a few blocks away. It became clear to me that the work I was doing in the clinic had become fully disconnected from the movement. It had never felt more urgent to connect with comrades in the streets.

In the following days, I received emails from the security unit of my clinic warning about the likelihood of increased chaos out front due to an uptick in clinic defenders. Not to worry, security said, the police were aware of the situation and they too would be present.

New York City for abortion rights, the organization I highlighted in this piece, embraced hundreds of new defenders after Roe fell. As expected, police were quick to arrest those who organized to defend bodily autonomy.

In our post-Roe world, there are no neutral positions. Reproductive justice will not be won without a fight, and the tradition of clinic defense reminds us how to step up.

GUERRILLA GIRLS
DEMAND A RETURN TO
TRADITIONAL VALUES
ON ABORTION.

Before the mid-19th century, abortion in the first few months of pregnancy was legal. Even the Catholic Church did not forbid it until 1869.*

* Carl N. Flanders. Abortion. Library in a Book. 1991.

A PUBLIC SERVICE MESSAGE FROM GUERRILLA GIRLS 532 LAGUARDIA PL. #237, NY 10012

In 1973 abortion became a constitutional right.
In 2022 the Extreme Court took it away.

What gives THE RIGHT the right
to take away WOMEN'S RIGHTS?

MAKING TROUBLE SINCE 1985   @guerrillagirls | guerrillagirls.com

TAP TAP

AHEM, UH...

I HAVE... DECIDED TO TRANSITION! ANY QUESTIONS?

YES, YOU, IN THE SHIRT!

HAVE YOU CONSIDERED, UH, MAYBE YOUR GENDER IDENTITY COMES FROM THE SAME PLACE AS INTERNALIZED MISOGYNY AND TRAUMA? AND YOUR TRANSITION IS A FORM OF UNRESOLVED SELF-HATRED OR SELF-HARM?

THE COMIC THAT DEFENDS SELF-HARM

BY ELIAS

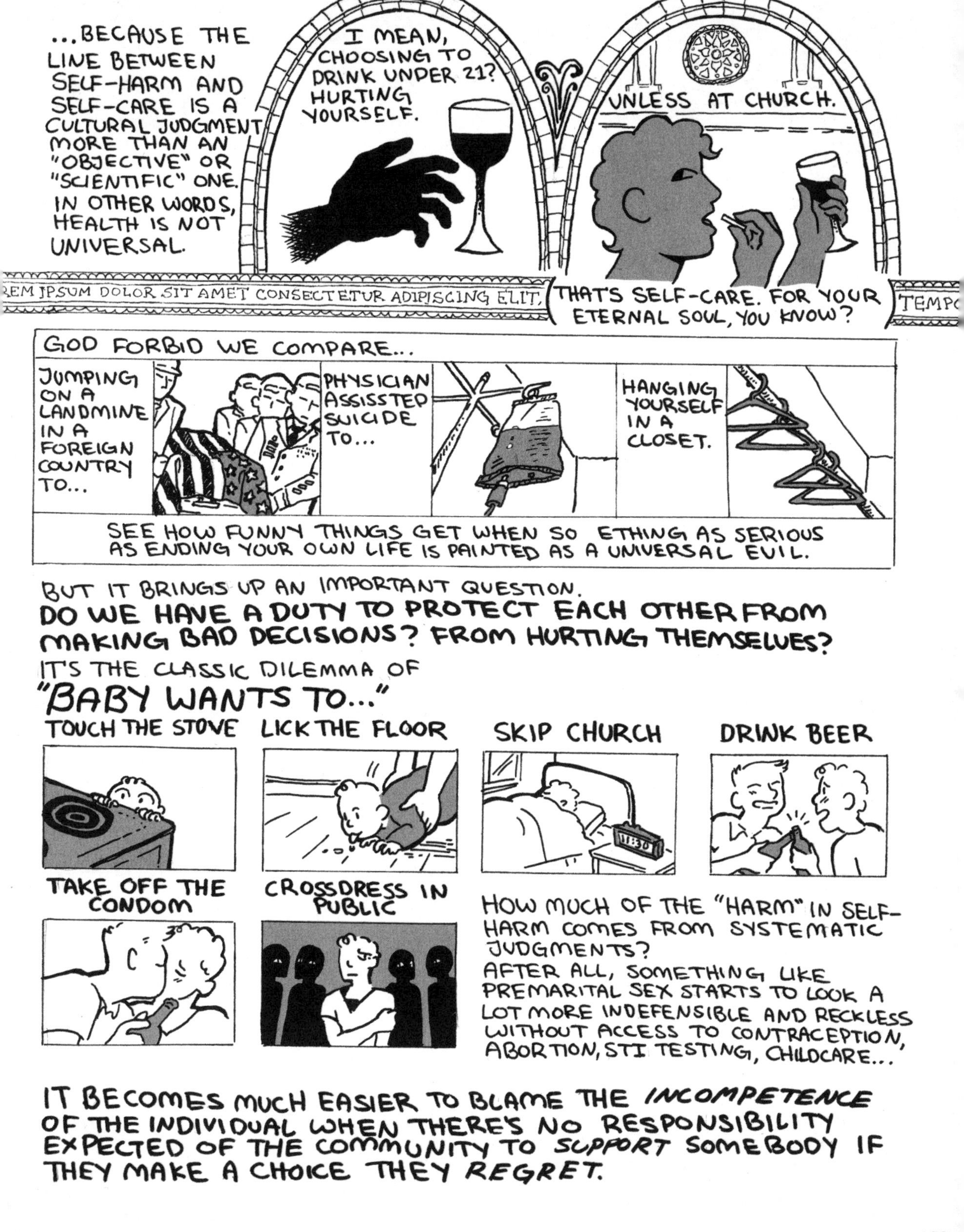
...BECAUSE THE LINE BETWEEN SELF-HARM AND SELF-CARE IS A CULTURAL JUDGMENT MORE THAN AN "OBJECTIVE" OR "SCIENTIFIC" ONE. IN OTHER WORDS, HEALTH IS NOT UNIVERSAL.
I MEAN, CHOOSING TO DRINK UNDER 21? HURTING YOURSELF.
UNLESS AT CHURCH.
REM IPSUM DOLOR SIT AMET CONSECTETUR ADIPISCING ELIT,
THAT'S SELF-CARE. FOR YOUR ETERNAL SOUL, YOU KNOW?
TEMPO
GOD FORBID WE COMPARE...
JUMPING ON A LANDMINE IN A FOREIGN COUNTRY TO...
PHYSICIAN ASSISSTED SUICIDE TO...
HANGING YOURSELF IN A CLOSET.
SEE HOW FUNNY THINGS GET WHEN SO ETHING AS SERIOUS AS ENDING YOUR OWN LIFE IS PAINTED AS A UNIVERSAL EVIL.
BUT IT BRINGS UP AN IMPORTANT QUESTION.
DO WE HAVE A DUTY TO PROTECT EACH OTHER FROM MAKING BAD DECISIONS? FROM HURTING THEMSELVES?
IT'S THE CLASSIC DILEMMA OF
"BABY WANTS TO..."
TOUCH THE STOVE
LICK THE FLOOR
SKIP CHURCH
11:30
DRINK BEER
TAKE OFF THE CONDOM
CROSSDRESS IN PUBLIC
HOW MUCH OF THE "HARM" IN SELF-HARM COMES FROM SYSTEMATIC JUDGMENTS?
AFTER ALL, SOMETHING LIKE PREMARITAL SEX STARTS TO LOOK A LOT MORE INDEFENSIBLE AND RECKLESS WITHOUT ACCESS TO CONTRACEPTION, ABORTION, STI TESTING, CHILDCARE...
IT BECOMES MUCH EASIER TO BLAME THE INCOMPETENCE OF THE INDIVIDUAL WHEN THERE'S NO RESPONSIBILITY EXPECTED OF THE COMMUNITY TO SUPPORT SOMEBODY IF THEY MAKE A CHOICE THEY REGRET.

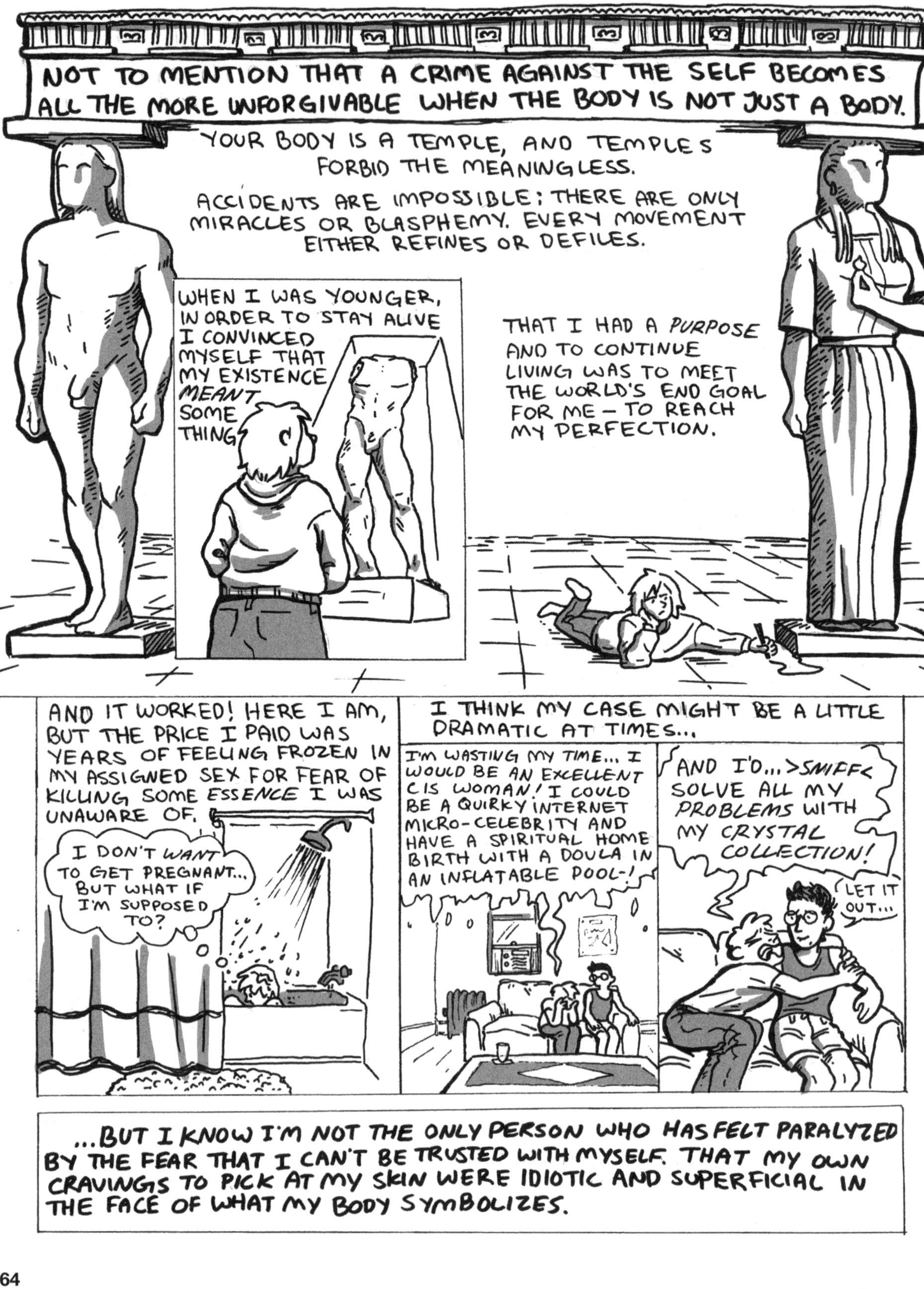
NOT TO MENTION THAT A CRIME AGAINST THE SELF BECOMES ALL THE MORE UNFORGIVABLE WHEN THE BODY IS NOT JUST A BODY.
YOUR BODY IS A TEMPLE, AND TEMPLES FORBID THE MEANINGLESS.
ACCIDENTS ARE IMPOSSIBLE: THERE ARE ONLY MIRACLES OR BLASPHEMY. EVERY MOVEMENT EITHER REFINES OR DEFILES.
WHEN I WAS YOUNGER, IN ORDER TO STAY ALIVE I CONVINCED MYSELF THAT MY EXISTENCE MEANT SOME THING
THAT I HAD A PURPOSE AND TO CONTINUE LIVING WAS TO MEET THE WORLD'S END GOAL FOR ME – TO REACH MY PERFECTION.
AND IT WORKED! HERE I AM, BUT THE PRICE I PAID WAS YEARS OF FEELING FROZEN IN MY ASSIGNED SEX FOR FEAR OF KILLING SOME ESSENCE I WAS UNAWARE OF.
I DON'T WANT TO GET PREGNANT... BUT WHAT IF I'M SUPPOSED TO?
I THINK MY CASE MIGHT BE A LITTLE DRAMATIC AT TIMES...
I'M WASTING MY TIME... I WOULD BE AN EXCELLENT CIS WOMAN! I COULD BE A QUIRKY INTERNET MICRO-CELEBRITY AND HAVE A SPIRITUAL HOME BIRTH WITH A DOULA IN AN INFLATABLE POOL-!
AND I'D... >SNIFF< SOLVE ALL MY PROBLEMS WITH MY CRYSTAL COLLECTION!
LET IT OUT...
...BUT I KNOW I'M NOT THE ONLY PERSON WHO HAS FELT PARALYZED BY THE FEAR THAT I CAN'T BE TRUSTED WITH MYSELF. THAT MY OWN CRAVINGS TO PICK AT MY SKIN WERE IDIOTIC AND SUPERFICIAL IN THE FACE OF WHAT MY BODY SYMBOLIZES.

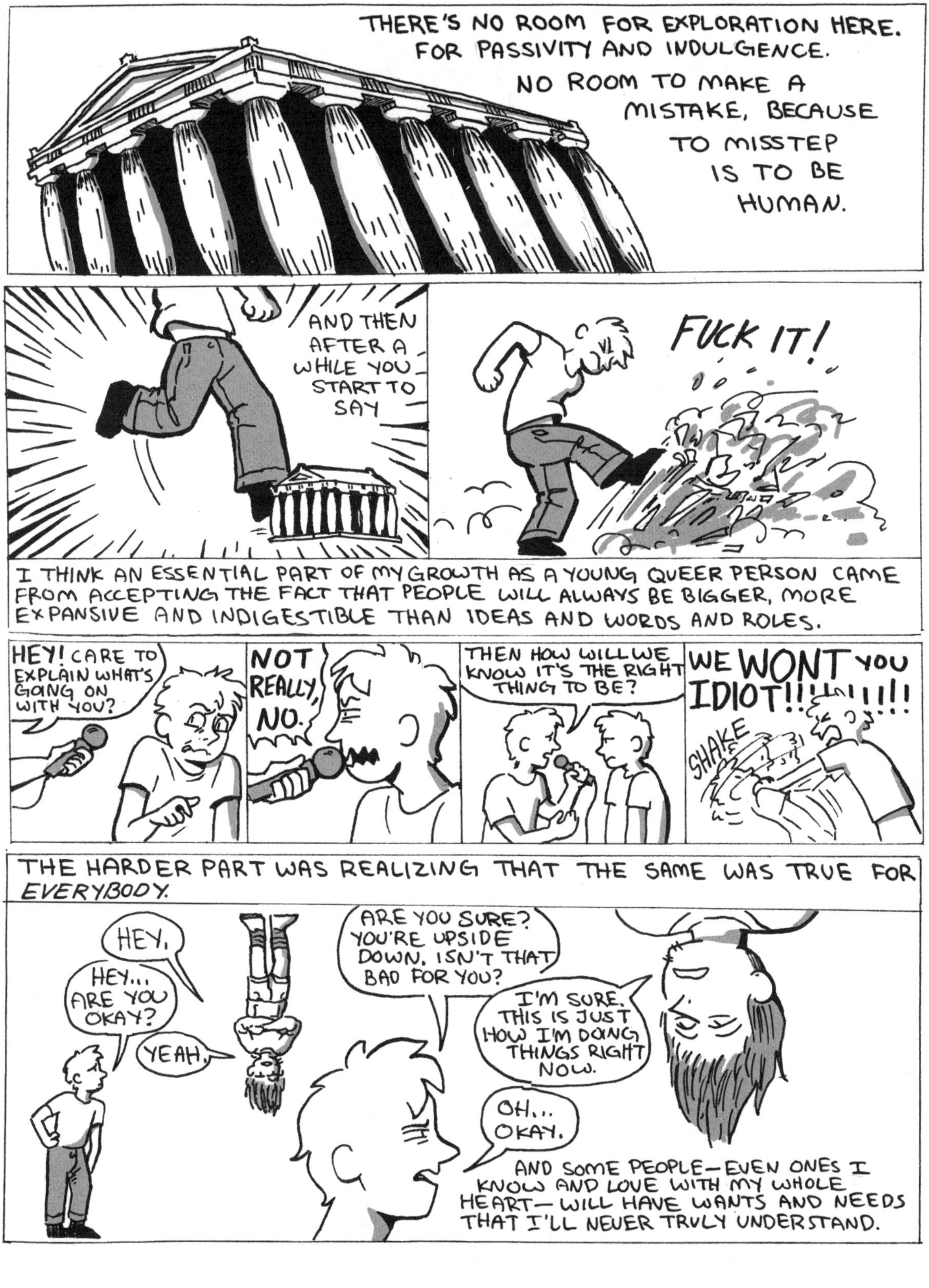
THERE'S NO ROOM FOR EXPLORATION HERE. FOR PASSIVITY AND INDULGENCE.
NO ROOM TO MAKE A MISTAKE, BECAUSE TO MISSTEP IS TO BE HUMAN.
AND THEN AFTER A WHILE YOU START TO SAY
FUCK IT!
I THINK AN ESSENTIAL PART OF MY GROWTH AS A YOUNG QUEER PERSON CAME FROM ACCEPTING THE FACT THAT PEOPLE WILL ALWAYS BE BIGGER, MORE EXPANSIVE AND INDIGESTIBLE THAN IDEAS AND WORDS AND ROLES.
HEY! CARE TO EXPLAIN WHAT'S GOING ON WITH YOU?
NOT REALLY, NO.
THEN HOW WILL WE KNOW IT'S THE RIGHT THING TO BE?
WE WONT YOU IDIOT!!!!!!!!!
SHAKE
THE HARDER PART WAS REALIZING THAT THE SAME WAS TRUE FOR EVERYBODY.
HEY.
HEY... ARE YOU OKAY?
YEAH.
ARE YOU SURE? YOU'RE UPSIDE DOWN. ISN'T THAT BAD FOR YOU?
I'M SURE. THIS IS JUST HOW I'M DOING THINGS RIGHT NOW.
OH... OKAY.
AND SOME PEOPLE—EVEN ONES I KNOW AND LOVE WITH MY WHOLE HEART—WILL HAVE WANTS AND NEEDS THAT I'LL NEVER TRULY UNDERSTAND.

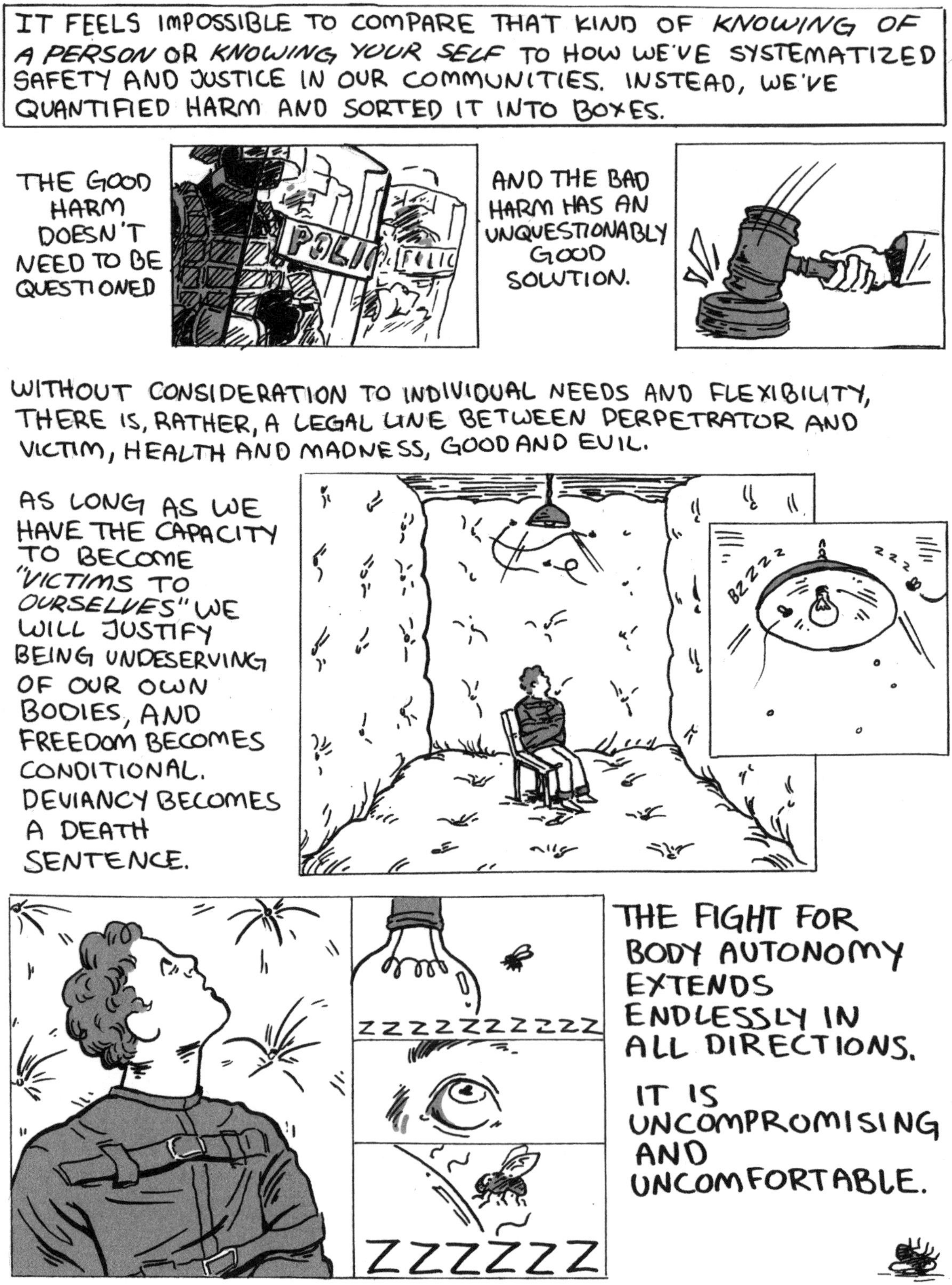
IT FEELS IMPOSSIBLE TO COMPARE THAT KIND OF *KNOWING OF A PERSON* OR *KNOWING YOUR SELF* TO HOW WE'VE SYSTEMATIZED SAFETY AND JUSTICE IN OUR COMMUNITIES. INSTEAD, WE'VE QUANTIFIED HARM AND SORTED IT INTO BOXES.
THE GOOD HARM DOESN'T NEED TO BE QUESTIONED
AND THE BAD HARM HAS AN UNQUESTIONABLY GOOD SOLUTION.
WITHOUT CONSIDERATION TO INDIVIDUAL NEEDS AND FLEXIBILITY, THERE IS, RATHER, A LEGAL LINE BETWEEN PERPETRATOR AND VICTIM, HEALTH AND MADNESS, GOOD AND EVIL.
AS LONG AS WE HAVE THE CAPACITY TO BECOME "*VICTIMS TO OURSELVES*" WE WILL JUSTIFY BEING UNDESERVING OF OUR OWN BODIES, AND FREEDOM BECOMES CONDITIONAL. DEVIANCY BECOMES A DEATH SENTENCE.
BZZZZ
ZZZ
ZZZZZZZZZZZ
ZZZZZZ
THE FIGHT FOR BODY AUTONOMY EXTENDS ENDLESSLY IN ALL DIRECTIONS.
IT IS UNCOMPROMISING AND UNCOMFORTABLE.

IT INCLUDES THE RIGHT TO STAY THE SAME...

END INTERSEX GENITAL MUTILATION NOW

PROTECT TRANS YOUTH

...OR NOT.

TO BOTH LIVE AND DIE ON YOUR TERMS.

THE RIGHT TO SAY NO, I WON'T CHANGE MY MIND...

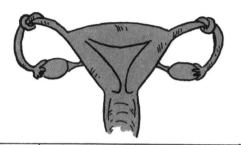

...AND THE RIGHT TO CHANGE IT.

ZRRRRR

ZZRRR

THE RIGHT TO BAD IDEAS AND SELF-DETERMIN-ATION.

TO BE SOMETHING THAT DOESN'T MAKE ANY SENSE.

HM...

...

AND HOW ABOUT A WORLD WHERE, EVEN AFTER EVERYTHING, YOU CAN STILL GO HOME AT THE END OF THE DAY.

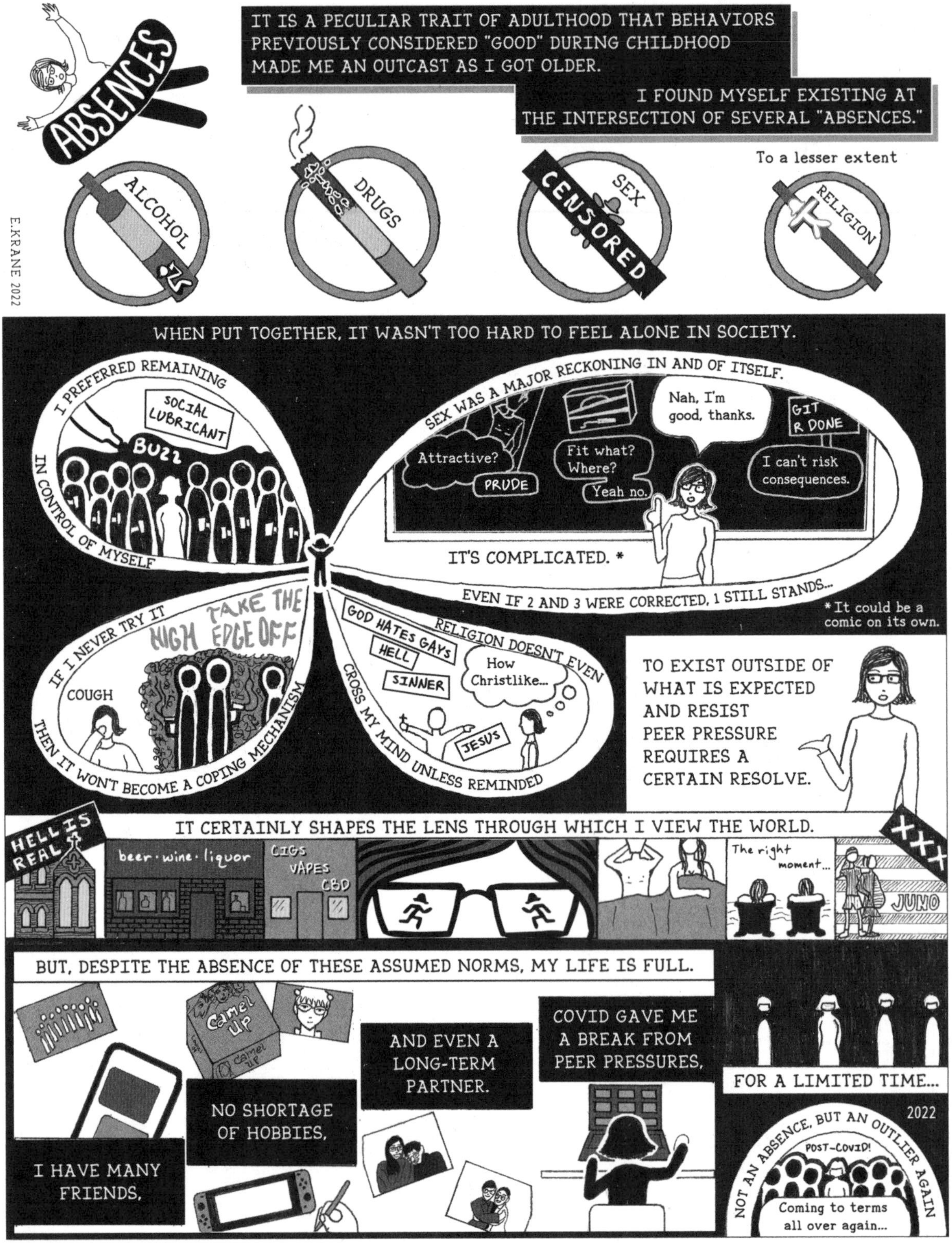

ABSENCES
IT IS A PECULIAR TRAIT OF ADULTHOOD THAT BEHAVIORS PREVIOUSLY CONSIDERED "GOOD" DURING CHILDHOOD MADE ME AN OUTCAST AS I GOT OLDER.
I FOUND MYSELF EXISTING AT THE INTERSECTION OF SEVERAL "ABSENCES."
ALCOHOL
DRUGS
SEX
CENSORED
To a lesser extent
RELIGION
E.KRANE 2022
WHEN PUT TOGETHER, IT WASN'T TOO HARD TO FEEL ALONE IN SOCIETY.
I PREFERRED REMAINING IN CONTROL OF MYSELF
SOCIAL LUBRICANT
BUZZ
SEX WAS A MAJOR RECKONING IN AND OF ITSELF.
Attractive?
PRUDE
Fit what? Where?
Yeah no.
Nah, I'm good, thanks.
GIT R DONE
I can't risk consequences.
IT'S COMPLICATED. *
EVEN IF 2 AND 3 WERE CORRECTED, 1 STILL STANDS...
*It could be a comic on its own.
IF I NEVER TRY IT THEN IT WON'T BECOME A COPING MECHANISM
TAKE THE EDGE OFF
HIGH
COUGH
RELIGION DOESN'T EVEN CROSS MY MIND UNLESS REMINDED
GOD HATES GAYS
HELL
SINNER
How Christlike...
JESUS
TO EXIST OUTSIDE OF WHAT IS EXPECTED AND RESIST PEER PRESSURE REQUIRES A CERTAIN RESOLVE.
IT CERTAINLY SHAPES THE LENS THROUGH WHICH I VIEW THE WORLD.
HELL IS REAL
beer · wine · liquor
CIGS VAPES CBD
The right moment...
XXX
JUNO
BUT, DESPITE THE ABSENCE OF THESE ASSUMED NORMS, MY LIFE IS FULL.
Camel Up
I HAVE MANY FRIENDS,
NO SHORTAGE OF HOBBIES,
AND EVEN A LONG-TERM PARTNER.
COVID GAVE ME A BREAK FROM PEER PRESSURES,
FOR A LIMITED TIME...
2022
NOT AN ABSENCE, BUT AN OUTLIER AGAIN
POST-COVID!
Coming to terms all over again...

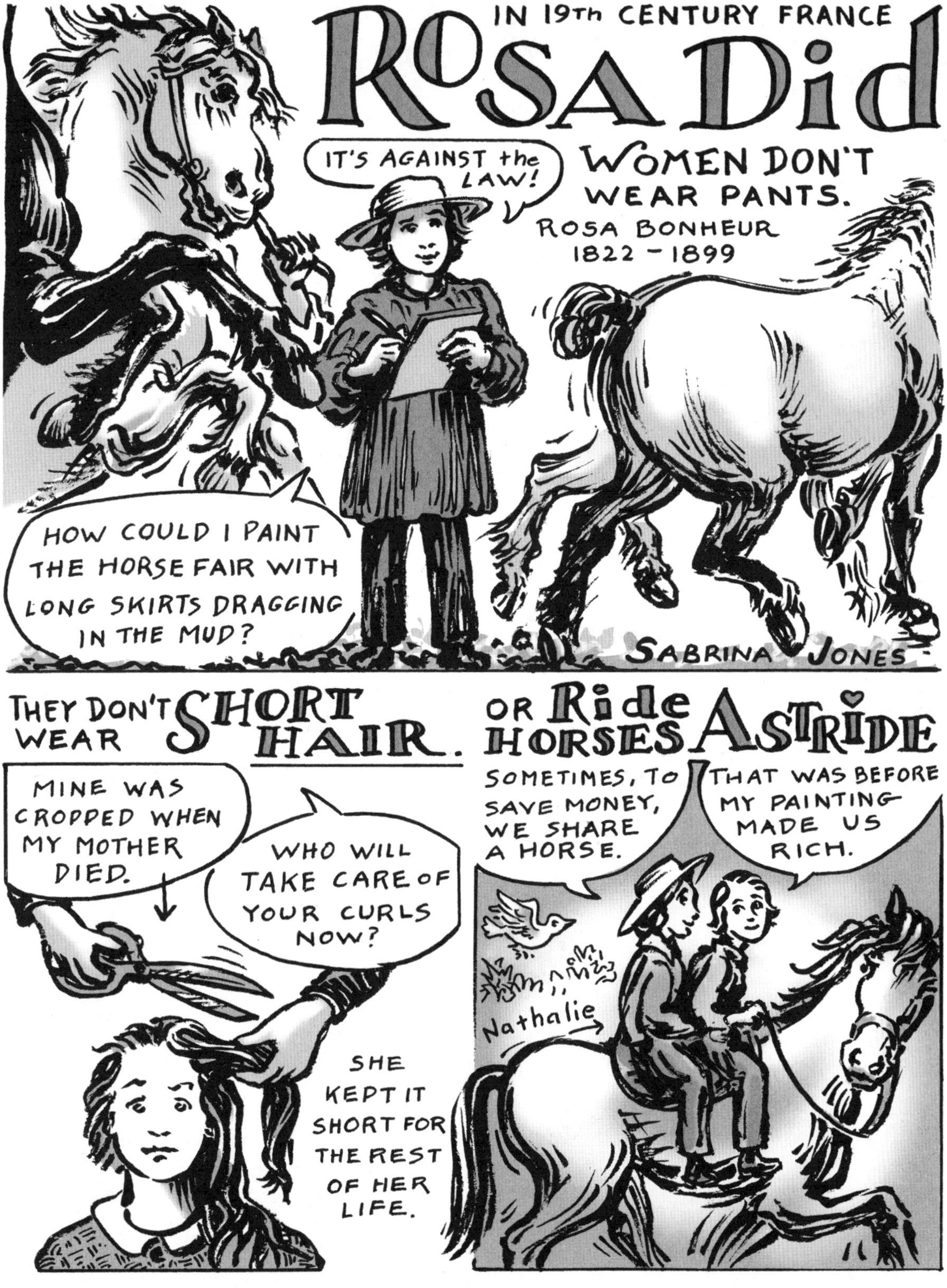

IN 19th CENTURY FRANCE
ROSA DID
WOMEN DON'T WEAR PANTS.
IT'S AGAINST the LAW!
ROSA BONHEUR 1822 – 1899
HOW COULD I PAINT THE HORSE FAIR WITH LONG SKIRTS DRAGGING IN THE MUD?
SABRINA JONES
THEY DON'T WEAR SHORT HAIR.
MINE WAS CROPPED WHEN MY MOTHER DIED.
WHO WILL TAKE CARE OF YOUR CURLS NOW?
SHE KEPT IT SHORT FOR THE REST OF HER LIFE.
OR RIDE HORSES ASTRIDE
SOMETIMES, TO SAVE MONEY, WE SHARE A HORSE.
THAT WAS BEFORE MY PAINTING MADE US RICH.
Nathalie

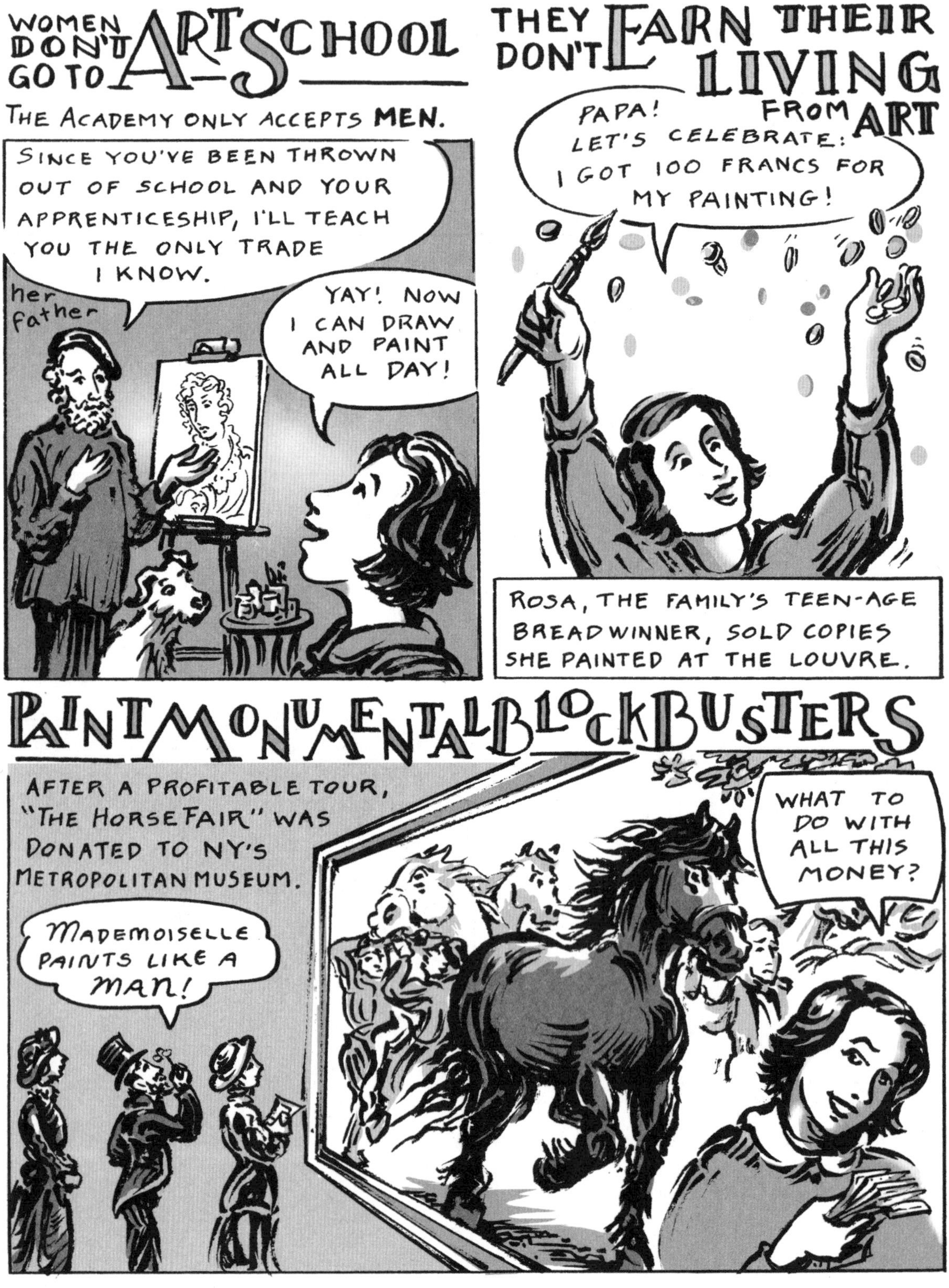
WOMEN DON'T GO TO ART SCHOOL
THE ACADEMY ONLY ACCEPTS MEN.
SINCE YOU'VE BEEN THROWN OUT OF SCHOOL AND YOUR APPRENTICESHIP, I'LL TEACH YOU THE ONLY TRADE I KNOW.
her father
YAY! NOW I CAN DRAW AND PAINT ALL DAY!
THEY DON'T EARN THEIR LIVING FROM ART
PAPA! LET'S CELEBRATE: I GOT 100 FRANCS FOR MY PAINTING!
ROSA, THE FAMILY'S TEEN-AGE BREADWINNER, SOLD COPIES SHE PAINTED AT THE LOUVRE.
PAINT MONUMENTAL BLOCKBUSTERS
AFTER A PROFITABLE TOUR, "THE HORSE FAIR" WAS DONATED TO NY'S METROPOLITAN MUSEUM.
MADEMOISELLE PAINTS LIKE A MAN!
WHAT TO DO WITH ALL THIS MONEY?

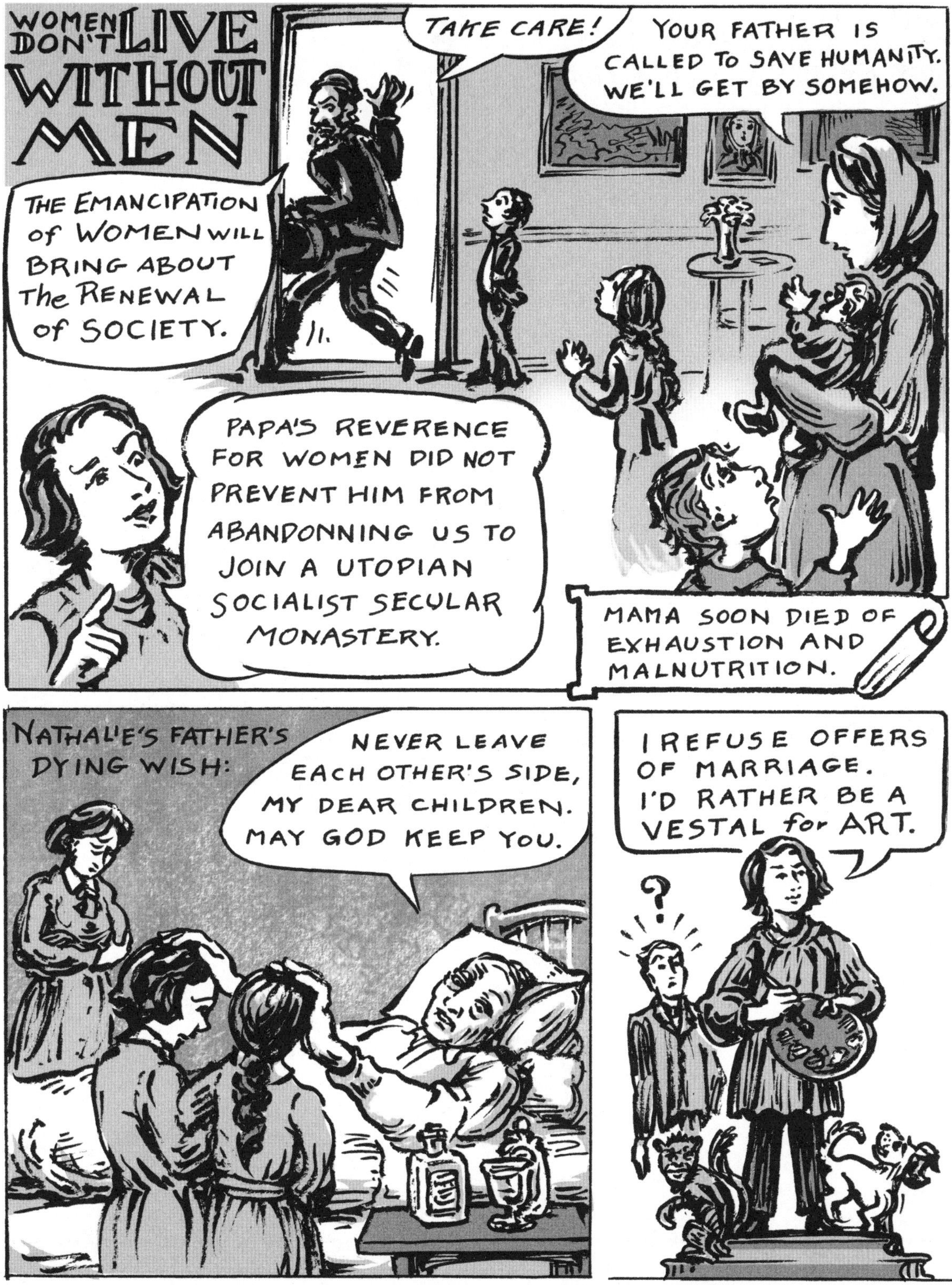
WOMEN DON'T LIVE WITHOUT MEN
TAKE CARE!
YOUR FATHER IS CALLED TO SAVE HUMANITY. WE'LL GET BY SOMEHOW.
THE EMANCIPATION of WOMEN WILL BRING ABOUT The RENEWAL of SOCIETY.
PAPA'S REVERENCE FOR WOMEN DID NOT PREVENT HIM FROM ABANDONNING US TO JOIN A UTOPIAN SOCIALIST SECULAR MONASTERY.
MAMA SOON DIED OF EXHAUSTION AND MALNUTRITION.
NATHALIE'S FATHER'S DYING WISH:
NEVER LEAVE EACH OTHER'S SIDE, MY DEAR CHILDREN. MAY GOD KEEP YOU.
I REFUSE OFFERS OF MARRIAGE. I'D RATHER BE A VESTAL for ART.
?

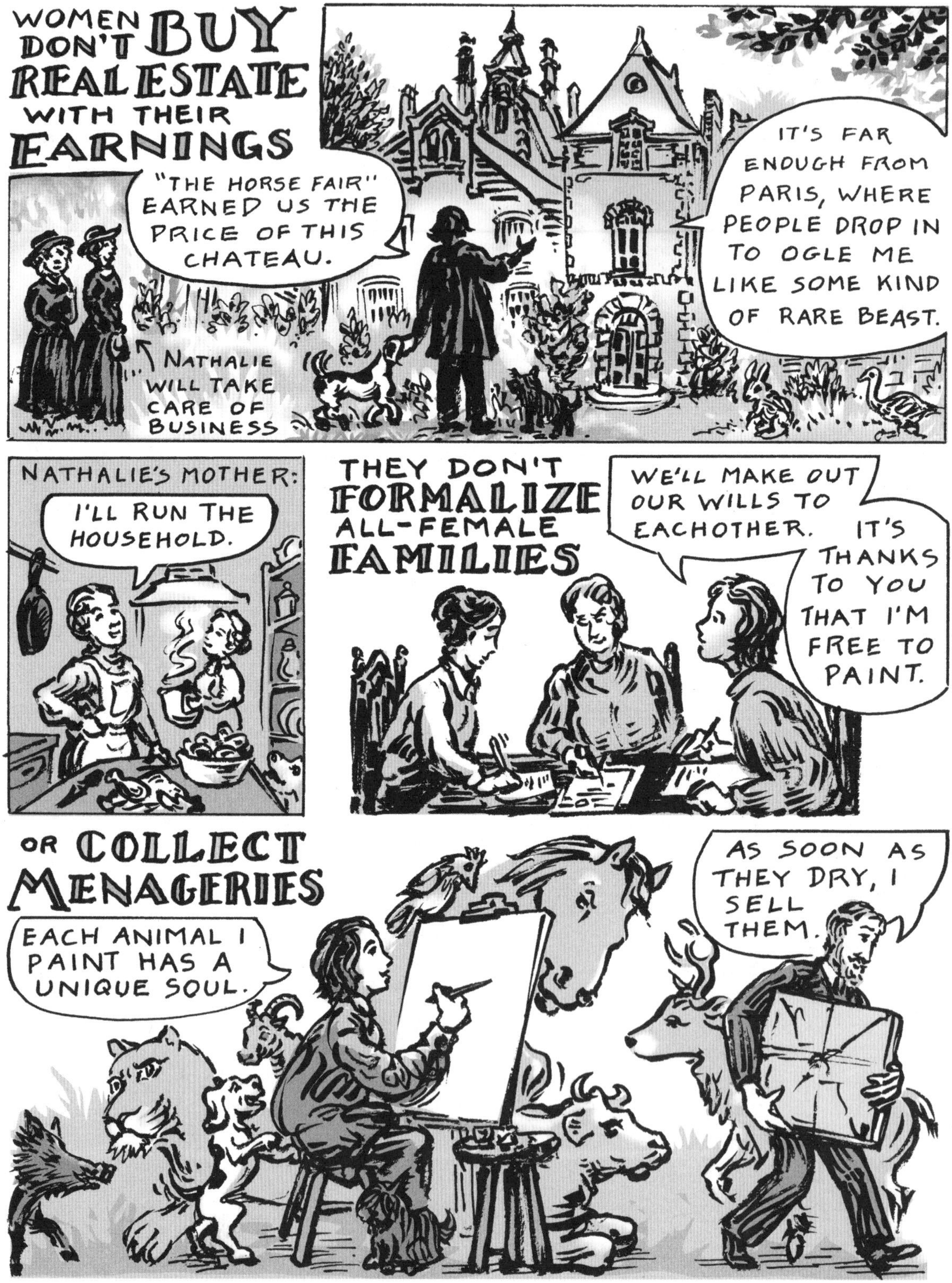
WOMEN DON'T BUY REAL ESTATE WITH THEIR EARNINGS
"THE HORSE FAIR" EARNED US THE PRICE OF THIS CHATEAU.
IT'S FAR ENOUGH FROM PARIS, WHERE PEOPLE DROP IN TO OGLE ME LIKE SOME KIND OF RARE BEAST.
NATHALIE WILL TAKE CARE OF BUSINESS
NATHALIE'S MOTHER:
I'LL RUN THE HOUSEHOLD.
THEY DON'T FORMALIZE ALL-FEMALE FAMILIES
WE'LL MAKE OUT OUR WILLS TO EACHOTHER.
IT'S THANKS TO YOU THAT I'M FREE TO PAINT.
OR COLLECT MENAGERIES
EACH ANIMAL I PAINT HAS A UNIQUE SOUL.
AS SOON AS THEY DRY, I SELL THEM.

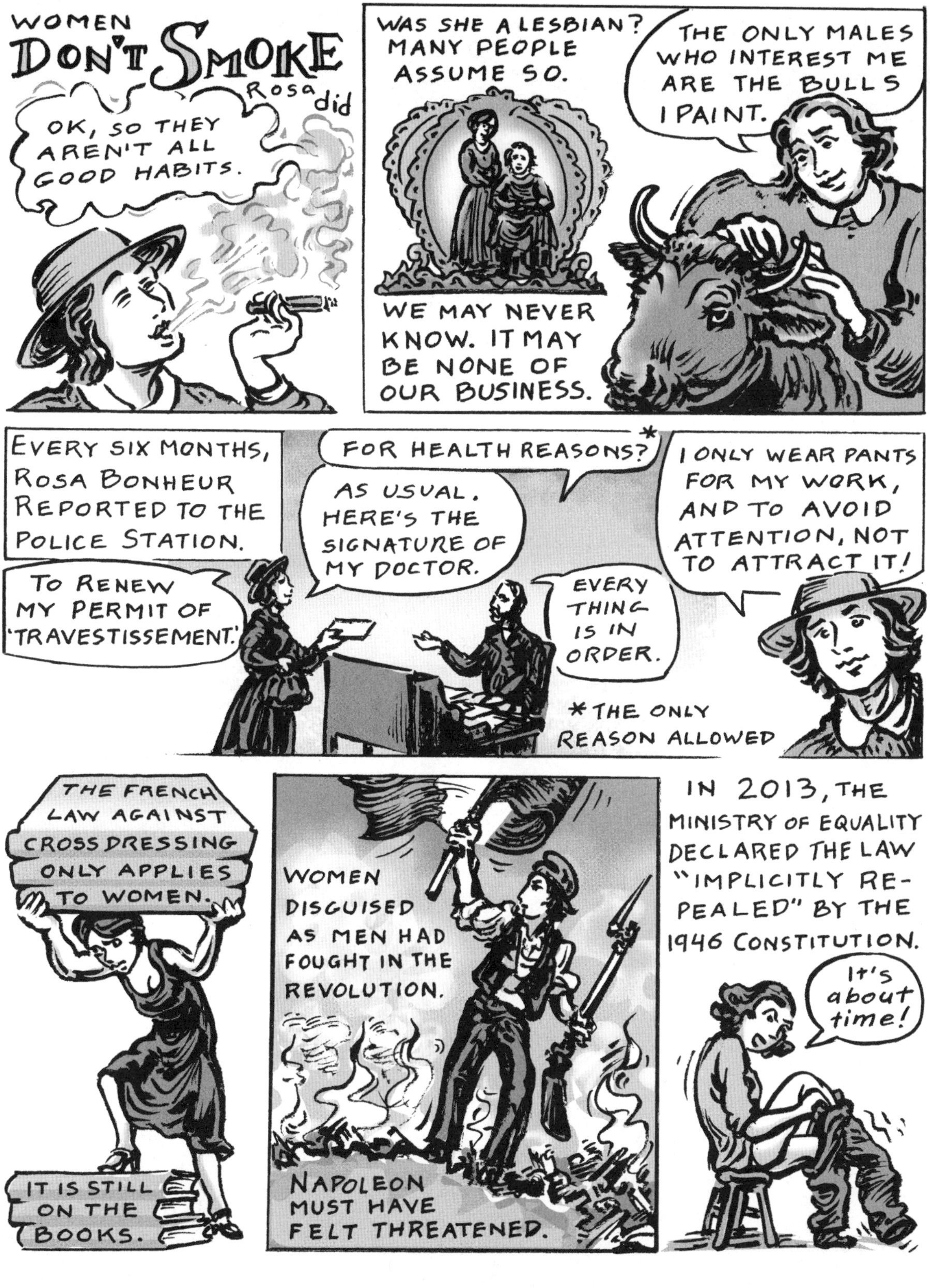

WOMEN DON'T SMOKE
Rosa did
OK, SO THEY AREN'T ALL GOOD HABITS.
WAS SHE A LESBIAN? MANY PEOPLE ASSUME SO.
THE ONLY MALES WHO INTEREST ME ARE THE BULLS I PAINT.
WE MAY NEVER KNOW. IT MAY BE NONE OF OUR BUSINESS.
EVERY SIX MONTHS, ROSA BONHEUR REPORTED TO THE POLICE STATION.
TO RENEW MY PERMIT OF 'TRAVESTISSEMENT.'
FOR HEALTH REASONS?*
AS USUAL. HERE'S THE SIGNATURE OF MY DOCTOR.
EVERY THING IS IN ORDER.
I ONLY WEAR PANTS FOR MY WORK, AND TO AVOID ATTENTION, NOT TO ATTRACT IT!
*THE ONLY REASON ALLOWED
THE FRENCH LAW AGAINST CROSSDRESSING ONLY APPLIES TO WOMEN.
IT IS STILL ON THE BOOKS.
WOMEN DISGUISED AS MEN HAD FOUGHT IN THE REVOLUTION.
NAPOLEON MUST HAVE FELT THREATENED.
IN 2013, THE MINISTRY OF EQUALITY DECLARED THE LAW "IMPLICITLY RE-PEALED" BY THE 1946 CONSTITUTION.
It's about time!

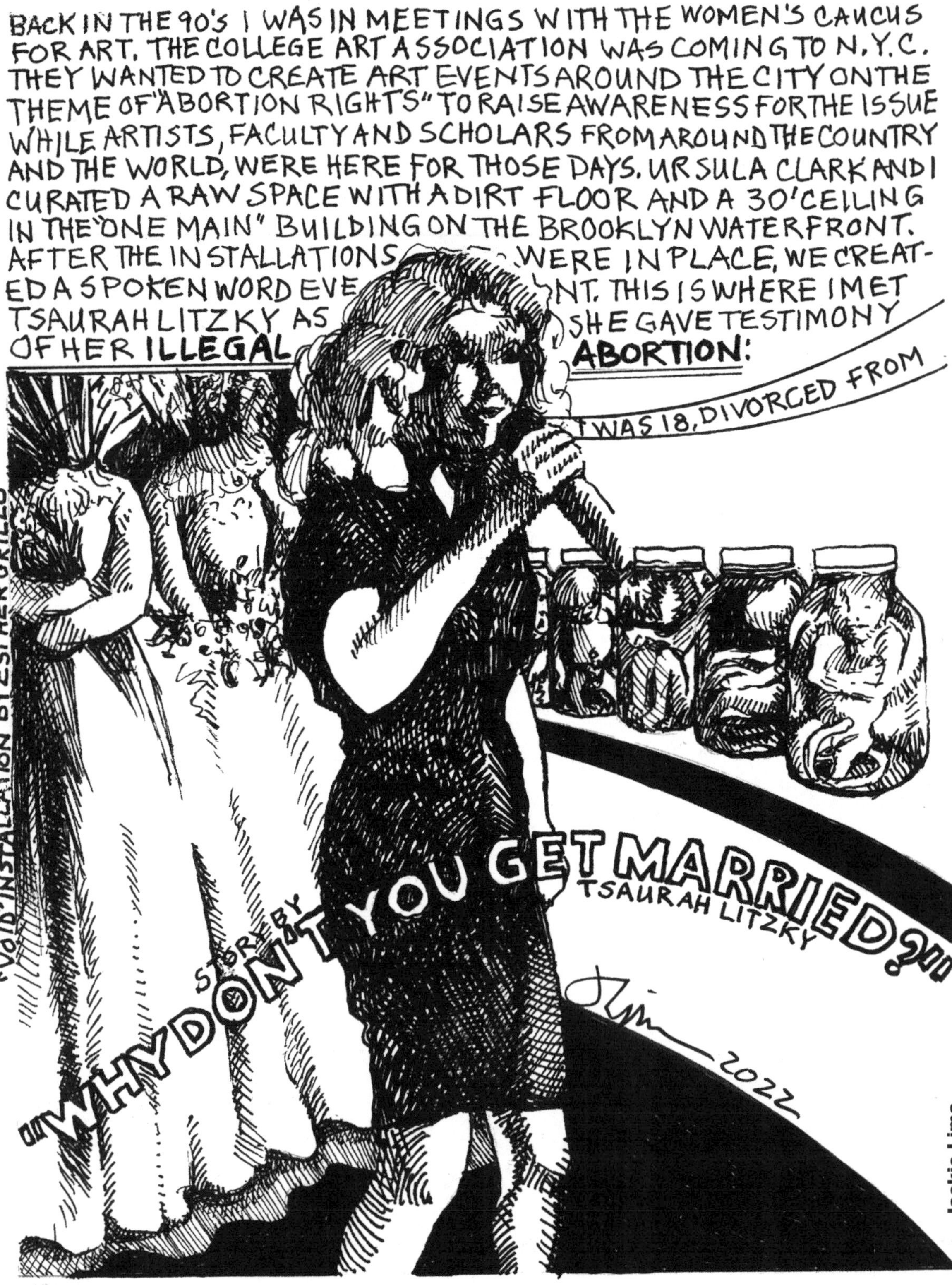
BACK IN THE 90'S I WAS IN MEETINGS WITH THE WOMEN'S CAUCUS FOR ART. THE COLLEGE ART ASSOCIATION WAS COMING TO N.Y.C. THEY WANTED TO CREATE ART EVENTS AROUND THE CITY ON THE THEME OF "ABORTION RIGHTS" TO RAISE AWARENESS FOR THE ISSUE WHILE ARTISTS, FACULTY AND SCHOLARS FROM AROUND THE COUNTRY AND THE WORLD, WERE HERE FOR THOSE DAYS. URSULA CLARK AND I CURATED A RAW SPACE WITH A DIRT FLOOR AND A 30' CEILING IN THE "ONE MAIN" BUILDING ON THE BROOKLYN WATERFRONT. AFTER THE INSTALLATIONS WERE IN PLACE, WE CREATED A SPOKEN WORD EVENT. THIS IS WHERE I MET TSAURAH LITZKY AS SHE GAVE TESTIMONY OF HER ILLEGAL ABORTION:
I WAS 18, DIVORCED FROM
"VOID" INSTALLATION BY ESTHER GRILLO
"WHY DON'T YOU GET MARRIED?!"
STORY BY TSAURAH LITZKY
2022
Jackie Lima

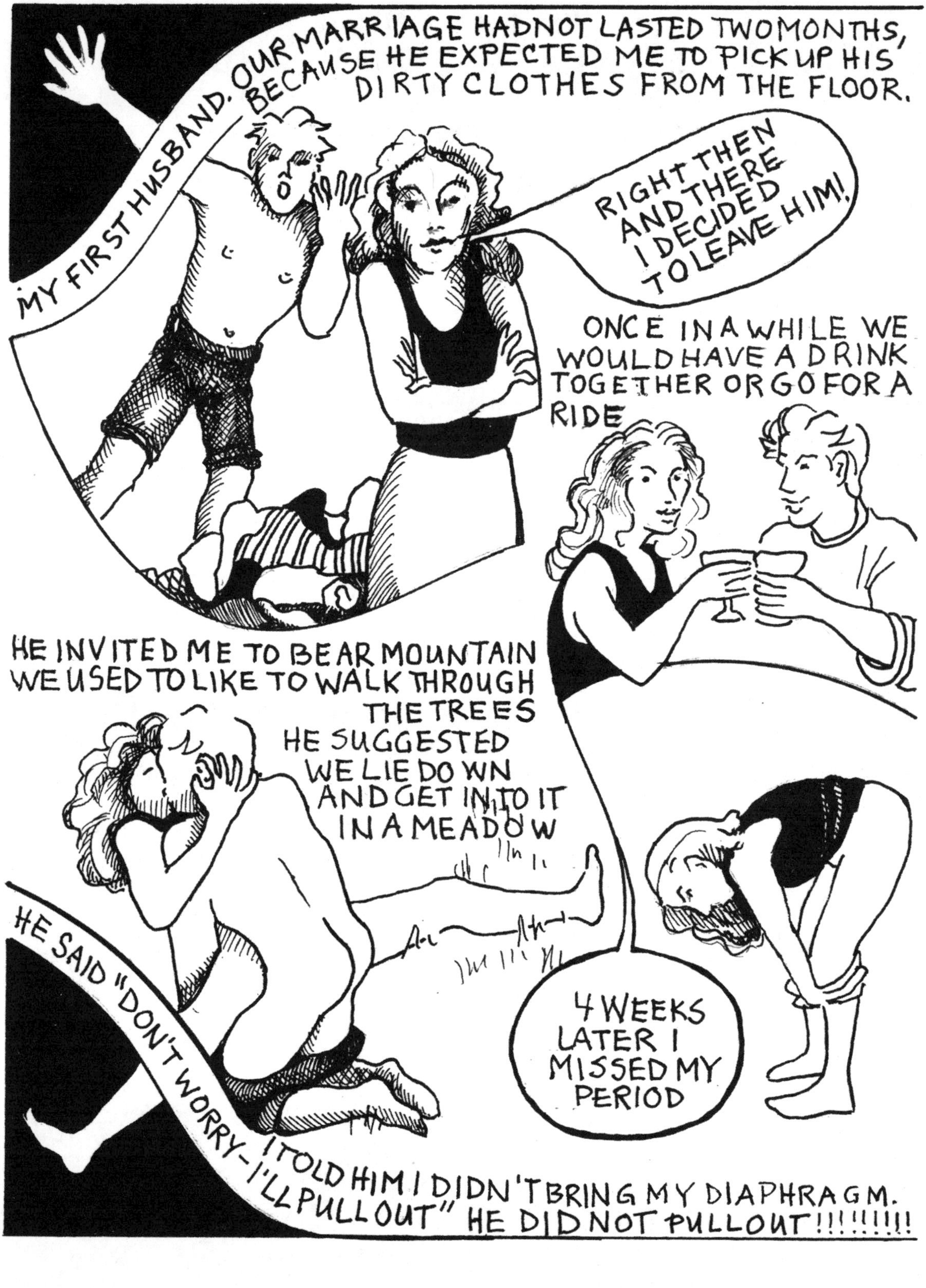
MY FIRST HUSBAND. OUR MARRIAGE HADNOT LASTED TWOMONTHS, BECAUSE HE EXPECTED ME TO PICK UP HIS DIRTY CLOTHES FROM THE FLOOR.
RIGHT THEN AND THERE I DECIDED TO LEAVE HIM!
ONCE IN A WHILE WE WOULD HAVE A DRINK TOGETHER OR GO FOR A RIDE
HE INVITED ME TO BEAR MOUNTAIN WE USED TO LIKE TO WALK THROUGH THE TREES
HE SUGGESTED WE LIE DOWN AND GET INTO IT IN A MEADOW
4 WEEKS LATER I MISSED MY PERIOD
I TOLD HIM I DIDN'T BRING MY DIAPHRAGM.
HE SAID "DON'T WORRY- I'LL PULL OUT" HE DID NOT PULL OUT!!!!!!!!

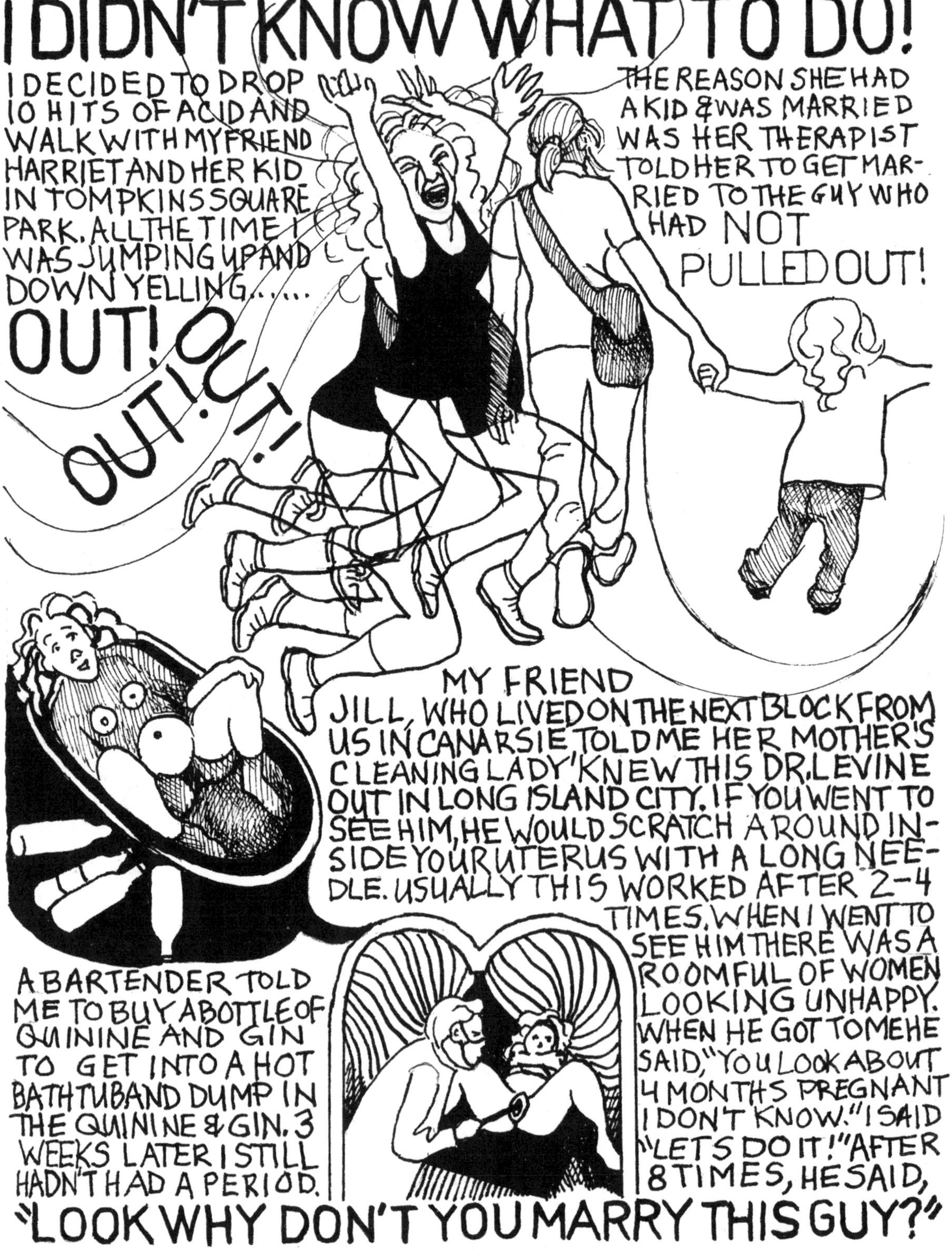

I DIDN'T KNOW WHAT TO DO!
I DECIDED TO DROP 10 HITS OF ACID AND WALK WITH MY FRIEND HARRIET AND HER KID IN TOMPKINS SQUARE PARK. ALL THE TIME I WAS JUMPING UP AND DOWN YELLING......
OUT! OUT! OUT!
THE REASON SHE HAD A KID & WAS MARRIED WAS HER THERAPIST TOLD HER TO GET MARRIED TO THE GUY WHO HAD NOT PULLED OUT!
MY FRIEND JILL, WHO LIVED ON THE NEXT BLOCK FROM US IN CANARSIE, TOLD ME HER MOTHER'S CLEANING LADY KNEW THIS DR. LEVINE OUT IN LONG ISLAND CITY. IF YOU WENT TO SEE HIM, HE WOULD SCRATCH AROUND INSIDE YOUR UTERUS WITH A LONG NEEDLE. USUALLY THIS WORKED AFTER 2-4 TIMES. WHEN I WENT TO SEE HIM THERE WAS A ROOMFUL OF WOMEN LOOKING UNHAPPY. WHEN HE GOT TO ME HE SAID, "YOU LOOK ABOUT 4 MONTHS PREGNANT I DON'T KNOW." I SAID "LETS DO IT!" AFTER 8 TIMES, HE SAID,
A BARTENDER TOLD ME TO BUY A BOTTLE OF QUININE AND GIN TO GET INTO A HOT BATHTUB AND DUMP IN THE QUININE & GIN. 3 WEEKS LATER I STILL HADN'T HAD A PERIOD.
"LOOK WHY DON'T YOU MARRY THIS GUY?"

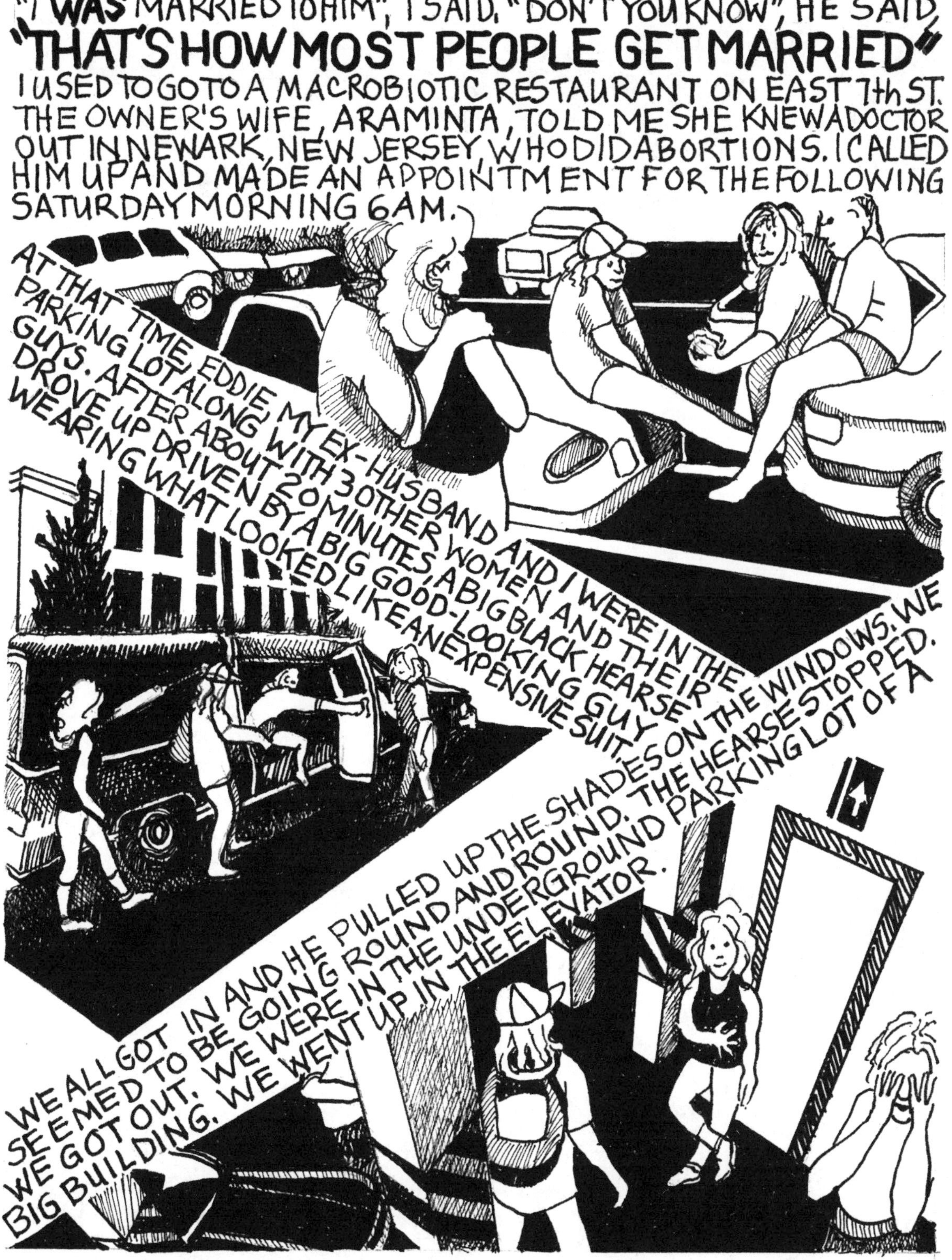
"I WAS MARRIED TO HIM", I SAID. "DON'T YOU KNOW", HE SAID,
"THAT'S HOW MOST PEOPLE GET MARRIED"
I USED TO GO TO A MACROBIOTIC RESTAURANT ON EAST 7th ST. THE OWNER'S WIFE, ARAMINTA, TOLD ME SHE KNEW A DOCTOR OUT IN NEWARK, NEW JERSEY, WHO DID ABORTIONS. I CALLED HIM UP AND MADE AN APPOINTMENT FOR THE FOLLOWING SATURDAY MORNING 6AM.
AT THAT TIME, EDDIE, MY EX-HUSBAND AND I WERE IN THE PARKING LOT ALONG WITH 30 OTHER WOMEN AND THEIR GUYS. AFTER ABOUT 20 MINUTES, A BIG BLACK HEARSE DROVE UP DRIVEN BY A BIG GOOD-LOOKING GUY WEARING WHAT LOOKED LIKE AN EXPENSIVE SUIT.
WE ALL GOT IN AND HE PULLED UP THE SHADES ON THE WINDOWS. WE SEEMED TO BE GOING ROUND AND ROUND. THE HEARSE STOPPED. WE GOT OUT. WE WERE IN THE UNDERGROUND PARKING LOT OF A BIG BUILDING. WE WENT UP IN THE ELEVATOR.

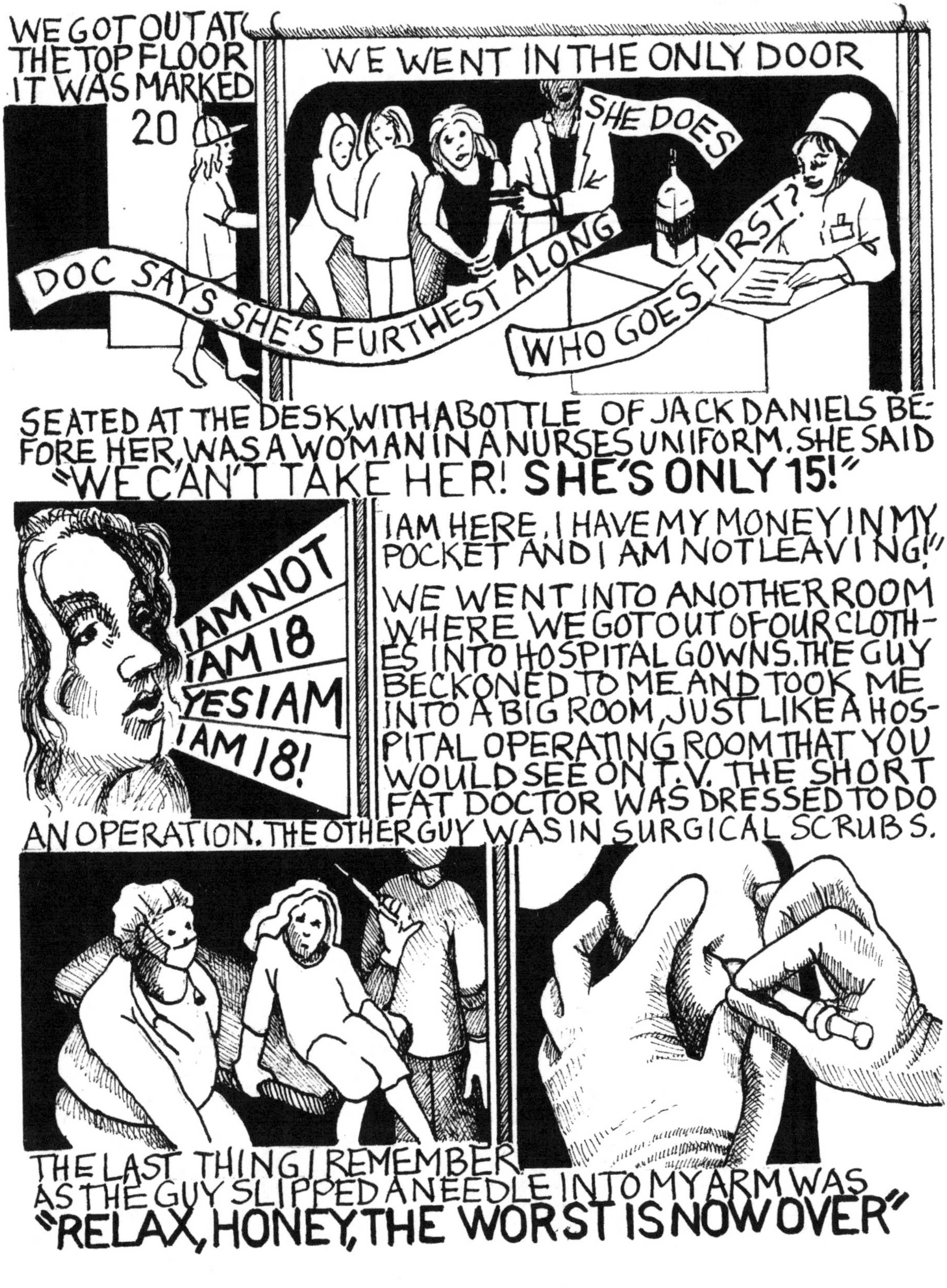
WE GOT OUT AT THE TOP FLOOR IT WAS MARKED
20
WE WENT IN THE ONLY DOOR
SHE DOES
WHO GOES FIRST?
DOC SAYS SHE'S FURTHEST ALONG
SEATED AT THE DESK, WITH A BOTTLE OF JACK DANIELS BEFORE HER, WAS A WOMAN IN A NURSES UNIFORM. SHE SAID
"WE CAN'T TAKE HER! SHE'S ONLY 15!"
I AM NOT
I AM 18
YES I AM
I AM 18!
I AM HERE, I HAVE MY MONEY IN MY POCKET AND I AM NOT LEAVING!"
WE WENT INTO ANOTHER ROOM WHERE WE GOT OUT OF OUR CLOTHES INTO HOSPITAL GOWNS. THE GUY BECKONED TO ME AND TOOK ME INTO A BIG ROOM, JUST LIKE A HOSPITAL OPERATING ROOM THAT YOU WOULD SEE ON T.V. THE SHORT FAT DOCTOR WAS DRESSED TO DO AN OPERATION. THE OTHER GUY WAS IN SURGICAL SCRUBS.
THE LAST THING I REMEMBER AS THE GUY SLIPPED A NEEDLE INTO MY ARM WAS
"RELAX, HONEY, THE WORST IS NOW OVER"

"THE NEXT THING I KNEW, I WAS AWAKE"

THE DOCTOR AND THE GUY WERE MARCHING ME UP AND DOWN IN THE ROOM WHERE WE HAD CHANGED OUR CLOTHES. THE OTHER WOMEN WERE STANDING BY, THEY WERE ALL DRESSED AND LOOKED HORRIFIED. THE DOCTOR AND THE GUY WERE SLAPPING ME – SLAPPING ME – SLAPPING ME – SLAPPING ME!

IF I DIDN'T WAKE UP, PROBABLY WHAT THEY WOULD HAVE DONE IS TAKEN ALL MY I.D. AND DUMPED ME SOMEPLACE IN A FIELD IN NEW JERSEY!

I WOKE UP.
THE GUY DROVE US ALL BACK TO THE PARKING LOT IN NEWARK. EDDIE AND THE OTHER MEN WERE WAITING IN THEIR CARS. EDDIE TOOK ME TO A DINER AND ORDERED ME A STEAK WHICH I DID NOT EAT. I JUST FELT WEIRD AND VERY WEAK. I ASKED EDDIE TO DRIVE ME BACK TO MY FAMILY HOME IN CANARSIE.

AT THE TIME, I WAS A SOPHOMORE AT BROOKLYN COLLEGE MAJORING IN PHILOSOPHY. MY PHILOSOPHY OF HISTORY CLASS PROFESSOR DID NOT LIKE ME. HE SAID, "I AM PASSING YOU WITH A "C" BUT YOU DO NOT HAVE THE STAMINA FOR A SERIOUS STUDENT OF PHILOSOPHY.

I SUGGEST YOU GET MARRIED"

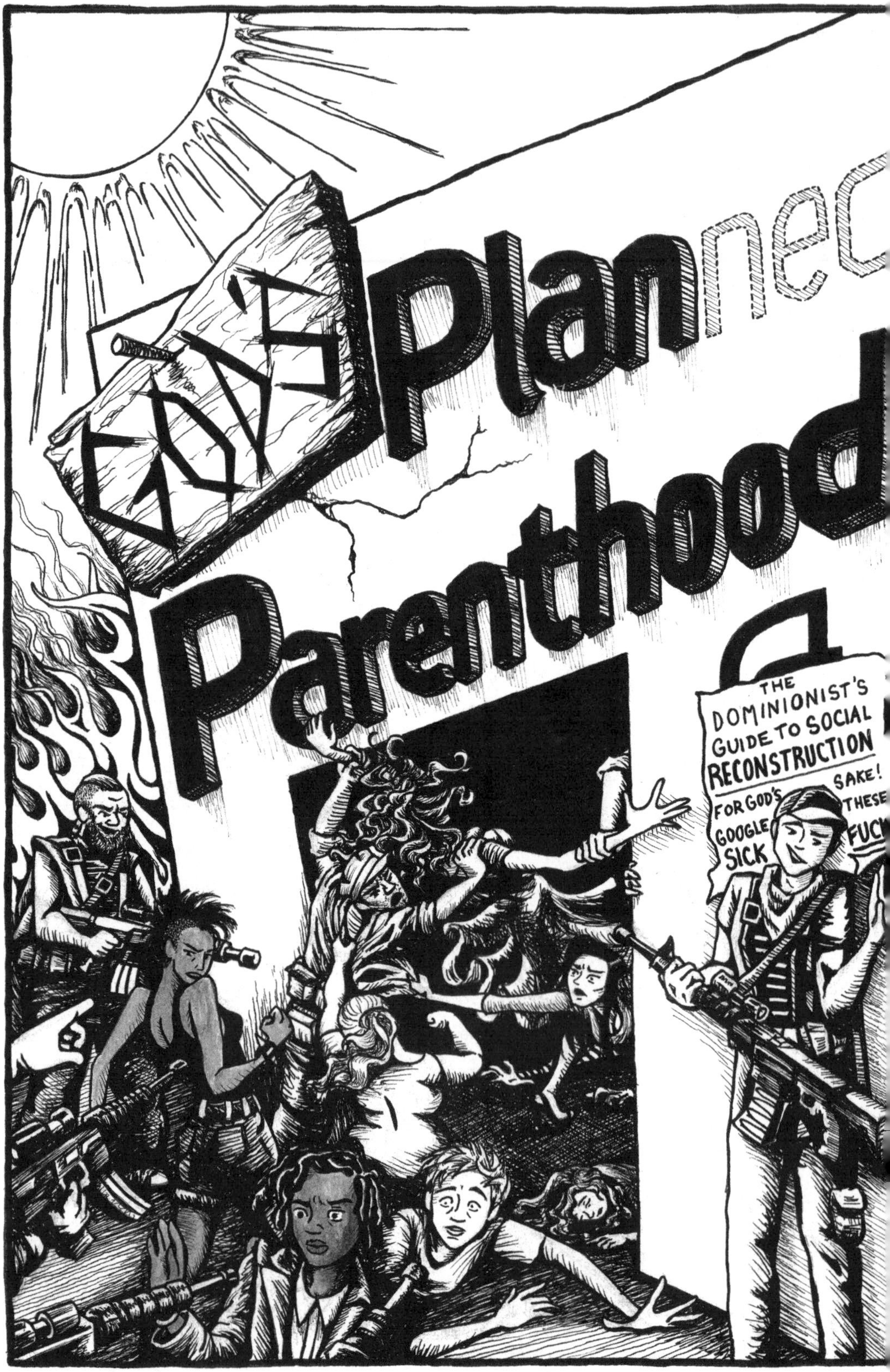
GOD'S
Planned
Parenthood
THE DOMINIONIST'S GUIDE TO SOCIAL RECONSTRUCTION
FOR GOD'S SAKE! GOOGLE THESE SICK FUCK

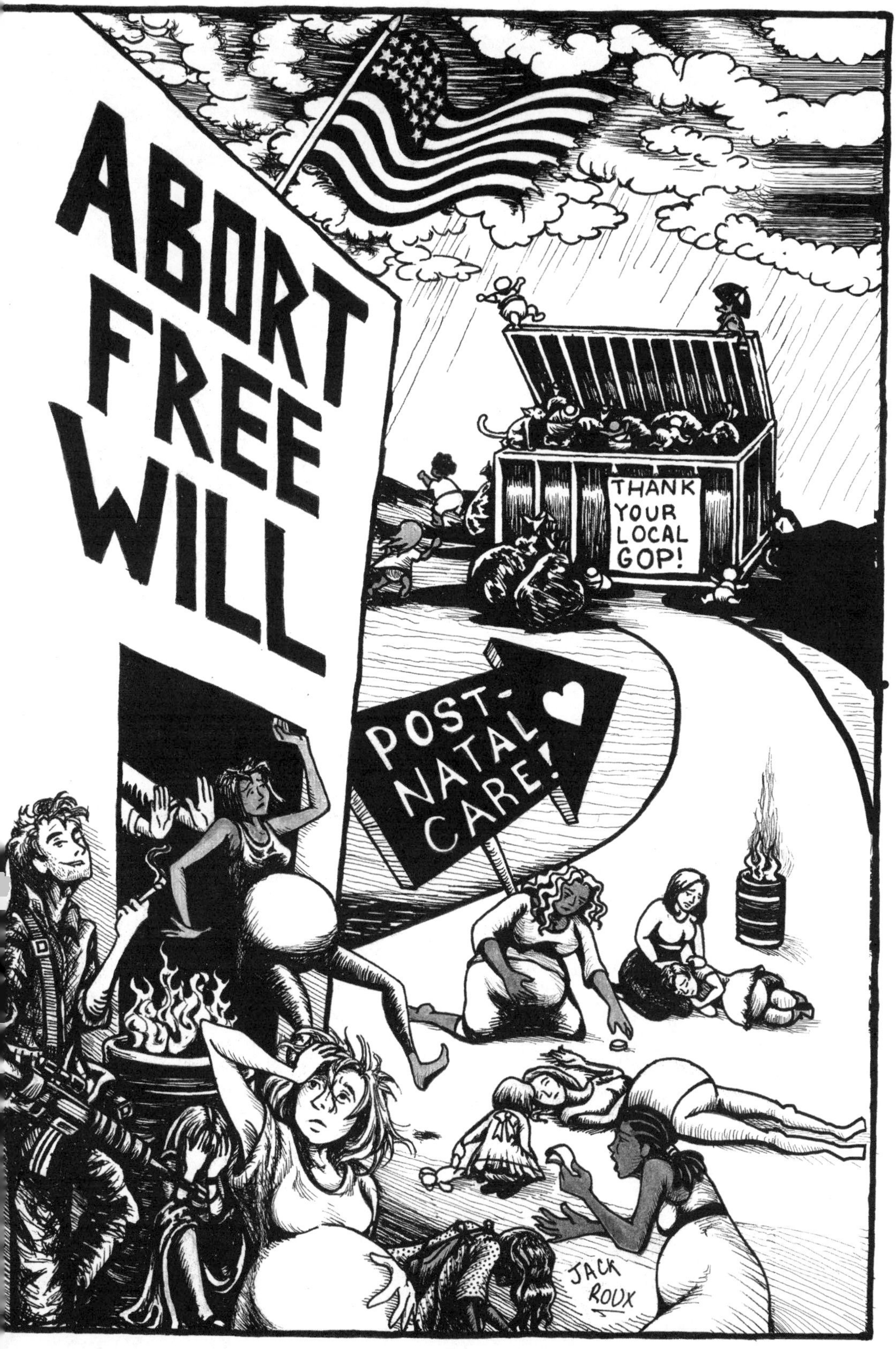
ABORT FREE WILL
THANK YOUR LOCAL GOP!
POST-NATAL CARE!
JACK ROUX

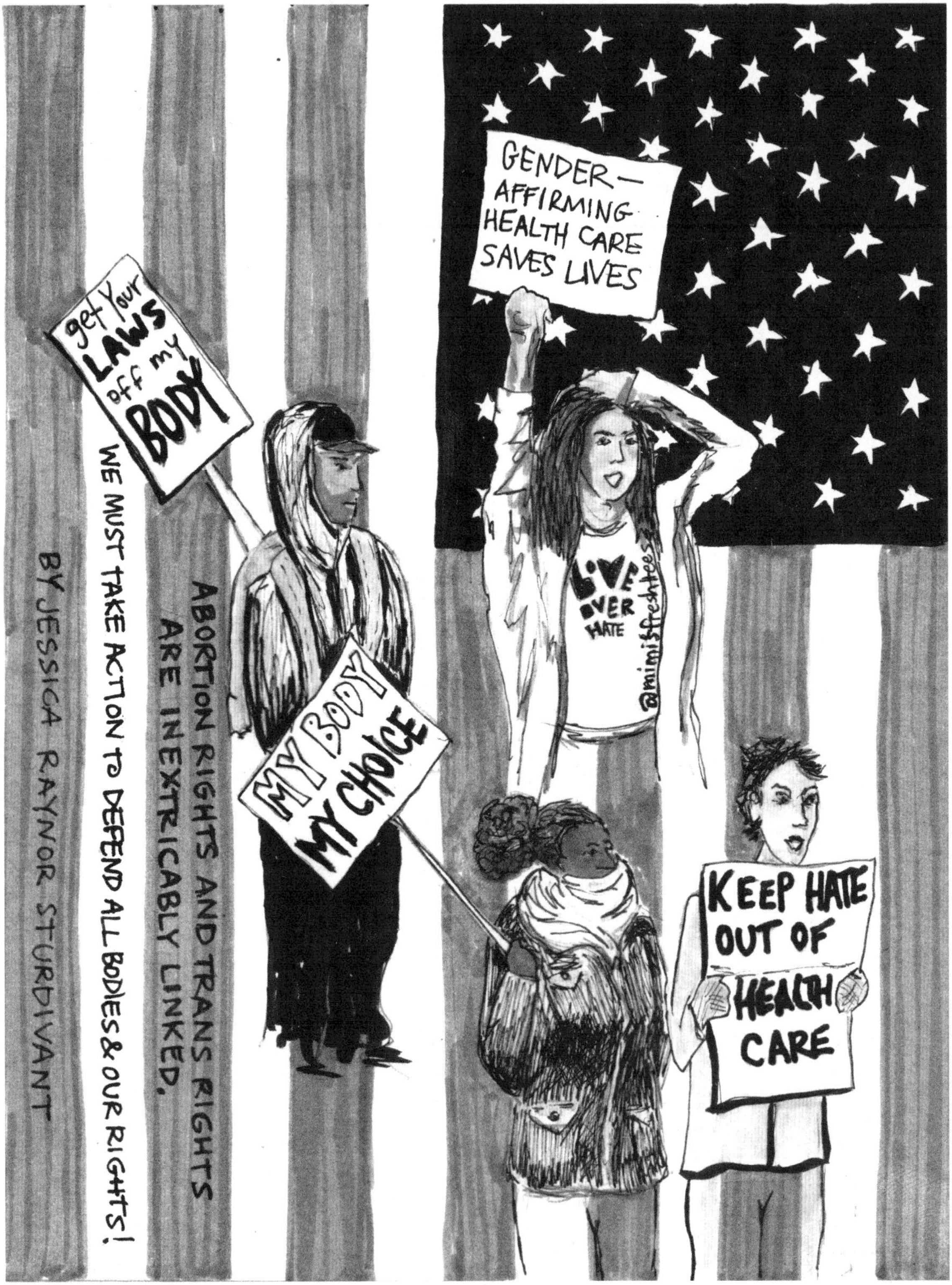
GENDER-AFFIRMING HEALTH CARE SAVES LIVES
get your LAWS off my BODY
LOVE OVER HATE
@mimisfreshtees
ABORTION RIGHTS AND TRANS RIGHTS ARE INEXTRICABLY LINKED.
WE MUST TAKE ACTION TO DEFEND ALL BODIES & OUR RIGHTS!
BY JESSICA RAYNOR STURDIVANT
MY BODY MY CHOICE
KEEP HATE OUT OF HEALTH CARE

WHEN A PERSON'S GENDER EXPRESSION[1] AND/OR GENDER IDENTITY[2] DOES NOT MATCH THE SEX THEY WERE ASSIGNED AT BIRTH[3], THIS CAN MAKE ACCESS TO HEALTH CARE, AND REPRODUCTIVE CARE, UNCOMFORTABLE, AND IN SOME CASES, IMPOSSIBLE.

[3] ASSIGNED SEX

IS A LABEL THAT YOU'RE GIVEN BASED ON MEDICAL FACTORS, INCLUDING YOUR HORMONES, CHROMOSOMES, AND GENITALS.

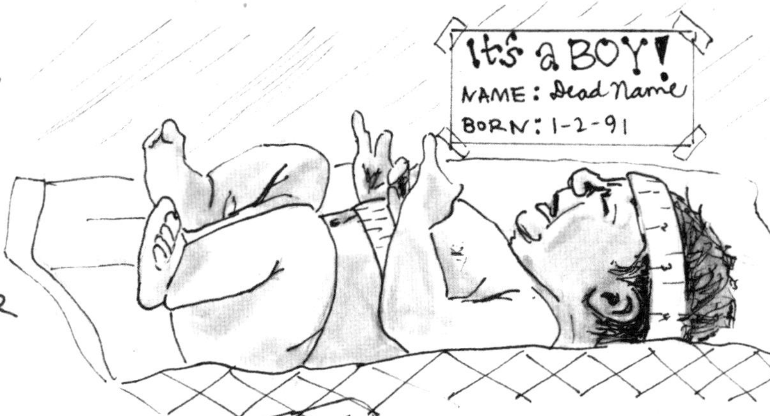
It's a BOY!
NAME: Dead Name
BORN: 1-2-91

[2] GENDER IDENTITY:

A PERSON'S DEEPLY HELD CORE SENSE OF SELF IN RELATION TO GENDER.

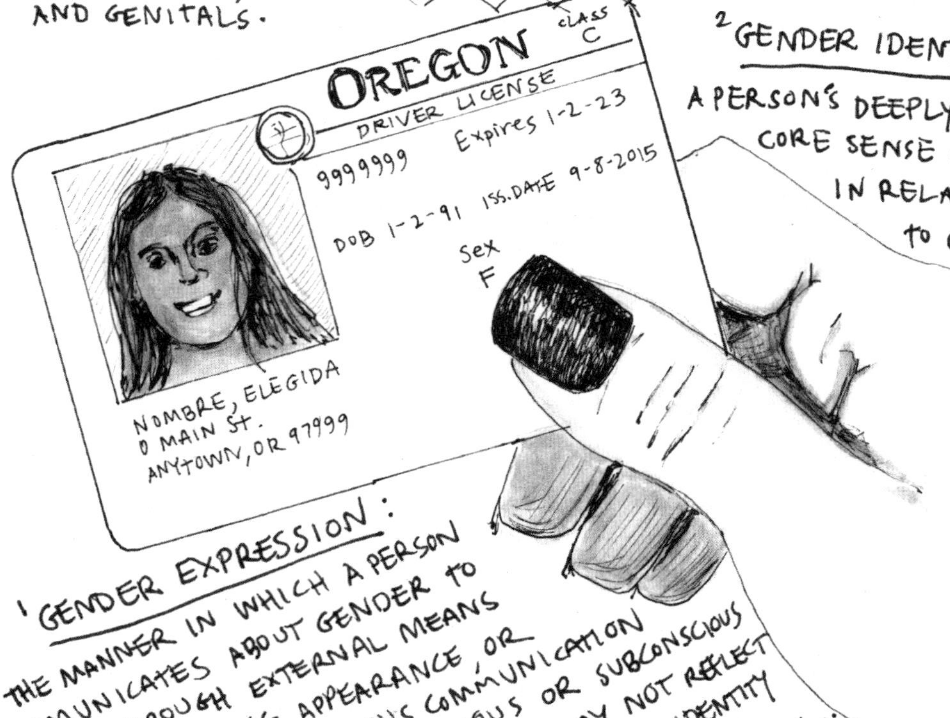
OREGON
CLASS C
DRIVER LICENSE
9999999
Expires 1-2-23
DOB 1-2-91
ISS.DATE 9-8-2015
Sex F
NOMBRE, ELEGIDA
0 MAIN ST.
ANYTOWN, OR 97999

[1] GENDER EXPRESSION:

THE MANNER IN WHICH A PERSON COMMUNICATES ABOUT GENDER TO OTHERS THROUGH EXTERNAL MEANS SUCH AS CLOTHING, APPEARANCE, OR MANNERISMS. THIS COMMUNICATION MAY BE CONSCIOUS OR SUBCONSCIOUS AND MAY OR MAY NOT REFLECT THEIR GENDER IDENTITY OR SEXUAL ORIENTATION...

1,2 HTTPS://PFLAG.ORG/GLOSSARY
3 HTTPS://PLANNEDPARENTHOOD.ORG

WHAT IS IN THE WAY OF TRANS AND NON-BINARY FOLKS' ACCESS TO HEALTH AND REPRODUCTIVE CARE?

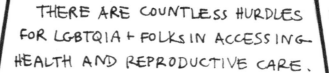

THERE ARE COUNTLESS HURDLES FOR LGBTQIA+ FOLKS IN ACCESSING HEALTH AND REPRODUCTIVE CARE.

TO NAME A FEW:

NON-INCLUSIVE LANGUAGE IN WRITTEN AND SPOKEN COMMUNICATION FROM HEALTH CARE PROFESSIONALS AND INSTITUTIONS

LACK OF LGBTQIA+ REPRESENTATION* IN LITERATURE ILLUSTRATIONS/PHOTOS AND ART ON WALLS OF HEALTH CARE FACILITY
* THEREFORE, ERASURE

CAUTION

TRANS MEN AND NON-BINARY FOLKS ASSIGNED FEMALE AT BIRTH ARE REQUIRED TO TEST FOR PREGNANCY PRIOR TO ANY OPERATION, CAUSING GENDER DYSPHORIA AND THEREFORE, TRAUMA

WHEN A PERSON'S GENDER ON THEIR ID CARD DOES NOT MATCH THEIR GENDER IDENTITY, THEY MAY NOT BE ALLOWED IN THE DOOR OF SOME ABORTION CLINICS

STOP

LACK OF PRIVACY IN ACCESSING HEALTH CARE IS AN ISSUE FOR TRANS AND NON-BINARY FOLKS, PARTICULARLY WHEN SEEKING ABORTION, FOR FEAR OF BEING OUTED

"**THE REASON YOU DON'T FIGHT FOR ME IS BECAUSE YOU'RE NOT FIGHTING FOR YOURSELF FULLY.** AND ANY MOVEMENT THAT'S TRYING TO EMANCIPATE MEN FROM THE SHACKLES OF HETEROPATRIARCHY OR EMANCIPATE WOMEN FROM TRADITIONAL GENDER IDEOLOGY HAS TO HAVE TRANS AND NON-BINARY PEOPLE AT THE FOREFRONT BECAUSE WE ARE ACTUALLY THE MOST HONEST. WE'RE TRACING THE ROOT, WHERE DID THESE IDEAS OF MANHOOD AND WOMANHOOD COME FROM? THEY COME FROM A BINARY STRUCTURE....

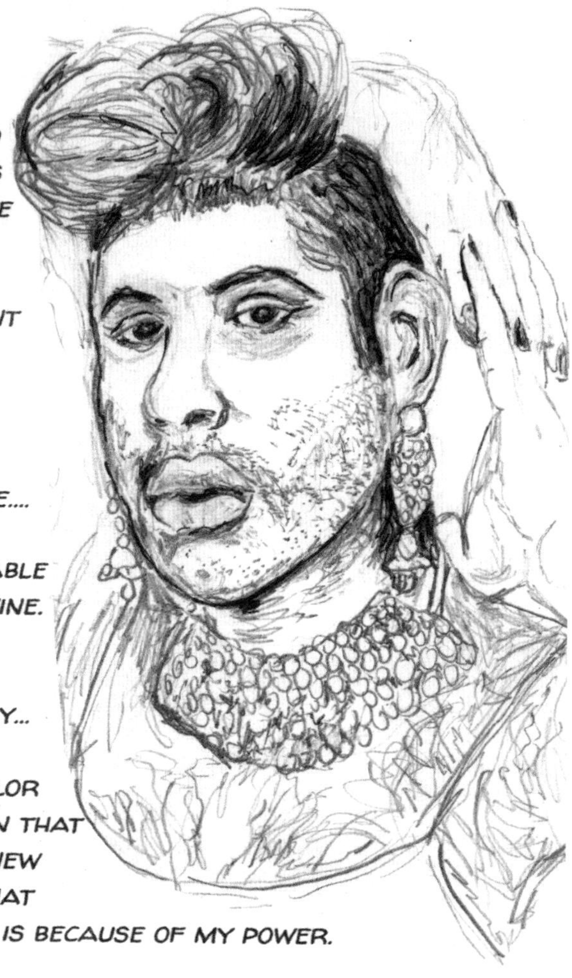

I HAVE AN UNSHAKABLE AND IRREVOCABLE SENSE OF WHO I AM BECAUSE I AM DIVINE. I COME FROM PEOPLE WHO WERE EXTERMINATED AND TARGETED BY COLONISTS BECAUSE THE GENDER BINARY... WAS SUPERIMPOSED ON BLACK PEOPLE, INDIGENOUS PEOPLE, AND PEOPLE OF COLOR EUROPEAN COLONISTS. AND THE REASON THAT THEY TARGETED US IS BECAUSE THEY KNEW OUR POWER, RIGHT? SO THE REASON THAT THERE'S SO MUCH ANIMUS AGAINST ME IS BECAUSE OF MY POWER.

I DON'T NEED TO BE LEGITIMIZED, OR I DON'T HAVE ANYTHING TO PROVE. ...**I DON'T THINK THE MAJORITY OF PEOPLE ARE READY TO HEAL AND THAT'S WHY THEY REPRESS US AS TRANS AND GENDER-VARIANT PEOPLE BECAUSE THEY'VE DONE THIS VIOLENCE TO THEMSELVES FIRST.** THEY'VE REPRESSED THEIR OWN FEMININITY, THEY'VE REPRESSED THEIR OWN GENDER NONCONFORMITY, THEY'VE REPRESSED THEIR OWN AMBIVALENCE, THEY'VE REPRESSED THEIR OWN CREATIVITY. AND SO **WHEN THEY SEE US HAVE THE AUDACITY TO LIVE A LIFE WITHOUT COMPROMISE**, WHERE WE SAY THERE ARE NO TRADE-OFFS, WHERE WE SAY WE ACTUALLY GET TO CARVE IN A MARROW OF THIS EARTH AND CREATE OUR OWN GODDAMN BEAUTY, INSTEAD OF SAYING, 'THANK YOU FOR TEACHING ME ANOTHER WAY TO LIVE', **THEY TRY TO DISAPPEAR US BECAUSE THEY DID THAT TO THEMSELVES FIRST**. SO I GUESS I WOULD REPHRASE YOUR QUESTION TO BE, 'CAN YOU HELP ME GET FREE?' NOT, 'CAN YOU HELP ME HELP YOU?'" – ALOK VAID-MENON

TRANS FOLKS CAN GET PREGNANT WHEN THEY CHOOSE TO HAVE THE KIND OF SEX THAT CAN MAKE A BABY (WHETHER FOR PLEASURE OR TO MAKE A BABY) AND WHEN THEY DO NOT CHOOSE TO DO SO (RAPE).

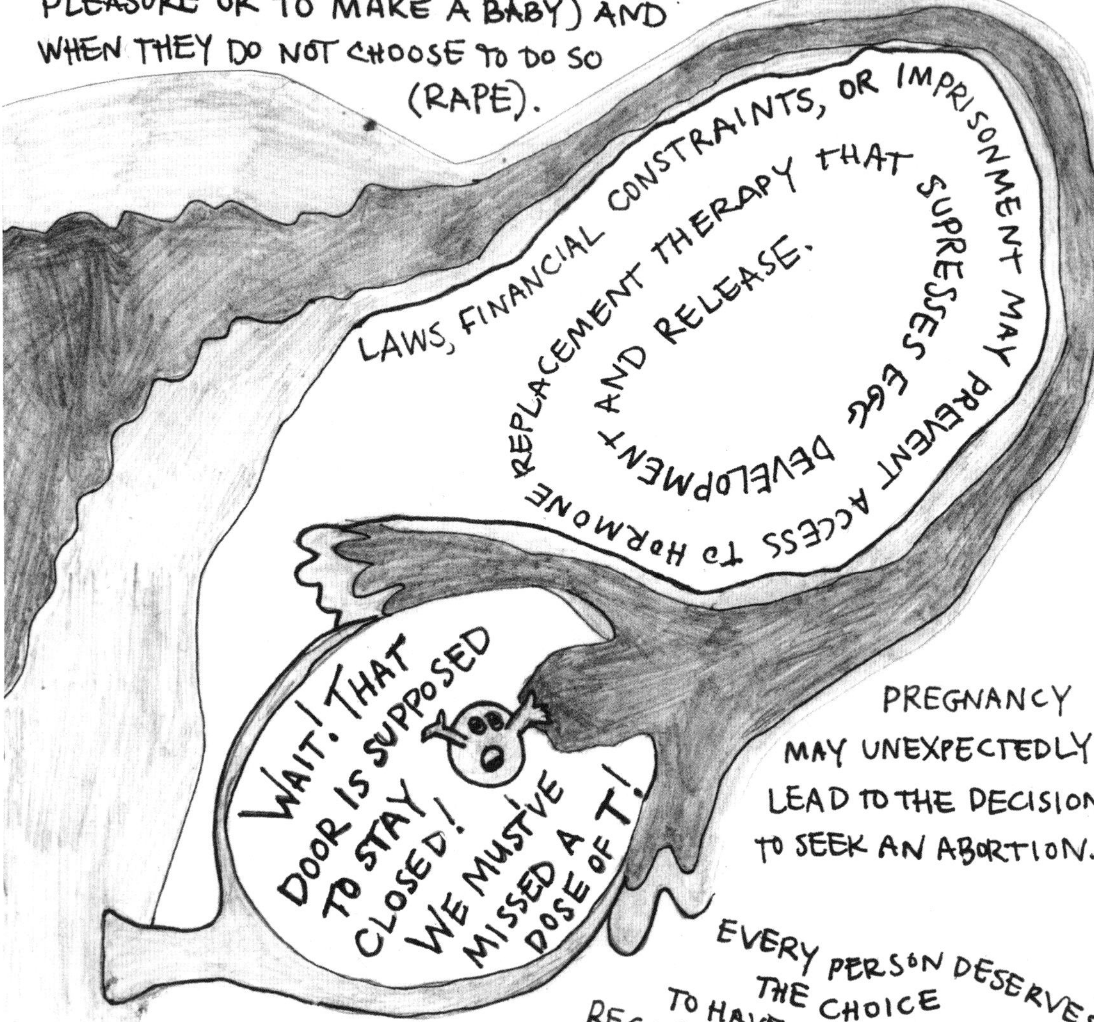

LAWS, FINANCIAL CONSTRAINTS, OR IMPRISONMENT MAY PREVENT ACCESS TO HORMONE REPLACEMENT THERAPY THAT SUPRESSES EGG DEVELOPMENT AND RELEASE.
WAIT! THAT DOOR IS SUPPOSED TO STAY CLOSED! WE MUST'VE MISSED A DOSE OF T!

PREGNANCY MAY UNEXPECTEDLY LEAD TO THE DECISION TO SEEK AN ABORTION.

EVERY PERSON DESERVES THE CHOICE TO HAVE AN ABORTION, REGARDLESS OF GENDER IDENTITY.

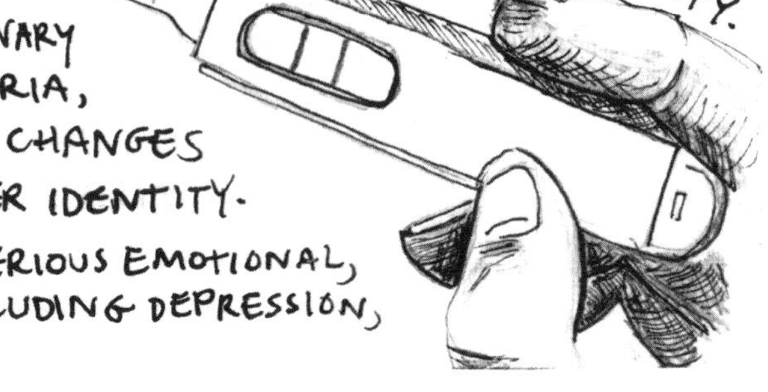

ALL PREGNANT FOLKS ARE SUSCEPTIBLE TO SCRUTINY AND QUESTIONING. TRANS AND NON-BINARY FOLKS ALSO FACE GENDER DYSPHORIA, AS PREGNANCY CAUSES BODILY CHANGES THAT MAY NOT ALIGN WITH GENDER IDENTITY.

GENDER DYSPHORIA MAY LEAD TO SERIOUS EMOTIONAL, SOCIAL, AND PHYSICAL RISKS, INCLUDING DEPRESSION, SELF-HARM, AND SUICIDE.

"I am a Black trans woman who believes in abortion. Not because I'll ever personally ever experience the threat of forced birth, but because I know what it's like to not be in control of my body. To have someone else decide my destiny, thrusting their dominion over my organs.

I am a Black trans woman who believes in abortion. Because i have loved too many people hwo have lived their whole lives with the possibility of needing one — my mama, my sisters, my friends, my good Judys, my boyfriends who were trans and non-binary and carried the risk more acutely for both of us.

I am a Black trans woman who believes in abortion. Because I've been pushed, pulled, prodded, pinned down, and afraid. I've been told to quiet down, and had my screams ignored. I've been told I can't be trusted to know what's right and what's wrong for me.

I am a Black trans woman who believes in abortion. Because this is all really just about power. Who gets to say how you should feel, what your body is good for, what your role is, who you can love, what you can do, who you can be, and when.

I am a Black trans woman who believes in abortion. Because it's not about scarcity, it's about abundance. A more expansive idea of reproductive justice. **It's about us all getting the care that we deserve.** Black mamas and parents, trans folks, non-binary folks, sex workers, disabled folks, incarcerated folks, detained folks, non-Christians, and on and on.

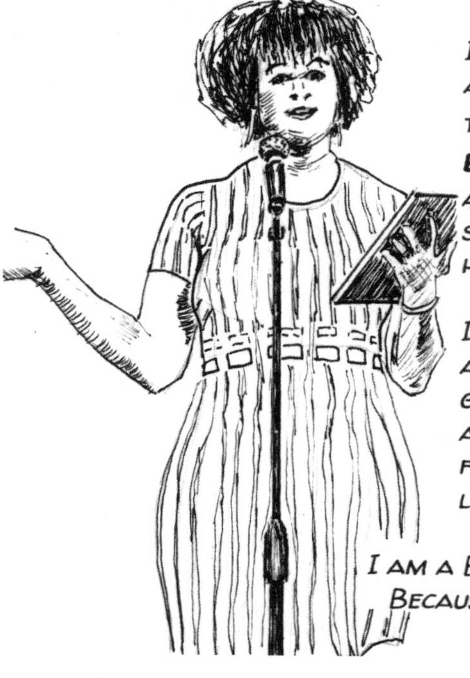

I am a Black trans woman who believes in abortion. Because lofty institutions fail me too. **It's about fighting not just your battle, but your neighbor's, too.** It's about destroying the white supremacist, the sexist, the ableist, the transphobe, the homophobe, the xenophobe in your head.

I am a Black trans woman who believes in abortion. Because it's about abolition and gender-affirming care. It's about democracy and real sex ed. It's about intersectional feminism and the environment. It's about Black lives, brown lives, and MeToo.

I am a Black trans woman who believes in abortion. Because it's not really just about abortion, is it?"

—Raquel Willis

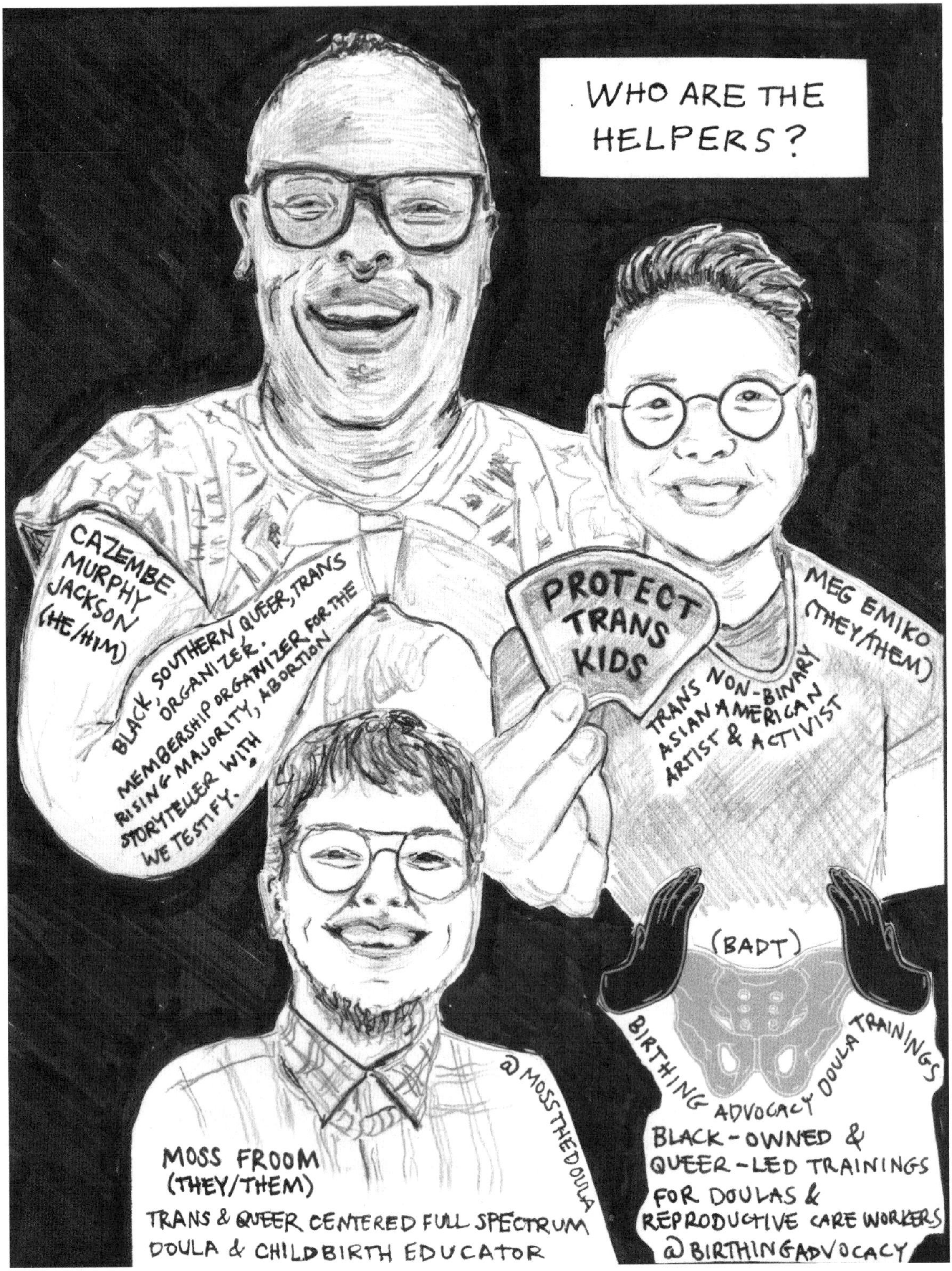
WHO ARE THE HELPERS?
CAZEMBE MURPHY JACKSON (HE/HIM)
BLACK, SOUTHERN QUEER, TRANS ORGANIZER.
MEMBERSHIP ORGANIZER FOR THE RISING MAJORITY, ABORTION STORYTELLER WITH WE TESTIFY.
PROTECT TRANS KIDS
MEG EMIKO (THEY/THEM)
TRANS NON-BINARY ASIAN AMERICAN ARTIST & ACTIVIST
MOSS FROOM (THEY/THEM)
TRANS & QUEER CENTERED FULL SPECTRUM DOULA & CHILDBIRTH EDUCATOR
@MOSSTHEDOULA
(BADT)
BIRTHING ADVOCACY DOULA TRAININGS
BLACK-OWNED & QUEER-LED TRAININGS FOR DOULAS & REPRODUCTIVE CARE WORKERS
@BIRTHINGADVOCACY

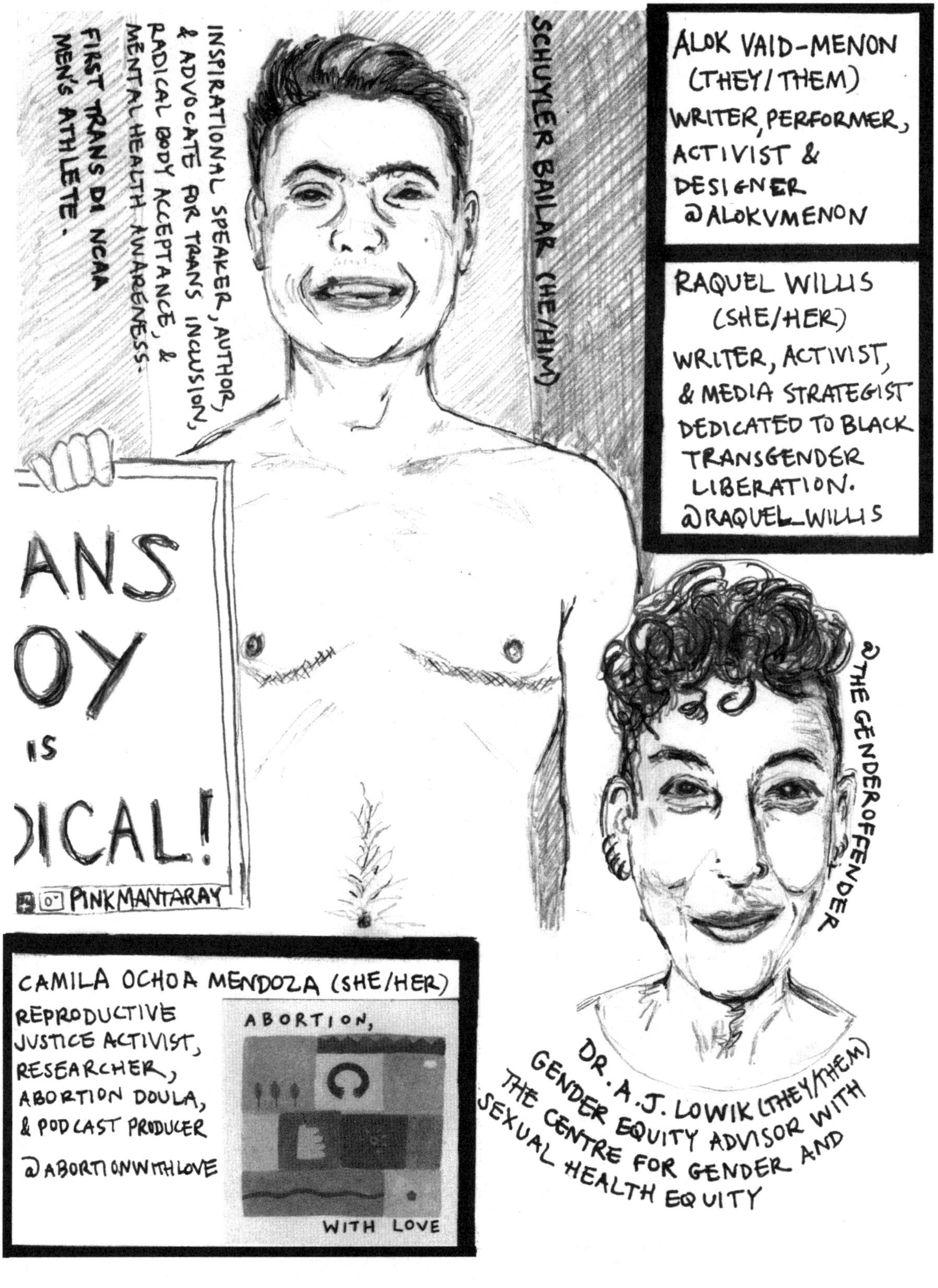
ALOK VAID-MENON (THEY/THEM)
WRITER, PERFORMER, ACTIVIST & DESIGNER
@ALOKVMENON
RAQUEL WILLIS (SHE/HER)
WRITER, ACTIVIST, & MEDIA STRATEGIST DEDICATED TO BLACK TRANSGENDER LIBERATION.
@RAQUEL_WILLIS
SCHUYLER BAILAR (HE/HIM)
INSPIRATIONAL SPEAKER, AUTHOR, & ADVOCATE FOR TRANS INCLUSION, RADICAL BODY ACCEPTANCE, & MENTAL HEALTH AWARENESS.
FIRST TRANS DI NCAA MEN'S ATHLETE.
ANS
OY
IS
DICAL!
PINKMANTARAY
@THEGENDEROFFENDER
DR. A.J. LOWIK (THEY/THEM)
GENDER EQUITY ADVISOR WITH THE CENTRE FOR GENDER AND SEXUAL HEALTH EQUITY
CAMILA OCHOA MENDOZA (SHE/HER)
REPRODUCTIVE JUSTICE ACTIVIST, RESEARCHER, ABORTION DOULA, & PODCAST PRODUCER
@ABORTIONWITHLOVE
ABORTION,
WITH LOVE

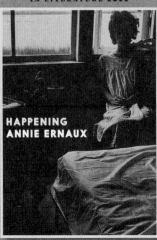

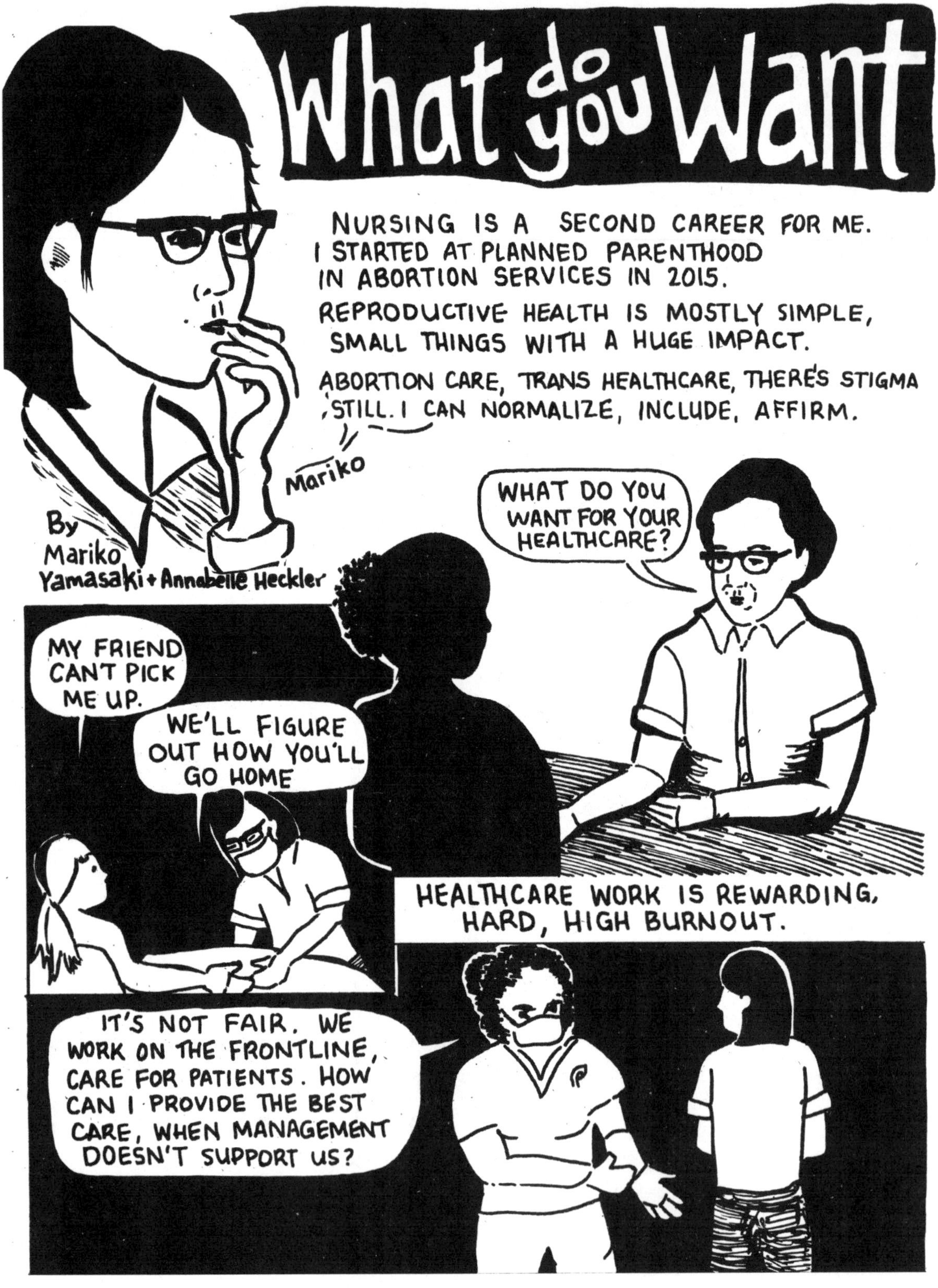
What do you Want
NURSING IS A SECOND CAREER FOR ME. I STARTED AT PLANNED PARENTHOOD IN ABORTION SERVICES IN 2015.
REPRODUCTIVE HEALTH IS MOSTLY SIMPLE, SMALL THINGS WITH A HUGE IMPACT.
ABORTION CARE, TRANS HEALTHCARE, THERE'S STIGMA STILL. I CAN NORMALIZE, INCLUDE, AFFIRM.
Mariko
By Mariko Yamasaki + Annabelle Heckler
WHAT DO YOU WANT FOR YOUR HEALTHCARE?
MY FRIEND CAN'T PICK ME UP.
WE'LL FIGURE OUT HOW YOU'LL GO HOME
HEALTHCARE WORK IS REWARDING, HARD, HIGH BURNOUT.
IT'S NOT FAIR. WE WORK ON THE FRONTLINE, CARE FOR PATIENTS. HOW CAN I PROVIDE THE BEST CARE, WHEN MANAGEMENT DOESN'T SUPPORT US?

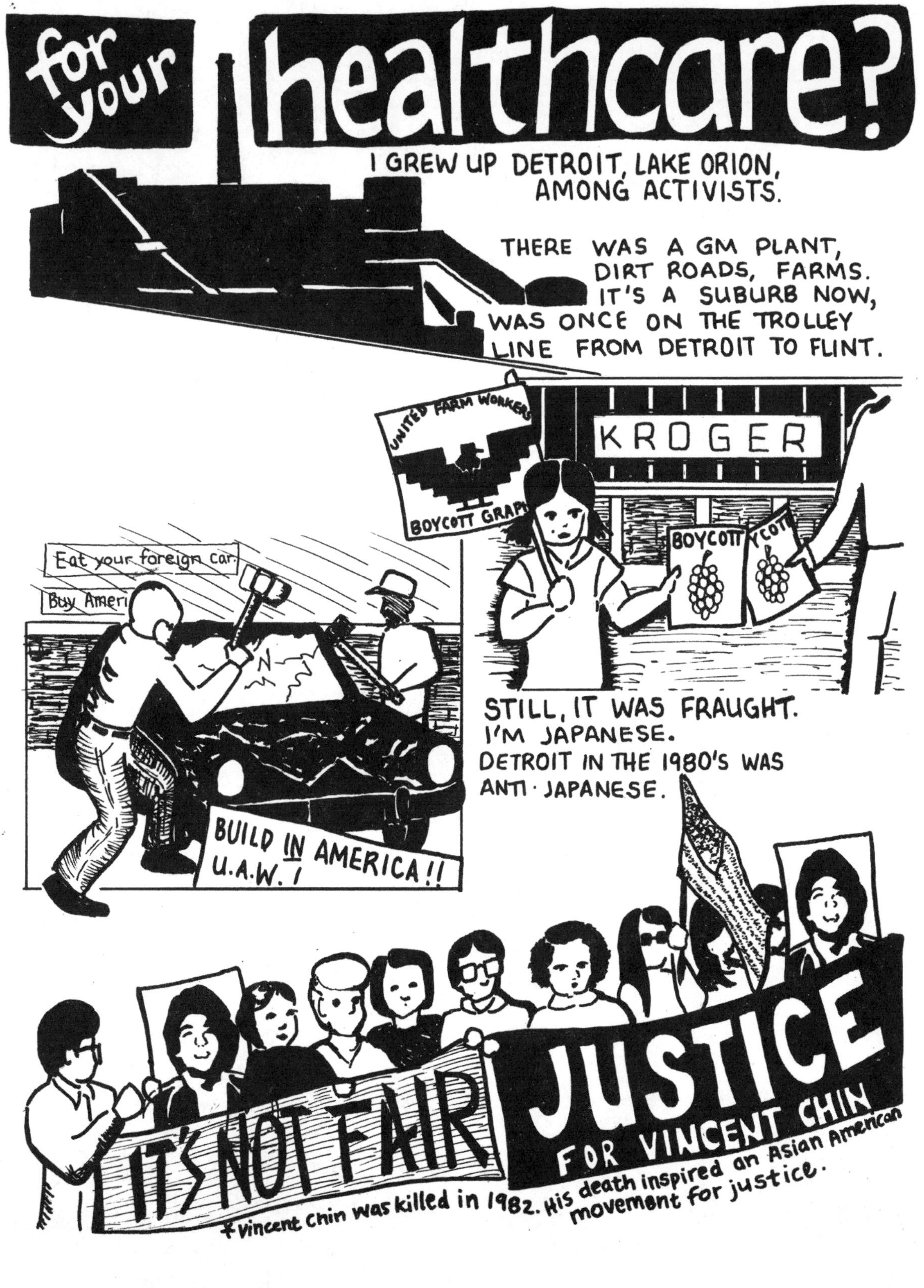

for your healthcare?
I GREW UP DETROIT, LAKE ORION, AMONG ACTIVISTS.
THERE WAS A GM PLANT, DIRT ROADS, FARMS. IT'S A SUBURB NOW, WAS ONCE ON THE TROLLEY LINE FROM DETROIT TO FLINT.
UNITED FARM WORKERS
BOYCOTT GRAP
KROGER
BOYCOTT
Eat your foreign car.
Buy Ameri
BUILD IN AMERICA!!
U.A.W. I
STILL, IT WAS FRAUGHT.
I'M JAPANESE.
DETROIT IN THE 1980'S WAS ANTI-JAPANESE.
IT'S NOT FAIR
JUSTICE FOR VINCENT CHIN
*Vincent Chin was killed in 1982. His death inspired an Asian American movement for justice.

WE COME FROM DIFFERENT COMMUNITIES. IN ALL OF OUR ROLES, WE CARE ABOUT OUR PATIENTS AND THE WORK WE DO.

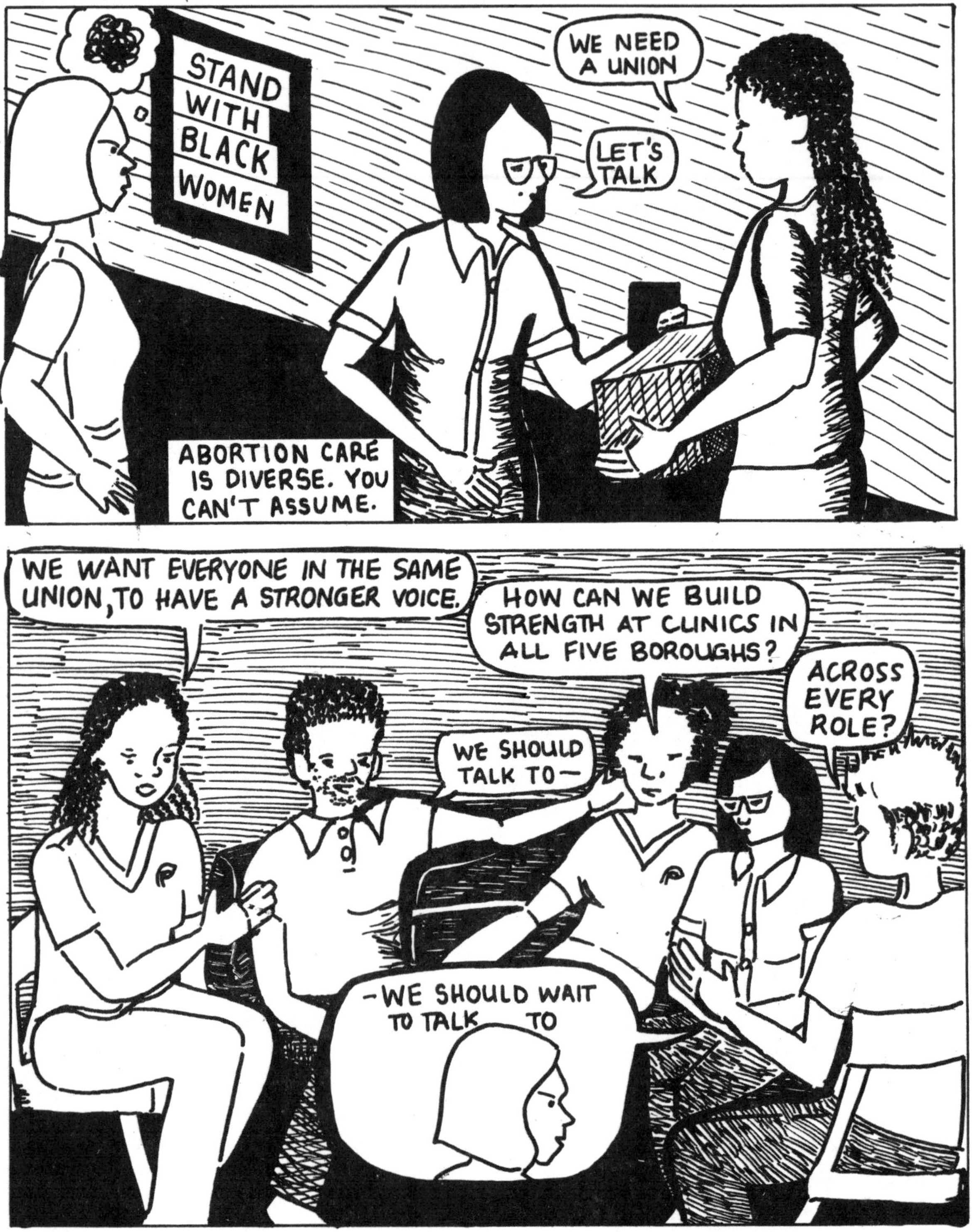
STAND WITH BLACK WOMEN
WE NEED A UNION
LET'S TALK
ABORTION CARE IS DIVERSE. YOU CAN'T ASSUME.
WE WANT EVERYONE IN THE SAME UNION, TO HAVE A STRONGER VOICE.
HOW CAN WE BUILD STRENGTH AT CLINICS IN ALL FIVE BOROUGHS?
ACROSS EVERY ROLE?
WE SHOULD TALK TO—
—WE SHOULD WAIT TO TALK TO

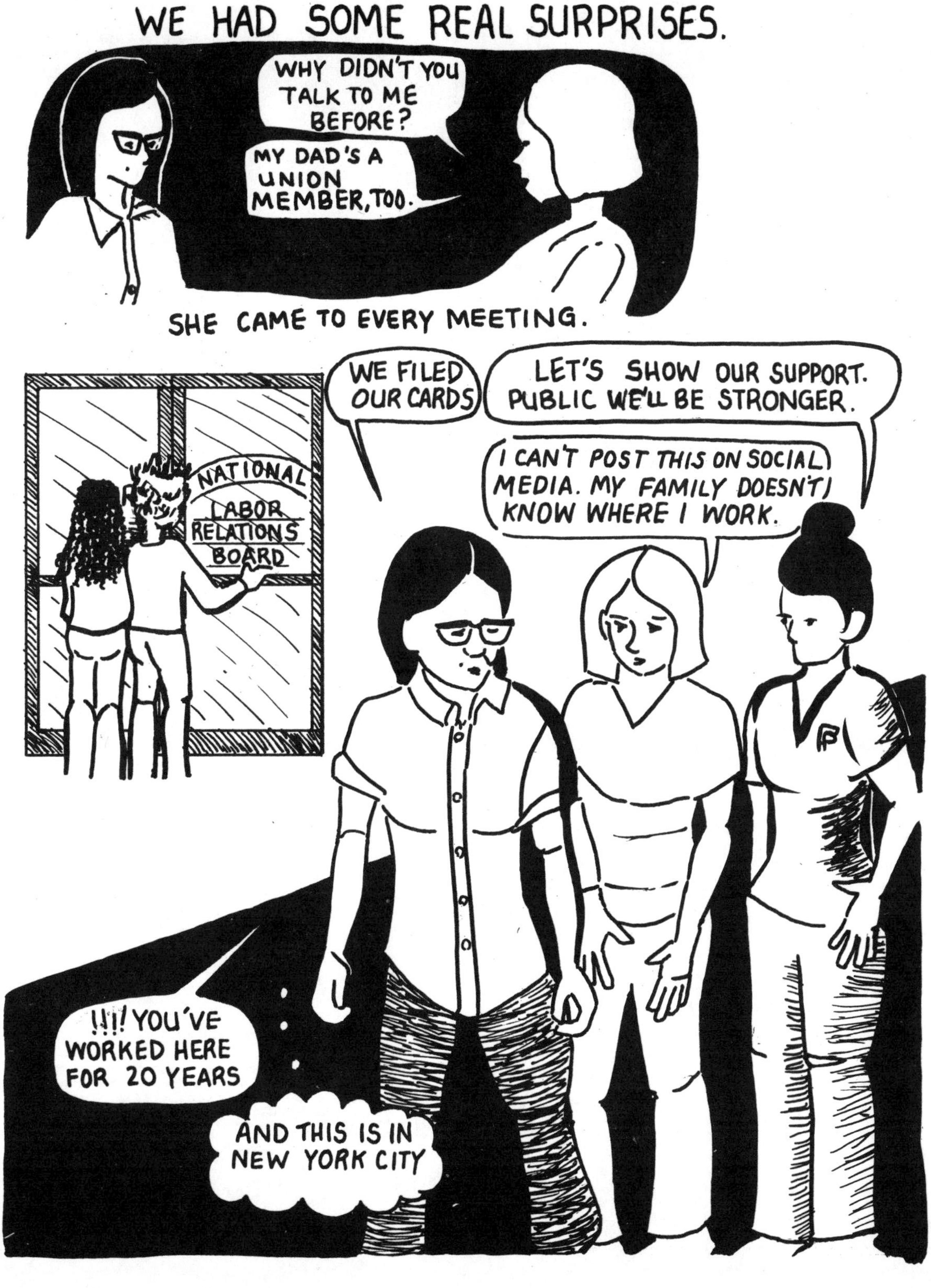
WE HAD SOME REAL SURPRISES.
WHY DIDN'T YOU TALK TO ME BEFORE?
MY DAD'S A UNION MEMBER, TOO.
SHE CAME TO EVERY MEETING.
NATIONAL LABOR RELATIONS BOARD
WE FILED OUR CARDS
LET'S SHOW OUR SUPPORT. PUBLIC WE'LL BE STRONGER.
I CAN'T POST THIS ON SOCIAL MEDIA. MY FAMILY DOESN'T KNOW WHERE I WORK.
!!!! YOU'VE WORKED HERE FOR 20 YEARS
AND THIS IS IN NEW YORK CITY

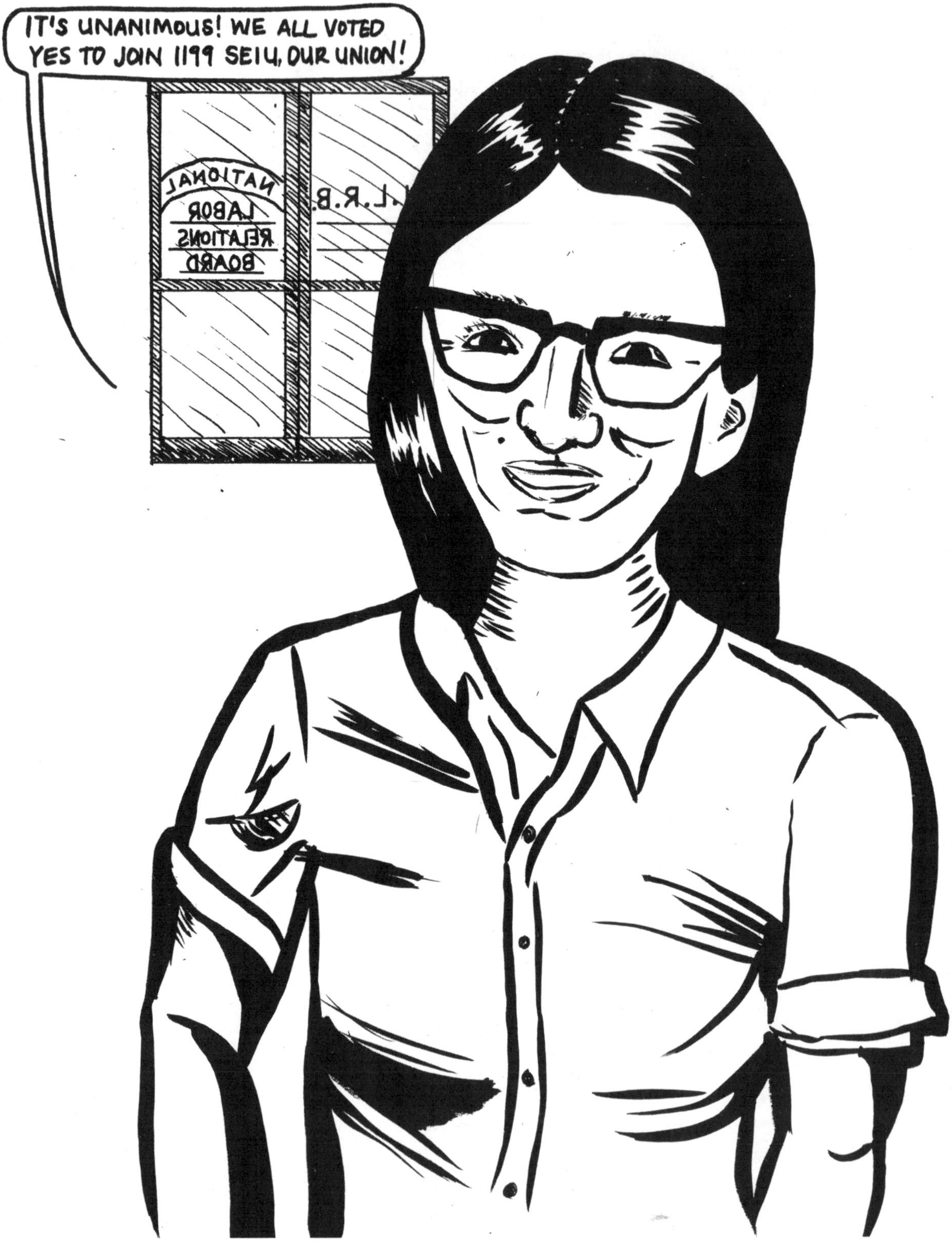
IT'S UNANIMOUS! WE ALL VOTED YES TO JOIN 1199 SEIU, OUR UNION!

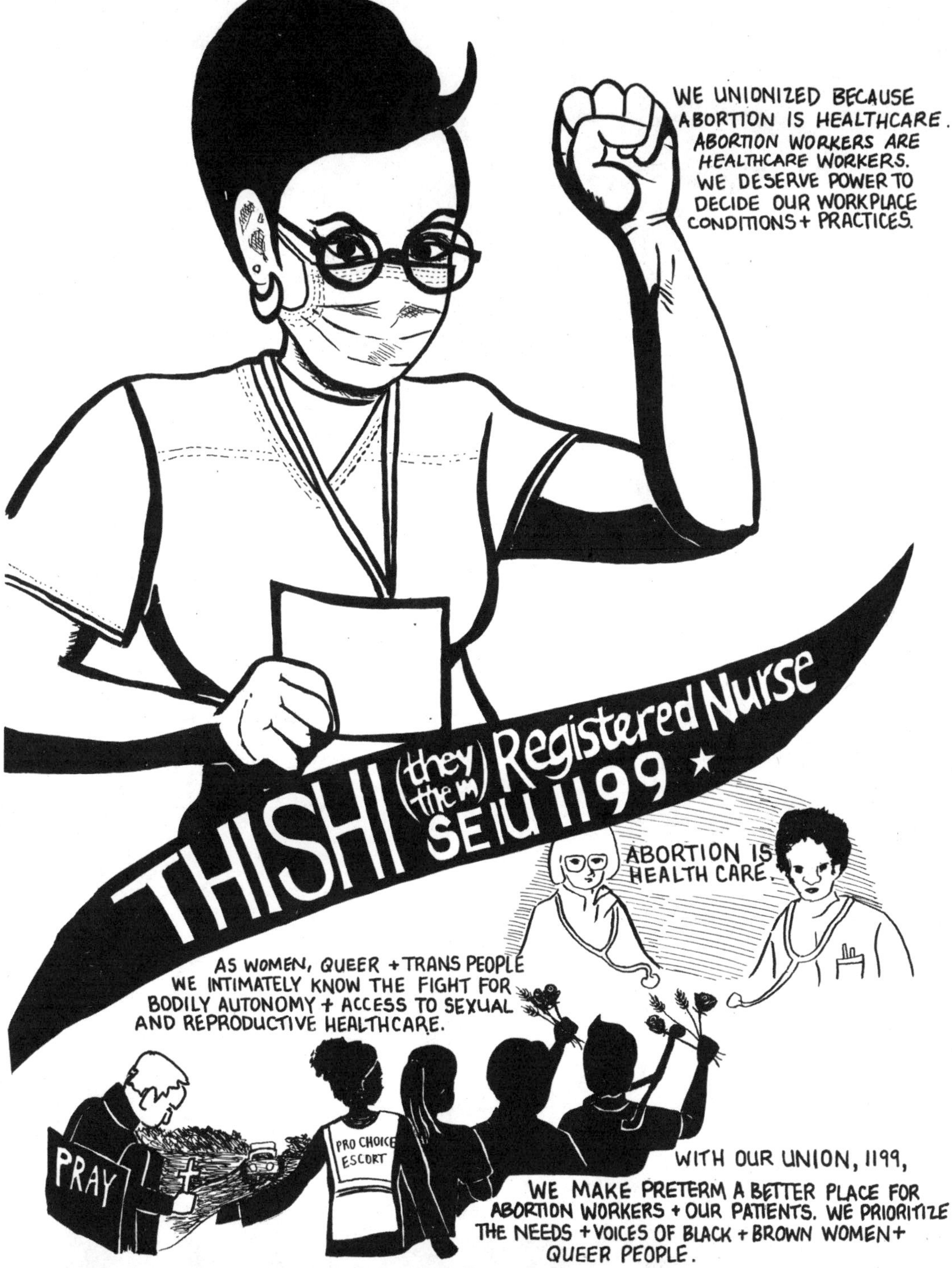

WE UNIONIZED BECAUSE ABORTION IS HEALTHCARE. ABORTION WORKERS ARE HEALTHCARE WORKERS. WE DESERVE POWER TO DECIDE OUR WORKPLACE CONDITIONS + PRACTICES.
THISHI (they them) Registered Nurse SEIU 1199 ★
ABORTION IS HEALTH CARE.
AS WOMEN, QUEER + TRANS PEOPLE WE INTIMATELY KNOW THE FIGHT FOR BODILY AUTONOMY + ACCESS TO SEXUAL AND REPRODUCTIVE HEALTHCARE.
PRAY
PRO CHOICE ESCORT
WITH OUR UNION, 1199, WE MAKE PRETERM A BETTER PLACE FOR ABORTION WORKERS + OUR PATIENTS. WE PRIORITIZE THE NEEDS + VOICES OF BLACK + BROWN WOMEN + QUEER PEOPLE.
POWER + LOVE TO ALL ABORTION WORKERS IN OHIO AND EVERYWHERE FIGHTING TO KEEP ABORTION CARE SAFE + ACCESSIBLE FOR ALL! ★
soli! Thishi + Annabelle

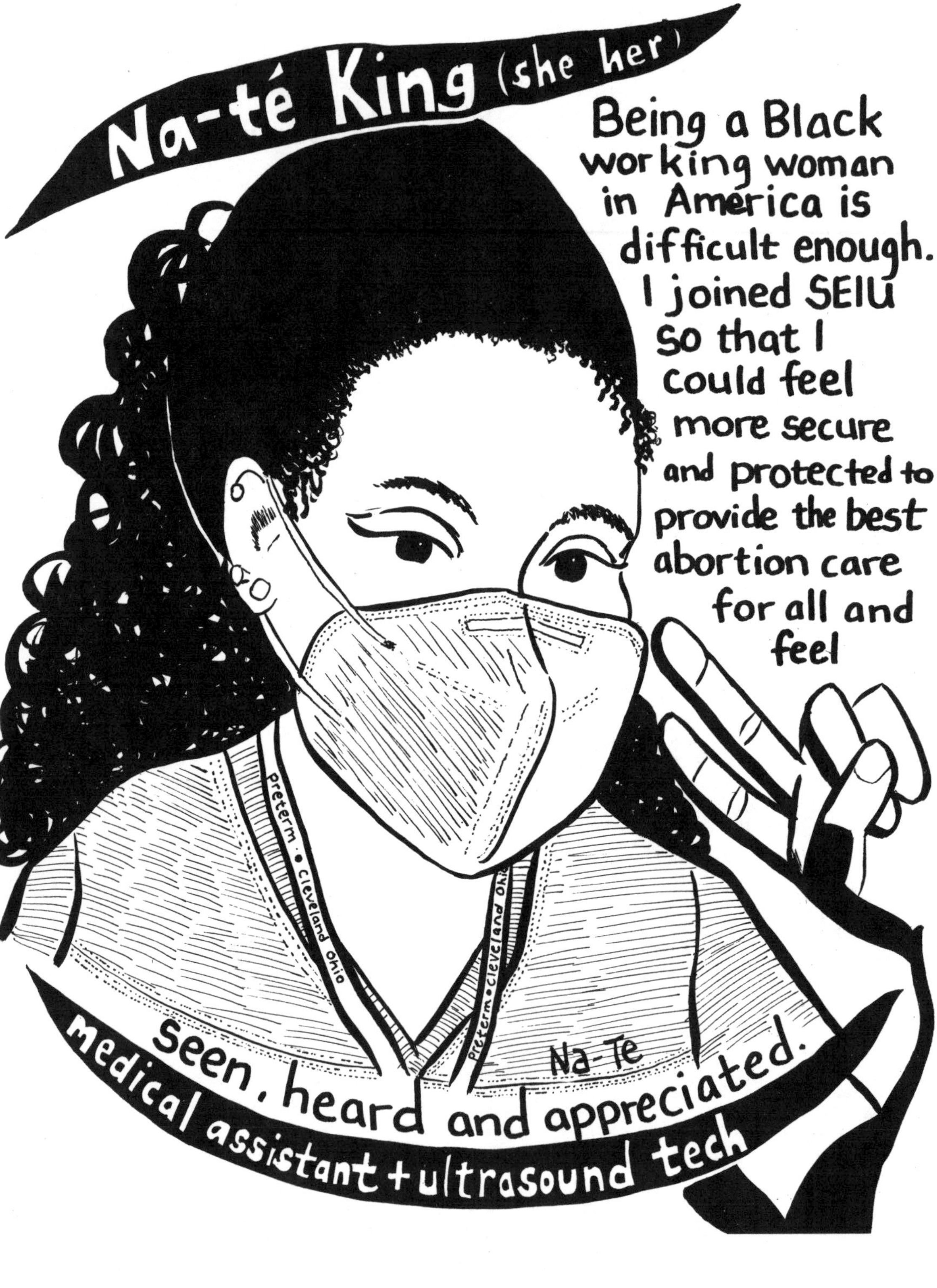

Na-té King (she her)
Being a Black working woman in America is difficult enough. I joined SEIU so that I could feel more secure and protected to provide the best abortion care for all and feel
seen, heard and appreciated.
medical assistant + ultrasound tech
preterm • Cleveland Ohio
Na-Te

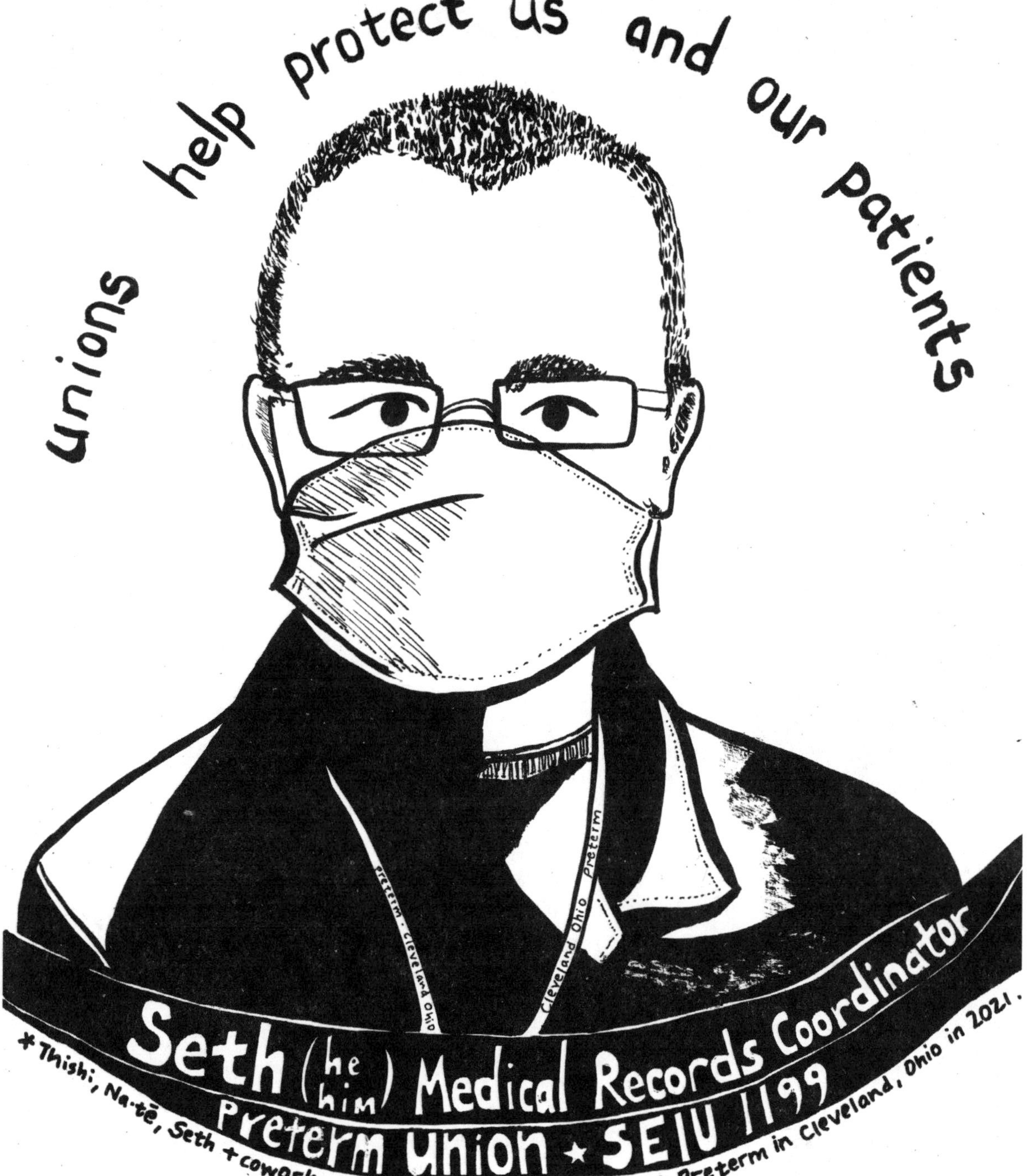
unions help protect us and our patients
preterm · Cleveland Ohio
Cleveland Ohio preterm
Seth (he him) Medical Records Coordinator
Preterm union ★ SEIU 1199
* Thishi, Na-tē, Seth + coworkers organized + won a union at Preterm in Cleveland, Ohio in 2021.

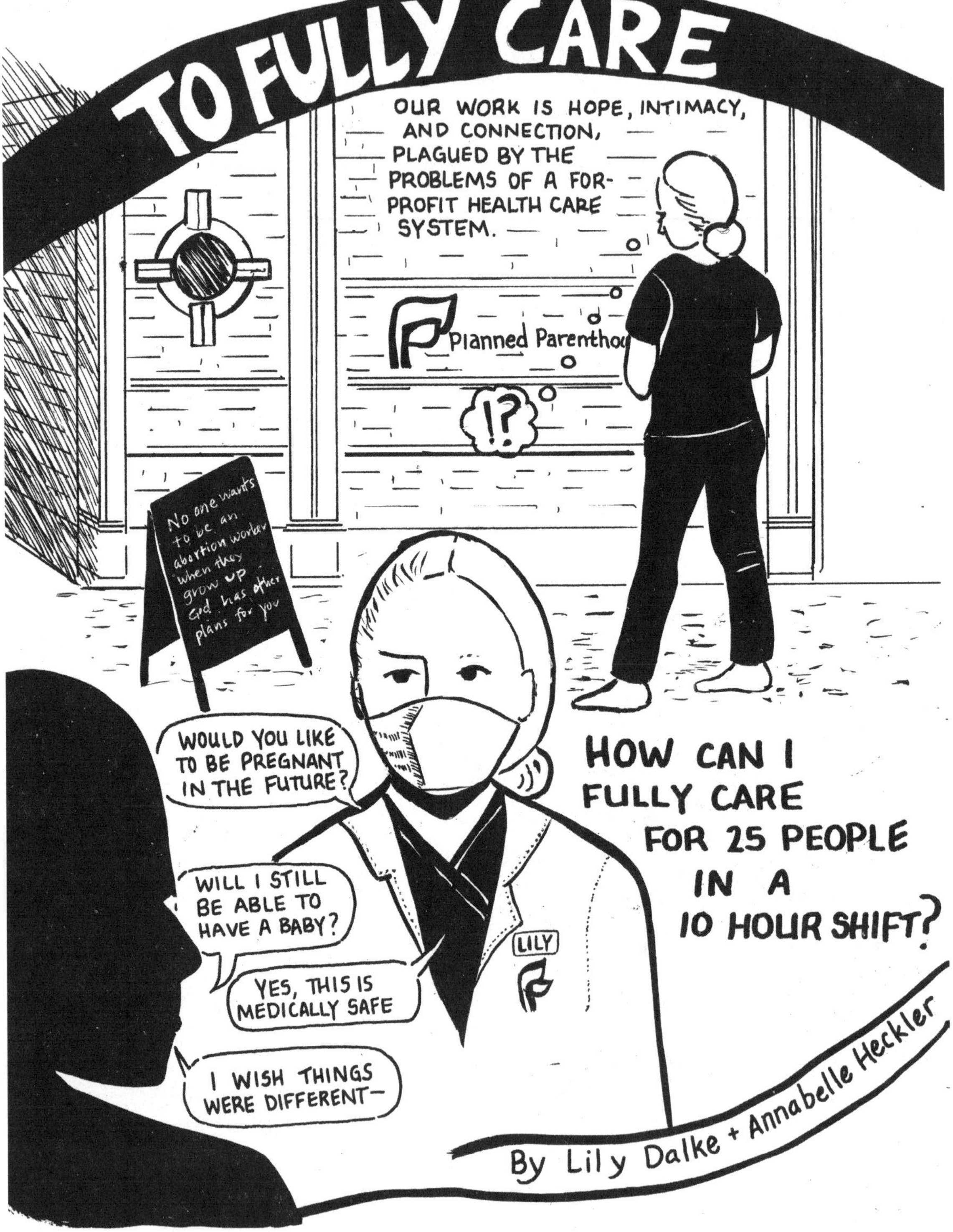
TO FULLY CARE
OUR WORK IS HOPE, INTIMACY, AND CONNECTION, PLAGUED BY THE PROBLEMS OF A FOR-PROFIT HEALTH CARE SYSTEM.
Planned Parenthoo
!?
No one wants to be an abortion worker when they grow up. God has other plans for you
WOULD YOU LIKE TO BE PREGNANT IN THE FUTURE?
WILL I STILL BE ABLE TO HAVE A BABY?
YES, THIS IS MEDICALLY SAFE
I WISH THINGS WERE DIFFERENT—
LILY
HOW CAN I FULLY CARE FOR 25 PEOPLE IN A 10 HOUR SHIFT?
By Lily Dalke + Annabelle Heckler

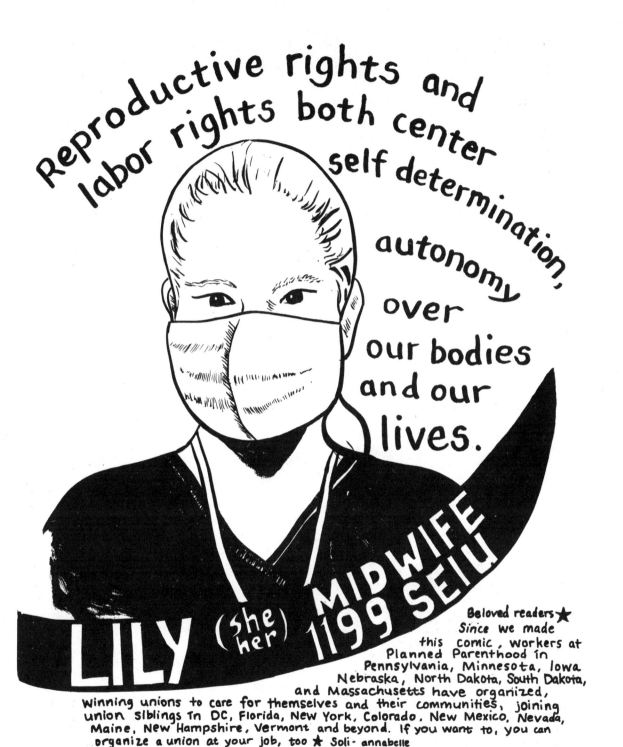

Reproductive rights and labor rights both center self determination, autonomy over our bodies and our lives.

LILY (she/her) MIDWIFE 1199 SEIU

Beloved readers ★ Since we made this comic, workers at Planned Parenthood in Pennsylvania, Minnesota, Iowa, Nebraska, North Dakota, South Dakota, and Massachusetts have organized, winning unions to care for themselves and their communities, joining union siblings in DC, Florida, New York, Colorado, New Mexico, Nevada, Maine, New Hampshire, Vermont and beyond. If you want to, you can organize a union at your job, too ★ Soli- annabelle

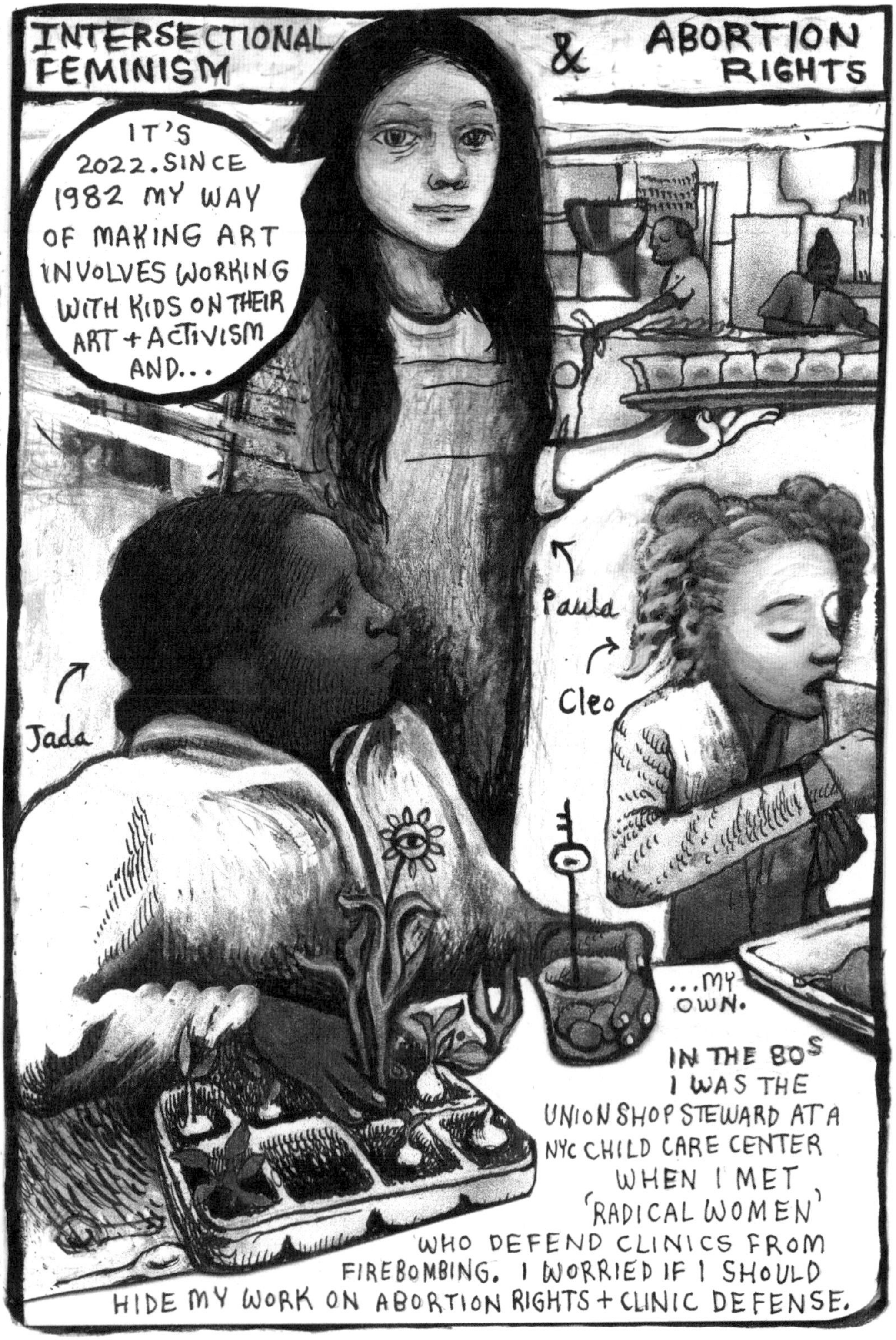
INTERSECTIONAL FEMINISM & ABORTION RIGHTS
IT'S 2022. SINCE 1982 MY WAY OF MAKING ART INVOLVES WORKING WITH KIDS ON THEIR ART + ACTIVISM AND...
Paula
Cleo
Jada
...MY OWN.
IN THE 80s I WAS THE UNION SHOP STEWARD AT A NYC CHILD CARE CENTER WHEN I MET 'RADICAL WOMEN' WHO DEFEND CLINICS FROM FIREBOMBING. I WORRIED IF I SHOULD HIDE MY WORK ON ABORTION RIGHTS + CLINIC DEFENSE.

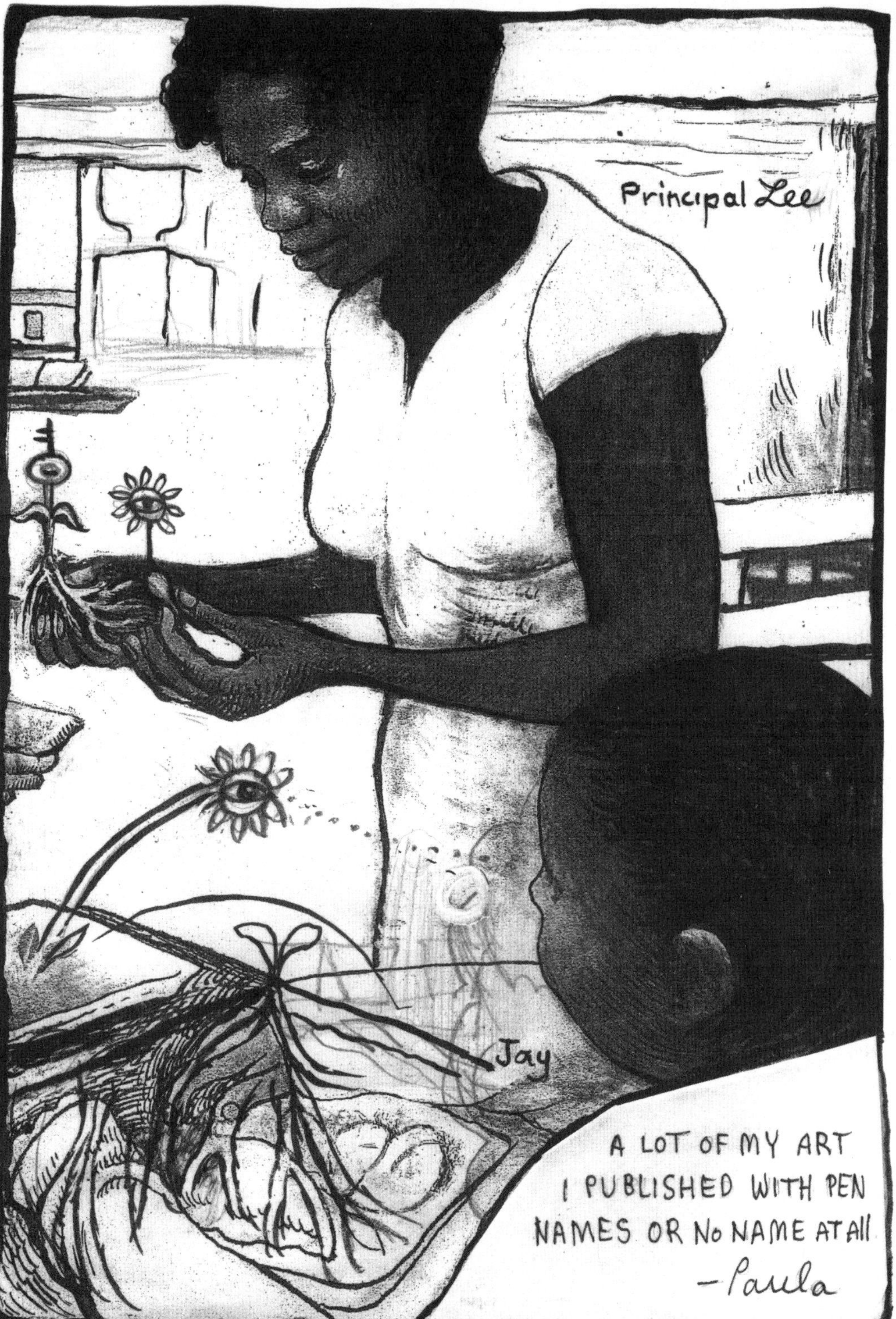
Principal Lee
Jay
A LOT OF MY ART
I PUBLISHED WITH PEN
NAMES OR NO NAME AT ALL
—Paula

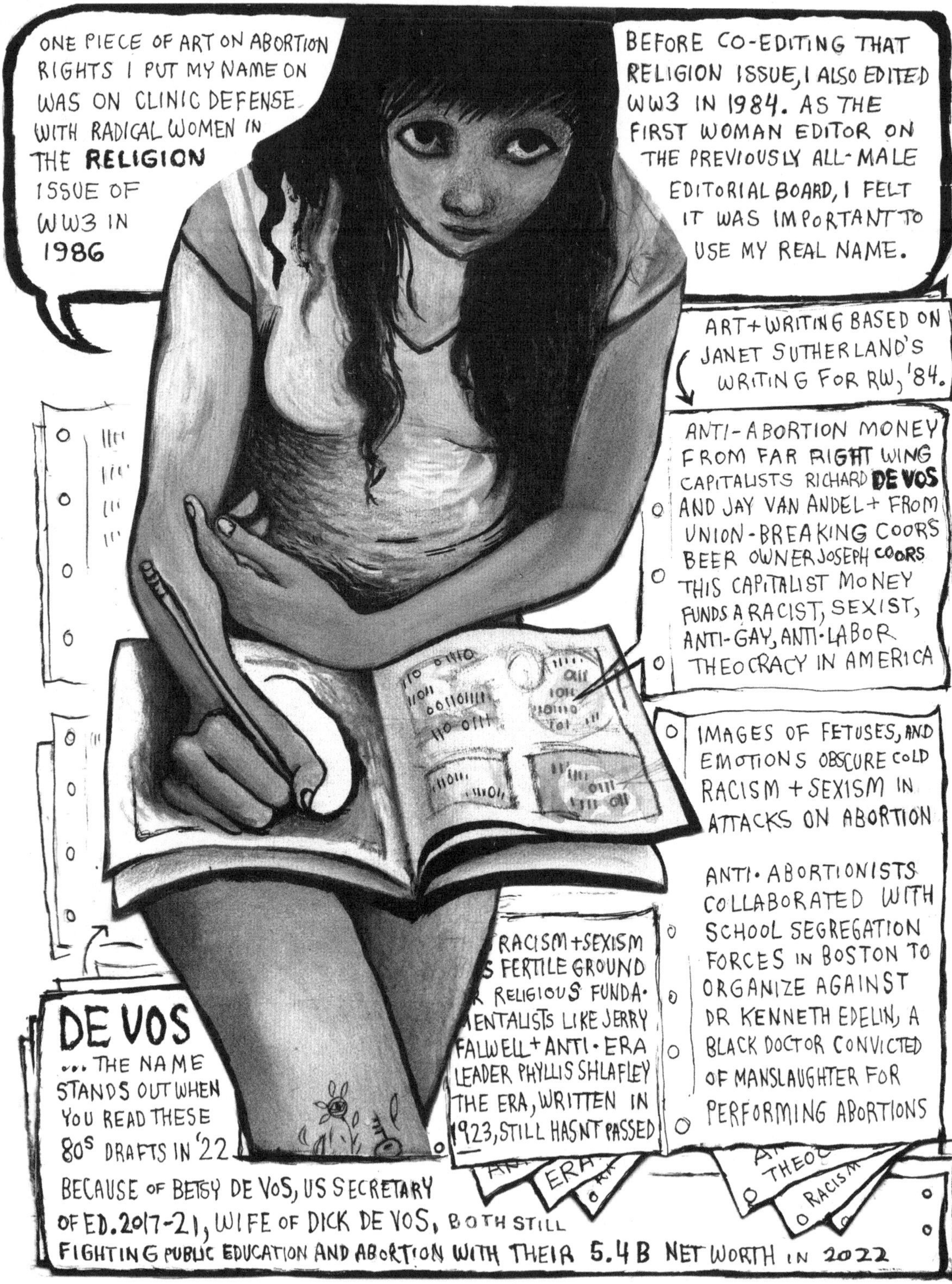
ONE PIECE OF ART ON ABORTION RIGHTS I PUT MY NAME ON WAS ON CLINIC DEFENSE WITH RADICAL WOMEN IN THE RELIGION ISSUE OF WW3 IN 1986
BEFORE CO-EDITING THAT RELIGION ISSUE, I ALSO EDITED WW3 IN 1984. AS THE FIRST WOMAN EDITOR ON THE PREVIOUSLY ALL-MALE EDITORIAL BOARD, I FELT IT WAS IMPORTANT TO USE MY REAL NAME.
ART + WRITING BASED ON JANET SUTHERLAND'S WRITING FOR RW, '84.
ANTI-ABORTION MONEY FROM FAR RIGHT WING CAPITALISTS RICHARD DE VOS AND JAY VAN ANDEL + FROM UNION-BREAKING COORS BEER OWNER JOSEPH COORS
THIS CAPITALIST MONEY FUNDS A RACIST, SEXIST, ANTI-GAY, ANTI-LABOR THEOCRACY IN AMERICA
IMAGES OF FETUSES, AND EMOTIONS OBSCURE COLD RACISM + SEXISM IN ATTACKS ON ABORTION
ANTI-ABORTIONISTS COLLABORATED WITH SCHOOL SEGREGATION FORCES IN BOSTON TO ORGANIZE AGAINST DR KENNETH EDELIN, A BLACK DOCTOR CONVICTED OF MANSLAUGHTER FOR PERFORMING ABORTIONS
RACISM + SEXISM S FERTILE GROUND R RELIGIOUS FUNDA-ENTALISTS LIKE JERRY FALWELL + ANTI-ERA LEADER PHYLLIS SHLAFLEY
THE ERA, WRITTEN IN 1923, STILL HASNT PASSED
DE VOS ... THE NAME STANDS OUT WHEN YOU READ THESE 80s DRAFTS IN '22
BECAUSE OF BETSY DE VOS, US SECRETARY OF ED. 2017-21, WIFE OF DICK DE VOS, BOTH STILL FIGHTING PUBLIC EDUCATION AND ABORTION WITH THEIR 5.4 B NET WORTH IN 2022

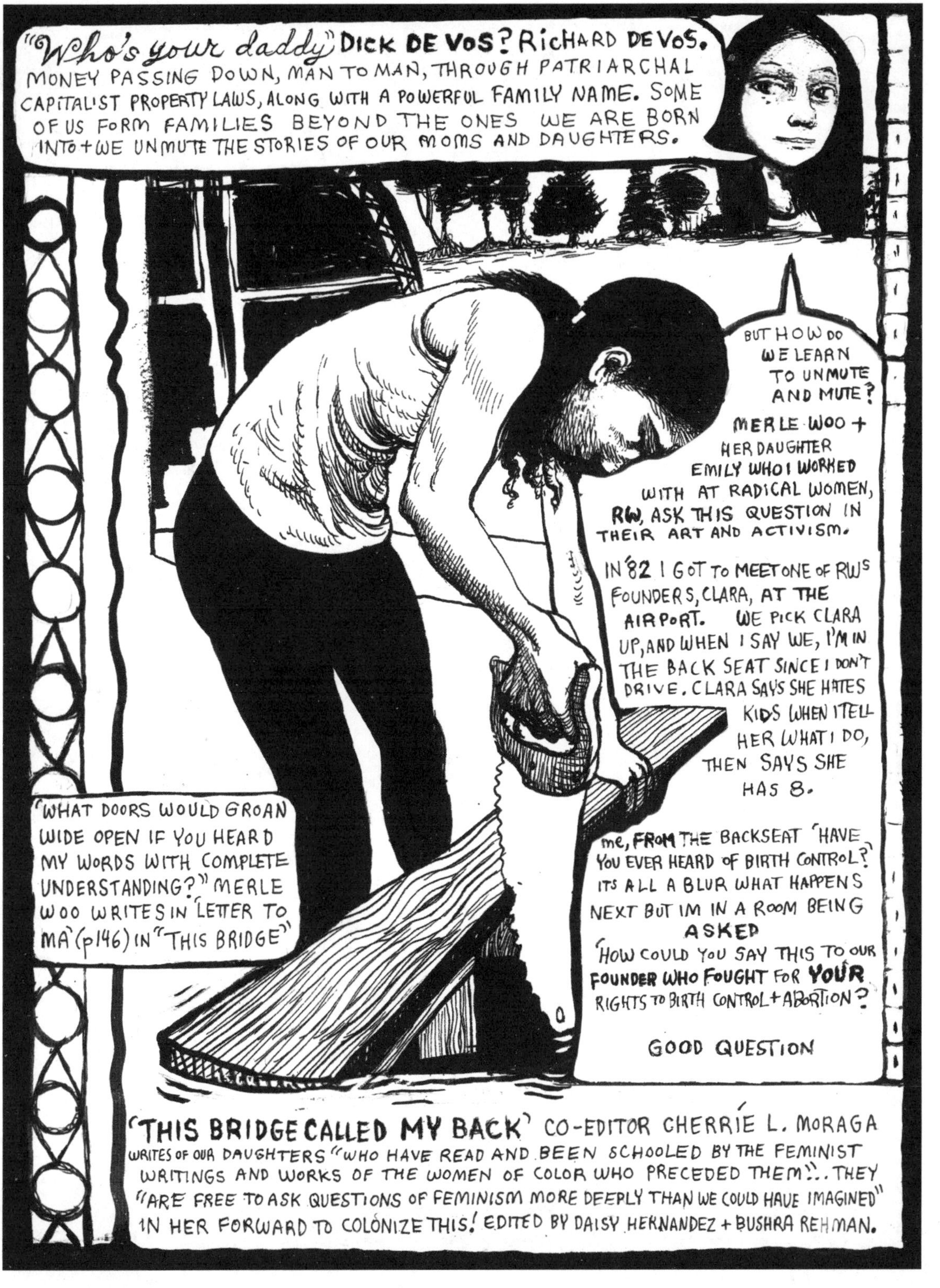
"Who's your daddy" DICK DE VOS? RICHARD DE VOS. MONEY PASSING DOWN, MAN TO MAN, THROUGH PATRIARCHAL CAPITALIST PROPERTY LAWS, ALONG WITH A POWERFUL FAMILY NAME. SOME OF US FORM FAMILIES BEYOND THE ONES WE ARE BORN INTO + WE UNMUTE THE STORIES OF OUR MOMS AND DAUGHTERS.
BUT HOW DO WE LEARN TO UNMUTE AND MUTE?
MERLE WOO + HER DAUGHTER EMILY WHO I WORKED WITH AT RADICAL WOMEN, RW, ASK THIS QUESTION IN THEIR ART AND ACTIVISM.
IN '82 I GOT TO MEET ONE OF RW'S FOUNDERS, CLARA, AT THE AIRPORT. WE PICK CLARA UP, AND WHEN I SAY WE, I'M IN THE BACK SEAT SINCE I DON'T DRIVE. CLARA SAYS SHE HATES KIDS WHEN I TELL HER WHAT I DO, THEN SAYS SHE HAS 8.
"WHAT DOORS WOULD GROAN WIDE OPEN IF YOU HEARD MY WORDS WITH COMPLETE UNDERSTANDING?" MERLE WOO WRITES IN 'LETTER TO MA' (p146) IN "THIS BRIDGE"
me, FROM THE BACKSEAT 'HAVE YOU EVER HEARD OF BIRTH CONTROL?' ITS ALL A BLUR WHAT HAPPENS NEXT BUT IM IN A ROOM BEING ASKED 'HOW COULD YOU SAY THIS TO OUR FOUNDER WHO FOUGHT FOR YOUR RIGHTS TO BIRTH CONTROL + ABORTION?'
GOOD QUESTION
'THIS BRIDGE CALLED MY BACK' CO-EDITOR CHERRÍE L. MORAGA WRITES OF OUR DAUGHTERS "WHO HAVE READ AND BEEN SCHOOLED BY THE FEMINIST WRITINGS AND WORKS OF THE WOMEN OF COLOR WHO PRECEDED THEM"... THEY "ARE FREE TO ASK QUESTIONS OF FEMINISM MORE DEEPLY THAN WE COULD HAVE IMAGINED" IN HER FORWARD TO COLÓNIZE THIS! EDITED BY DAISY HERNANDEZ + BUSHRA REHMAN.

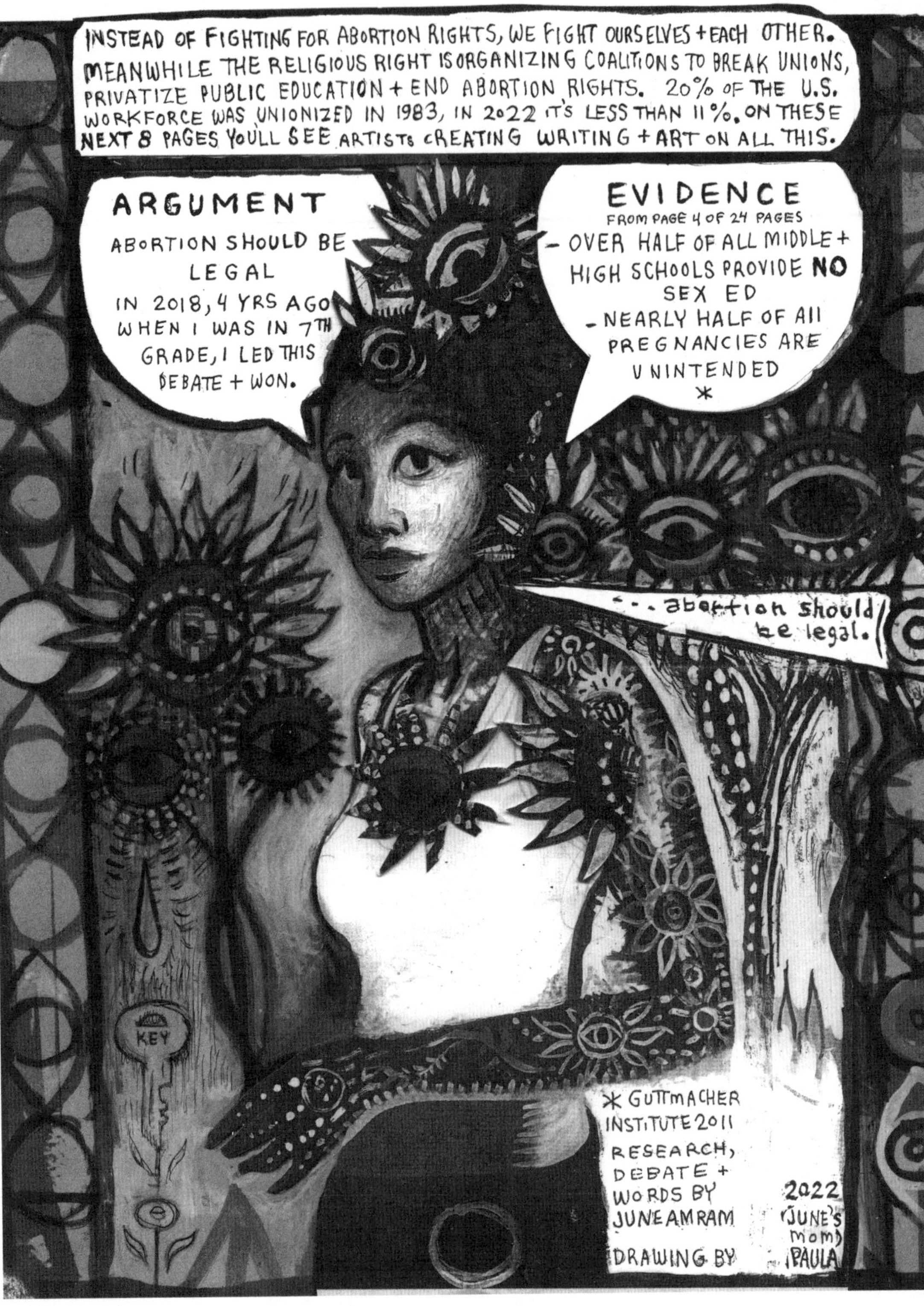
INSTEAD OF FIGHTING FOR ABORTION RIGHTS, WE FIGHT OURSELVES + EACH OTHER. MEANWHILE THE RELIGIOUS RIGHT IS ORGANIZING COALITIONS TO BREAK UNIONS, PRIVATIZE PUBLIC EDUCATION + END ABORTION RIGHTS. 20% OF THE U.S. WORKFORCE WAS UNIONIZED IN 1983, IN 2022 IT'S LESS THAN 11%. ON THESE NEXT 8 PAGES YOU'LL SEE ARTISTS CREATING WRITING + ART ON ALL THIS.
ARGUMENT
ABORTION SHOULD BE LEGAL
IN 2018, 4 YRS AGO WHEN I WAS IN 7TH GRADE, I LED THIS DEBATE + WON.
EVIDENCE
FROM PAGE 4 OF 24 PAGES
- OVER HALF OF ALL MIDDLE + HIGH SCHOOLS PROVIDE NO SEX ED
- NEARLY HALF OF ALL PREGNANCIES ARE UNINTENDED *
...abortion should be legal.
KEY
* GUTTMACHER INSTITUTE 2011
RESEARCH, DEBATE + WORDS BY JUNE AMRAM
DRAWING BY
2022 (JUNE'S MOM) PAULA

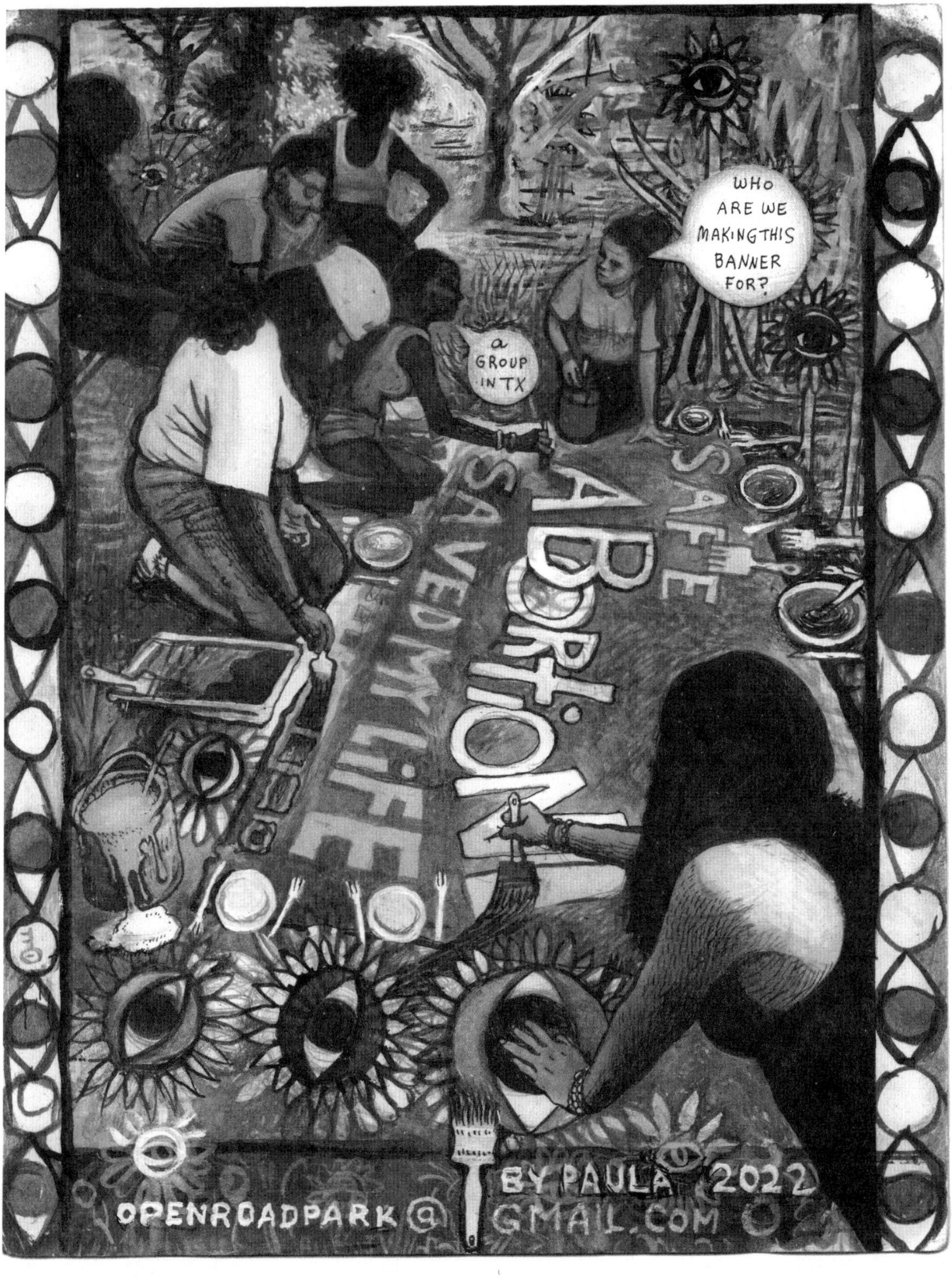
WHO ARE WE MAKING THIS BANNER FOR?
a GROUP IN TX
SAFE ABORTION
SAFE ABORTION SAVED MY LIFE
BY PAULA 2022
OPENROADPARK@GMAIL.COM

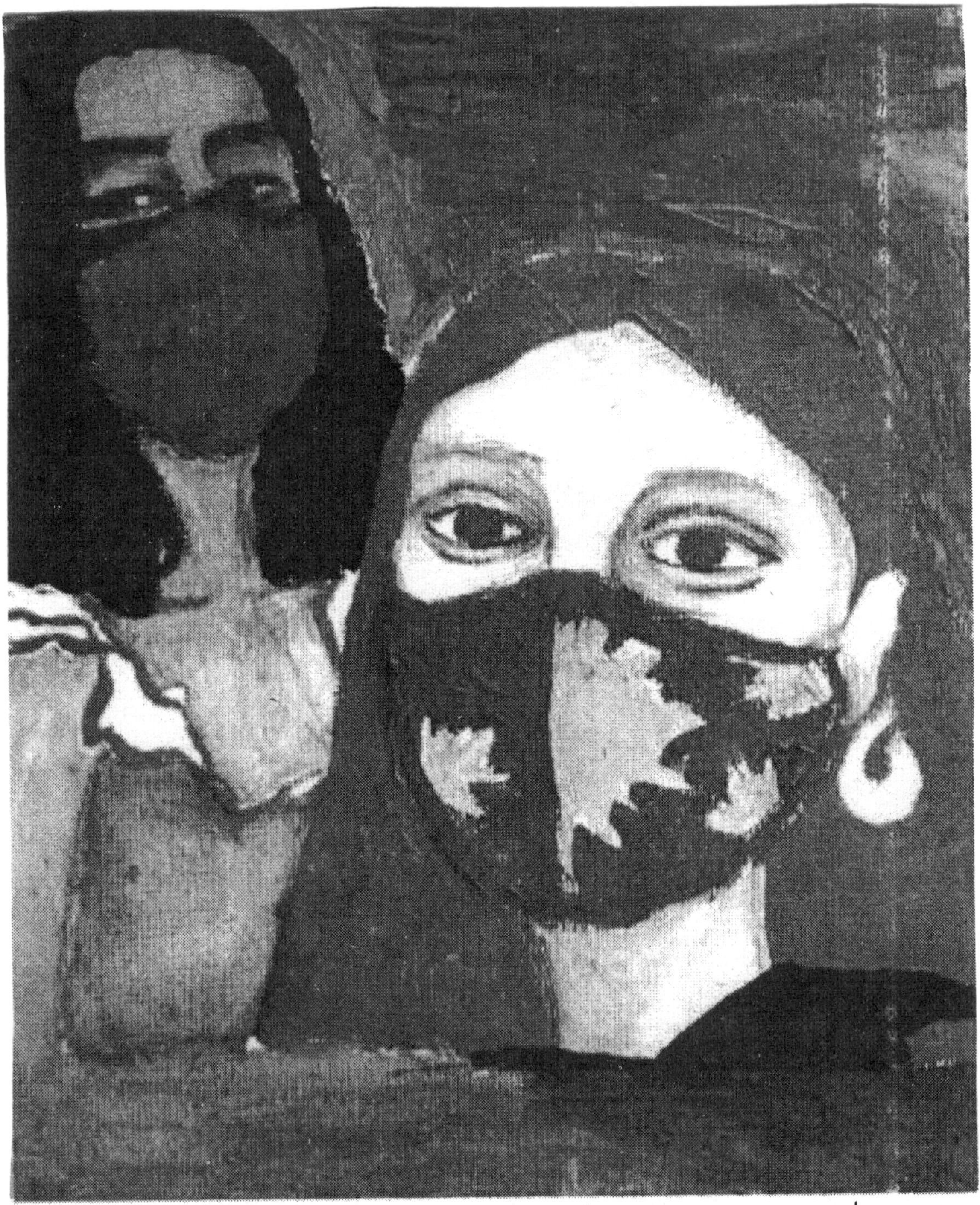

ART BY JUNE AMRAM OF JUNE + SYLVIA ARRINGTON 2022

UNMUTE

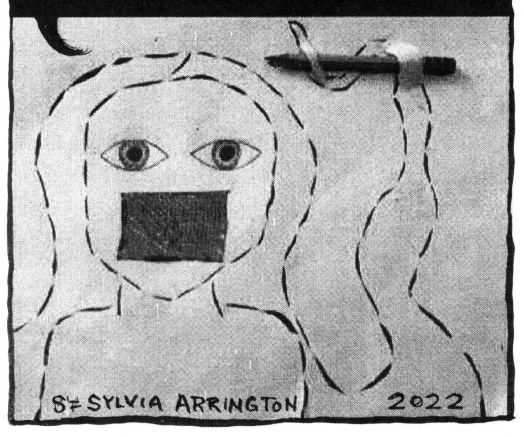

THE E.R.A. We lobbied for the Equal Rights Amendment to the NYS Constitution. The ERA will "*prohibit discrimination based on a person's ethnicity, national origin, age, disability, and sex — including their sexual orientation, gender identity, gender expression, pregnancy & pregnancy outcomes*"

Painting, left, by June Amram of June, 16 and S, 14
Art of cut paper, tape, pencil "Unmute" by S, below.

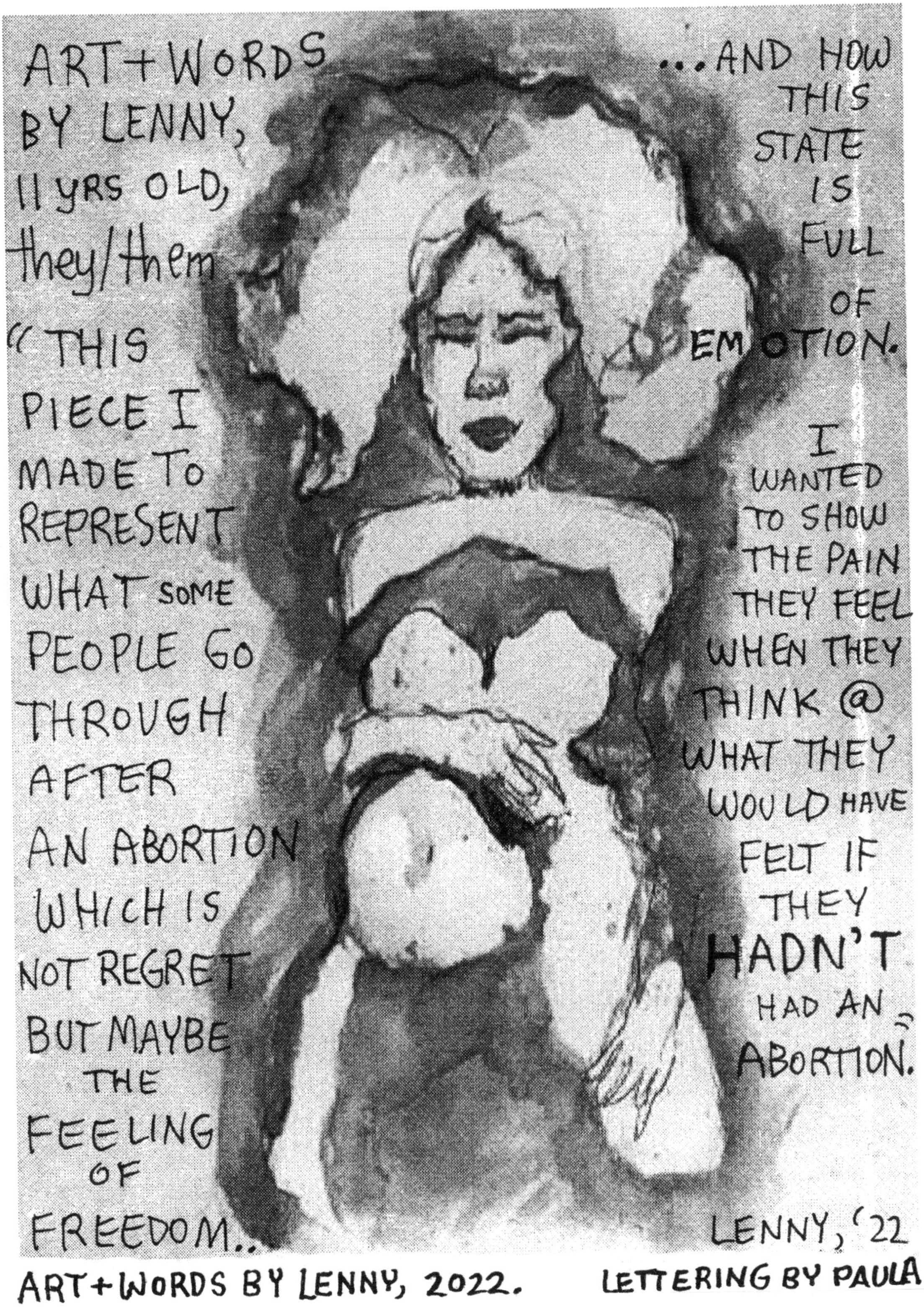
ART + WORDS BY LENNY, 11 YRS OLD, they/them
"THIS PIECE I MADE TO REPRESENT WHAT SOME PEOPLE GO THROUGH AFTER AN ABORTION WHICH IS NOT REGRET BUT MAYBE THE FEELING OF FREEDOM...
...AND HOW THIS STATE IS FULL OF EMOTION.
I WANTED TO SHOW THE PAIN THEY FEEL WHEN THEY THINK @ WHAT THEY WOULD HAVE FELT IF THEY HADN'T HAD AN ABORTION."
LENNY, '22
ART + WORDS BY LENNY, 2022. LETTERING BY PAULA

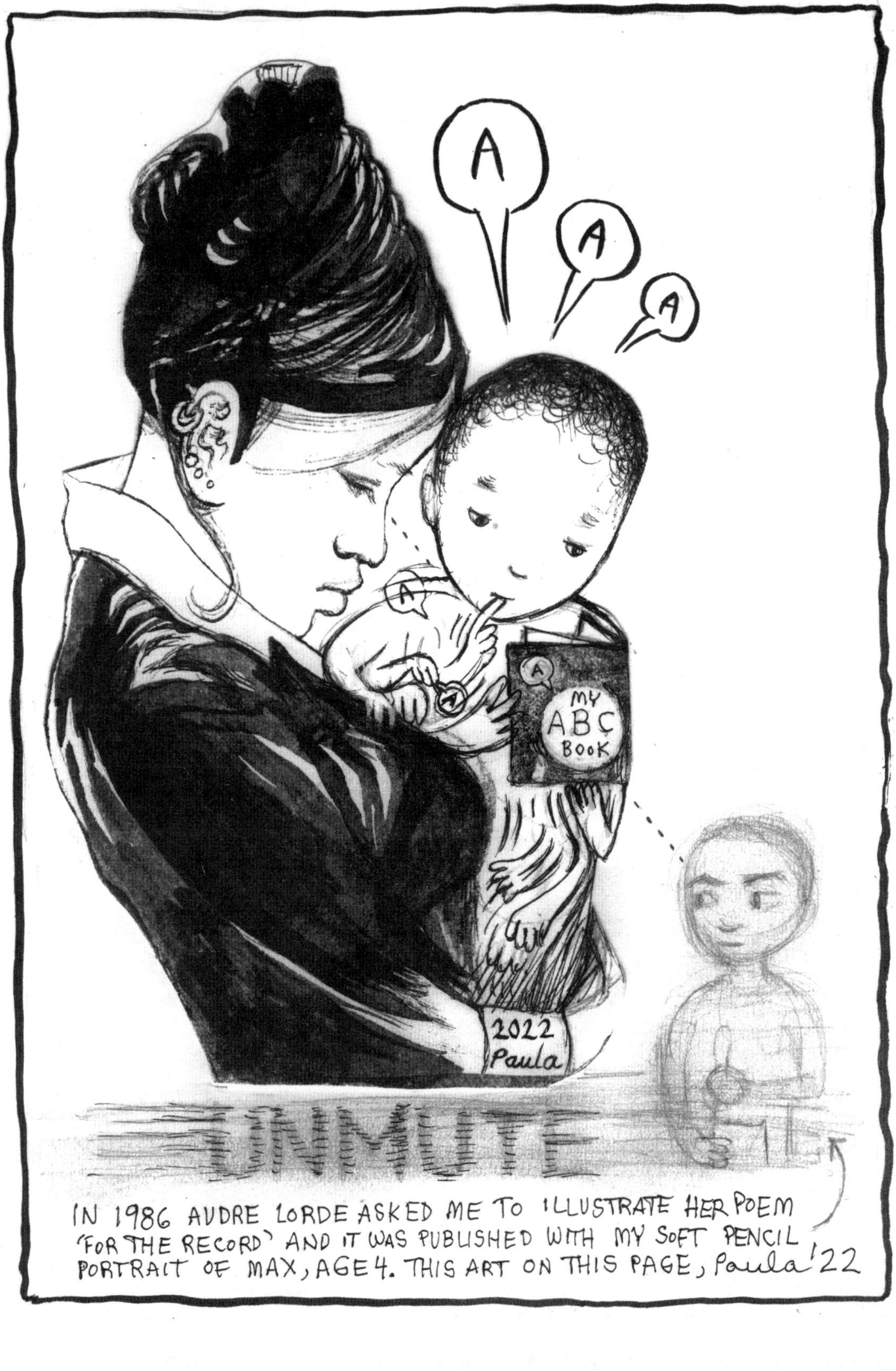
A
A
A
A
A
A
MY ABC BOOK
2022 Paula
UNMUTE
IN 1986 AUDRE LORDE ASKED ME TO ILLUSTRATE HER POEM 'FOR THE RECORD' AND IT WAS PUBLISHED WITH MY SOFT PENCIL PORTRAIT OF MAX, AGE 4. THIS ART ON THIS PAGE, Paula '22

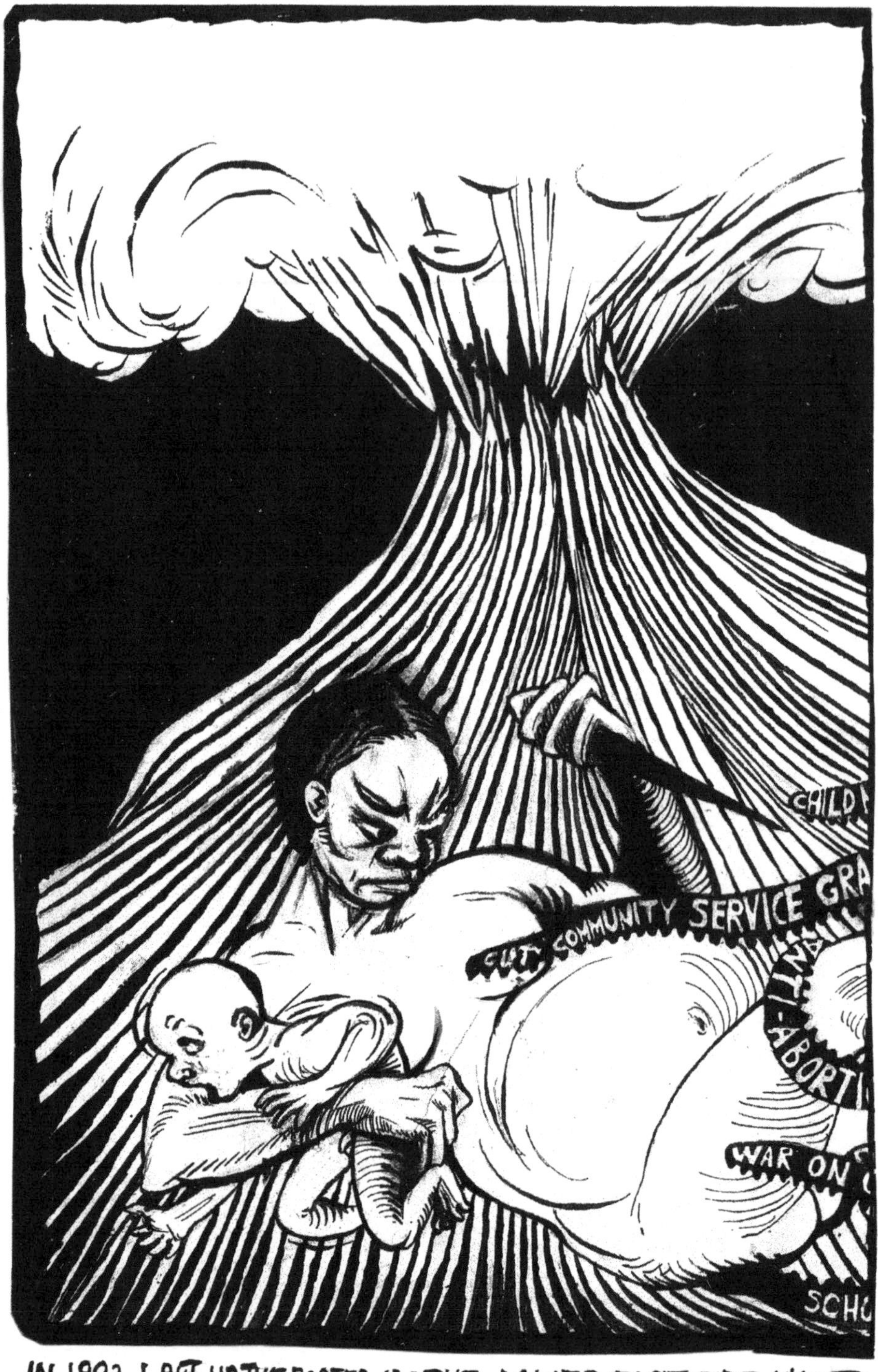
CHILD
COMMUNITY SERVICE GRA
ANTI-ABORT
WAR ON
SCHO

IN 1982 I PUT UP THIS POSTER IN THE LOWER EAST SIDE NYC TO FIGHT ATTACKS ON OUR BODIES. THE SPINE OF THIS BOOK IS FIGHTING THIS OCTOPUS BY CUTTING ITS LEGS DOWN THE MIDDLE BETWEEN THESE TWO PAGES.